D1588559

REBUILDING THE KIRK

PRESBYTERIAN REUNION IN SCOTLAND 1909–1929

REBUILDING THE KIRK

PRESBYTERIAN REUNION IN SCOTLAND
1909–1929

DOUGLAS M. MURRAY

SCOTTISH ACADEMIC PRESS
EDINBURGH

Published by
Scottish Academic Press Ltd
22 Hanover Street
Edinburgh EH2 2EP

ISBN 0 7073 0774 0

British Library Cataloguing in Publication Data

A catalogue record for this book is available
from the British Library

Typeset by Trinity Typesetting, Edinburgh
Printed in Great Britain by Polestar AUP Aberdeen Limited

Contents

Acknowledgements

I am most grateful to the University of Glasgow and my colleagues in the Faculty of Divinity for making it possible for me to undertake two periods of study leave in 1996 and 1998 when much of the research for this book was carried out. In addition I am indebted to the Humanities Research Board of the British Academy for a grant towards the cost of the first of these periods which was spent in Edinburgh. I wish to acknowledge my gratitude, too, to the Board of Practice and Procedure of the General Assembly, the Hope Trust and also to The Drummond Trust, 3 Pitt Terrace, Stirling, for generous financial assistance towards the cost of the publication of this study.

I wish to thank the members of the Faculty of Divinity at New College in Edinburgh for electing me as a Visiting Research Fellow in 1996 and for their warm welcome and kind hospitality during that period. I am particularly grateful to Professor Stewart J. Brown and Professor Duncan B. Forrester of New College for their interest in this project. Professor Brown encouraged me not only to examine the process of Presbyterian reunion in the 1920s, but also to provide the background to those developments. I owe a significant debt of gratitude to my former teacher at Edinburgh, Professor Alec C. Cheyne. He has been a source of encouragement during the writing of this book, and he kindly read and commented on the first drafts of parts of two of the early chapters. In the final stages prior to publication I received the invaluable services of the Rev. J. Ainslie McIntyre, who acted as copy editor and proof reader, and the Rev. Valerie G. C. Watson who helped with the Index. And I must thank Dr Douglas Grant of the Scottish Academic Press for all that he has done in seeing the book through to publication.

I wish to acknowledge the assistance of all those who have enabled me to consult the archive material which has been used in this study. My principal debt is to the Librarian and staff of New College Library, for their help in consulting the main sources, the papers of Alexander Martin and John White. I am also grateful to the Librarians and staff of the Special Collections at the University Libraries of Glasgow, Edinburgh, Aberdeen and St Andrews, to the Keeper of the Records and the staff of the Scottish Record Office, Edinburgh, and of the Glasgow City Archives, and the Archivist and staff of the Glasgow University Archives. I wish to thank the Rev. John Fulton, Secretary of the United Free Church of Scotland, for making the records and papers of the United Free Church (Continuing) and of the United Free Church Association readily available to me, and the Rev. Alan Birss of Paisley Abbey for his help in consulting the papers of the Scottish Church Society. I am grateful, too, to the Clerks and the staff of the Presbyteries of Glasgow and Hamilton for their help in trying to trace the relevant presbytery minutes of the period.

Several people have generously helped me in the course of writing this book. I wish to thank the Rev. Dr Finlay A. J. Macdonald, Principal Clerk of the General Assembly of the Church of Scotland, and the Rev. Marjory A. MacLean, Depute Clerk, for so readily answering my queries. As with my previous study in this area, I am grateful to the former Principal Clerk, the Very Rev. Dr James L. Weatherhead, for generously discussing the points which I raised about the scope of the Articles Declaratory. And I wish to thank the Rev. Robert J. M. Anderson for giving me references to the debates in parliament and for correspondence about recent legislation concerning the European Convention of Human Rights and its relation to the Church of Scotland Act. Finally, throughout the four years it has taken to carry out the research and the writing of this book I have relied greatly on the understanding, encouragement and support of my wife Freya.

DOUGLAS M. MURRAY

Abbreviations used in the footnotes and the bibliography

(AUC)   University of Aberdeen, Minutes of the University Court, 1924–36, Vols. X–XII, Aberdeen University Library.

AGA   Church of Scotland, *Principal Acts of the General Assembly of the Church of Scotland* (Edinburgh, 1908–29).

(BAL)   Lord Balfour of Burleigh's Papers, New College Library, Edinburgh.

C of S   The Church of Scotland.

C of S Min.   The Church of Scotland, Minutes of the Committee to Confer with the United Free Church of Scotland, John White's Papers, New College Library, Edinburgh.

C of S Rep.   *Reports on the Schemes of the Church of Scotland* (Edinburgh, 1908–29), and *Reports to the General Assembly of the Church of Scotland* (Edinburgh, 1930–).

Cox   J. T. Cox, ed., *Practice and Procedure in the Church of Scotland*, 6th edn. (Edinburgh, 1976).

DSCHT   Nigel M. de S. Cameron, ed., *Dictionary of Scottish Church History and Theology* (Edinburgh, 1993).

(EUC)   University of Edinburgh, Signed Minutes of the University Court, 1924–34, Vols. XIV–XVI, Edinburgh University Library.

(EUD)   University of Edinburgh, Minutes and Papers of the Faculty of Divinity, 1927–58, Edinburgh University Library.

FR   Douglas M. Murray, *Freedom to Reform: the 'Articles Declaratory' of the Church of Scotland 1921* (Edinburgh, 1993).

(GUC)   University of Glasgow, Camera Minutes of the University Court, 1926–34, C1/2/9–10, Glasgow University Archives.

Hansard HC   *Parliamentary Debates*, Official Report, Fifth and Sixth Series, House of Commons (London).

Hansard HL   *Parliamentary Debates*, Official Report, Fifth Series, House of Lords (London).

(IRV)   Papers of Principal Sir James Irvine, UY 875 Irvine, St Andrews University Library.

(JC)   The Diaries and Papers of James Cooper, Aberdeen University Library, Special Collections and Archives, MS.2283/1–44 and Box.

JW   Augustus Muir, *John White CH, DD, LLD* (London, 1958).

Layman's Book   Church of Scotland, *The Layman's Book of the General Assembly* (Edinburgh, 1909–29).

(LS)	Lord Sands' Papers, Scottish Record Office, Edinburgh, CH1/10/1–25.
LW	*Life and Work.*
(M)	Alexander Martin's Papers, New College Library, Edinburgh, Boxes 1–21.
(PGA)	Papers of the General Assembly of the Church of Scotland, Scottish Record Office, Edinburgh, CH1/25/1–4.
PRS	Rolf Sjölinder, *Presbyterian Reunion in Scotland 1907–1921, Its Background and Development* (Edinburgh, 1962*).*
Record	*The Record* of the United Free Church of Scotland.
RSCHS	*Records of the Scottish Church History Society.*
(StAUC)	University of St Andrews, Minutes of the University Court, 1927–34, UY505, St Andrews University Library.
SCS	The Scottish Church Society.
(SCS)	The Papers and Memoranda of the Scottish Church Society relating to Church Union, The Secretary of the Scottish Church Society, Paisley Abbey, Paisley.
SLPF	Scottish Land and Property Federation.
(SLPF)	Records of the Scottish Land and Property Federation, Scottish Record Office, Edinburgh, GD325/1/203, 305, 327–8.
UFC	The United Free Church of Scotland.
UFC Handbook	*The Handbook of the United Free Church of Scotland (Continuing) and of the United Free Church of Scotland, 1931–9,* The Offices of the United Free Church of Scotland, Glasgow.
UFC Min.	United Free Church of Scotland, Minutes of the Committee for Conference with the Church of Scotland, 1908–29, Scottish Record Office, CH3/1389/1–3.
UFC Proc.	United Free Church of Scotland, *The Proceedings and Debates of the General Assembly* (Edinburgh, 1909–29).
UFC Rep.	*Reports to the General Assembly of the United Free Church of Scotland* (Edinburgh, 1908–29).
(UFC)	United Free Church of Scotland Papers, New College Library, Edinburgh.
UFCA	United Free Church Association.
UFCA Min.	The Minutes of the United Free Church Association, 1919–29, The Offices of the United Free Church of Scotland, Glasgow.
(UFCA)	Papers of the United Free Church Association, 1919–29, The Offices of the United Free Church of Scotland, Glasgow.
(W)	John White's Papers, New College Library, Edinburgh, Boxes 1–106.

Preface

One of the most significant events to have shaped the life of the Kirk during the twentieth century was the union in 1929 of the Church of Scotland and the United Free Church. To the present generation of church members the impact of the union may not always be evident. It is often assumed that certain principles and practices have 'aye been' whereas they are the result of the decisions made at that time. I thought it would be interesting and instructive to see what these decisions were and how they were reached. It has been said that the union of 1929 has produced a Church which is both national and free. The Church of Scotland can be referred to as the National Church or as the Established Church. What is its relationship to the State? With the decline in church membership can it still claim to be 'a national Church representative of the Christian faith of the Scottish people'? And in what sense is the Kirk free? Is it free to make changes in matters of doctrine and government and is it free to unite with other Churches which are not Presbyterian?

I had previously published a short study of the framing and subsequent impact of the Articles Declaratory of the Constitution of the Church of Scotland in Matters Spiritual. This document was recognised by parliament in the Church of Scotland Act of 1921 and set out the claim of the Church to spiritual independence. It thus provided the framework for the subsequent union to take place. The book was entitled *Freedom to Reform*, and was based on the Chalmers Lectures of 1991. In researching that subject I discovered a great deal of material relating to the discussions which took place after the Articles had been approved. There were two distinct stages in the movement for reunion. In the first place the Church of Scotland had to be free to unite with another Church, and thus its spiritual freedom had to be recognised and its property and finances had to be made over to it by the State. Only then could detailed discussions of union between the two Churches take place. The removal of the second obstacle, which was accomplished with the passing of an Act dealing with the property and endowments of the Church, and the preparation of the Basis and Plan of Union itself, have not been fully studied before.

The most comprehensive work on this subject is that by the Swedish scholar, Rolf Sjölinder, *Presbyterian Reunion in Scotland 1907–1921*, published in 1962, which takes the story of union as far as the recognition by parliament of the Articles Declaratory. The only book to deal with the course of the union up to 1929 is the short study by J. R. Fleming, *The Story of Church Union in Scotland*, which was brought out just after the event in 1930. It was based upon a series of articles which had been published in *The Record* of the United Free Church of Scotland. Clearly Fleming's account, although that of a contemporary witness, could not be based on the papers and other records which are now available. The best description of the process of reunion after 1921 is found in the biography of one the leading figures, *John White, CH, DD, LLD* by Augustus Muir, published in 1956. The story, however, is told necessarily from the point of view of the main character. I therefore saw the need for a close examination of the movement for reunion up to 1929.

I soon realised, however, that to make sense of the 1920s some background had to be provided about what had gone before. I therefore decided to cover the whole period of the negotiations, from 1909 to 1929. This means that there is inevitably some overlap with my previous book, *Freedom to Reform*. Some sections of chapters 3 and 4 contain material which is found in a slightly different form in that book. That study was concerned primarily, however, with the subject of spiritual freedom in relation to doctrine, and it did not deal with the other aspects such as the national recognition of religion. In addition it did not describe the earlier discussions prior to the framing of the Articles Declaratory.

The focus of this study is on the discussions of the two committees on union as they sought to rebuild the Kirk, to provide a foundation and a structure for the united Church. It is thus necessarily concerned with the framing of the various documents which set out those fundamental matters, and how they were received in the general assemblies of both Churches. This examination is based primarily on the extensive archive material, both official and unofficial, which has been left by those who were most closely involved in the movement, John White and Alexander Martin. They began as the clerks and later became the conveners of the two committees. It has not been possible to cast the net wider and examine the reception of the union proposals at the level of the presbyteries and kirk sessions of the two Churches. Hopefully what has been set out here will provide a framework for such further study to take place. In addition, while the social and political factors of the time are referred to, it has also not been possible to enter into a more wide-ranging discussion of their relevance. This study is therefore limited, but it deals with what must be the starting point for any consideration of this subject, the discussions which enabled the union of 1929 to be accomplished.

The task of bringing about Presbyterian reunion in Scotland was not an easy one and it took twenty years to bring about. But the final result was a great achievement, in that the Church's freedom from the State, and its spiritual freedom within its own sphere, were set out in its constitution and recognised by parliament. The Church since then has not always realised the nature and scope of this freedom. If this study leads to a greater understanding of the way in which the Kirk was rebuilt in 1929, and to a process of continuing reform and renewal in the life of the Church, then it will not have been in vain.

Chapter 1

Celebrating the event: the day of union 1929

On Wednesday, 2nd October 1929, the city of Edinburgh witnessed yet another important event in the history of Scotland, the union of the two largest Presbyterian Churches after almost two centuries of separation. The day began with separate meetings of the general assemblies of the Church of Scotland and the United Free Church of Scotland. The ministers and elders then filed out of their respective assembly halls in the Lawnmarket and on the Mound to meet at the junction of the High Street and Bank Street. In the view of at least one observer, the moment when the two moderators met and clasped hands seemed to be the 'practical consummation' of union.[1] Large crowds had gathered undeterred by the wind and the rain, and they were rewarded with a clear spell and some glimpses of sunshine as the procession then made its way to St Giles' Cathedral for a service of thanksgiving.[2] The significance of the moment was appreciated by some of the spectators who broke out spontaneously in singing the words of psalm 133:[3]

> Behold, how good a thing it is,
> And how becoming well,
> Together such as brethren are
> In unity to dwell.

The service in St Giles' was a simple one of prayers, scripture readings and praise. The leaders of the two Churches were able to reflect on the completion of a long and difficult undertaking that had begun with the first discussions in 1909. Much still remained to be done, since union had never been seen as an end in itself. It was carried out in order that the Church might serve the people of Scotland more faithfully, more energetically, and more

---

[1] Gordon Quig, 'The Union Assembly' in *LW*, November 1929, p. 266.
[2] John Buchan and George Adam Smith, *The Kirk in Scotland 1560–1929* (Edinburgh, 1930), p. 127.
[3] Ibid.; G. M. Reith, *Reminiscences of the United Free Church General Assembly* (Edinburgh and London, 1933), p. 342.

efficiently. It was for that reason that those most involved in the movement had undertaken the task of rebuilding the Kirk, and it was for that reason that they had persevered through all the difficulties and delays of the previous twenty years.

The two assemblies met in joint session later that day in the only building large enough to hold them, the Industrial Hall in Annandale Street, which had been built as an exhibition centre and later became a bus garage. It was cleverly transformed with banners and other decorations designed by the Scottish landscape artist and church elder, Sir David Young Cameron. The Lord High Commissioner was the Duke of York, the future King George VI, accompanied by his wife Elizabeth, who had returned to her native Scotland for the occasion. Lord Sands, an elder and a former Procurator of the Kirk, the layman who had done most for the cause, moved the resolution in favour of union. He spoke of the three great tasks that lay before the united Church.[4] First, there was the duty of home mission, of carrying the gospel into every home in the land by intensive territorial work. Secondly, the Church had to gain and keep a hold upon the rising generation. And thirdly it was commissioned to take the gospel to the far flung corners of the world.

These concerns were echoed by John White, one of the chief architects of the union, in his opening address as the first moderator of the general assembly of the united Church. He spoke of the 'churchless million' as the real object of reunion and as the first challenge which faced the Kirk.[5] In meeting this challenge the Church also had to use its resources more efficiently, a theme which John White had developed in his closing address as moderator at the general assembly of the Church of Scotland in 1925.[6] In arguing the case for union during the previous years he had often spoken eloquently of the wastage of people and resources by the unnecessary duplication of ministers and congregations throughout Scotland while other needy areas remained unprovided.[7]

Regardless of the future, however, the achievement of bringing the two Churches together was a remarkable one. At that first assembly Lord Sands recalled the ecclesiastical scene in Scotland at the end of the previous century, when division was the norm and when rivalry and jealousy were the order of the day.[8] In view

[4] Church of Scotland, *Proceedings of the Union Assembly 1929* (Edinburgh, 1929), p. 4.

[5] Ibid., p. 18.

[6] John White, *Efficiency*, Address delivered at the Close of the General Assembly, May 28, 1925 (Edinburgh and London, 1925).

[7] *JW*, p. 87.

[8] Church of Scotland, *Proceedings of the Union Assembly*, p. 3.

of the disunity of the recent past, he said, the day of union was 'a high day in the history of the people and of our Church'. According to Sands, they were celebrating 'a great historical event'. He spoke of each body entering the union on equal terms and with equal respect for the ideals of both Churches. The two Churches represented different traditions and stood for different principles. The genius of the union of 1929, according to those who promoted it, was that both traditions and both principles were enshrined in the united Church. How had that been achieved?

The clerk of the United Free Church committee, Andrew N. Bogle, had had the task of commending the union to the readership of his Church's magazine in 1925.[9] He, too, began his argument by illustrating the need for union because of the wasteful duplication of resources by the two Churches. He then made the point that in any union of this kind compromise was essential. The United Free Church was the successor of the main strands of the secession Churches of the eighteenth century, which had first united in 1820 and then again in 1847 to form the United Presbyterian Church, and of the Free Church which was the result of the Disruption of 1843. For all those who had left the Established Church at different times, he said, the fundamental principle was that of the spiritual freedom of the Church. The Church of Christ had to be able to carry out its work free from interference by the State. The Church of Scotland was the Established Church and those who remained within it did so, according to Bogle, not because of the material advantages of this position, or because of a love of strife, but because they attached fundamental importance to the principle of the national recognition of religion.[10] In order to maintain the practical embodiment of this principle the Church of Scotland had been willing to undergo certain limitations upon its freedom as a Church in its alliance with the State.

As Bogle pointed out, there were only three possible ways in which union could be achieved. Either the United Free Church had to accept the position of the Church of Scotland; or the Church of Scotland would have to accept the position of the UF Church; or 'some third position must be found which both could accept'.[11] Clearly only the third possibility offered any hope of success, and even that had appeared a distant prospect when the discussions began. Yet that was what had been achieved in 1929. The leaders of the union committees of both Churches had sought to find a

---

[9] A. N. Bogle, 'Church Union in Scotland: An Account of the Movement and Present Position' in *Record*, September 1925, pp. 383–6.

[10] Ibid., p. 384.

[11] Ibid.

middle way between establishment on the one hand and disestablishment on the other. They had tried to rebuild the Kirk by combining the best features of their different traditions in a new way.

It was the criticism of those who were opposed to this policy that such a *via media* was neither possible nor desirable. There was a minority in the UF Church, some of whom in the end refused to enter the union and continued in being as a separate Church, while there were those in the Church of Scotland who remained within the united Church as a somewhat disaffected group. For the members of the UF minority the compromise settlement meant that the united Church was still tied to the State, and they were opposed to such a connection. Only the second of the three options would have been acceptable to them and clearly such was impossible as a basis of union. For the minority members in the other Church the establishment of religion was a vital principle and they did not wish to see the Kirk's position modified in any significant way. For them the first option was the preferred solution, and this, too, would not have been an acceptable method of union. Only the third option offered a possibility of reconciling the different traditions.

The solution to the differences between the two Churches came down to this question. Was the Church of Scotland willing to meet the United Free Church with regard to spiritual freedom, and was the United Free Church willing to meet the Church of Scotland with regard to the national recognition of religion? In view of some important recent developments there was a new willingness to explore how the two different principles might be reconciled in the one Church. One event was the union of 1900 between the Free Church and the United Presbyterian Church to form the United Free Church. This union showed that the reconciliation of differences was possible. The Established Church, too, had made overtures towards reunion although these had not led to positive results, partly because the Kirk envisaged the other Churches accepting an establishment of religion.

These developments were the result of a general change in theological thought and ecclesiastical policy away from division and towards union as the best way forward for Scottish Presbyterianism. There had been a new emphasis in biblical studies upon the nature of the Kingdom of God as a corporate entity that was to be realised in the present and not just in the future. The divided state of the Church was seen as a serious obstacle to the realisation of the Kingdom.[12] In addition the setting

---

[12] *PRS*, p. 154.

up of the Kingdom in the world involved concern for the moral and social, as well as religious, well-being of people. The Church was therefore seen to have a vital role to play in seeking 'the Christian good of Scotland', a role which would be carried out more effectively if it was united. The nineteenth century had also seen an emphasis upon the doctrines of the incarnation and the humanity of Christ, pioneered in Scotland by ministers such as John McLeod Campbell and Edward Irving. It was important that the spiritual unity of the Church be expressed in outward form. The Church was seen as the body of Christ and as such it should take on the characteristics of Christ's life. Outward unity was one such feature. Following the work of Professor William Milligan of Aberdeen, the Scottish Church Society was formed by high churchmen in 1892 to emphasise the divine nature of the Church and to promote its unity.[13] High churchmen, or Scoto-Catholics as they were sometimes called, would play a prominent role in the Church of Scotland's union committee. The unity of the Church was also thought to be important in view of its witness to a divided world. Christ himself had prayed that his followers should be one in order that the world might believe.[14] This prayer was one of the chief motives which led to the reunion of the Churches, and it was referred to in some of the key documents in 1929.[15]

The Churches in Scotland were also influenced by the fact that their missionaries had already begun working together abroad, including in India where they were both part of the Indian Presbyterian Church.[16] In the work of evangelisation in other cultures, the divisions imported from home seemed less significant. A year after the discussions between the Churches began, the World Missionary Conference was held in the United Free Church assembly hall in Edinburgh. The impact of the 1910 conference upon the union movement was considerable. The conference reminded the Churches of the call to take the gospel to the rest of the world and of the necessity of presenting a united front in that task. The conference was an example, too, of the wider ecumenical movement that would develop into the World Conference on Faith and Order. Delegates from the two Scottish Presbyterian Churches would attend the important preliminary Faith and

---

[13] *PRS*, pp. 75–6. See further, Douglas M. Murray, 'The Scottish Church Society, 1892–1914: the High Church Movement in the Church of Scotland' (Cambridge Ph.D. thesis, 1975).

[14] *PRS*, p. 154. John 17: 20–1.

[15] E.g. Article VII of the Articles Declaratory, in Appendix I, p. 286.

[16] *PRS*, p. 157.

Order meeting held at Geneva in 1920. In addition, the Lambeth Conference of the Anglican Church would in the same year issue its famous 'Appeal to all Christian People'. These international developments could not fail to have an impact on the movement for Presbyterian union in Scotland.

Throughout the negotiations, too, the needs of the nation and the duplication of the work of the Church were never far from the minds of those involved. The population of Scotland had doubled during both the eighteenth and nineteenth centuries and by 1910 it was estimated at 4,800,000.[17] By the beginning of the twentieth century the bulk of the population lived in the cities and the densely populated areas, with around seventy-five per cent living in the central belt of the country. The Presbyterian Churches had sought to meet the challenges of this growing and changing population. Over 2,000 new churches had been built since the Disruption, to add to the 1,000 or so original parishes. But it was realised that the major weakness of this activity was that these buildings belonged to three denominations, and that they were not necessarily placed in the situations of greatest need.[18] In many rural areas churches stood side by side competing with each other for the allegiance of the same small number of people. Each of the three denominations built fewer churches in relation to the size of the population in the cities than in the rest of the country. For example, in the presbytery of Glasgow the Free Church built only four new churches between 1879 and 1891, or one for every 34,062 of the increase in the population.[19] In 1914 the Church of Scotland had ninety-two churches for Glasgow's one million inhabitants and 1,400 to serve the rest of the population. Hence in Glasgow the Kirk provided one minister for every 10,000 people, while in the rest of Scotland the ratio was 1:2,700.[20] There was an overall decline in the membership of the Presbyterian Churches in relation to the growth of population, and a decrease in church attendance and in the numbers of children attending Sunday School. In addition the Roman Catholic population had increased considerably during the second half of the nineteenth century due largely to Irish immigration.[21] But of greatest concern was the number of people who had no contact with any Church. While in 1900 the Church of Scotland had 660,000 members, and the

---

[17] *C of S Rep.*, 1910, p. 1055.

[18] Ibid., p. 1056.

[19] *PRS*, p. 53.

[20] *PRS*, pp. 53–4.

[21] Andrew J. Campbell, *Two Centuries of the Church of Scotland 1707–1929* (Paisley, 1930), p. 308.

United Free Church had nearly 490,000, it had been estimated by the statistician Robert Howie that in 1891 over 1,500,000, or 37.7 per cent of the population, had no church connection at all.[22] Howie's figures were queried at the time,[23] but even so the number of 'unchurched' was alarmingly high and posed a challenge to the Presbyterian Churches. The question remained as to whether the Kirk would meet that challenge in the years which lay ahead.

A more immediate factor in propelling the United Free Church towards reunion with the Church of Scotland was the House of Lords decision in 1904 in the Free Church Case. One result of the union of 1900 was that a minority of the former Free Church claimed to be the true successors of the Disruption. The 'Wee Frees' argued that by entering the union the majority had departed from the original constitution of the Free Church and was therefore no longer entitled to its property and assets. The fact that their case was upheld in the highest court in the land showed that a so-called 'free' Church was not free from the adverse judgements of the courts of the land. As Bogle put it:[24]

> a Church might claim to be free and might make great sacrifices for freedom, and find itself able to exercise its freedom only by the loss of all its property. The bondage of a constitution might be quite as real as the bondage of a special statute.

Following this case, in 1906, the United Free Church assembly passed an Act anent the Spiritual Independence of the Church in which it set out its historic claim to freedom from state interference. At this time, too, the Church of Scotland was finding that its status as an established Church had one serious disadvantage, that it could not alter its doctrinal position without reference to parliament.

Discussions began in 1909 to discover the causes which kept the Churches apart, but the key suggestion as to how the reunion of the Kirk might be achieved was set out in 1912 by Lord Sands in what came to be known as 'The Memorandum'. This document, in turn, was based on several important suggestions which had been contained in the first joint report of the two committees in the

---

[22] Robert Howie, *The Churches and the Churchless in Scotland* (Glasgow, 1893), p. 119.

[23] Donald J. Withrington, 'The Churches in Scotland, c. 1870–1900: Towards a New Social Conscience?', in *RSCHS*, 19 (1977), p. 58 n. 5.

[24] Bogle, 'Church Union in Scotland', p. 384.

previous year. If the Kirk was to become one body then the obstacles in the way of this task had first to be removed. Two obstacles to reunion were identified: the lack of freedom of the Church of Scotland in relation to the State, and in relation to its property and endowments. The Memorandum provided the preamble to a possible bill by which parliament would recognise the freedom of the Kirk and then later deal with the endowments. With regard to the first obstacle, the Church would draw up a declaration of its spiritual freedom and character as a national Church, and the State would recognise this constitution as the lawful constitution of the Church.

Work was begun on the drafting of this constitution, but these discussions were interrupted by the outbreak of war in 1914. The First World War had several effects in relation to the process of union.[25] The absence of ministers who were serving as chaplains or in the ranks of the armed services led to many vacancies in the home congregations. The continuing unnecessary duplication of resources was shown up in even sharper relief. There was, however, an increasing amount of co-operation both at home and on the front. Joint services were held in some parishes when the minister of the other Church was away, and chaplains worked closely together to serve the troops. A gathering of both general assemblies was held in 1916, at which the Church of Scotland moderator, John Brown of Bellahouston Church in Glasgow, said that 'There was no bond of union stronger than that which was formed by the endurance of a common trial or a common sorrow.'[26] A meeting of chaplains and other workers of the two Churches in 1918 expressed a desire to continue with the level of collaboration which had been experienced during the war. Following the end of hostilities, too, the Churches would be faced by the task of reconstruction and renewal, a task which could be carried out more effectively together than apart.

Discussions resumed in earnest in 1918 and the statement of the Church's freedom, the Articles Declaratory of the Constitution of the Church of Scotland in Matters Spiritual, was finally agreed in 1919. The Articles enshrined the claim to spiritual freedom which was found in the UF Act of 1906 and, of fundamental importance, it set out the 'the right to change the constitution itself'.[27] This right of change was subject to only one limitation, that any modification had to be in harmony with the provisions of the first Article. This Article contained a declaration of catholic

---

[25] *PRS*, pp. 276–8.
[26] John White, The War and Union (W) 100.
[27] Bogle, 'Church Union in Scotland', p. 384.

doctrine and the drafting of this statement caused the most difficulty during the discussions. In essence the Article declared that the Church would lose its identity if it ceased to be Trinitarian and Protestant. The Articles Declaratory also referred to the distinct but complementary roles of the Church and the State, and spoke of the Church of Scotland as a national Church representative of the Christian faith of the Scottish people.

The Articles embodied the principles of the two Churches and were recognised by parliament in the Church of Scotland Act of 1921. There remained the question of the support of the Church by the State. The property and endowments of the Church of Scotland had to be made over to the Church itself so that it was master of its own house in this respect. Both Churches recognised that this was a matter for parliament to deal with and they had to wait while the legislative process was completed. As Bogle pointed out,[28] each Church had its own condition relating to this issue. The UF Church laid down that the united Church would be assigned its funds and properties in the same way as it held its funds and properties. The Church of Scotland insisted that its endowments were not to be secularised. With these conditions the Churches accepted the terms of the Church of Scotland (Property and Endowments) Act of 1925.

The two obstacles to union had now been removed, at least in the eyes of the leaders and of a majority in the assemblies of both Churches. The way was thus open for talks regarding the union of the two Churches. New committees were appointed and a Basis and a Plan of Union were drawn up. Both Churches, after all, were very close in outlook and practice and, the two main differences of principle having been removed, there was little to keep them apart. Certainly the Basis and Plan of Union were ready within a year. After the time that had been taken in the preliminary stages, the leaders were anxious to avoid any further delay when the ball was finally in their court. But one reason why this stage of the negotiations did not take long was that certain differences between the two Churches were left over to be dealt with by the united Church, rather than resolved beforehand. There was something to be said for this procedure since the united Church could more easily decide matters for itself. Yet the question remained as to whether these issues would be settled after mature reflection and deliberation or simply left to be resolved by use and wont.

The Basis of Union dealt with those fundamental matters which were the foundation of the Church, its underlying constitution and its standards relating to doctrine, worship,

[28] Ibid., p. 385.

government and discipline. It was important from a legal point of view that the union of 1929 was seen to be in continuity with the union of 1900, and with the union of 1847 by which the United Presbyterian Church had been formed. The Basis of Union thus had to deal with the same matters and take a similar form to these previous agreements. The Plan of Union dealt with more practical matters which it was necessary to settle so that the united Church could begin its work, and which could be changed later in the light of experience. The Plan included issues such as the ordination and training of ministers, the composition of the general assembly and the other courts of the Church, and the amalgamation of the Church's central structures and finances. The Basis and Plan of Union were finally approved by both assemblies in May 1929 thus paving the way for the union to take place later that year.

Throughout the process minorities in both Churches presented difficulties for the two committees. The minority in the United Free Church was larger and consisted of those who represented the more extreme voluntary position. In the end some of the minority members would settle for nothing less than the disestablishment and disendowment of the Church of Scotland. Although not as large, the Church of Scotland minority wished the Kirk to maintain its previous position in relation to the State without significant change. Those representing the high church tradition had argued in the earlier discussions for a distinctive statement of catholic doctrine to be made in the constitution of the Church, and their position was recognised in the contents of the first of the Articles Declaratory. In both Churches concessions by the majority reduced the size of the opposition, although these measures could not prevent a relatively small number staying out of the union as the United Free Church (Continuing). Although the Kirk had been reunited, the previous history of ecclesiastical division had not been healed in the complete way that the leaders of the union movement had hoped. In order to set the scene for the making of Presbyterian reunion it is necessary to look at how these divisions had resulted from the relations of Church and State in Scotland since the Reformation, and how the process of rebuilding the Kirk had begun.

Chapter 2

Setting the scene: the background to reunion

(a) the need for reunion: Church and State in Scotland 1560–1843

It could be said that the aim of the union of 1929 was to heal the breach in the Kirk caused by the Disruption of 1843 when a large number of ministers, elders and members left to form the Free Church. But that would only refer to part of the story. The United Free Church was the result of a union between the Free Church and the United Presbyterian Church, itself a union of various secession bodies which had left the Established Church during the eighteenth century. In order to understand the background to the event of 1929 one has to appreciate something of the reasons for the previous divisions in the Kirk and, indeed, the history of relations between Church and State in Scotland from the time of the Reformation. It is worth noting that G. D. Henderson, in his masterly account of the Disruption, entitled *Heritage*,[1] gave a full account of the development of the 'Scottish tradition' of the Kirk since 1560 before he dealt with the events of 1843. We therefore need to draw attention to several key features of this story which make sense of the union movement in the early twentieth century.

Henderson points out that there have been several theories about the relationship between Church and State in the history of the Christian Church.[2] There has been 'Hildebrandism', named after the eleventh century pope who claimed the supremacy of the spiritual power of the Church over the temporal authority of the emperor. The opposite view, 'Erastianism', associated with the Swiss physician of the sixteenth century, Dr Thomas Erastus, makes the State supreme over the Church. A third view advocates the complete separation of Church and State, and is associated with the Anabaptists and Independents of the sixteenth and seventeenth centuries. In Scotland, on the other hand, an attempt was made to combine aspects of the different systems, following

[1] G. D. Henderson, *Heritage, A Study of the Disruption* (Edinburgh and London, 1943).
[2] Ibid., pp. 14–15.

the Genevan model of John Calvin and his successor Theodore Beza. This view was based on a partnership between Church and State in which each recognised the distinctive authority of the other and each supported the other in appropriate ways. It thus rejected the supremacy of the Church and the supremacy of the State, and the complete separation of the two, but sought to do justice 'both to the ideal of the national recognition of religion and to the doctrine of spiritual independence'.[3] Since this relationship depended on the twin spheres of authority and of mutual recognition and support, it would always be difficult to define exactly the boundaries of the spheres and the nature of the support. There would be a danger that the pendulum would swing more in one direction than in the other. The history of the relations between Church and State in Scotland could be described in those terms, with the pendulum at times swinging more in favour of the Church and at other times more in favour of the State. A completely satisfying solution to this problem may not be attainable, but, says Henderson, 'Scotland made a substantial contribution at the Union of 1929'.[4] According to John White, the union of 1929 was based on a 'right concordat' which had settled the issue of the relations between Church and State in Scotland.[5]

The Reformation in Scotland was carried out by an armed revolution against the crown but was then recognised by parliament, and the Kirk sought to receive the benefits of state support. The official statement of the reformed faith, the Scots Confession, declared that Christ is the only Head of the Church, yet it also spoke of the duty of the magistrate to further the cause of the true religion.[6] The Scots reformers thus wished to combine the freedom of the Church in its own sphere with the recognition and support of the Church by the State. There was no thought of any separation between the two institutions since Church and nation were co-terminous and the Church and the State 'were but different aspects of one and the same society'.[7] When conflict arose between the representatives of the civil and the ecclesiastical authorities, however, John Knox for one felt it necessary to emphasise the spiritual independence of the Kirk. After a difficult period following the Concordat of Leith, which allowed for the

---

[3] Ibid., p. 15.

[4] Ibid.

[5] John White, 'Church and State' in *Scottish Legionary*, 1949, p. 17.

[6] *The Scots Confession of 1560*, A modern translation by James Bulloch (Edinburgh, 1984), XVI, XXIV.

[7] Gordon Donaldson, *The Scottish Reformation* (Cambridge 1960), p. 131.

appointment of bishops, the Second Book of Discipline of 1578 not only rejected Episcopacy in favour of a Presbyterian system, but also set out a clear distinction between the different jurisdictions of Church and State.[8] The ensuing struggle between James VI and Andrew Melville and the second generation of reformers was thus an extension of the already existing tension evident in the position of Knox and the first generation of reformers. On one famous occasion Melville called the king 'God's sillie vassall' and spoke of the 'twa Kingdomes in Scotland'.[9] In the Kingdom of Christ, the Kirk, said Melville, the King was not a king, nor a lord, nor a head, but a member.

According to John White, the view of Melville was 'more helpful' than the alternatives of Hildebrandism or Erastianism.[10] Melville promulgated a high doctrine of the Church which some have seen as a Protestant version of Hildebrandism, favouring a new form of clerical absolutism.[11] But White instead saw Melville's two kingdoms theory as the 'foster-parent of democracy and civil liberty'.[12] According to White, Melville's view of the two kingdoms contained 'the principles which the Church of Scotland has always contended for'.[13] The Second Book of Discipline was recognised by parliament in 1592 and again in 1690 and was listed in the Basis and Plan of Union in 1929, along with the First Book of Discipline, the Scots Confession and Knox's Book of Common Order, as a document 'held in honour as having an important place in the history of Scottish Presbyterianism'.[14] The model of Church-State relations which was the basis of the Union of 1929 was thus that of the 'two kingdoms', a mutual recognition by both of the independent sphere of the other. The question remains as to how successfully the concordat of 1929 defined the nature of the relationship between the two jurisdictions.

The so-called 'Golden Act' of 1592 marked the high-water mark of Scottish Presbyterianism and of the recognition by the State of the spiritual claims of the Church. This act spoke of the 'liberties, privileges, immunities and freedoms' which had been 'given and granted' by the King to the Church.[15] The interpretation

[8] James Kirk, ed., *The Second Book of Discipline* (Edinburgh, 1980), X. 5, 8, pp. 214–5. White, 'Church and State', p. 17.

[9] Robert Pitcairn, ed., *The Autobiography and Diary of Mr James Melvill* (Edinburgh, 1842), p. 370.

[10] White, 'Church and State', p. 16.

[11] Gordon Donaldson, *Scottish Church History* (Edinburgh, 1985), p. 235.

[12] White, 'Church and State', p. 16.

[13] John White, Church and State (W) 40.

[14] Cox, p. 389; Henderson, *Heritage*, p. 23.

[15] T. Thomson, ed., *The Acts of the Parliament of Scotland* (London, 1814), Vol. III, p. 541.

of this act, as Henderson notes, would be one of the matters on which the parties differed in 1843, and it would be a matter of discussion prior to the union in 1929.[16] This act would be mentioned in Article III of the Articles Declaratory as an important landmark in the relationship between Church and State in Scotland.

Following the achievements of the Act of 1592, the Presbyterian party led by Melville overreached itself and the King was able to exert his authority over the Kirk. Bishops were introduced to work along with presbyteries. The pendulum swung now in favour of the royal supremacy which was expressed even more forcefully by Charles I. His policy was challenged in the National Covenant of 1638. For the Covenanters, Scotland was to be a covenanted nation under God. The initial success of the Covenanters, and their alliance with the English parliamentarians in the Solemn League and Covenant of 1643, turned Scotland, in Henderson's words, into something of a theocracy. The pendulum had swung to the other extreme, towards the supremacy of the Church over the State.[17] One result of the English alliance was the Scottish acceptance of the documents of the Westminster Assembly of Divines as the Kirk's standards in matters of doctrine, worship, and church government. The Restoration of Charles II saw the renewal of the claim to royal supremacy in matters of religion and the reintroduction of bishops into the Kirk. The policies of his brother James VII, however, led to the Revolution of 1688–9 in both England and Scotland.

The Revolution Settlement in Scotland saw the final victory of Presbyterianism, which was recognised as the form of government of the Kirk, and adherence to the Westminster Confession was enshrined in statute law. Yet while Presbyterianism had been triumphant, its victory had come by way of establishment. The Presbyterian Church was 'by law established' and owed its position to statute, and the notion of a covenanted nation was abandoned.[18] The Settlement was thus a defeat for the Covenants, and a loyal covenanting remnant stayed out of the Kirk. The Settlement, too, could not be said to be Erastian in character since the Church had a large measure of self-government. But while the Settlement was moderate it was an establishment of religion. The character of the Kirk was further protected by the Act of Security passed in relation to the Treaty of Union of 1707. The union of the parliaments of Scotland and England had deliberately left the Kirk out of its scope, and, in order to safeguard the Church, the Act of

[16] Henderson, *Heritage*, p. 23; see below, pp. 99–100.
[17] Ibid., p. 27.
[18] Ibid., p. 30.

Security provided for the continuation of the Presbyterian religion in Scotland, and enacted that all university professors in Scotland should subscribe to the Westminster Confession of Faith.

It could be said that the seeds of the future difficulties between Church and State stemmed from the terms of the Revolution Settlement and the Treaty of Union. In spite of the Act of Security, the parliament at Westminster would alter the position of the Kirk. In particular, patronage, which had been abolished in 1690, was restored by act of parliament in 1712, an act against which the general assembly of the Kirk annually protested for over seventy years without success. The issue of patronage would be the presenting cause of the principal secessions from the Church. Patronage had existed in the Church from the beginnings of the parish system. It gave the right of presentation to a vacant living to a lay patron, usually a local landowner. By the time of the Disruption in 1843, a third of patronages belonged to the crown, nearly two-thirds to the landed aristocracy and gentry, and a small number were owned by burgh councils and universities.[19] The Scots reformers had tried unsuccessfully to abolish patronage and to give congregations the right to elect their own ministers. The Second Book of Discipline had declared patronage to be a grievance and it had again been abolished in 1649 during the Presbyterian ascendancy in the Kirk. The Revolution Settlement had placed the right of presentation in the hands of the elders and heritors or landowners of the parish. The act restoring patronage seemed to the Kirk to be an unwarranted intrusion into its internal affairs. Not only that, but another act was passed in 1712 giving toleration to Episcopalians in Scotland under certain conditions, and this measure also seemed to fly in the face of the Act of Security.

It was in relation to patronage that the two main secessions took place in Scottish Presbyterianism during the eighteenth century. The first was led by Ebenezer Erskine in 1733 and followed the assembly's passing of an act in the previous year which seemed to acquiesce in patronage. The second followed the deposition in 1752 of Thomas Gillespie, who had refused to obey the assembly as part of his presbytery's struggle regarding patronage and the rights of congregations. The Relief Church which was subsequently formed was strongly opposed to the interference of the State in the affairs of the Church. In contrast,

---

[19] Stewart J. Brown, 'The Ten Years' Conflict and the Disruption of 1843' in Stewart J. Brown and Michael Fry, eds., *Scotland in the Age of the Disruption* (Edinburgh, 1993), p. 6.

the policy of the Kirk was under the control of the Moderate party which came to favour patronage as a means by which the Church could be more closely related to the society of the day. It should be noted, too, that those who left in 1733 did so, not just because of patronage, but because they considered that the headship of Christ was not adequately asserted, that the Covenants were disregarded, and that the Church had too readily accepted establishment at the hands of the state.[20] In other words, the particular issue of patronage was simply one factor in their overall concern to emphasise the spiritual nature of the Church in relation to the State.

The principle of spiritual independence lay behind the largest secession of all, the Disruption of 1843, when a third of the ministers and a similar proportion of the elders and members of the Kirk left to form the Free Church of Scotland. The Evangelical Revival had led to the Evangelicals becoming the dominant party in the Kirk instead of the Moderates. On gaining a majority in the assembly in 1834, the Evangelicals set about implementing the policies which they felt were for the good of the Church. By the Veto Act the assembly declared the principle that a minister should not be 'intruded on any congregation contrary to the will of the people'.[21] According to this act a majority of male heads of families could veto the choice of the patron as minister. The Evangelicals thus did not seek to abolish patronage, but rather to make it more responsive to local opinion. The Veto Act introduced an element of popular choice, or rather a negative voice, as an expression of the principle of non-intrusion. In addition the Chapel Act gave chapels of ease, or church extension congregations, full status as parishes *quoad sacra* with jurisdiction over spiritual affairs, while civil functions such as poor relief and education remained with the old parishes. The new parishes would have their own kirk sessions and their ministers would be able to sit on presbytery and attend the general assembly. Although some legal opinions had voiced caution on both these measures, saying that they were matters for parliament to deal with, the Evangelicals went ahead. In due course both acts would be declared illegal in the civil courts thus bringing the majority in the assembly into conflict with the State.

The legality of the Veto Act was challenged in a number of cases, one of the most significant being that of Auchterarder where the patron's choice of minister was vetoed by a majority of male heads of families. The Court of Session ruled in 1838 by a

---

[20] Henderson, *Heritage*, p. 36.
[21] Ibid., p. 65.

majority of eight to five that the assembly had no authority to legislate with regard to this matter, and that the rights of patrons, having been established by act of parliament, could only be modified by parliament. The Church 'had exceeded its rights and entered into the province of the State'.[22] As Henderson points out, the Auchterarder decision marked the point where the interest shifted from the problem of the intrusion of ministers into parishes to that of spiritual independence.[23] The Veto Act had been passed on the assumption of the two kingdom theory, the belief in two separate but parallel and complementary jurisdictions. On the other hand many of the lawyers in the Church—and the judgements in the cases seemed to support this outlook — tended to the Erastian view in which the State had ultimate authority over the Church. The Moderates did not share the enthusiasm of the Evangelicals for the two kingdom view because they feared that it could so easily develop into the Hildebrandine position. In their opinion too much power was being claimed by the Church and there had to be some other sphere of jurisdiction which would counterbalance its authority. The legislature seemed to be the best alternative, although there might be occasions when conscience would dictate otherwise.[24] In addition there were some Evangelicals who also thought that the Church's claim to spiritual independence could not be absolute. They would form themselves into a Middle Party and, led by Matthew Leishman of Govan, they urged compromise instead of secession.[25] For the Evangelical leadership, however, there was no going back. The 'sole headship of the Lord Jesus Christ' was at stake and the spiritual independence of the Church had to be recognised by the State. If these decisions stood the Church was not free to carry out its work in the way it thought best.

An appeal against the Auchterarder decision was taken to the House of Lords but was rejected. The government was approached to see if legislation could be introduced to alleviate the position in which the Church found itself. The government did not act and other attempts at legislation failed. The case at Marnoch in the presbytery of Strathbogie, where a majority of ministers upheld the decisions of the civil courts rather than the ecclesiastical courts and were subsequently deposed by the assembly, only served to harden attitudes on all sides of the dispute. The voice of moderation

[22] Ibid., p. 69.
[23] Ibid., p. 70.
[24] Ibid., p. 71.
[25] Douglas M. Murray, 'Matthew Leishman of Govan 1821–1874: the Middle Party and the middle way', *Society of Friends of Govan Old*, Sixth Annual Report, 1996, pp. 12–14.

and compromise was drowned out in the extreme language used in the pamphlet war of the time. The assembly presented its case to the government for the last time in 1842 in the Claim of Right. In this document the Evangelicals referred to the various acts of parliament which, in their view, recognised the independent spiritual jurisdiction of the Church. The intrusion of ministers on unwilling congregations was declared to be a fundamental matter. The Church would rather give up the advantages of establishment than yield on this issue. The document made clear that it was because of its adherence to the doctrine of the sole headship of Christ that the Church was now in peril.

The final decision which made the Disruption inevitable was over the Chapel Act, which was declared illegal by the Court of Session in January of 1843 in the Stewarton Case. The local heritors and kirk session had objected to the setting up of another parish in Stewarton to accommodate a former secession congregation. The decision in this case was perhaps even more significant in terms of the relationship between Church and State. One of the principal concerns of Andrew Melville, as expressed in the Second Book of Discipline, was that the civil authorities should not interfere in the membership of ecclesiastical courts. Yet by this decision the civil courts ruled that chapel ministers could not sit in presbyteries and the general assembly. The State was thus regulating the membership of the courts of the Church. This matter was one which had to be addressed before the union of 1929, and Article IV of the Articles Declaratory would contain a reference to the Church's right to determine 'the constitution and membership of its Courts'.[26] There seemed to be no alternative for the Evangelicals but to leave the establishment since the Church was not free within its own sphere. Thus at the assembly in 1843 the retiring moderator, Professor David Welsh, tabled a Protest signed by over 200 commissioners, and left to form the Free Church of Scotland. Presbyterianism in Scotland was now tragically divided from top to bottom.

(b) the early moves towards reunion 1847–1900

It could be said that the first step towards Presbyterian reunion in Scotland had already taken place in 1820, before the Disruption, with the formation of the United Secession Church, a union of two bodies which were the successors of the First Secession of 1733. A further important stage was reached in 1847, only four years after the Disruption, with the union of that body with the Relief Church

---

[26] See below, p. 67.

to form the United Presbyterian Church. One of the features which these various strands of Presbyteriansim had in common was an espousal of the voluntary position. The Free Church had made it clear, as the first moderator Thomas Chalmers said in 1843, that although they had left the establishment they had done so on the establishment principle. They believed in an establishment of religion but they held also to the spiritual independence of the Church. The State should support but not interfere with the Church. While they had left a vitiated establishment, they would rejoice in returning to a pure one. They were not voluntaries.[27]

Voluntaryism could take different forms. It was in essence and in origin a protest against compulsion in the sphere of religion. It was 'the repudiation of the use of the coercive powers of the State in the interests of a particular Church.'[28] It was a protest against State Churches which were regarded as compulsory Churches, supported by the State rather than by the voluntary contributions of members. It could also take a more extreme view, that the State should have nothing to do with religion, but the majority of seceders in Scotland held that the civil authorities should promote the Christian religion, only not by favouring one particular Church.[29] According to Robert J. Drummond, who became one of the joint conveners of the UF committee and whose background was United Presbyterian, the early seceders wished to see a proper relation between Church and State, not an absence of such a relationship.[30] The Basis of Union of the United Presbyterian Church, while accepting the Westminster Confession and Catechisms, also rejected 'compulsory or persecuting and intolerant principles in religion' and maintained that the Church should be supported by the voluntary contributions of its members.

Voluntaryism also came to influence the Free Church. It was difficult for a *de facto* voluntary Church not to become one in principle as well. And so the majority of the assembly of the Free Church decided in favour of disestablishment in the 1870s, while a significant mainly highland minority remained true to the views of the founding fathers of the Free Church. It had been this minority, led by James Begg, which had blocked the moves for union between the two Churches. In seeking to bring about union, the joint committee of the Churches had in 1869 come to an

[27] Hugh Watt, *Thomas Chalmers and the Disruption of 1843* (Edinburgh, 1943), p. 306.

[28] David S. Cairns, *Life and Times of Alexander Robertson MacEwen, D.D.* (London, 1925), p. 174.

[29] David Woodside, *The Soul of a Scottish Church* (Edinburgh, 1919), pp. 92–3.

[30] Robert J. Drummond, *Lest We Forget* (London, 1951), p. 139.

agreement with regard to national religion.[31] This statement said that civil government is an ordinance of God and that the civil magistrate ought himself to embrace and profess the religion of Christ and further its interests among his subjects. However, as he has no authority in spiritual things, he cannot compel or impose upon his subjects any particular observance of religion or interfere in the government of the Church. There were, however, certain areas where laws ought to be framed in the light of the Word of God, and those concerning marriage, the observance of the Sabbath, and the keeping of days of humiliation and thanksgiving, the fast days, were instances of such legislation. The document rejected both Erastiansim and the spiritual supremacy of the Church and spoke instead of the independent spiritual authority of the Church and the separate authority of the State. Church and State, however, though distinct, owed mutual duties to each other. Here was a statement of the moderate voluntaryism which the Free Church as a whole came to adopt. It was one which still had a definite role for the national recognition of religion, and it was on this basis that the union of the Churches in 1929 would be constructed.

In spite of the failure of the earlier moves towards reunion, the Free Church majority eventually passed a Declaratory Act in relation to the Westminster Confession in 1892, thus bringing it into line with the other Church both in relation to certain doctrinal matters such as the extent of the atonement, and also in relation to the civil magistrate. The Free Church Act was very similar in content to that of the UP Declaratory Act of 1879. The UP Act stated that the Church disapproves of all compulsory or persecuting and intolerant principles in religion, while the Free Church Act stated that 'this Church disclaims intolerant or persecuting principles'.[32] The passing of this act, however, provoked a small number of highlanders to form the Free Presbyterian Church in the following year. The way was now open for the union of the Churches to take place and this was achieved in 1900. The mainly highland minority, however, stayed out of the union as the Free Church or 'Wee Frees'. The establishment of religion was therefore an open question in the United Free Church, and was the reason for the claim by the minority that the majority had abandoned the fundamental principles of the Disruption upon which the Church was founded.

---

[31] Articles of Agreement as to National Religion, in *Selected Documents Bearing on the Question raised by the Communication from the Church of Scotland* (1908), pp. 14–15 (UFC).
[32] Declaratory Act of the United Presbyterian Synod anent the Confession of Faith, 1879, 5, and Declaratory Act of the Free Church of Scotland, 1892, in Cox, pp. 435–7.

Meanwhile the Established Church succeeded in having patronage abolished by parliament in 1874, thus seeming to open the way for a return by those who had left at the Disruption. This expectation, however, proved to be misplaced since hardly any ministers and only a few members of the Free Church returned to the Kirk.[33] In welcoming the repeal of the patronage act, the assembly hoped that the way would be open for 'the healing of the divisions which so greatly weaken the influence of the Church of Christ in the land.'[34] In addition the assembly in 1870 had received several overtures on the subject of union. It agreed to take all possible steps 'consistently with the principles on which this Church is founded, to promote the reunion of Churches having a common origin, adhering to the same Confession of Faith and the same system of government and worship.'[35] A committee was set up which decided that an approach should be made to the other Presbyterian Churches in Scotland with a view to union on any basis 'which is consistent with its historic principles'.[36] It was not until 1878 that an approach was made to the other Churches and replies received from them, but the basis of the initiative was the 'support of an establishment of religion'.[37] The synod of the United Presbyterian Church welcomed the approach and favoured greater co-operation by the three large Presbyterian Churches, but said that it was impossible for the synod 'to contemplate sharing with the Established Church the trust reposed in it by the State'.[38] The Free Church assembly spoke against the evils of division and in favour of co-operation. It also affirmed the principle of the national recognition of religion. But in the light of the Claim of Right and the Protest of 1843 it was unable to support 'the maintenance of the existing establishment as at present constituted'.[39] The Church of Scotland assembly did not realise that the issue of spiritual independence and establishment of religion still required to be addressed if the heirs of the Secessions and the Disruption were to consider reunion.

The next moves from the Auld Kirk took place in 1886 following the general election in 1885 which had been fought in Scotland in

[33] I. G. C. Hutchison, *A Political History of Scotland 1832–1924* (Edinburgh, 1986), p. 116.

[34] *AGA*, 27 May 1875, p. 63.

[35] *AGA*, 27 May 1870, p. 64; John White, Union Efforts, p. 1 (W) 97.

[36] *C of S Rep.*, 1875, p. 619. Cf. *AGA*, 31 May 1875, p. 80; *C of S Rep.*, 1875, p. 621; White, Union Efforts, p. 4.

[37] *AGA*, 31 May 1878, p. 82.

[38] 'Answer from the United Presbyterian Church', 8 May 1879, in *Selected Documents*, p. 5 (UFC). Cf. Woodside, *Soul of a Scottish Church*, p. 298.

[39] 'Answer by the Committee of the Free Church Assembly on Assembly Arrangements', 30 May 1879, in ibid., pp. 6–7.

part on the issue of disestablishment. The campaign for the disestablishment of the Church was waged enthusiastically by the two other Presbyterian Churches and came to be supported by the Liberal Party in Scotland. The subject was a central issue in the general election campaigns between 1874 and 1892 and reached its height in 1885.[40] The Church of Scotland assembly had appointed a Church Interests Committee in 1882, and a Church Defence Association was also formed to resist these proposals. Although the issue continued to be discussed, and various parliamentary measures were introduced, it was dead in terms of practical politics after 1886.[41] The assembly of the Church of Scotland thus decided once again to approach the question of reunion on the basis of establishment.[42] The Free Church replied that it was still convinced of the 'propriety and necessity' of disestablishment and disendowment, but that it would consider an approach to union where the differences between the Churches were treated as open for discussion.[43] The Church of Scotland's Church Interests Committee responded by pointing out the benefits of establishment which the Kirk was willing to share with other Presbyterian Churches, but recognised that there was no common ground on which to proceed.[44] The synod of the United Presbyterian Church was also unable to respond on the basis outlined by the Church of Scotland.[45] One attempt in parliament to remove an obstacle to reunion also took place in 1886. A bill was introduced by R. B. Finlay, member for the Inverness Burghs who later became Lord Finlay, to declare the spiritual independence of the Church. The assembly's Church Interests Committee generally welcomed the bill and said that, should it be passed, the Church of Scotland should take the opportunity to enter into conference with the other Churches that 'they may be incorporated into one National Church'.[46] However the measure failed, partly because it was seen as a means by which parliament would confer freedom upon the Church rather than recognising its existence in the Church.[47] It still referred to the Church 'as by law established'.

[40] Ian Machin, 'Voluntaryism and Reunion, 1874–1929', in Norman Macdougall, ed., *Church, Politics and Society: Scotland 1408–1929* (Edinburgh, 1983), pp. 225–6.

[41] A. L. Drummond and James Bulloch, *The Church in Late Victorian Scotland 1874–1900* (Edinburgh, 1978), pp. 123, 125.

[42] *AGA*, 26 May 1886, p. 44.

[43] 'Reply of the Free Church', 28 May 1886, in *Selected Documents*, p. 10.

[44] 'Reply of the General Assembly of the Church of Scotland's Committee on Church Interests', 15 November 1886, in ibid., pp. 11–12.

[45] 'Reply of the Synod of the United Presbyterian Church', 26 May 1886, in ibid., p. 13. Cf. Woodside, *Soul of a Scottish Church*, p. 300.

[46] *C of S Rep.*, 1887, pp. 589–90.

[47] *C of S Rep.*, 1887, pp. 587–8; John White, Finlay's Bill 1886 (W) 46; Drummond and Bulloch, *Church in Late Victorian Scotland*, p. 123.

Perhaps of greater significance was the holding of informal discussions between representatives of the three main Presbyterian Churches in the mid-1890s. These meetings were private and unofficial and thus could not, by definition, achieve anything tangible of themselves. But the nature of the discussions showed both the extent of the agreement between the Churches and the matters which still remained to be resolved between them. They also showed the need for compromise if union was to be achieved.[48] In addition they produced a suggestion which would prove to be the means by which the union of 1929 would in the end be brought about. One of the participants was Professor A. R. McEwen of the United Presbyterian Church. He found that there was a large measure of agreement on the two main issues of national religion and spiritual independence.[49] It was agreed that the Christian religion ought to be acknowledged by the State, and that the State should also recognise the Church as a divine institution and the chief means whereby righteousness and godliness should be promoted. The spiritual independence of the Church should therefore be recognised, facilities for the religious education of the young should be provided, measures should be promoted for the moral and social improvement of the people, and religious ordinances should be supplied in the armed forces of the Crown. There was also a unanimous statement on spiritual independence which asserted that Christ had appointed for his Church a government distinct from that of the State, with a purely spiritual jurisdiction. Each Church must therefore guard its rights in all matters spiritual such as doctrine, discipline, worship, and government, and equally the Church must not interfere with the legitimate exercise of power by the State. It was made clear that the Church's authority was not unlimited or arbitrary but consisted simply of freedom to obey the Word of God, a freedom which had been conferred by Christ. This last point is worth noting since the limitations of the freedom of the Church in relation to doctrine would be one of the most difficult issues to be resolved in the drafting of the Articles Declaratory.

These statements showed a considerable amount of agreement and formed a useful starting point for the formal discussions between the Churches. But on the issue of establishment the representatives of the Churches were still far apart, and, in the words of Professor David S. Cairns of the United Presbyterian Church, the report of the discussions on this issue broke up 'like an exploding shell'.[50] The Church of Scotland members did,

[48] Lord Sands, *Dr. Archibald Scott of St George's, Edinburgh, and his times* (Edinburgh and London, 1919), p. 196.
[49] Cairns, *Life of McEwen*, p. 179.
[50] Ibid., p. 180.

however, present what was in effect a moderate view of the question. They stated that establishment was not inimical to the spiritual freedom of the Church and that it was necessary for the protection of the Church's independence. The non-established Churches might find themselves in conflict with the laws of the land without some special agreement. Such, indeed, proved to be the case for the United Free Church with the House of Lords decision in 1904. They defined establishment as the State approving of the creed and constitution of the Church, guaranteeing the independence of its courts, and accepting its legislation so long as duly pronounced in accordance with the creed and constitution of the Church.[51] As Cairns pointed out, however, everything turned on the ambiguous word 'approves'. Taken in the sense of 'recognises', however, we have the basis of the Church of Scotland Act of 1921. Establishment would depend on a special and binding compact, the State bestowing certain privileges in return for the Church fulfilling certain obligations. The fact that this agreement was made with only one Church was not thought to be unfair. The non-established Churches either could not or would not undertake to perform the spiritual work which the State deemed essential to the nation, and therefore could not expect the same advantages as those who did.

The Free Church members said that such a compact should be made with all Christian Churches and not just with one, and that the preferential treatment of one Church at the hands of the State was a great obstacle to union. Here, indeed, was evidence of how far the Free Church had moved from the time of the Disruption when the establishment principle was still held.[52] The United Presbyterians also maintained the principle of religious equality, that a State's testimony to Christianity was impaired when it dealt unequally with its citizens and selected one Church for special privileges. They affirmed their adherence to the principle of the national recognition of religion, but could not agree to the application of that principle in an established Church. Just as the Church of Scotland members had said that they could not consent to disestablishment, so the United Presbyterians could not entertain the idea of entering an established Church.

The two positions were thus clearly defined. The one side could see no disadvantages in their non-established state while the other side could see no disadvantages in their established position. But, as Cairns pointed out, the disadvantages in both these positions would be shown up within the next ten years.[53]

[51] Ibid., p. 181.
[52] JW, p. 99.
[53] Cairns, *Life of McEwen*, p. 186.

The whole relationship of the Churches to the law had to be clarified before any of the Churches could rest on a 'secure foundation'. As he said, 'both the constitutional position of the Church of Scotland and the legal position of the Free Church in view of the Spiritual Independence which it asserted were fundamentally insecure'. The position of the United Presbyterian Church was only different inasmuch as it had avoided the legal difficulty by vesting its congregational properties in the hands of trustees who held them nominally in their own name but in reality on behalf of the Church. The 'fundamental insecurity' of the non-established Churches would be shown up mercilessly by the House of Lords decision in 1904, and the disadvantages of the Established Church would be shown up when it sought to modify its doctrinal position. The former would lead the UF Church to see the merits in its spiritual freedom being recognised by the State, while the latter would show the Church of Scotland that it was not really free in spiritual terms. Both Churches would be prepared to re-examine their previous suppositions in the light of these events and be prepared for open-ended and unrestricted conference on union. No longer would either establishment or disestablishment be prior conditions for discussion.

In addition the way by which reunion might be achieved by the Churches was pointed to during these informal discussions by Professor Henry Calderwood of the United Presbyterian Church. He said:

> In the event of the reunion of the Presbyterians of Scotland, the British Legislature, on memorial from the Established Church, and on concurrence of the sister Presbyterian Churches, may recognise the reconstituted Presbyterian Church as *de facto* the 'National Church', thereby acknowledging that the Scottish nation is Protestant in faith and Presbyterian in Church government, and that the reconstituted Church stands in historic continuity with the Church of the Reformation, whose position and interests were provided for in the Treaty of Union between Scotland and England.[54]

These words made a great impression upon one young Church of Scotland minister, John White, about to begin a court case with the heritors in his parish of Shettleston over the building of a new church, a struggle which would not have been necessary had Calderwood's idea of a united *de facto* National Church been realised.[55] Calderwood's idea would become almost exactly the

[54] *JW*, p. 100.
[55] Ibid.

way which would be followed by the Church of Scotland in removing the main obstacle to union with the United Free Church. The Established Church, in consultation with its sister Church, would prepare a new statement of its constitution in terms of spiritual freedom and the national recognition of religion, and these 'Articles Declaratory' would be recognised by parliament in the Church of Scotland Act of 1921. The united Church would thus be recognised as a national Church, in continuity with the Church 'which was reformed in 1560, whose liberties were ratified in 1592, and for whose security provision was made in the Treaty of Union of 1707'.[56]

(c) the immediate factors in reunion

Two events served to shake both the United Free Church and the Church of Scotland out of their complacency and make them open to consider reunion in a new light. For the UF Church the event was the decision of the House of Lords in the Free Church Case in 1904. By this decision the whole of the property and assets of the former Free Church were awarded to the largely highland minority who had remained out of the union in 1900. The minority had argued—and their case was upheld by the Lords—that in uniting with the United Presbyterian Church, the majority had departed from the founding principles of the Free Church and were therefore no longer the true successors of the Disruption. One respect in which the majority had changed was, it was argued, in terms of its view of establishment. This was now an open question in the UF Church and was no longer held to be a matter of principle. At the time of the Disruption, however, the Free Church had maintained the establishment principle, even although it had left the Established Church. The address by Thomas Chalmers at the first assembly of the Free Church on this subject was used to support this contention. The other respect in which the majority was said to have abandoned the founding principles of the Church was with regard to doctrine. The Declaratory Act of 1892 had modified the Church's adherence to the doctrines of the Westminster Confession of Faith, particularly with regard to the atonement, whereas in 1843 the Church had accepted the teaching of the Confession without exception. The minority represented those within the Church who remained faithful to the Calvinism of the Westminster standards and were unaffected by views concerning the universal scope of the atonement which had gained in popularity during the nineteenth

[56] Article III of the Articles Declaratory, in Appendix I, p. 285.

century. On both issues, it was maintained, the majority of the former Free Church had departed from the original principles of the Disruption and had therefore forfeited the property of the Church.

Underlying this view, however, was a more basic principle, that of Church and creed, which has been identified by Kenneth Ross in his study of the Free Church Case.[57] By 'creed' in this context is meant the fundamental principles of a Church which cannot be changed without the Church losing its identity. The creed of the Free Church, it was argued, was that of the Westminster Confession and the way in which it was interpreted in 1843. Thus both matters on which the majority had departed from the Confession, the establishment of religion and the doctrine of the atonement, were simply instances of this deeper principle. The Church did not have the liberty to change its 'creed'. The majority, now in the United Free Church, argued that the Church did have the power to alter its understanding of the Confession, and that it had the power to develop and change as new insights and understandings were gained. The Church was not tied to the way in which these matters were understood in 1843 or even in 1647 when the Westminster Confession had first been accepted by the Kirk. In other words, the Church had 'the power of change'.[58] There were fundamental principles which could not be departed from without the Church ceasing to be a Christian Church, but this 'creed' consisted of more fundamental matters relating to the nature of Christian belief itself, not to matters such as an establishment of religion and the extent of the atonement. On these secondary matters there could be differences of opinion and the Church could change and develop its position.[59] The case in the end turned upon whether or not the Free Church could change or whether it was tied to the position it had taken in 1843. Although the case of the minority had been dismissed in the Court of Session it was upheld by a majority in the House of Lords in 1904.

The verdict was a devastating blow to the United Free Church. Its entire property, churches, manses, offices, theological colleges, and all its funds, rightfully belonged to a small minority. In terms of natural justice the verdict was seen by many to be flawed. In addition it could be argued that, in terms of the law relating to trusts on which the judgement was based, the purpose of a trust must be carried out in its entirety or not at all. Such a small minority was not able to execute all the terms of the trusts in

[57] Kenneth R. Ross, *Church and Creed in Scotland: the Free Church Case 1900–1904 and its Origins* (Edinburgh, 1988). Cf. *FR*, pp. 13–16.
[58] *FR*, p. 15.
[59] *FR*, p. 38.

question and thus forfeited its legal right to them.[60] Following the recommendations of a royal commission, the Churches (Scotland) Act was passed by parliament in 1905 and an executive commission was set up to allocate the property in an equitable way in relation to the due performance of the purposes for which the funds had been raised.[61] The significance of this act was not lost on the majority. Here was a 'free' Church depending upon parliament to restore its property which it had lost through an action in the civil courts. Not only could such an action not have been taken against the Established Church, since its property and other rights were themselves protected by legislation, but the Church had had to look to the State to intervene on its behalf. The constitution of the Church was not secure in relation to the law and there would always be uncertainty over whether the claims of the Church to spiritual freedom would be recognised by the courts in the way in which the Church recognised them. The advantages of the freedom of the Church being recognised by parliament were only too apparent to the United Free Church, and thus reunion with the Church of Scotland on that basis became an attractive proposition.

In order to try and prevent such a case arising again, although it was realised that without statutory recognition such could not be guaranteed, the UF Church passed an act in 1906 anent the Spiritual Independence of the Church.[62] By this act it was stated that the Church has under Christ as its only Head 'independent and exclusive jurisdiction and power of legislating in all matters of doctrine, worship, discipline, and government of the Church'. The Act went on to state that it was a 'fundamental principle and rule of this Church that,

> in dependence on the grace of God, recognising the authority of the Word of God, contained in the Scriptures of the Old and New Testaments, as the supreme unchangeable Standard, and looking to the Head of the Church for the promised guidance of the Holy Spirit, this Church has the sole and exclusive right and power from time to time, as duty may require, through her Courts to alter, change, add to, or modify, her constitution and laws, Subordinate Standards and Formulas, and to determine and declare what these are, and to unite with other Churches ...

The United Free Church thus enacted that the right to change its doctrinal and other standards was a 'fundamental principle' of the Church, that the Church had the power of change as it had

---

[60] Ross, *Church and Creed*, p. 49.
[61] Ibid., p. 52.
[62] *UFC Proc.*, 1906, pp. 289–90; cf. *FR*, pp. 15, 24–5. The act is found as Appendix II, pp. 288–9.

argued before the House of Lords. The wording of the act is important since much of it would be reflected in the Articles Declaratory of the Constitution of the Church of Scotland in Matters Spiritual. Having emerged from the trauma of the Free Church Case, and having set out its claim to spiritual freedom in such an uncompromising way, the UF Church would not be willing to retreat from this stance when it considered reunion with the Established Church. Thus the Articles setting out the constitutional position of the Kirk had to contain a similarly clear and unambiguous statement regarding the freedom of the Church in relation to doctrine, worship and government. The terms of Articles IV and V echo the language of the UF Act. The significance of this Act in relation to the composition of the Articles Declaratory has not always been recognised but is crucial to their interpretation. If the Articles had not taken the same position with regard to spiritual independence as the UF Act of 1906, then reunion would not have been possible.[63]

Was there, then, nothing that had to remain, was the position one of complete flux? The 1906 Act did wish to give the Church the power in future to make any change in relation to its doctrine, life, and government. It will be noted, however, that certain things were mentioned as a permanent reference in relation to such change. The Church's right to change was to be carried out in dependence on the grace of God, recognising the authority of the Word of God, looking to the Head of the Church, and with the guidance of the Holy Spirit. The Act was thus not bereft of any doctrinal reference, but such references were just that, references, and would require considerable interpretation by the Church. When it came to discussing the limitations of the Church's freedom in relation to doctrine during the union negotiations, these references were referred to by those who sought to include a statement of faith in the Articles Declaratory.[64] Thus the Act was not only the model for the Articles in relation to spiritual freedom, but also in relation to those doctrines which were to be regarded as fundamental, from which the Church could not depart without losing its identity as a Church. There was still a 'creed', but that 'permanent substratum' would not in future be the Westminster Confession, as it had been for the minority in the Free Church Case, but the declaration of the catholic faith set out in the Church's constitution. The doctrinal reference in the Articles would be made in a similar way to that of the 1906 Act, but it

[63] *FR*, esp. pp. 31–2.
[64] *FR*, pp. 38–9.

would be considerably expanded, made more explicit, and its status would be enhanced.[65]

The United Free Church thus approached the question of reunion more aware of the drawbacks of being a free Church without any statutory recognition, and having agreed to an uncompromising statement of spiritual freedom from which it was not willing to retreat. The Church of Scotland was also more open to the drawbacks of being an established Church because of its desire to modify its adherence to the Westminster Confession. If the UF Church had run into legal problems because it had departed from the Confession, the Established Church found it was unable to alter its adherence to the Confession because of its legal position. As we have seen, the Revolution Settlement of 1690 enshrined the Westminster Confession as the Kirk's standard of faith. In addition, the subscription of ministers to the Confession was laid down by an act of 1693 by which every minister had to subscribe to the Confession as the confession of his faith. The Church itself had introduced an even stricter formula in 1711 which it was able to depart from in 1889 without reference to parliament. But to change the formula of 1693, an act of parliament was required; the Church was not free to make this change itself.[66] The irony of the situation was that it was only because an act was going through parliament to deal with the outcome of the Free Church Case that the Church of Scotland was able to achieve this measure of relief. An additional clause of the Churches (Scotland) Act of 1905 gave the Kirk the ability to change the way in which ministers subscribed to the Westminster Confession. After much discussion the assembly in 1910 agreed that in future a minister would subscribe the Confession 'declaring that I accept it as the Confession of this Church, and that I believe the fundamental doctrines of the Christian Faith therein'.[67]

The significance of this change was twofold. The Church of Scotland had been brought face to face with one of the major disadvantages of being an established Church. It had found that it was not free to make a change in the doctrinal subscription of ministers. It could no longer claim that establishment was not a restriction on the exercise of its freedom as a Church. It was indeed a serious disability for a Church not to be able to make changes in this sphere. The more progressive voices within the Kirk welcomed the opportunity to seek recognition by the State of

---

[65] *FR*, pp. 40–1, 71–2.
[66] *FR*, p. 16.
[67] *AGA*, 1910, Act XIII, p. 30.

a full measure of spiritual freedom which would include the area of doctrine as well as other aspects of the life of the Church. But there were other more conservative voices in the councils of the Church who were unhappy about the Church being given unlimited freedom in the doctrinal sphere.

We therefore come to the second significance of this episode for the question of reunion. In discussing the content of the new formula of subscription to be required of ministers, the Church of Scotland was faced with the question of what constituted the fundamentals of the faith and how adherence to these essential beliefs should be expressed. Ministers would no longer be required to subscribe to the whole of the Confession, but how were they still to adhere to a basic minimum of belief? This question occupied a great deal of time in the discussions concerning the new formula.[68] In particular the high churchmen on the committee, such as Professor James Cooper of Glasgow, wished to include a reference to the fundamental doctrines of the catholic faith as the basic minimum to be required. For Cooper and his fellow Scoto-Catholics the faith was prior to the Church, and no Church had liberty to depart from that faith. The Church of Scotland's adherence to these doctrines was made by its holding to the Westminster Confession which contained the catholic faith, although it also contained much more. Once it was proposed to alter the way in which ministers subscribed to this document, a way had to be found for them still to acknowledge the catholic faith. Cooper would have wished, ideally, for subscription to be made instead to the Nicene Creed, the doctrinal symbol of the undivided Church which contained the catholic doctrines of the trinity and the incarnation. At any rate he wished a more explicit statement of the fundamental doctrines of the faith to be included in the new formula. Yet in the end he and his colleagues agreed to the final version which contained a general rather than a specific reference to the 'fundamental doctrines of the Christian Faith' contained in the Confession. Cooper was concerned that the fundamentals had not been defined, but he took comfort from the fact that the formula must surely include adherence to such doctrines as the trinity, the divinity of Christ, and the incarnation.[69] Cooper would later regret that he had not stood out for a more explicit statement of catholic doctrine. Thus when it came to discussing the doctrinal reference in the Articles Declaratory, Cooper would insist on what he regarded as a satisfactory statement of certain doctrines. Without the previous discussions

[68] Sands, *Archibald Scott* , ch. 10.
[69] *FR*, pp. 35–6.

regarding the formula of subscription it is difficult to understand Cooper's role in the drafting of the Kirk's constitution and the final form which that constitution would take, especially the doctrinal declaration in Article I.[70] Not only had the Church of Scotland realised the need for the Church to have spiritual freedom, it had also realised the limits to that freedom.

(d) the first steps towards reunion

The plight of the United Free Church as a result of the House of Lords decision brought out a wave of sympathy in the Church of Scotland. Lord Balfour of Burleigh, the prominent Kirk elder, offered to mediate between the two sides.[71] Offers of accommodation were made to those who were forced to leave their buildings, including one to the headquarters staff to share the Church offices in Queen Street in Edinburgh.[72] These practical gestures of friendship were greatly appreciated and 'caused many to wonder whether the two Churches could not come closer together, in one way or another, in spite of constitutional differences.'[73] There was, too, the growing co-operation of the Churches in various fields, particularly those of foreign missions and social work. A special committee of the Church of Scotland assembly would later say that in foreign mission the Church had advanced the farthest in terms of co-operation and union with other Churches.[74] One joint meeting, held by the two presbyteries of Edinburgh in March 1906 to consider social questions, made a considerable impression on one of those present, Archibald Scott, minister of St George's Parish Church. After the meeting he said that the time was ripe for getting the assembly to do on a national scale what had been done at this local level.[75] At the meeting of the presbytery of Edinburgh on 27th March 1907 he moved that the assembly be overtured to hold a conference with the United Free Church with a view to greater co-operation between the Churches, thereby laying a foundation upon which Presbyterian reunion might be built. His motion was challenged by John White who wished the invitation to be extended to other Churches and that the conference should be held on reunion, not just on co-operation. After informal consultation the terms of Scott's motion were altered to read that agreement be sought as to how the existing relationship of the

[70] *FR*, pp. 48–9.
[71] P. Carnegie Simpson, *The Life of Principal Rainy* (London, 1909), II, pp. 391–2.
[72] *JW*, p. 104.
[73] Ibid.
[74] *C of S Rep.*, 1908, p. 1283.
[75] Drummond, *Lest We Forget*, p. 132.

Churches might be so adjusted 'as to provide a foundation upon which they can begin to build a satisfactory structure of comprehensive reunion'.[76] In his speech Scott said that the maintenance of the *status quo* was not desired in any of the Churches:

> They wanted the Churches to consider the existing state of things, and to move forward to a position in which, under Divine guidance, they could reconstitute the old national Church and inaugurate an era of reform among the people.[77]

He also said that he wanted to avoid using the terms 'establishment' and 'disestablishment' which had become shibboleths. According to Dr. Norman Macleod, the senior clerk of the assembly, this last statement had caused some disquiet and could be easily misunderstood.[78]

At the assembly overtures along similar lines were received from two other presbyteries and seven synods, but in view of the continuing difficulties between the Free Church and the United Free Church it was decided that no action be taken meantime. Instead a committee was formed with Norman Macleod as convener to consider co-operation and reunion in general terms.[79] On the report of this committee in 1908, the assembly issued its invitation to both the UF and the Free Church to confer on the present ecclesiastical situation in Scotland and consider how greater co-operation could be brought about which would lead to the 'union for which many hearts long and pray'.[80] A minority report, signed by James Cooper and three other high churchmen, called for the committee to enter on the subject of reunion rather than start with the question of co-operation.[81] In spite of support from John White and William Mair, the assembly preferred the more cautious approach of the committee to that of the minority. William Mair, the veteran expert on church law, had been waging a one-man campaign on behalf of union for some time.[82] A former staunch defender of the Established Church, he had written a series of articles in *Blackwood's Magazine*[83] in which he no longer insisted on reunion 'on the basis of a return to the maternal home

---

[76] *JW*, p. 110.

[77] *The Scotsman*, 25 April 1907.

[78] Sands, *Archibald Scott*, p. 233.

[79] *AGA*, 24 May 1907, p. 51.

[80] *AGA*, 22 May 1908, p. 57.

[81] *C of S Rep.*, 1908, p. 1304. In addition to Cooper, the minority report was signed by R. S. Kirkpatrick, G. W. Sprott, and H. J. Wotherspoon.

[82] *JW*, p. 114.

[83] Three of these articles were subsequently published as *Churches and the Law* (Edinburgh, 1904) and *The Scottish Churches: Two Papers* (Edinburgh, 1907).

of daughters who had strayed'.[84] Mair had earlier written to Scott in those terms and had held a private meeting at his home in Edinburgh of leading ministers of both Churches which had endorsed this view.[85] As it was, the wording of the assembly's motion in 1908 was superseded by the reply from the United Free Church in the following year. While the 'Wee Frees' declined the invitation — in the words of John White they sent us 'a post-card to say NO'[86] — the UF Church declared in favour of unrestricted conference on union. The assemblies of both Churches now appointed committees with the remit:[87]

> To enter into unrestricted conference on the existing ecclesiastical situation and on the main causes which keep the Churches apart; in the earnest hope that, by God's blessing, misunderstandings and hindrances may be removed, and the great object of Presbyterian reunion in Scotland thereby advanced.

For the first time the suggestion had been made, and had been accepted, that establishment should be an open question. In the opinion of Lord Sands, if antecedent conditions had been announced, the proposed conference would have failed. 'No accommodation', he said, 'was ever arrived at where the parties to the negotiation announced irreducible conditions at the outset as the condition of negotiation.'[88] Could the ancient relationship with the State be modified in such a way as to be acceptable to both Churches?[89] The discussions were to begin but it was not clear at first that a way towards union could be found.

---

[84] Sands, *Archibald Scott*, p. 210.
[85] Ibid., pp. 214, 221.
[86] Why are other Presbyterian Churches given the same opportunity as the United Free Church to consider Re–union with the Church of Scotland? (W) 97. *JW*, p. 114.
[87] *AGA*, 27 May 1909, p. 68.
[88] Sands, *Archibald Scott*, p. 237.
[89] *JW*, pp. 114–15.

Chapter 3

Surveying the ground: the early discussions on reunion 1909–13

(a) procedures and personalities

The first meeting of the two committees took place on 9th November 1909 on neutral ground in the Goold Hall, part of the Bible Society premises at St Andrew Square in Edinburgh.[1] Subsequent meetings were held in the Library Hall of New College, which is now known as the Martin Hall. After the opening praise, the scripture lesson was read from John's Gospel chapter 17, and prayer was led by Principal Alexander Whyte and by James Robertson of Whittingehame, the moderator of the general assembly of the Church of Scotland.[2] Not all in the room would live to see the eventual outcome. Of the 210 ministers and elders who entered upon the discussions, ninety-five died during the progress of the work, and only fifty-six were still in active service when the task was completed twenty years later.[3] Some of those who gathered knew each other quite well, some not at all. It took time for the participants to get to know one another and to take the measure of each other. It was inevitable that the first meetings were exploratory by nature, a testing time for everyone. Wallace Williamson of St Giles', who became one of the joint conveners, later told the Church of Scotland assembly that it was the queerest meeting he had ever attended:[4]

> We looked into each other's faces, strangers many of us, and perhaps not altogether unsuspicious of each other; the air was certainly electric and the heat was suffocating…We passed from that stage of suspicion to a stage of watchfulness….

[1] *JW*, p. 115.
[2] J. R. Fleming, *The Story of Church Union in Scotland*, its origins and progress 1560–1929 (London, 1929), p. 66; G. F. Barbour, *The Life of Alexander Whyte, D.D.* (London, 1923), p. 517.
[3] Fleming, *Story of Union*, p. 66.
[4] *Layman's Book*, 1913, p. 87.

John White spoke of the members of the two committees cautiously pacing round in a circle and eventually coming back to the point from which they had started. But the suspicion and ignorance would gradually disappear as they came to know each other better. As White would later say: 'Personal acquaintance destroyed many a prejudice.'[5] In reading the minutes of these meetings, one certainly has the impression that the discussions often covered the same ground time and again until the majority of the committee reached a common understanding of the points at issue.

It was clear that in terms of procedure the joint committee was too large for a thorough discussion of the weightier matters, although the comprehensiveness of the main committees, or 'hundreds' as they were called, would be important in providing a representative sounding board of opinion in both Churches. If the proposals for union met with the approval of the hundreds, it was likely they would meet with acceptance in the Churches as a whole. In order to do the initial groundwork, a sub-committee was appointed to examine the remit more closely and twenty-five members were appointed from each side.[6] Seven meetings were held during the first year. It was soon decided that the topics for discussion were the two principles set out by both assemblies in 1908 as necessary to be conserved in any reunion, the national recognition of religion and the spiritual freedom of the Church. A smaller sub-committee of twelve was appointed to examine more closely one aspect of the question, the liberty of the Church in relation to creed, and the other meetings were devoted to the national recognition of religion. An interim report was presented to the assemblies in 1910 and a much fuller joint report in 1911.

Since some of those who were present at that first meeting would become prominent in the following negotiations it is as well at the outset briefly to identify the leading personalities in both Churches. One of the joint conveners of the Church of Scotland committee was Norman Macleod (1838–1911), minister in Inverness, moderator in 1900, and the principal clerk of the assembly since 1907. Macleod was not destined to play a large part in the movement since he died only two years after the committee began its work. A member of that highland ecclesiastical dynasty which has given so many leaders to the Kirk, Macleod was a quiet, friendly man who confided his anxieties about the outcome of the union movement to John White.[7] In particular he

---

[5] *JW*, p. 119.
[6] Norman Maclean, *The Years of Fulfilment* (London, 1953), p. 111.
[7] *JW*, p. 118.

was anxious lest the high churchmen on the committee would press their desire for a credal statement to such an extent as to make the success of the enterprise extremely doubtful. He had some sympathy with this position since he also wished the Church to adhere explicitly to a credal formula in any reunion.[8]

He was succeeded as joint convener by Andrew Wallace Williamson (1856–1925), minister of St Giles' Cathedral in Edinburgh, who had supported the policy of the committee from an early stage. According to his biographer, Lord Sands, his contribution to the movement for union was 'inspirational rather than constructive'.[9] While not an innovator or a noted back-room negotiator, he brought zeal, enthusiasm, and a gift of oratorical expression to the task. In debate he could lift the subject of reunion above the realm of practical ecclesiastical arrangements to the higher level of the spiritual nature of the Church. He proved to be a valuable spokesman for the committee at the assembly. He was a moderate high churchman who had left the Scottish Church Society because he did not think it should form a party or pressure group within the Kirk. Like his predecessor as convener, therefore, he was sympathetic to the demand for a doctrinal statement in the framing of the Church's constitution.[10] Free of a direct link to the Scoto-Catholic minority, he was able to gain the confidence of a wide cross-section of the committee and still remain loyal to the catholic faith and to the traditions of the Kirk. His seeking of conciliation and brotherhood in the committee also contributed to the success of the movement. Without his influence, said Sands, the course of events in the committee, the assembly and the Church might have been very different.[11]

The other joint convener at the start of the discussions was Alexander Hugh Bruce, Lord Balfour of Burleigh (1849–1921), a leading Conservative politician who had served as Scottish Secretary from 1895 to 1903, and who provided a valuable link between the Church and parliament on several occasions. He placed his recognised qualities of shrewdness and business ability at the disposal of the Church.[12] He had already served as the convener of the Committee on the Formula, and of the Church Interests Committee where he was known as a stout defender of

---

[8] *JW*, pp. 118–9. Cf. *FR*, pp. 32–3.
[9] Lord Sands, *Life of Andrew Wallace Williamson, K.C.V.O., D.D.* (Edinburgh, 1929), p. 270.
[10] Murray, 'Scottish Church Society', pp. 68, 124–8.
[11] Sands, *Wallace Williamson*, pp. 270–1.
[12] Lady Frances Balfour, *A Memoir of Lord Balfour of Burleigh, K.T.* (London, 1924), p. 147.

the Kirk in the disestablishment campaign. His father was a member of the Established Church but his mother belonged to the Free Church. Part of his commitment to union was a desire to heal the breach which had led his parents to attend different places of worship.[13] In the work of the committee he was, according to Lord Sands, 'strong yet conciliatory, resolute yet diplomatic, resourceful yet cautious'.[14] Although his intellect might not be 'as keen as a razor', his advice was usually 'weighty with the wisdom of much experience of the ways of men'.[15] Like Norman Macleod and Wallace Williamson he was anxious to secure some place for doctrine in the statement of the Church's freedom, although he would be accused by James Cooper of trying to set up a 'creedless' Church!

One of the joint conveners of the United Free Church committee was George Robson (1842–1911), formerly minister of the United Presbyterian Church in Inverness and Perth, and editor of *The Record*, the magazine of the UF Church. Like Norman Macleod, Robson would not live long enough to have a lasting impact on the negotiations. He was not considered by one observer to be 'a particularly heavy gun' on the committee.[16] He was a key figure in organising the 1910 World Missionary Conference in Edinburgh, which did much to promote the cause of church unity in general and was an encouragement to those engaged in the particular task in Scotland.[17] It was Robson's 'intense spirituality and missionary fervour' which impressed many members of the committee.[18] One person to be encouraged in this way was Lord Sands who received an unexpected and brief visit from him while he was struggling to draft an early document for the committee.[19] Robson had felt impelled to call on Sands to tell him to be of good courage, and that those who were for him were far greater than those against him. Sands later said that it was the shortest visit he had ever received in terms of time but the longest in import, since he took up his task 'with hope renewed and with the assurance of final victory'. Robson was succeeded by John Young (1844–1930), another minister of the former UP Church who had become home mission secretary in 1889 and was moderator in 1910. His more extreme voluntaryism eventually led him to resign as convener and become an opponent of the committee's policy on union.

---

[13] Ibid., p. 32.
[14] *LW*, August 1921, p. 117.
[15] Maclean, *Years of Fulfilment*, p. 114.
[16] A. Fleming to J. White, undated, 1929 (W) 11.10.
[17] The Church Union Association, *The Coming of One United Church for Scotland* (rev. ed. 1910), pp. 10–11.
[18] *JW*, p. 116.
[19] Maclean, *Years of Fulfilment*, p. 126.

The other joint convener was Archibald Henderson (1837–1927), minister of the former Free Church in Crieff, principal clerk of the general assembly, 1900–16, and moderator in 1909, who played a most significant role in the movement for union. He had an incomparable knowledge of church law and history,[20] and was a man of 'wide learning, acute judgement, robust common sense, and forceful personality'.[21] His caution was also evident throughout the discussions. He advised the secretary of the committee, Alexander Martin, to 'gang warily' when dealing with the statutory proposals which might affect their Church; caution, he said, did not mean hostility.[22] That the minority in the UF Church thought of him as a 'wily ecclesiastic' is a tribute to his astute mind.[23] He had a clear-cut, legal style which pierced directly to the heart of the subject under discussion.[24] John White never forgot the role Henderson played in reminding the committee of the need for union. At one early meeting, when discussions were seeming to get nowhere and there might even be the danger of collapse, Henderson produced a map of Scotland which showed the mass of the population between the Forth and Clyde valleys and the corresponding density of the effort of the Churches which was in other areas. This reminded the members of the two committees how urgent was their common task. He had said to White on that occasion: 'I charge you to keep the united Church alive to the need—the ever-increasing and intensifying need — of the neglected of our land.' In recalling this incident much later White said: 'I have tried'.[25]

It was, however, the two clerks who made the most important contribution to the union for they each became the conveners of their respective committees in due course. They saw the movement through to the end and, starting off on opposite sides, ended up together in the battle with the opponents of union in each Church. John White was appointed for his ability to stand up to the clerk of the United Free Church committee, Alexander Martin, who, it was thought, might dominate the discussions by virtue of his sharp intellect.[26] Lord Balfour of Burleigh had said, 'We must have a man of standing who can hold his own with Professor Martin.'[27] White had a high regard for Martin,[28] and paid tribute

[20] UFC Min., 27 April 1927.
[21] *LW*, June 1927, p. 130.
[22] A. Henderson to A. Martin, 25.10.21 (M) 10.
[23] Reith, *Reminiscences*, p. 126.
[24] Alexander Gammie, ed., *General Assemblies Annual, 1929* (Glasgow, 1929), p. 36.
[25] Dr White's reference to Dr Henderson (W) 9.4. See below, p. 153.
[26] *JW*, p. 117.
[27] *The Scotsman* 12.11.25.
[28] John White, Alexander Martin (W) 40.

to his gifts, alertness, eminent fairness, deliberate manner and thoroughness. White appreciated the fact that Martin, like Henderson, never viewed reunion merely from a church angle but from the angle of the religious need of Scotland.[29]

Alexander Martin (1857–1946) became minister of Morningside Free Church in Edinburgh in 1884 and was appointed professor of Apologetics and Practical Theology at New College in 1897, becoming principal in 1918. As can be gathered from White's reference to his colleague's deliberate manner, Martin could be rather ponderous and long-winded in his advocacy of the cause. His successor at Morningside, R. E. McIntyre, spoke of the 'daunting length' of his speeches at the assembly.[30] But, in McIntyre's view, this was because Martin was less concerned to score debating points off his opponents than to do justice to the truth. He had a wider concern: 'Reconciliation was his object, persuasion his weapon.'[31] Another colleague said that, as a speaker, Martin was clear and conclusive rather than eloquent and passionate, and that he moved slowly, like a ship getting under way.[32] He was described at one assembly as 'winding himself into his subject like a serpent' and as requiring time to develop his case.[33] His treatment of a subject was marked by comprehensiveness, thoroughness, and mastery, which in their cumulative effect were inevitably impressive.[34] Like Henderson he was cautious by nature.[35] This quality, allied to his intellectual gifts, was of particular value in explaining the reasons for union and pleading its cause to his brethren in the UF Church in the 1920s, when the ball was finally in the court of that Church. Martin published a series of weighty and influential pamphlets at that time.[36] He exercised a crucial role, too, in seeking if at all possible to meet the demands of the minority in his Church, and in trying to prevent the emergence of a continuing UF Church. Adam Welch, one of his professorial colleagues at New College, spoke of the patience and courtesy which Martin had showed towards those who did not agree with him.[37] Adam Renwick, who in the end supported the union, spoke

---

[29] John White, The Very Rev. Principal Alexander Martin, D.D., LL.D. (W) 49.
[30] LW, August 1946, pp. 179–80.
[31] Ibid., p. 180.
[32] Gammie, General Assemblies Annual, 1929, p. 36.
[33] Record, July 1927, p. 310.
[34] Ibid.
[35] Chair of Apologetics and Practical Theology, New College, Edinburgh, Testimonials in favour of Rev. Alexander Martin, M.A. (M) 3.
[36] Alexander Martin, Church Union in Scotland: the first phase (Edinburgh, 1923); Church Union in Scotland: the first stage completed (Edinburgh, 1925); Church Union in Scotland: nearing the goal (Edinburgh, 1928).
[37] Record, January 1929, p. 11.

this word to the future historian of the movement from the viewpoint of the minority:[38]

> I would like to tell him.... of the part taken in that high enterprise by Principal Martin: the boundless patience, the readiness to consider a problem from our point of view, and the steadfast adherence to the supreme aim.

If Martin's intellect was rather ponderous, White's was agile and sharp. As his biographer put it, he was[39]

> quick to lay down the law, impatient, sometimes too impatient, curbing himself with difficulty when things did not go the way he thought they should, afire at all times with a zeal for union, a vital figure in every debate.

In his contributions to debate he was likened to a razor-edged hatchet, cleaving between 'what really matters and what doesn't matter at all'.[40] He brought his sharp mind to bear on the issue of union, a mind steeped in the law and history of the Church.

John White (1867–1951) became minister of Shettleston in 1893, of South Leith in 1904 and then of the prestigious Barony Church in Glasgow in 1911. He had emerged victorious from the celebrated Shettleston Case in which he had taken on the local heritors of his first parish when they had refused to rebuild the church. Partly as a result of his involvement in this case he had become knowledgeable on the law relating to the endowments of the Kirk. This expertise proved invaluable when it came to the preparation of the bill relating to these matters. He was recognised as an invaluable man to have on board by his colleagues in the committee, although they might at times regret his sharpness and impatience. His friend and ally Norman Maclean told of how he had played his part of counterpoint to Alexander Martin with too great an enthusiasm at one of the early meetings of the committee. This had prompted an elder present to comment that there was no need for the committees to proceed any further since they had fulfilled their remit to find out the causes which kept the two Churches apart: 'the two Clerks'![41] White's role in the cause of union cannot be underestimated. He played the most significant individual part of any of the participants and this was recognised when he was nominated by his opposite number, Alexander Martin,

---

[38] A. Renwick to A. Martin, 30.4.28 (M) 20.5/1.
[39] *JW*, p. 116.
[40] A. W. Ferguson, in *The British Weekly*, 3 October 1929.
[41] Maclean, *Years of Fulfilment*, p. 116. Cf. *JW*, p. 117, where a similar point was made by William Mair.

as the first moderator of the general assembly of the united Church in 1929.[42]

White played a crucial role in the negotiations at two particular points. One was when there was an impasse over the content of the doctrinal statement to be included in Article I of the Articles Declaratory in 1918. White moved successfully that the doctrinal content be removed altogether. In his words, this motion 'worked a cure' and led to a satisfactory resolution of the issue.[43] The other time when his intervention was crucial was during the seemingly endless discussions with the landowners over the question of the teinds. It was White who grasped the nettle and agreed to a continuing charge on land rather than a once-and-for-all payment.[44] On each occasion decisive action by White had rescued the situation and put the process of reunion on track once more. Both measures involved a certain amount of risk, but White was always conscious of the larger picture and he calculated that the risk was worth taking. Although impatient at times with the pace of the movement, White could be very long-suffering with individual members of the committee, as he was with the high churchmen James Cooper and Arthur Wotherspoon. He was also careful not to offend unnecessarily the minority in his own Church which led Martin to think that, although White was a strong man, he could be 'quite timid' at times![45]

White emerged as the key figure in advocating the cause of union to his own Church and this was recognised when he was appointed as a kind of roving ambassador for the Basis and Plan of Union in 1927. To carry out this task he was released from his parochial duties with the agreement of the kirk session of the Barony.[46] By this time White was also convener of the Church and Nation Committee where he exercised a somewhat conservative influence.[47] In politics he was a Tory and his political outlook coloured his views in several respects. He also became convener of the Business Committee and hence 'Leader of the House'. The dominance of John White at one assembly was noted by one observer:[48]

> As he sat in the place of leader of the House, at the head of the table of the circumtabular oligarchy, his hand was ever on the pulse of the Assembly. His pre-eminence has never been more pronounced.

[42] Church of Scotland, *Proceedings of the Union Assembly 1929*, pp. 7–8.
[43] *FR*, p. 61.
[44] See below, pp. 133–4.
[45] Alexander Martin, Notebook, 7 May 1928 (M) 2.6.
[46] *JW*, p. 256.
[47] Stewart J. Brown, 'The Social Vision of Scottish Presbyterianism and the Union of 1929' in *RSCHS* XXIV (1990), pp. 77–96.
[48] *JW*, pp. 255–6.

It is because of the meticulous way in which both clerks, Martin and White, carried out their work, and then left their papers for posterity, that a full account can be given of the making of the union of the Churches.

Another participant whose papers have been preserved was the advocate Christopher N. Johnston (1857–1934), who became Lord Sands in 1917 on being elevated to the bench. As Procurator, and then as a member and as joint convener of the committee, Lord Sands played, after John White, the most crucial role on the Established Church side. He had a considerable knowledge of church law and of the Church's relation to statute law. He was consulted constantly about these matters during the discussions and produced many a memorandum for the use of the committee. As can be seen from his biographies of Archibald Scott and Wallace Williamson, he also had a keen insight into theological and ecclesiastical matters. He has the notable distinction for an elder of receiving the degree of Doctor of Divinity from Edinburgh University. His legal mind and theological understanding were brought to bear on the union discussions at several important points. He was the author of the Memorandum of 1912 which showed the way forward for the movement at a crucial time. Sands' document gave it a new impetus and direction, and set it on the right track. Then, too, he did much to solve the doctrinal question when it threatened to put an end to the discussions in 1918. If White's intervention was the negative factor in breaking the impasse, it was Sands who provided the positive solution to the problem with another important memorandum.[49] This document was in many ways more significant than the Memorandum of 1912, since its composition required theological as well as legal skills.[50] It was Sands, too, who identified the nature of the doctrinal statement in Article I as a 'keynote' or 'declaration' rather than a definition of the fundamental doctrines of the faith.[51] Archibald Henderson recognised his role in the framing of the Memorandum and the Articles when he wrote to him in 1919: 'I am sure you must feel rewarded in the achievement of your offspring.'[52] Sands had also won the confidence and respect of the UF committee members. He attributed this to the fact that he was asked to open the discussion on the subject of spiritual freedom when the committees first met in 1909. The ministerial members of his committee had an inferiority complex on this issue since

[49] *FR*, p. 62.
[50] *FR*, pp. 62–3.
[51] *FR*, pp. 63, 66.
[52] A. Henderson to Lord Sands, 27.5.19 (LS) 9.

their UF counterparts had been studying it for years and saw themselves as experts. Sands took up the challenge and was able, while expounding the principles of his own Church, to understand and appreciate the point of view of the other side.[53] Sands continued to play an important part in the negotiations and became joint convener of the union committee of the Church of Scotland. It was fitting that he was asked to propose the motion for union at the joint assembly in 1929. It is worth noting, too, that the two laymen who played significant roles in the movement for reunion, Lord Balfour and Lord Sands, were both elders of the Church of Scotland. The United Free Church, in spite of its high view of the eldership, did not provide an elder who took such a leading part in the negotiations.

Two other figures should be mentioned as the outstanding representatives of the minorities in both Churches. On the Church of Scotland committee the most prominent member of the Scoto-Catholic minority was James Cooper (1846–1922). Cooper had been minister of St Stephen's in Broughty Ferry and of East St Nicholas Church in Aberdeen before becoming professor of Ecclesiastical History at the University of Glasgow in 1898. He was moderator of the general assembly in 1917. Cooper was greatly influenced by the Episcopal Church of his native Morayshire and was something of a romantic who was passionately interested in the middle ages.[54] He was devoted to the study of liturgy and church architecture. He was an active member of the Church Service Society, and founded the Aberdeen Ecclesiological Society in 1886. To come across Cooper in the Church of Scotland, it was said, was like 'coming upon an old-fashioned cathedral, with its air of calm grandeur and mellowed beauty, in the midst of the staring red-brick buildings of a brand new manufacturing town.'[55] Cooper was also an enthusiastic promoter of church unity. He wished above all to see a union between the Church of Scotland and the Church of England, what he called a 'United Church for the British Empire'.[56] He was a frequent visitor south of the Border and had many friends among the clergy of the Anglican Church. Such an ecumenical prospect was not a practical possibility at the time, and so Cooper was

---

[53] *British Weekly*, 3.10.29.

[54] H. J. Wotherspoon, *James Cooper: A Memoir* (London, 1926), pp. 15, 60; Douglas M. Murray, 'James Cooper (1846–1922) at Glasgow: Presbytery and Episcopacy', in William Ian P. Hazlett, ed., *Traditions of Theology in Glasgow 1450–1990* (Edinburgh, 1993), p. 71.

[55] James F. Leishman, *Linton Leaves* (Edinburgh, 1937), p. 145. Cf. Murray, 'James Cooper at Glasgow', pp. 71–2.

[56] James Cooper, *A United Church for the British Empire* (Forres, 1902).

prepared to work for what was on offer, which was a purely Presbyterian reunion. But his main concern was for the place of doctrine in the life of the Church and this was most clearly expressed in his association with the Scottish Church Society, of which he became the first secretary in 1892. The society was formed to defend and advance the place of 'catholic' doctrine in the Kirk, and this aim goes far to explain Cooper's role in the union negotiations.[57] Cooper stood out for what he considered to be an adequate statement of the catholic faith in the first of the Articles Declaratory. It was only when he was satisfied with the content of that Article that he agreed to the document. Along with his fellow high churchman, Arthur Wotherspoon, he was also concerned with the established position of the Church. It was, however, the doctrinal issue which was always the most important, and in the end he acquiesced when he had achieved the security for the faith which he considered necessary for the Church. Cooper was single-minded in his pursuit of this goal and the other members of the committee could be exasperated by his stance. To someone like Lord Balfour, Cooper seemed to pose as the sole defender of doctrinal orthodoxy.[58] Yet he was also a very gracious man and he was respected by those who disagreed with his position. John White had to cope with his obstinacy more than most, yet he never lost his affection for Cooper whom he described as a 'dear man'.[59] The references in Article I to the doctrines of the trinity and the incarnation are an abiding legacy of Cooper's role in the discussions.

James Barr (1862–1949) was by far the most outspoken and prominent member of the minority in the United Free Church. He was president of the United Free Church Association, formed in 1919 to oppose union on the basis of civil establishment, and he became the first moderator of the general assembly of the United Free Church (Continuing). He was widely respected for his commitment to social issues and many enjoyed his speeches because of his sense of humour.[60] It would be wrong to assume that Barr represented the traditional United Presbyterian position on church-state relations, since he was brought up in the Free Church and entered its ministry before the union of 1900. As he said at one assembly, he had been brought up to hold the view of a pure establishment and he held by that view until he came to see that it was 'civilly unjust and constitutionally impossible'.[61] He

[57] Murray, 'Scottish Church Society', p. 2.
[58] *FR*, p. 50.
[59] *FR*, p. 51.
[60] Reith, *Reminiscences*, p. 214.
[61] *UFC Proc.*, 1913, p. 261.

served first of all at Wamphray, and then the Glasgow congregations of Dennistoun and Govan, before becoming a full-time deputy of the Home Mission Committee. He was one of the few Scottish ministers of any Church to oppose the First World War, although his three sons all volunteered for active service, and James, the youngest, was killed in action when only nineteen years old.[62] Before the war Barr was a member of the Liberal Party, but he joined the Independent Labour Party in 1920. He served as Labour MP for Motherwell and Wishaw from 1924 to 1931 and spoke against the property and endowments bill. He later served as Labour member for Coatbridge and Airdrie from 1935 to 1945. It has been pointed out, however, that to think of Barr as being first and foremost a voluntaryist who opposed the Established Church would be to fail to see him in the proper light. Barr was essentially 'an evangelist who saw politics as the means through which he could establish the Kingdom of God'.[63] Hence his opposition to the union and his career in politics must be seen as only one expression of his conviction that the Christian faith had to be related to public issues and social concerns. It may be that he was influenced by the thinking of the social gospel movement which he came across during an early visit to North America.[64] For him the voluntary position was bound up with his main concern for the work of the Church. Only a Church supported voluntarily and free from a connection with the State could witness effectively to the gospel and express such concern in appropriate action. Only a voluntary Church would support causes such as pacifism, temperance, and the abolition of capital punishment. Only when the Church was disestablished would the working class take the gospel seriously. Thus while others argued that it was division which prevented the Church exercising an effective influence in society, Barr argued that it was establishment. It is significant that the final two chapters of his early book, *The Scottish Church Question*, published shortly after the founding of the United Free Church Association, were entitled 'Reaching the Masses' and 'Religious Equality'.[65]

(b) principles

(i) spiritual freedom
As Lord Sands recalled, the Church of Scotland committee turned in the first instance to him to present a preliminary paper on the

[62] William H. Marwick, 'James Barr: Modern Covenanter', in *Scottish Journal of Science*, 1 (1973), p. 183.
[63] Albert Bogle, 'James Barr, B.D., M.P.' in *RSCHS*, 21 (1983), p. 204.
[64] Ibid., pp. 190–1.
[65] James Barr, *The Scottish Church Question* (London, 1920), chs. 24 and 25.

subject of spiritual freedom to the conference on 22nd December 1909.[66] The United Free Church had already set out its claim to spiritual freedom in its Act anent Spiritual Independence in 1906. In view of the difficulties it had suffered as a result of the House of Lords decision in 1904 it could not go back on that position. The question was whether the Church of Scotland could incorporate this claim in its own constitution in view of its relationship with the State. Sands pointed out that the establishment of the Church in Scotland was based upon certain statutes. The Church regarded these statutes as recognising the Reformation and as accepting the Confession of Faith and constitution which the Church had framed for itself. This was, in his view, a spiritual freedom larger than that enjoyed by any other Protestant State Church. It still meant, however, that the Church of Scotland could not alter its Confession of Faith, its Presbyterian form of church government, or its endowed parish ministry, without obtaining the permission of parliament. These restrictions, however, had not been imposed upon the Church by the State but were the result of parliament coming in, at the request of the Church, to protect its liberties against the encroachments of the crown. There were negative aspects of this statutory position since the Church was not fully free in spiritual matters. But this effect was incidental and was not the object of these statutes. The restraints were ones which the Church had imposed upon itself. It followed, however, that if the Church now wished to remove these restrictions upon its freedom, then it had a perfect right to do so since these limitations were the result of legislation which the Church itself had requested.

According to Sands, there were also positive aspects to the Church's position. The separate jurisdiction of the courts of the Church in spiritual matters was recognised by the State. There would be disagreement over what constituted a spiritual matter from time to time, but this was the case with non-established Churches as well. But with regard to the Established Church, the civil courts would not interfere with the way in which it carried out its jurisdiction. This was not the case with the courts of a non-established Church since the governing body of that Church was not recognised by the civil courts as having a jurisdiction. To support his view he quoted several legal opinions of judges, all since the Disruption, which showed a recognition of the separate jurisdiction of the church courts. He concluded that the issue of spiritual freedom did not present any insuperable barrier to

[66] Lord Sands, Spiritual Freedom in the Church of Scotland, in Church of Scotland, *Papers prepared provisionally for the use of the Sub-Committee in Conference with the United Free Church*, pp. 13–18 (W) 76 and (LS) 20/36.

union and that, if the two Presbyterian Churches which represented a majority of the Scottish people were to approach parliament, their request would not be refused.

The essence of Sands' argument was that there were certain matters in which the Established Church was not free from the State, and that an approach should be made to parliament to recognise this freedom. Yet there would also be an advantage to such a recognition, since the Church would not be subject to the kind of legal decision which had affected the United Free Church in 1904. There still remained, however, the nature of the relationship with the State which would result from such an approach to parliament. In what sense would the Church of Scotland be the 'National Church' and would it still be 'established' and tied to the State in some way?

Norman Macleod, in a paper for the committee, drew attention to more recent legal enactments, such as that regarding patronage in 1874, which in his view reversed the previous decisions of the Disruption.[67] He also pointed out that the legal advantages lay with the Established Church rather than with the non-established Churches. The united Church would, in his view, possess all the rights and privileges of jurisdiction presently enjoyed only by the Auld Kirk. Macleod, however, made a point which Sands had not made. Even were the full spiritual freedom of the Church to be recognised by parliament, there would be limitations on that freedom which the Church would impose on itself. Spiritual freedom was never absolute. It was *spiritual* freedom, the freedom of the Church, and hence there would be self-imposed restrictions of liberty in relation to its creed. The Church could not be free to believe what it wished, but only to be the Church, in continuity of faith with the catholic Church down through the centuries. He made clear that he was speaking of the Church accepting the creed of its own volition; he was not speaking of a creed imposed by the State. He said, 'If there be such a body of truth as "the Faith once for all delivered", why should we hesitate to avow it?'[68] And he continued:[69]

> Greater liberty we all desire, but only, I hope, with due regard to the 'sum and substance' of Reformed Evangelical doctrine, which is truly catholic. I am all for liberty, but liberty without licence.

[67] Memorandum by Dr Norman Macleod in ibid., pp. 19–26.
[68] Ibid., p. 23. Cf. *FR*, pp. 25–7.
[69] Ibid., p. 25. Cf. Arthur Gordon, Spiritual Independence: its nature and limits, in ibid., pp. 31–50.

There was thus a concern among some of the leaders of the Church of Scotland side from the very beginning that there should be a credal limitation upon the spiritual freedom of the Church. The Established Church was not free to change its doctrinal position at present because its Confession of Faith was enshrined in statute law as part of its relationship to the State. This guaranteed, in Macleod's words, 'a certain *fixity* of creed' (his italics). But if the relationship to the State was to be modified, as it would have to be if the demands of the United Free Church were to be met, then some other way of guaranteeing the Church's adherence to the catholic faith had to be found. In other words, since the Church would have the freedom to change its standards of doctrine, worship and discipline, the Westminster Confession of Faith could itself be replaced by another statement. If this was not the case then much of the discussions which followed, and the final form of the Articles Declaratory, cannot be understood.

Hence there was the need for the subject of 'Liberty in relation to Creed' to be considered by a special sub-committee. In these discussions serious differences of opinion emerged between the two high churchmen, James Cooper and Arthur Wotherspoon, and the rest of the committee. The two representatives of the Scoto-Catholic position believed that the Church was obliged to 'keep whole and undefiled the Faith once delivered to the saints, and to bear explicit witness to the same'.[70] In their view the Church was not at liberty to depart from adherence to the catholic faith as set out in the creeds of the undivided Church, and they thought that the Church of Scotland should explicitly recognise the Nicene Creed. The opposite view was found on the United Free side and was expressed by Professor James Denney of the Glasgow College. He moved in the sub-committee that all references to doctrine be deleted.[71] A more mediating position was taken by Professor W. P. Paterson of Edinburgh University. He maintained that the Church would enjoy doctrinal liberty by its continuing recognition of the Westminster Confession, but with the ability to 'modify, abridge, or supplement' it within the limits of its adherence to the substance of the Reformed Faith which the Church would declare.[72] As would become apparent, however, he thought that such an adherence could be in general

[70] Reasons of Dissent from the Findings adopted by a Majority of the Joint Conference on Thursday, 15th September 1910, I (M) 6.

[71] Minutes of the Joint Sub-Committee, 15 July 1910 (M) 6. Cf. Report by the Joint Sub-Committee on Liberty in Relation to Creed, 15 September 1910, p. 5 (M) 6.

[72] W. P. Paterson, Ascertained Differences as to Spiritual Independence and the possibility of reconciling these, in *Papers prepared provisionally for the use of the Sub-Committee*, pp. 27–9.

terms to the 'fundamentals' or to the 'substance' of the faith, without spelling out what constituted that core of belief. In this he would be strenuously opposed by James Cooper.

The matter was fully set out in an explanatory minute of the joint sub-committee.[73] It was pointed out that the statement of spiritual freedom in the UF Act of 1906 did not preclude the Church from reserving certain fundamental doctrines. Indeed the Act itself said that the Church's freedom to alter its subordinate standards was subject to the divine headship of Christ, the work of the Holy Spirit, and the supreme authority of the Word of God contained in the scriptures. William Mair pointed out to Alexander Martin that, since the UF Church did not have an absolute doctrinal freedom, it would be possible to agree to a fuller statement.[74] Thus a declaration of fundamental doctrines in any future union would not be a departure from this principle.

Two methods of making such a doctrinal declaration were possible. One would be in the form of a definitive statement of the fundamentals of the faith. Such a statement, however, would create a number of problems. If all essential doctrines were included, then there would be an end to doctrinal freedom in the Church. There would also be difficulty in coming to an agreement over what should and what should not be included. The other alternative was that of following the precedent of the 1906 Act. In this case certain doctrines would be placed in such a relation to the declaration of freedom that they must be held to be necessarily excluded from its ambit and to be regarded as fundamental in the Church.[75] The heart of the problem was thus identified and it was crucial as far as the future doctrinal position of the Church was concerned. The position of the Westminster Confession had to be taken into account. If union took place on the basis of that document as the subordinate standard of the Church, unqualified by any statement of liberty, then the Confession would, in the eyes of the civil courts, be the unalterable standard of the Church. This, said the minute, was a position 'which cannot be accepted'.[76] If such was the case, then the position of the Church would be no different from that of the United Free Church in the Free Church Case. There had to be some declaration of liberty in relation to the Confession of Faith. Yet how was such an affirmation to be framed? An unqualified declaration of freedom had not even

---

[73] Joint Sub-Committee on Liberty in Relation to Creed, Minute Explanatory of Discussion in Sub-Committee (M) 8. Cf. *FR*, pp. 39–41.

[74] *FR*, p. 39.

[75] Minute Explanatory of Discussion, p. 3.

[76] Ibid., p. 4.

been made by the United Free Church, and in any case it would not be accepted by the Church of Scotland. There had to be some qualification. The suggestion was therefore made 'that certain fundamental doctrinal positions should in any Act of Union be placed in such a relation to the declaration of liberty therein contained as not to be subject to it.'[77] This would not be a new confession or doctrinal standard but a 'Treaty of Union' accepted by and binding upon those 'who united to form the Church, and upon all others who might join the Church'.

The question then arose as to what form this doctrinal declaration should take. It could take the form of a general statement such as 'the sum and substance of the doctrine of the Reformed Churches'. Depending on how it was interpreted, this could be a more stringent limitation upon liberty than was desired, or alternatively it could turn out to be valueless as a safeguard. On the other hand, if certain doctrines were enumerated, this would be no different from the previous proposal to define the substance of the faith in a permanent way. It had to be remembered that what was being suggested was a doctrinal 'testimony' rather than a formal 'statement'. The model of the 1906 Act could be followed. Alternatively, a declaration might be made to the effect that the Churches united 'upon the basis of a common faith in a, b, c; in which faith, once delivered unto the Saints and received in the Church in all ages, this United Church shall always abide.'[78]

It was this method which would be used in the framing of the first of the Articles Declaratory of the Constitution of the Church in Matters Spiritual. So both the declaration of spiritual freedom, and the way by which a doctrinal testimony was made, would be modelled upon the 1906 Act of the United Free Church. Thus the main matters to be dealt with in the new constitution of the Church had been outlined, and the way in which they would be dealt with had been identified. The basis of the Articles Declaratory is found already, therefore, in this minute.

(ii) national recognition of religion
The other main subject for discussion had been identified as the national recognition of religion. In a preliminary paper for the Church of Scotland committee, Professor Henry Cowan of Aberdeen University had referred to the agreement reached at the informal conference in 1896. This agreement stated that 'in the case of a Christian nation, the State ought to avow itself subject to

[77] Ibid.
[78] Ibid., p. 5.

the law of Christ, and is bound to embody and apply the spirit and the principles of that law in its own legislation and procedure.'[79] There were certain expressions of this principle, he said, about which there was unlikely to be disagreement. These included the place of prayer on certain public occasions, the observance of the Lord's Day, the keeping of days of national humiliation and thanksgiving, the provision of chaplains in the armed forces, the framing of marriage laws, and the presence of a royal commissioner at the meetings of the general assembly of the Church. It was important, in his view, that this principle be exercised through the recognition of one Church, the one which had that national character by reason of history and present circumstances. It was the view of W. P. Paterson that the reunited Church would have an irresistible claim to be recognised as the National Church. It would not be a case of parliament arbitrarily choosing one Church as such, he said, but simply endorsing 'a selection which has been providentially made in the history of our country'.[80] In reply to those who said that this would involve injustice towards other Churches which did not share these privileges, the main consideration must be, not the competing claims of the Churches, but the greatest good of the Scottish people. It would be desirable, in his view, for the Church of Scotland to support proposals which would improve the legal status of other Churches.

In the United Free Church the more extreme voluntary position was expressed by John Young. In a statement made to the committee in March 1911,[81] he agreed that the State should have a religious character, that it should protect the exercise of religion, and that it should reflect religious values in its laws on such matters as the Sabbath and marriage. But it was important to keep these matters distinct from the spiritual task of the Church. A union of Church and State hindered rather than furthered the spiritual work of the Church. He pointed out that there was an increasingly non-Presbyterian element in the Scottish population to which a national Presbyterian Church would offer little appeal. In addition a national Church tended to encourage a nominal church connection, a use of the Church for ceremonies such as baptisms and weddings, and what he called a 'ratepayers' attitude to the work of the Church. In his view a spiritual renewal in the life of the Church was never possible on the basis of a state connection.

[79] Memorandum by Rev. Prof. Cowan on the National Recognition of Religion, in *Papers prepared provisionally for the use of the Sub-Committee*, pp. 51–2.
[80] National Religion and Establishment, heads of a statement made by Professor Paterson, in ibid., p. 73.
[81] Statement by Dr Young, March 1911 (M) 11.4.

Although he also came from the background of the UP Church, Professor A. R. McEwen of New College expressed a much more positive view of a future national Church than that of Young. In a paper dealing with the continuity of the Established Church with the Church of the Reformation, the Revolution Settlement, and the Treaty of Union, McEwen pointed out that the United Free Church was in continuity with those who were the successors of the Secessions of the eighteenth century and of the Disruption of 1843.[82] It would not be necessary, he said, for this continuity to be included in a statute. It would be sufficient for parliament to recognise that, in uniting with another Presbyterian Church, the Church of Scotland did not lose its identity with the Church of the past. Would the reunited Church possess privileges? Clearly the Church of the Reformation was regarded as the Church of the nation in an exclusive sense. The ancient statutes, such as that of 1592, not only conferred privileges on one Church, they also expressly refused status to any other. Not only would some statutes which restricted the freedom of the Church have to be repealed, but those which conferred exclusive privilege would have to be modified. There were elements of the Revolution Settlement which resulted in the control of the Church by the government, but it was clear, said McEwen, that the Kirk did not wish to identify with these aspects, but rather with the more positive aspects of the Treaty of Union. The Act of Security was intended to protect the Presbyterian Church from domination by Episcopacy. This act had already been modified in relation to university tests and a further modification might therefore be made. A recognition of identity would in his view require specification. Thus the door was not closed to an acceptance of a national recognition of religion; its character, however, would have to be clearly specified. He thought that with the repeal of certain statutes, and the improved legal status given to other Churches, such a recognition could be acceptable.

At the meetings of the joint sub-committee in November and December 1910, the United Free Church representatives agreed that recognition by the State of the Church's spiritual authority could be accompanied by a recognition of its role as a national Church.[83] Recognition, however, also had to be given to other Churches in their spiritual character, and not just as 'lay corporations'. For the United Free Church representatives, much would depend on the way in which the united Church was recognised as 'national'.

---

[82] Memorandum by Professor A. R. McEwen, to be considered by Sub-Committee (M) 14.1.
[83] The National Recognition of Religion (M) 12.3.

(c) proposals

(i) the joint report of 1911
The lines on which the discussions for union would proceed were clearly set out in the joint report of 1911:[84]

> The Church of Scotland would, it is believed, approve a fresh declaration of Spiritual Freedom being embodied in the Constitution of a reunited Church in such comprehensive terms as would include all matters spiritual, always consistently with the Word of God and in fidelity to the substance of the Reformed Faith, being the fundamental doctrines of the Christian faith contained in the common Standards of the conferring Churches. This freedom would include the power of the Church to modify the Constitution under the conditions laid down in the Constitution itself.

Such restrictions upon the freedom of the Church, as in relation to its doctrinal and other standards, its constitution, the composition of its courts, and in relation to ministers and parishes and unions with other Churches, would all be met, in the view of the Church of Scotland, 'without any sacrifice of principle or breach of the historical continuity of the National Church'. It was also stated that parliament would be asked to acknowledge the constitution agreed by the uniting Churches as the constitution of the Church of Scotland. Yet there were matters to which the Church must still adhere, no matter what its relation to the State might be. There must still be certain doctrines which were the fundamental basis of its communion and the marks of its identity as a Church. Differences of opinion had arisen as to the content and form of the doctrinal testimony, but it was hoped that, in view of the common standards of the two Churches, these differences could be reconciled. Agreement should be found regarding both the principle of spiritual freedom and the testimony of the Churches to their common faith. It was clear from the discussions that the differences on the matter of doctrine cut across both Churches. The two extreme positions on this issue—those advocating complete liberty such as James Denney, and those wishing adherence to the Creeds such as James Cooper—were found in the United Free Church and the Church of Scotland respectively. Yet the variations of opinion between those extremes, including those who wished to find a compromise, were also to be found within both Churches.

---

[84] *C of S Rep.*, 1911, pp. 936–7.

The joint report recognised that there was common ground that 'the nation, acting in its corporate capacity, ought to render homage to God and to promote in all appropriate ways the interests of His Kingdom'.[85] A nation was obliged to advance God's kingdom by so ordering its policy, its institutions and its laws, in accordance with the principles of justice and humanity. There should also be specific ways in which the nation would express its faith. The form which this took could not satisfactorily be one which tolerated all religious beliefs, but rather one which specifically honoured Christianity and in particular the Protestant faith of the nation.

In what way should such recognition be given? It was the view of the Church of Scotland that the most satisfactory form was by the recognition of the Protestant and Presbyterian Church as the National Church. A reunited Presbyterian Church would represent both the faith of the vast majority of the population and the different streams of national tradition, and would be particularly well equipped to meet the spiritual needs of the people of Scotland. Such a reunited Church would have a separate and exclusive jurisdiction in spiritual matters recognised by parliament. The question of injustice to other Churches was raised by the recognition of one Church as the National Church. But in the circumstances of a union of the Churches such an objection could not be made:[86]

> State recognition of the reunited Church as the National Church could not under these conditions be represented as giving to one Church a privilege denied to the other Churches which have an equal claim to it; for whilst other Churches might claim to be recognised as Christian Churches, no other Church could claim to be recognised as the National Church representative of the past religious history and the present religious life of the Scottish people.

The recognition of the united Church by the State would not be a matter of preferential choice but the acceptance of a fact. The union could create a completely new situation along with an important element of continuity. The united Church would be both the Church of a large section of the population and the successor to the National Church of the past.

The Church of Scotland representatives realised that a large readjustment would be required in the relation of the Church to the State. Not only was it important that recognition be given to

---

[85] Ibid., p. 939.
[86] Ibid., pp. 940–1.

the continuity of the Church with the past, it was also important that the Church be recognised as undertaking the provision of religious ordinances and pastoral care for the people of Scotland in the present. It was vital that the Church be seen as possessing a separate and exclusive jurisdiction in matters spiritual, and that the endowments be conserved for the united Church and used towards the support of religious ordinances in a territorial system. It was felt, in conclusion, that should the spiritual independence of the Church be recognised in a way satisfactory to the United Free Church, they would feel that State recognition of the national character of the Church could also be secured by the existing statutes as modified by the declaration of liberty.

That the content of the joint report was mainly from the Church of Scotland side was due to the fact that the UF representatives had interpreted the remit given to the committee quite strictly. They thus limited themselves to examining the existing ecclesiastical situation and the main causes which were keeping the Churches apart. As John White said at the assembly of the Established Church in 1911, it had been a pity that their colleagues in the other Church had not felt able, as they had done, to offer constructive suggestions as to how the situation of the Churches could be remedied. Instead, he said, they had restricted their remit to criticism of the present position of the Kirk [87] But, as White told the assembly, the Church of Scotland had made substantial proposals towards removing the difficulties in the way of reunion. They were not proposing to unite on the existing constitution of the Kirk but on one which would be altered to take account of the criticisms of their brethren. White emphasised the magnitude of the step which the Kirk was proposing to take. The Church was going to draw up a new constitution which it would place before parliament for ratification. There was no question of the State conferring powers on the Church; on the contrary there was an acknowledgement that the Church possessed these powers inherently as a Church of Christ. Nor was there any question of the Church being disestablished; it would remain the National Church in continuity with the Church of the Reformation. Furthermore this would place other Churches on a correct footing with regard to the law, since as the United Free Church pointed out the established position of the Church of Scotland at present failed to give due recognition to other Churches as Churches of Christ. In addition the statutes, or at least certain clauses in them, which were inconsistent with the spiritual liberty of the Church would be repealed.

[87] *JW*, p. 131.

As White's biographer rightly points out, the Church of Scotland's position as set out in 1911 did not alter in any fundamental way from this point onwards. White was criticised, no doubt with some justification, for saying in his farewell sermon to his congregation of South Leith in 1911 virtually what he had said at the previous meeting of the assembly:[88]

> The Church of Scotland has given a full and practical expression to her desire for Union. She has indeed gone a generous length. I think she has gone as far as she need go. She must take her stand where she now is.

No doubt the statement was an example of White's impetuosity and bluntness. William Mair wrote to him to say that if what had been reported of his sermon was true, there was no need for the committees to meet again.[89] But White was right. The Church of Scotland did not in fact change its stance in any fundamental way during the remainder of the union discussions. It was the United Free Church 'that moved step by step nearer to this position until at last the two Churches stood steadfastly together'.[90] On the other hand, it could be argued that in taking up this position the Church of Scotland representatives had moved significantly towards the outlook of the United Free Church. It took time for their colleagues in the other Church to realise that such a significant movement on their part had taken place.

(ii) the Memorandum of 1912

Partly as a result of the cautious approach on the part of the UF Church, the remit which was sought from both assemblies in 1911 was fairly limited. The report was commended to the serious and prayerful consideration of church members and the committees were asked 'to watch over the matter and report'.[91] Henderson had been anxious not to appear to be pushing matters in his Church and White could sympathise with this view.[92] The members of the Church had to have time to consider the contents of the report and not feel pressurised into supporting a movement which they had had little time to consider. At the assembly of the UF Church Archibald Henderson said that they should welcome the proposals made by the Church of Scotland for a fresh declaration of spiritual freedom being embodied in the constitution

---

[88] *JW*, p. 136.
[89] Ibid.
[90] *JW.*, p. 137.
[91] *C of S Rep.*, 1911, p. 920; *UFC Proc.*, 1911, p. 266.
[92] *JW*, p. 138.

of the united Church.[93] This liberty, he pointed out, would include the ability to change its subordinate standards and to alter the constitution of the Church itself, and it would be free from all external authority. From the discussions of the joint committee he felt that this was made in sincerity and he was hopeful that further progress could therefore be made.

John White was of the view that, although the Churches must be allowed time to consider the issues raised by the joint report, it was important that progress should be continued otherwise it might not be possible to restart the talks at a future date. He appreciated the caution which Henderson had to use with his own Church but did not feel that the same restraint need apply in the Established Church.[94] An enlarged Business Committee was thus instructed to 'draft a series of Propositions on the leading points dealt with in the Report to the last General Assembly'.[95] Lord Balfour of Burleigh had been in correspondence with Henderson urging that some action be taken, and it seems that he played a significant role in getting Lord Sands to draft what became known as 'The Memorandum'.[96]

The Memorandum did not contain anything which was not already to be found in the 1911 report, but it set out a draft preamble to a bill which demonstrated how the proposals could be given legislative shape. It showed that the Auld Kirk representatives were serious about the approach to parliament and went far to convince the other side of their firm intention.[97] The author of the document, Lord Sands, included a summary of its contents in his biography of Wallace Williamson, the first three points of which are as follows:[98]

(1) The pressing problem in relation to Union is the adjustment of State relations in a manner acceptable to both Churches.
(2) It would be difficult, if not indeed impracticable, to secure concurrence in an attempt to define special State relations in a modern statute. The problem must therefore be approached on the footing of modifying and adapting what is old and not of attempting to create something new.
(3) A constitution might be framed and adopted setting forth the spiritual liberty claimed by the Church. This

---

[93] United Free Church of Scotland, *Speeches delivered by Archibald Henderson, John Young and James Denney at the General Assembly, 30 May 1911* (Edinburgh, 1911), p. 6.

[94] *JW*, p. 139.

[95] Ibid.

[96] Ibid.; A. Henderson to A. Martin, 16.11.27 (M) 20.2/17.

[97] *JW*, pp. 140–1. The text of the Memorandum was printed in *C of S Rep.*, 1912, pp. 1216–21, and is found as Appendix III, pp. 290–4.

[98] Sands, *Wallace Williamson*, p. 256.

constitution might be recognised by Parliament as lawful, and all statutory provisions inconsistent therewith might be declared to be repealed.

In addition, the Memorandum referred to the position of other Churches, and the need for a statutory disclaimer of any exclusive claim of the Church of Scotland to recognition by the State. It also said that, with regard to the endowments of the Church, the Church of Scotland would only go forward on the footing that these should be conserved for the united Church and not secularised.

Many in the United Free Church realised the importance of the document in setting out in practical terms what would be involved in the course which the Established Church was proposing to follow. Several speakers at the assembly in 1912 said that the Memorandum was a bold and courageous step for the Church of Scotland to take.[99] The leading members of the committee had a number of questions about the meaning of the document, almost all of which were satisfactorily answered by their colleagues in the Auld Kirk. It was important for Henderson that the recognition of the Church's freedom by the State be just that, and that it could in no way be taken as a gift by the State to the Church.[100] It was thus essential that there be no ambiguity in the language used so that the Church was not limited or restrained in any way regarding its legislation or administration. Similarly any repeal of acts of parliament had to be so definite as to leave no room for interference by the civil courts. According to Lord Sands, a general repeal clause by itself was unreliable and what would be necessary would be a positive assertion of spiritual freedom in the constitution itself.[101]

Martin recognised that it was the intention of the Church of Scotland to seek 'the recognition of true and full autonomy', but a mere enlargement of liberty would leave untouched the nature of the Church as a state institution based on statute law. He asked: is this what is meant by the Church continuing to be the 'National Church'?[102] The courts of the Church must be recognised as having an inherent authority, not one conferred by the State. There must be no appearance of the State investing rights or powers in the Church as an institution. The United Free Church, he said, was a national Church, 'an embodiment of the religious

---

[99] *UFC Proc.*, 1912, pp. 282, 284.
[100] Memorandum: Notes for the Sub-Committee by Dr Henderson (M) 14.4.
[101] Notes of Procurator's Speech at Conference, 9.1.13 (M) 14.1.
[102] The Memorandum of the Church of Scotland: the Claim to Nationality. Notes of Professor Martin's Speech, November 7th, 1912. (M) 14.1.

genius of the nation, standing in the mid-stream of the nation's religious history, and fulfilling a national function in as much as we minister the Gospel to all sorts and conditions of people in every part of the land.' But the Church of Scotland at present had the character of a 'Parliamentarily-created corporation'. He wondered whether this character would be retained as part of the Church's claim to be a national Church. It would be possible to eliminate this element and retain the essence of the recognition of the principle. In Martin's view the UF Church could agree to the proposal if it meant three things. These were the public recognition of God's providence and care in the nation, the protection of the Church in the exercise of its functions as the Church of Christ, and the retention of Presbyterian worship as the organ of worship on public occasions. If to that list was added the duty of the Church to minister to the nation by a territorial ministry, then that was in essence the position of the Kirk which would be set out in its constitution. Martin had already recognised this aspect as part of the UF Church's role as a national Church. For McEwen the statutory disclaimer which was proposed in relation to other Churches was a 'fertile phrase', since it would be impossible to go through all the statutes and remove the offending phrases. A general clause abolishing privilege would suffice and would have a relation, too, to the continuing of the Treaty of Union. In his view the Church of Scotland would be more, not less, national than at present. The statutory disclaimer was absolutely essential if the UF Church was to assent to a recognition by the State of continuity and identity with the Church as established in 1592.[103]

That the questions of the UF representatives were answered by the other side is apparent by examining two documents, their Provisional Statement and their final Statement on the Memorandum.[104] The Provisional Statement said that a general repeal of statutes was not sufficient to safeguard the spiritual freedom of the Church. There should be a distinct article in the constitution to the effect that the decisions of the Church courts would be final in terms of doctrine, worship, and government. It should also be clear that recognition of the constitution by the State would not render it unalterable except with the sanction of Parliament. With regard to national recognition of religion, there

[103] Professor MacEwen's Notes, (Nov. 7th, 1912). (M) 13.1.

[104] United Free Church of Scotland, Provisional Statement on the Memorandum of the Church of Scotland, 13 February 1913 (M) 3; Statement on Church of Scotland Memorandum (M) 8. Cf. Notes and Suggestions regarding portions of the Memorandum of the Church of Scotland bearing on the State Relationship, Prepared with a view to further conference, 5.12.12 (M) 14.1 and (UFC).

was an important distinction between a national Church recognised *de facto* as the representative of the religious life of the nation, and one constituted *de jure* as the National Church. It was repeated that such recognition should not be exclusive and that other Churches should also be recognised.

The final Statement was more positive. It was accepted that the Church of Scotland realised that the full spiritual freedom of the Church in terms of doctrine, worship, government, membership of its courts, and in relation to its own constitution, would require to be recognised by the State. In addition, it had been explained in conference that the recognition of the Church of Scotland as national should not imply a denial of the role of other Churches as Churches of Christ making their own contribution to the life of the nation. It had also been clearly explained that the Church of Scotland would 'in no sense be an institution constituted or controlled by the State, or deriving powers from the State, or in any way limited in its actions by a special State relation.' The united Church would in fact be eminently national in character and service. Such a recognition would not compromise the freedom of the Church or the State, nor would it place the Church in an invidious relation to other Churches, since it would rest upon the fact of its being 'the most adequate representative of the Christianity of the nation'. In other words, it would be a *de facto* rather than a *de jure* recognition. The statutes which were 'ratified, approved and confirmed' by the Treaty of Union would be repealed in so far as they were inconsistent with the freedom of the Church and conferred a religious monopoly on the Church of Scotland. The value of the joint conference with the Church of Scotland representatives on the Memorandum was stated at the end of the document. It said: 'the Conferences have materially helped to make clearer what would be the relation to the State of a United Church were the proposals and the suggestions of the Memorandum realised.' The hesitations and questions of the UF committee had been dealt with and the members were now prepared to go forward to help the Church of Scotland draft its new constitution. It remained for them to convince the assembly.

In the view of White's biographer we come to the second point at which the movement towards union took a significant step forward.[105] The first was when the Church of Scotland had boldly decided to approach parliament with a new statement of spiritual freedom. The second was when the United Free Church decided to assist them in this task. Archibald Henderson gave 'one of the most persuasive and sweetly reasonable of all that prodigality of

[105] *JW*, p. 148.

speeches on Church Union delivered in the twenty years of striving between 1909 and 1929.'[106] He pointed out the extent of freedom which would be recognised as belonging to the Church of Scotland, including the power to alter the constitution. Yet the Church also wished to claim continuity with the Church of the Reformation. The members of the Church of Scotland could not be asked to give up their ideals of Church and State. After all, the establishment of religion was an open question in their own Church; they could not ask them to say that 'their fathers were all wrong and that our fathers were all right'.[107] In the debate which followed counter-motions were put from the voluntary position, including one by James Barr.[108] James Denney made a powerful plea for a new way of looking at the relation of the Church to the State. In his view there was nothing in the proposals as outlined in the Memorandum to which objection could be taken:[109]

> A Church which had complete spiritual freedom, a Church which was not constituted or controlled by the State, a Church which recognised the title of all Churches to recognition by the State, a Church which said to all Churches, 'Claim for yourself in your constitution the same kind of recognition that we claimed', a Church which said in the report of its committee that under the scheme contemplated by the memorandum any appeal to civil authority would be to the authority of general law and not to a special statutory relationship of the Church to the State — that was not what they ever meant by a State Church or what they ever assailed as being a privileged State Church.

In the end all the contrary motions were withdrawn and the assembly came to a unanimous finding. This was in contrast to the previous year, after the Memorandum had just been published, when opposition had been pressed to a vote, although only thirteen supported a hostile amendment in a house of over one thousand.[110] The next stage of the movement towards reunion could begin, the removal of the first of the obstacles in the way of rebuilding the Kirk, the drafting of a constitution for the Church of Scotland.

---

[106] Ibid.

[107] Speech by Archibald Henderson at the General Assembly of 1913, in United Free Church of Scotland, *The Present Ecclesiastical Situation in Scotland* (Edinburgh, 1913), p. 9.

[108] Reith, *Reminiscences*, pp. 144–5.

[109] *UFC Proc.*, 1913, p. 266.

[110] *UFC Proc.*, 1912, p. 285; Reith, *Reminiscences*, p. 137.

Chapter 4

Removing the obstacles: the Articles Declaratory 1913-26

Two distinct stages in the process of reunion can be identified. First, the Church of Scotland would seek to remove the obstacles to reunion, which would involve approaching parliament to pass two acts: one recognising the spiritual freedom of the Church, and one dealing with its property and endowments. Secondly, following the passing of both acts, negotiations would be carried out regarding the union as such. During this second stage the Church of Scotland would be free to unite with another Church without reference to the State. As Archibald Henderson put it:[1]

> The State would not be there. It would not be in the matter at all. When the Churches united they would not ask the leave of any one but of Him who was their only Master.

The two phases would not always be seen as distinct and it had been hoped at the outset that they might be conflated. The procedure which was followed meant that the clearing of the obstacles was carried out by the Church of Scotland, although the United Free Church was consulted about the proposals and gave them final approval before they were passed into law. The members of the UF Church did not therefore have to make a commitment to discussing the terms of union until both acts were passed and the Church of Scotland had formally adopted the Articles Declaratory in 1926. Only then was the ball finally in their court and only then was it apparent that a minority within their ranks might in the end refuse to enter the union. The Church of Scotland, on the other hand, had already faced difficult decisions and made radical changes in its constitution. Clearly the first stage, that of drafting the constitution, was crucial, and the previous major study of the union, as we have already noted,[2] only takes the story as far as 1921 when the first obstacle was removed with the passing of the Church of Scotland Act.

[1] *UFC Proc.*, 1919, p. 250. Cf. *FR*, p. 78.
[2] See above, p. xiv.

As the biographer of John White, Augustus Muir, put it, there had been no deliverance of the general assembly of the Church of Scotland since the Disruption which was more important than that of 1913 which instructed the union committee to draft a constitution and place it before the next assembly.[3] In addition the draft constitution was to be transmitted to the assembly of the United Free Church. As Lord Sands would note, the Memorandum had originally contemplated the drafting of Articles which would be ostensibly joint and which would become the constitution of the united Church on their adoption by both general assemblies.[4] But following representations by leading members of the UF Church, the drafting was left to the Established Church committee on its own. The UF leaders no doubt felt that their Church should not be seen to be closely identified with solving what was a problem for the Church of Scotland. In addition, if the Articles were to be the constitution for the united Church, their Church would be virtually agreeing to union on these terms, a step which the Church was not ready to take. In view of the subsequent opposition to the union within the UF Church, their assessment of the situation was correct.

According to Sands, however, the procedure whereby the Church of Scotland went it alone to begin with had two unfortunate consequences.[5] Since the document, although meant to apply to both Churches, had to take the form of a constitution for the Church of Scotland alone, an impression of arrogance was created. The Articles could not refer, for example, to the common standards of the two Churches. In the second place the procedure made it much more difficult to move conservative sentiment in the Church of Scotland. He put the problem in legal terms:

> It is easier to influence a man who is making a document which takes the form of a mutual contract than the man who is framing a document which takes the form of a will. In the mind and the mouth of the latter there is always the retort 'This is my will'.

Sands' view was formed after the first year of attempts to draft the constitution during which the committee had experienced the difficulties of satisfying the 'more conservative' sentiment in the Kirk. A minority report was presented to the assembly in 1914 by the two high churchmen, James Cooper and Arthur Wotherspoon, who were concerned for the place of the catholic faith, along with others who were concerned for the established position of the Church. Sands was referring to the fact that compromise is often

---

[3] JW, p. 150.
[4] Lord Sands, Notes on the Established Church Articles, June 1914 (M) 11.4.
[5] Ibid.

easier to reach when a higher aim is in view, in this case church union, than if there is no other such purpose in mind. Compromise is also more likely to be achieved when discussions are held directly with the other side. Even so, it is unlikely that agreement would have been reached on the final form of the Articles, particularly the doctrinal content, had the goal of union not been the ultimate purpose. His point remains, however, that the drafting of the constitution could well have been easier had the discussions been held jointly from the start.

Work was begun by the Church of Scotland committee in 1913 on drafting what came to be known as the Articles Declaratory of the Constitution of the Church of Scotland in Matters Spiritual. John White surprised his fellow committee members at their first meeting by producing a draft constitution which he had prepared. This draft would provide the basis for the discussions and its structure and content would be reflected in the final version of the Articles.[6] The first draft by the committee was presented to the assembly in 1914 and it was sent to the presbyteries for comment along with the minority report of that year.[7] The proposals were also communicated to the United Free Church. Following a break in discussions because of the outbreak of war, a revised version of the Articles was presented in 1918 and the comments of presbyteries were again invited. The final version of the Articles in 1919 was sent down to presbyteries for approval, but not formally under the Barrier Act, although such had been the original intention. Lord Sands pointed out that since they had not yet been recognised as lawful by parliament, it would be technically illegal for the Church to approve of them formally in this way. The results of this process were to be considered by a commission of assembly so that parliament could be approached without further delay. The Articles were also welcomed by the UF assembly in the same year. Parliament was then approached and the Church of Scotland Act was passed in 1921.[8] The Act however did not come into force until the Church had formally adopted the Articles using the Barrier Act procedure. This was carried out between the assemblies of 1925 and 1926 following the passing of the second act concerning the property and endowments of the Church. With these acts in place the Church of Scotland was free to recognise the Articles as setting out its constitution in matters spiritual and the discussions on union as such could then begin. The Act was then made effective by an Order of Council in 1926.

[6] JW, pp. 469–71.
[7] The text of the draft Articles of 1914 is found in Appendix IV, pp. 295–7.
[8] The text of the Church of Scotland Act and of the Articles Declaratory is found in Appendix I, pp. 283–7.

It is important to understand the overall aim of the new constitution. John White made some preliminary points in this regard to the committee in 1913.[9] The draft constitution, he said, should be as short as possible, and there should be no attempt to frame a new constitution dealing in detail with the general organisation of the Church. 'We must avoid', he said, 'falling into the mistake of treating the matter on such a basis as if we were preparing a new Constitution for a new Church, or a Constitution which is to supersede the existing Constitution of the Church of Scotland as a whole.' There was only one point which had to be dealt with, that 'liberty in relation to the State must... be clearly defined'. The committee did not have to deal with the government, doctrine or discipline of the Church — these were all found in the standards, and would remain. The document did, however, have to make clear that the Church was free in its own sphere in all these matters.

It was even suggested during the later stages of the drafting of the Articles that they should be described as Articles Declaratory of the Freedom, rather than of the Constitution, of the Church.[10] The purpose of the Articles, it was said, was to deal not with the constitution generally, but with the single point of freedom in relation to the State. This point had been made when the committee presented the first draft of the Articles in 1914: 'Apart from the declaration of liberty in matters spiritual, these Articles do not deal, and were not intended to deal, with the general question of State relations.'[11] Not only did the Articles not attempt to restate the constitution of the Church as a whole, they did not even deal with the issue of spiritual freedom in a comprehensive way. They were concerned only with certain elements of the position, namely, with liberty from civil control. The change in the title was not agreed, but from the outset the specific purpose of the document was accepted. It was a far-reaching statement in one way, but its importance lay in that one direction, the freedom of the Church in relation to the State. The Church of Scotland had come to accept that its relationship to the State did curtail its freedom in certain important respects, yet a complete break with the State was not desired. John White rejected the suggestion that acceptance of the Articles would 'disestablish' the Church.[12] He wished there to be

[9] John White, Notes and Suggestions to assist the Committee in framing the draft of such a Constitution as is suggested in the Memorandum, November 1913 (W) 98.

[10] Suggestions towards the Amendment of the 'Articles Declaratory of the Constitution of the Church of Scotland in Matters Spiritual', 1918 (LS) 20.2.

[11] *C of S Rep.* 1914, p. 1172.

[12] Transmission of Report and Articles to Presbyteries and to UF Assembly in 1914 (W) 97.

a right relationship, rather than an absence of relationship, between Church and State. But he did not like the unintentional limitations that the present State connection imposed.

(a) the freedom of the Church in relation to the State

The aim of the Articles Declaratory was thus to deal with the issue of spiritual freedom in such a way as would meet the objections of the United Free Church. That Church had declared its position in the 1906 Act anent Spiritual Independence. The constitution of the Church of Scotland had to embody the principles set out in that document. It followed, therefore, that the Articles echoed much of the content of the Act in the clauses dealing with the Church's liberty. Article IV, which outlined the Church's freedom in relation to the State, did not change materially from the first to the final draft. The Church of Scotland, like the United Free Church, claimed that the Lord Jesus Christ had appointed the government of the Church as distinct from and not subordinate to civil government. The Church

> receives from its Head and from Him alone the right and power subject to no civil authority to legislate, and to adjudicate finally, in all matters of doctrine, worship, government, and discipline in the Church, including the right to determine all questions concerning membership and office in the Church, the constitution of its Courts, and the mode of election of its office-bearers, and to define the boundaries of the spheres of labour of its ministers and other office-bearers.[13]

The Article specified the range of the freedom of the Church to include all matters of doctrine, worship, government and discipline, and in particular the membership of its courts. This last point was included to refer to the issues raised by the Stewarton Case on which judgement was given by the Court of Session in 1843. One of the results of this case was that ministers of chapel-of-ease congregations, which had been raised to full ecclesiastical status by the Chapel Act, were debarred from sitting in the courts of the Church. The mode of election of office-bearers was included in the light of the judgements which followed from the Veto Act, by which the manner of appointing ministers had been challenged by the civil courts. In this way the Articles sought to deal with the issues which had been raised by the legal judgements during the Ten Years' Conflict prior to the Disruption.[14]

The one major change made to this Article from the first draft in 1914 concerned the reference to the civil magistrate which was later made into a separate paragraph as Article VI. In addition, Article V in the draft of 1914 was placed within Article IV in the final

---

[13] Article IV. See Appendix I, p. 285.
[14] See above, pp. 16–18.

version which meant that the issue of spiritual freedom was dealt with in the one Article. This clause made clear that recognition by the civil authority did not in any way 'affect the character of this government and jurisdiction as derived from the Divine Head of the Church alone and not from any civil authority'. It was important for the United Free Church that this remaining link of the Church of Scotland with the State, the recognition of its spiritual independence, did not in any way imply the authority of the State over the Church or the right of interference by the State in the affairs of the Church. In an early draft of the constitution, it was noted that this clause was the 'crux of the matter so far as the distinctively Free Church section of the UF Church' was concerned.[15] Those belonging to this section held that the jurisdiction of the Church had been derived from statute law under the Act of 1592, and they were therefore wary of any form of recognition by the State.

It was also important that the State should recognise and not confer freedom upon the Church. Spiritual freedom in the areas of doctrine, worship, government and discipline belonged to the Church as the body of Christ and was not conferred upon it by the State. The minority in the Church of Scotland committee proposed at one stage that the new constitution had to be ratified by parliament.[16] If this motion had been carried, the whole value of the Articles would be destroyed. The Articles would then not be the inherent right of the Church, but only held by permission of the State. If the State was said to have conferred freedom upon the Church, it would have a statutory right to interfere in future in the Church's exercise of that freedom.

Article IV stated that the Church has the right and power to legislate in all matters of doctrine, worship, government and discipline. The Church of Scotland could rightly claim that the consequences which flow from a recognition of spiritual freedom had been identified and affirmed. John White, in an earlier memorandum, had identified these consequences as follows:[17]

(1)   That the composition of Church Courts would no longer be regulated by civil law;

(2)   that the election and appointment of Ministers would be governed solely by the law of the Church which the Church might alter;

(3)   and that the Church's power in regard to doctrinal definitions as set forth in its own Articles would not be controlled by the Parliamentary ratification of the Confession of Faith.

[15] Sketch Constitution C (W) 104.
[16] John White, Church Union. The Articles (W) 97.
[17] Consequences which flow from Provisions Securing Spiritual Freedom (W) 32.

The first two of these consequences have already been noted and the third was the subject of Article V.

(i) freedom to change the doctrinal standards of the Church
Article V stated the Church's freedom in relation to its own doctrinal standards, in particular its Confession of Faith. The Article stated the Church's ability

> to frame or adopt its subordinate standards, to declare the sense in which it understands its Confession of Faith, to modify the forms of expression therein, or to formulate other doctrinal statements, and to define the relation thereto of its office-bearers and members …

It was important, in view of the arguments in the Free Church Case, that the Church be recognised as having the power to alter its subordinate standards, particularly in doctrinal matters. It had been argued before the House of Lords that the Free Church did not have the power to change its adherence to the Westminster Confession as it had done in 1892 when it passed the Declaratory Act. In addition the Church of Scotland had had to approach parliament for legislation which would allow it to change the formula of subscription to the Confession. And so now it was specifically stated that the Church had the power to 'declare the sense in which it understands its Confession of Faith'. It also had the power, more basically, to frame or adopt its subordinate standards and formulate other doctrinal statements, which would mean that the Church could replace the Westminster Confession with another document. George Robson had identified this issue as the crux of the matter so far as the freedom of the Church in relation to the State was concerned. If the Church of Scotland representatives agreed that there had to be power in the constitution to change the Confession of Faith, then, he said, 'they practically yield the key to the position of the establishment'.[18] This position was appreciated at an early stage by at least one member of the Church of Scotland committee, Professor William A. Curtis, then of Aberdeen and later of Edinburgh University. He pointed out to Lord Sands that the other side would never accept the position whereby the State would be the judge in doctrinal matters.[19] Only the Church could perform that function for itself in the future, even if there was the risk of seeming to have an absolute spiritual authority like that of the papacy.

The only qualification was that such changes as might be made in the future should be 'in agreement with the Word of God and the fundamental doctrines of the Christian Faith contained in the

[18] G. Robson to A. Martin, 27.12.09 (M) 6. Cf. *FR*, p. 29.
[19] W. A. Curtis to Lord Sands, 1.12.13 (LS) 11. Cf. *FR*, p. 30.

said Confession, of which agreement the Church shall be sole judge ...' Those who prepared the minority report in 1914 did not think that this clause was sufficient, since it treated the Confession merely as a table of contents. They thought that it should read 'the Christian faith *as* contained in the Confession' or 'doctrines ... *according to* the Confession'.[20] James Cooper later wished to add the word 'as' to the sentence in order to link the fundamental doctrines more firmly to the way in which they were stated in the Westminster Confession.[21] This, however, would not have given the Church the liberty to depart from the understanding of the doctrines as held by the Westminster divines. As Lord Sands pointed out, with reference to the doctrine of creation, every Christian would wish to hold a doctrine of creation, but no one except a 'Wee Free' would wish to hold it *as* contained in the Confession.[22] Such a view would involve a literal understanding of the six days of creation. The purpose of drafting the Articles was to allow the united Church the freedom to depart from what the continuing Free Church would regard as doctrinal orthodoxy without being challenged in the civil courts as had happened to the United Free Church. The addition of the word 'as' would take that freedom away from the Church.

Members of the United Free Church, in commenting on the first draft of the Articles, also wished to be sure that the Articles allowed the Church in future to replace the Westminster Confession with another doctrinal standard. They asked about the extent of the doctrinal liberty claimed in this Article:[23]

> Does it include the power to substitute for the Westminster Confession of Faith another doctrinal standard, or to modify the terms in which adherence to the Westminster Confession is required?

The Article did not refer to the Westminster Confession by name, but rather to the Confession of Faith of the Church. If the Church were to change its standard in doctrinal matters, this Article would not require to be changed since it would then refer to the new Confession and not the previous one. If, however, the Church

---

[20] William Swan and A. W. Wotherspoon, *Nec Tamen Consumebatur. Statement differentiating the Minority Report from the Majority Report of the Church Union Committee* (Edinburgh and London, 1914), p. 7.

[21] *FR*, pp. 59-60.

[22] *FR*, p. 60.

[23] United Free Church of Scotland, Memorandum of Comments and Suggestions of Inquiry made in the Committee of the United Free Church on the Articles Declaratory, 1914 (M) 8. Cf. Church of Scotland Articles: Points which have emerged in discussion as occasioning difficulty, 1914 (M) 14.1.

were to depart from a Confession of Faith altogether, then the wording of this Article would also require to be changed. As it was, the Westminster Confession was mentioned in Article II as being the principal subordinate standard, 'containing the sum and substance of the Faith of the Reformed Church', and it would thus be this Article which would require to be altered. This possibility was outlined by Lord Sands:[24]

> If it were desired to go so far in the direction of new doctrinal statement as to substitute a new Confession for the Westminster Confession as the principal subordinate standard, the procedure would not be under Article V but under the power to alter Article II conferred by Article VIII.

In the 1918 draft of the Articles, however, an indirect reference had been made to the Confession of Faith in Article I which stated that the Church adhered to the fundamental doctrines of the Christian faith 'contained in its own Confession'. Since Article I would have a different status from the other Articles, and be a constant factor in the Church's constitution, this reference to the Confession would mean that the Confession, too, could not be changed. At the request of the office-bearers of the United Free Church, this reference to the Confession was deleted and the fundamental doctrines were stated to be those 'founded upon the Word of God'.[25] The first reference to the Westminster Confession was thus in Article II which was subject to change in the same way as the remaining Articles. Those who were most responsible for framing the Articles wished there to be no doubt about the Church's freedom in relation to its doctrinal standards.

(ii) freedom to unite with other Churches
The Church of Scotland also had to be recognised as having the freedom to unite with other Churches in the future, following upon the union with the United Free Church. There had to be a recognition, too, that such a union would be carried out on the Church's own terms, not on terms laid down by the State. The Church had to be able to unite with another Church without losing its identity in the eyes of the law. This had been the issue in the Free Church Case, and the UF representatives understandably did not wish to risk a repetition of that judgement. By uniting with

---

[24] Notes by Lord Sands upon the United Free Church Memorandum on the Church of Scotland draft Articles, November 1918 (M) 8. Cf. John White, Safeguards (W) 32; *FR*, p. 109.

[25] Notes on Informal Conference held at 4 Heriot Row, 5th December 1918 (M) 8. Cf. *FR*, p. 64.

the United Presbyterian Church in 1900, the Free Church was declared to have changed its identity since in terms of its creed, both as regards its doctrinal position and its view of establishment, it had departed from the principles upon which it had been formed in 1843.

The Article dealing with the unity of the Church remained in essence unchanged from, although shorter than, the first draft of 1914. Several features of this Article can be noted.[26] First, unity was said to be an obligation laid upon the Church since it was 'the will of Christ that His disciples should all be one in the Father and in Him'. The spiritual basis of Church unity was thus clearly stated, the same underlying motivation for union which had led the Churches to enter into discussions in the first place. That same theological imperative was to inspire the Church in future to seek unity with other branches of the Church of Christ. Yet, secondly, there were qualifications. Union was to be sought with Churches in which the Church of Scotland found 'the Word to be purely preached, the sacraments administered according to Christ's ordinance, and discipline rightly exercised'. These were the three 'notes' of the Church identified by the Scots Confession of Faith as marks by which the true Church might be known.[27] Furthermore, in the third place, it was up to the Church itself to judge whether the terms on which union would be carried out were 'consistent with these Articles'. The Church, and not the State, would be the 'sole judge' of whether or not such a union was consistent with its constitution. The question of church union was therefore to be decided on the same basis as changes to the subordinate standards. Speaking at the assembly of the United Free Church in 1919, Archibald Henderson said that this clause on unity 'was straight in the face of the House of Lords — and that it was meant to be — because they must be safe against a repetition of any such aggression of the civil courts upon the spiritual rights of the Church.'[28]

(iii) freedom to change the government of the Church
A future union, however, might not simply involve two Presbyterian Churches as was the case in 1929. The Church of Scotland might wish to unite with a Church which had a different form of government and discipline, and other changes might have to be made to facilitate this outcome. Church union might involve a change in church government. It was therefore important,

---

[26] See below, Appendix I, p. 286.
[27] *Scots Confession of 1560*, XVIII, p. 18.
[28] *UFC Proc*, 1919, p. 250. Cf. *FR*, p. 78.

in the eyes of the United Free Church representatives, that the Church's ability to change its form of government should also be stated clearly in the Articles. There was no specific Article which dealt with the Church's freedom to change its form of government, as was the case with its doctrinal standards. Article II, as well as referring to the Westminster Confession as the principal subordinate standard, also stated that 'the government of the Church is Presbyterian, and is exercised through Kirk Sessions, Presbyteries, Provincial Synods, and General Assemblies'. This sentence appeared in the draft of 1914 and remained unchanged. The procedure to be adopted with regard to any change in the government of the Church would therefore be by the alteration of this Article. The only change made so far to the Articles Declaratory has been of this nature. The abolition of provincial synods in 1992 involved the deletion of the words referring to those courts in this Article and the mechanism for change outlined in Article VIII had to be employed.[29]

Was it intended, however, that Presbyterianism itself might be radically changed rather than simply altered in a relatively minor way? In the final Article of the draft of 1914 it was stated that 'Presbyterian Church government being agreeable to the Word of God and consonant with the religious traditions of the Scottish people is the only form of government of the Church of Scotland'. This Article sought to deal with what were considered to be the permanent features of the Church's constitution, and it had been understood that these would be solely of a doctrinal character. Yet here was a reference to forms of church government, which the UF representatives had thought would be able to be changed. In their comments on this draft they said that this clause could 'restrict unduly the rightful liberty of the Church in matters concerning government'.[30] If this clause remained, Presbyterianism would become a 'permanent mark' of the identity of the Church and any change to the government of the Church could be subject to challenge in the civil courts. This clause was removed from future drafts of the Articles, leaving the sole reference to Presbyterianism in Article II.

In the Church of Scotland committee John White had to justify the decision not to include a reference to Presbyterianism among the constant features of the constitution. No one on either side of the discussions, after all, was proposing that the united Church should cease to be Presbyterian. White replied by quoting Lord Sands who had said:

[29] *FR*, pp. 115-18.
[30] Memorandum of Comments and Suggestions on the Articles, 1914.

Perhaps it may be asked why, seeing that there is no desire to subvert Scottish Presbyterianism, and any such subversion is not within the sphere of practical politics, room should have been allowed for this specious objection. Why was Presbyterianism not declared to be unalterable? The answer is that, to some of the staunchest adherents of Presbyterianism who were parties to the negotiations, it seemed that such a provision would be inconsistent with the genius of Presbyterianism and with the ideas of freedom with which Presbyterianism is identified.[31]

Alexander Martin was of the view that, according to the Articles, not only was the Church able to replace the Westminster Confession but 'also to modify and alter the Presbyterian government of the Church'.[32] This was important, in the view of Archibald Henderson, since it gave the Church of Scotland the ability to unite with other Churches which might not necessarily be Presbyterian in government or even accept the Westminster Confession of Faith.[33]

The strength of feeling on this issue among the UF representatives was shown by their reaction to the first draft of the preamble to the bill which would recognise the Articles. This stated that the Articles had been prepared with a view to 'the union of other Presbyterian Churches with the Church of Scotland'.[34] Martin wrote to both the Secretary for Scotland, Robert Munro, and to Lord Sands, objecting strongly to the inclusion of the word 'Presbyterian' in the preamble as it limited the freedom of the Church to unite with other Churches as outlined in Article VII.[35] If the bill remained as it was, future unions could only take place with those Churches which a civil court would regard as 'Presbyterian'. The ability of the Church to decide this matter for itself would be removed. After being told by Lord Sands and John White that the Church of Scotland committee had agreed 'reluctantly' to its omission, the Scottish Secretary said that he was willing to drop the term from the bill.[36] The State therefore recognised that the Church of Scotland had the freedom to unite with another Church which it regarded as being in agreement with the Articles or which was prepared to unite on the basis of the Articles.

[31] John White, Safeguards and Article I (W) 32. Cf. *FR*, pp. 80-1.
[32] Memo re Church of Scotland Articles and the Statutes, 10.2.19 (M) 8. Cf. *FR*, pp. 79-80.
[33] *FR*, p. 83.
[34] *FR*, p. 81.
[35] A. Martin to R. Munro, 18.3.21 (LS) 25; A. Martin to Lord Sands, 16.3.21 and 19.3.21 (LS) 9.
[36] Lord Sands, Private Memo, and J. White to R. Munro, 23.3.21 (LS) 25; R. Munro to A. Martin, 18.4.21 (M) 18.10/72. Cf. *FR*, pp. 81-3.

(iv) freedom to change the constitution of the Church

Since the Church was to be recognised as free in relation to its own constitution, the power to change the constitution had to be stated in some way. It was a prerequisite of the Church's freedom that the State should not be able in future to intervene to prevent the Church in the exercise of its freedom. The United Free Church representatives were anxious to avoid a repetition of the judgement in the Free Church Case whereby the House of Lords had denied that the Church had the power to change its position in certain respects. Counsel for the UF Church had argued that the power of change was present in the constitution of the Church.[37] This power of change had thus to be stated explicitly in the Articles Declaratory. The draft of 1914 stated in Article VIII that the Church 'has the right to interpret these Articles and, subject to the safeguards for deliberate action and legislation provided by the Church itself, to modify or add to them …' The Church was recognised as having the freedom to interpret its own constitution and to change it using its own legislation. This referred to the Barrier Act by which new legislation had to receive the approval of a majority of the presbyteries of the Church before it could be enacted by a subsequent general assembly. Thus any change to the Articles would follow the same procedure as other enactments.

A significant change was made to this Article, however, in the draft of 1919 and was made by the Church of Scotland representatives without consultation with their colleagues in the United Free Church. The mechanism whereby the Articles could be changed now involved an enhanced Barrier Act procedure. Any proposal to change the Articles had to receive a two-thirds, rather than a simple, majority of presbyteries, and this had to be achieved in two successive years rather than in one. Lord Sands justified this measure by saying that safeguards for the constitution had to be in the constitution itself.[38] Ordinary legislation could not be the basis of extraordinary safeguards. A future assembly might repeal the Barrier Act. This view had a certain logic to it, but it was his further argument, that the enhanced safeguards would assist in gaining the approval of the presbyteries for the Articles, which was the real reason for the introduction of this procedure.

At least one member of the Church of Scotland committee, William Curtis, disagreed with this change to Article VIII. It was in his view unnecessary and was 'a reprehensible procedure … to impose upon the future a more stringent demand for approximate unanimity than the Church has required either in the past or in the

[37] *FR*, p. 15.
[38] Lord Sands, Notes on Safeguards (W) 105. Cf. *FR*, p. 73

present vital instance.'[39] It went without saying that the representatives of the United Free Church were unhappy with the enhanced Barrier Act procedure. It made any change to the position of the Westminster Confession all the harder to achieve, and they resented the fact that the measure had been sprung upon them without warning.[40] They realised, however, that it was important for the Church of Scotland to have such a safeguard and they reluctantly agreed to its inclusion. They noted that this procedure applied only to the Articles, and that in practice the Church had never made a constitutional change which went against the opinion of more than one-third of the presbyteries.[41] They were also able to obtain some modification of the proposal. They pointed out that, under the Barrier Act, presbyteries could make suggestions for the improvement of the legislation being considered. This suggestion was incorporated into the final version of Article VIII at the assembly in 1919 and made the first approach to presbyteries more of a consultative process.[42] Archibald Henderson was able to commend this revised version of Article VIII to the assembly of the United Free Church.[43] The members of the UF minority, however, objected strongly to the inclusion of the enhanced Barrier Act procedure. It meant that any change in the constitution was very difficult to achieve.[44]

In addition, the United Free Church committee members could comfort themselves with the thought that the mechanism for change in Article VIII was itself capable of change using its own procedure.[45] In the debate on the Articles in the House of Lords, however, Lord Finlay voiced the opinion that the safeguards of Article VIII could not themselves be subject to modification.[46] This had not been the understanding of the matter at the time of the framing of the Articles by the representatives of either Church. In the view of the UF committee it was doubtful whether the interests of the Church would suffer, even if such a view were upheld. Any change to the Articles should command a large measure of support throughout the Church.[47] No serious change

[39] William A. Curtis, 'Reunion in the Scottish Church and the proposed Articles', in *The Hibbert Journal*, 18 (1919-20), p. 256.
[40] *FR*, pp. 74-5.
[41] Memorandum for the Use of Deputies (1919) (M) 14.1.
[42] *C of S Rep.*, 1919, p. 570.
[43] *UFC Proc.*, 1919, p. 251.
[44] *UFC Rep.*, 1922, p. 10; Barr, *Scottish Church Question*, pp. 154-6.
[45] *FR*, pp. 75-6.
[46] Hansard HL, 45, 19 July 1921, Col. 1162.
[47] Draft Statement on The Present Position in light of the Passing of the Church of Scotland Act, 1921, For Meeting of Committee on October 20th, 1921 (M) 12.1. Cf. Draft Statement for consideration in Sub-Committee, 6 July 1921 (UFC).

would be made in future 'unless it had in its favour a greater weight of opinion than would be necessary to satisfy the special safeguards of Article VIII.'[48] Members of the UF minority did not accept the assurance that the Church could modify Article VIII procedure and they continued to quote what had been said by Lord Finlay in the Lords.[49] John Young said at the UF assembly in 1922 that Articles I and VIII formed a contract of 'perpetual bondage' to the State in spiritual matters.[50] Even if Lord Finlay was correct, Archibald Henderson did not think that such was a sufficient reason to withdraw from the discussions on union.[51] He thought that Young's raising of the issue was not part of a concern about the constitution of a united Church but simply part of his 'anti-union arguments and devices'.[52]

One fundamental difficulty for the UF minority was that the constitution could not be changed except by act of parliament.[53] At a meeting of the sub-committee dealing with the Basis and Plan of Union in January 1927, James Barr made the point that, in contemplating union, the two Churches had to adhere to the constitution set out in the Articles.[54] There could not be a free negotiation between the Churches and in the future the united Church would be similarly constrained by the Act of 1921. In the view of the members of the United Free Church Association, the Articles would form the only legal basis for the union between the two Churches.[55]

Lord Sands gave a detailed answer to these arguments in the personal memorandum he drew up in relation to the opinion of counsel sought by the United Free Church in 1927–8.[56] It was, said Sands, based on a misconception if it was being argued that the Church of Scotland was under a special disability with regard to its constitution. The same restriction applied to every Church. This situation did not result from the Articles being recognised by parliament, but because they had been adopted by the Church as its constitution. If a Church wished to alter its constitution other

[48] UFC, Committee for Conference with the C of S on Union (1921) (M) 14.2.

[49] UFCA, *Annual Report and Statement.* Cf. J. Barr to A. Martin, 1.10.21 (M) 19.1/9.

[50] UFCA, *"Establishment with Freedom".*

[51] A. Henderson to A. Martin, 19.1.22 (M) 19.2/1.

[52] A. Henderson to A. Martin, 15.10.21 (M) 91.1/22.

[53] Statement authorised by the Minority, 29 January 1927.

[54] Minority re Statutory Position of the Articles etc. Excerpt From Minute of Joint Conference of Sub-Committees No. 1, 10 January 1927 (M) 14.3. Cf. James Barr, *The Scottish Church Question* (London, 1920), pp. 150-3.

[55] Minutes of UFCA, 11 May 1921.

[56] Personal Memorandum by Lord Sands for the information of Mr H. B. Macmillan, K.C. (W) 10.6.

than was provided for in the constitution, or to unite with another Church on terms inconsistent with that constitution, recourse must be made to parliament. Such had happened in the case of the bodies which formed the United Methodist Church. The minority refused to recognise this point and persisted in their belief that the Church of Scotland was in a quite different position in relation to its constitution from that of the voluntary Churches.

(b) the freedom of the Church in relation to creed

The declaration of freedom in the Articles, however, was not acceptable to some in the Established Church without some qualification. Since the restrictions of the relationship to the State were being removed, they were frightened by what seemed to be a claim by the Church to unlimited powers in spiritual matters without any restraint whatsoever. In expressing this fear they were echoing the concerns of those ministers at the time of the Disruption who felt that the Evangelicals who would form the Free Church were claiming an absolute liberty for the Church unchecked by any other authority. In particular, members of the Middle Party, formed in 1842 by Matthew Leishman of Govan, spoke of the need for the freedom of the Church to be limited in some way, especially with regard to matters of the faith.[57] The power was being expressed in the constitution to change the constitution, and hence to change the subordinate standards of the Church which were listed in the constitution. The Church would no longer be bound to the Westminster Confession as its doctrinal standard because it was enshrined in statute law by the Act of 1690 which was in turn included in the Act of Security. Some other safeguards had therefore to be found for the Church's adherence to the fundamental doctrines of the faith.

Lord Sands pointed out that the mere assertion of freedom could not be the basis of a Church.[58] A Christian Church had to remain a Christian Church; it did not have the freedom to become something else. Although Alexander Martin had at first argued that it was difficult to conceive of an autonomous body which was limited as to its power to change its constitution, he would later agree with Sands that there was no such thing as absolute freedom.[59] John White expressed it thus:

[57] E.g. Robert Lee, *The Popery of Spiritual Independence* (Edinburgh, 1845). Cf. Murray, 'Matthew Leishman of Govan'.

[58] Lord Sands, Notes on the Established Church Articles, June 1914 (M) 8; Notes by Lord Sands upon the United Free Church Memorandum on the Church of Scotland Draft Articles, November 1918 (M) 8.

[59] Martin, *Church Union: nearing the goal*, p. 11. Cf. *FR*, p. 27.

> Spiritual Freedom is an important principle which must have an important place in the Articles and be clearly and unambiguously stated, but Spiritual Freedom cannot alone be the basis of a Christian Church.[60]

But how was the limitation upon the Church's liberty to be defined? Much of the time of the committee responsible for drafting the Articles was spent seeking an answer to that question.

The constitution had to state the nature of the Church of Scotland as a Christian Church and that led immediately into the realm of doctrine. It was agreed that the first Article should refer to the fundamental doctrines of the faith which would remain outwith the scope of the Church's freedom. But it proved almost impossible to find agreement on the content of such a statement. According to Lord Sands, the doctrinal question caused 'far more trouble to the Church of Scotland Committee than all the other contents of the Articles', and John White agreed with this assessment.[61] They both thought also that, without some such doctrinal declaration as was eventually agreed in Article I, it would have been impossible for the Church of Scotland to go forward without the prospect of a 'protracted and bitter domestic conflict'.[62] The final version of Article I was, said White, not fully satisfactory to any one, but it was 'the very best settlement that would be arrived at, and it was only reached in a spirit of concession and brotherhood'.[63]

It had been pointed out in the earlier discussions that the United Free Church Act anent Spiritual Independence of 1906 was not devoid of doctrinal content. Lord Sands noted that the Act left excluded from its ambit the being of God, the headship of Christ, the authority of the Scriptures and the operation of the Holy Spirit.[64] The proposal which found most acceptance was that of taking the 1906 Act as a model and expanding it by making the doctrinal reference more explicit. Thus the Article would not be a definitive statement of fundamental doctrines but a 'keynote' setting out the essential nature of the Church of Scotland as part of the Catholic Church and those elements which were outwith the ambit of the Church's freedom in spiritual matters.[65] That is,

---

[60] John White, Article One (W) 32.
[61] Notes by Lord Sands, November 1918; White, Article One, and John White, Personal Reminiscences (W) 84. Cf. *FR*, p. 68.
[62] Notes by Lord Sands, November 1918; White, Article One; *FR*, p. 68.
[63] White, Article One.
[64] Ibid. Cf. *FR*, pp. 26-7.
[65] Memorandum by Lord Sands as to the Position of the Doctrinal Question, March 1918 (M) 8.

it would be a fuller description of the nature of the Church for which freedom was being claimed, a delineation of the identity of the Kirk which would always remain.

An early draft of the constitution began by stating that 'The Church of Scotland is a branch of the Holy Catholic Church'.[66] It was a similar statement which would remain at the beginning of Article I in each of the drafts, only it would be greatly expanded to include a reference to the catholic faith in the final version. This, however, would be the only 'statement' as such, since the expanded doctrinal content would be included as a description of the nature of the Church. The final version of Article I thus stated that 'The Church of Scotland is part of the Holy Catholic or Universal Church' and then went on to describe certain characteristics of that Church in subordinate clauses, all of which were introduced by verbs in the present continuous tense: 'worshipping one God … adoring the Father … confessing our Lord Jesus Christ … glorying in His Cross … trusting in the promised renewal and guidance of the Holy Spirit … proclaiming the forgiveness of sins … and labouring for the advancement of the Kingdom of God'. Within this sentence two doctrines in particular were given some definition, and these were the doctrines of the trinity and the incarnation. Thus the Father, the Son, and the Holy Ghost were said to be 'the same in substance, equal in power and glory' and Jesus Christ was said to be 'the Eternal Son, made very man for our salvation'.

It was the doctrines of the trinity and incarnation which Cooper and Wotherspoon insisted must be stated in a certain way, and the committee eventually agreed. Yet these doctrines were included within the description of the nature of the Church as catholic; they were not to be seen as definitive statements in themselves. The doctrines of the trinity and the incarnation were, however, seen as the foundation of all others and hence their inclusion in this way was justified. Other doctrines were referred to, such as those of the atonement, the resurrection, and the Holy Spirit, but they did not receive further elaboration. As John White said, the doctrines mentioned in Article I 'are not theologically defined, and their interpretation is with the Church'.[67] There was nothing in the Article to prevent the Church setting forth the Christian faith in other statements since, in White's view, there was 'no System of Christian Doctrine, no definition of theological dogma', in Article I.[68] James Denney, too, thought that its terms were in religious rather than in theological language.[69]

[66] Sketch Constitution C.
[67] White, Article One.
[68] Ibid.
[69] Dr Denney's Note on Articles I and VIII (M) 14.1.

It was important, too, that the doctrinal references should not be taken as the Church's definitive statement of the fundamental doctrines of the faith. The Article was a testimony or declaration, a keynote rather than a catalogue; it was not a comprehensive definition and was not an exhaustive list of all such doctrines. The Article, according to White, was not intended either as a formal or a complete doctrinal statement. It was, rather, 'an avowal of the fundamental doctrines of the Christian faith'.[70] The purpose of the Article, in Sands' view, was to meet the need for a declaration in regard to the trinity and the incarnation which would satisfy the minority and, at the same time, 'avoid any appearance of an attempt at a statement of fundamental doctrines which would in any way supersede the reference to the fundamental doctrines contained in the Confession of Faith.'[71]

In order to avoid the Article being taken as an enumeration of fundamental doctrines, a second sentence was added which referred to the fundamental doctrines in general terms. Thus it was stated that the Church of Scotland 'avows the fundamental doctrines of the Catholic faith founded thereupon', that is, founded upon the Word of God. Lord Sands explained that if Article I was limited 'to a purely doctrinal statement, however brief, this might tend to create the impression that the Article is designed as a complete summary of fundamental doctrines'.[72] The Church could therefore, at different times and for certain purposes, draw up statements of what it considered to be those fundamental doctrines, provided, of course, that such statements were consistent with the declaration made in Article I. White was clear on this point:[73]

> In framing our Articles on Spiritual Freedom we did not stand on the old ground of Christian Apology, but claimed the right to re-state theological arguments and to substitute, if and when necessary, a living power of adaptation and advance for a dead conservative tradition. All this to be consistent with the fundamental doctrines enumerated, but not finally defined, in Article I.

Because of the difficulty of reaching agreement on this issue, such a statement of fundamental doctrines has not been approved by the Church since the Articles were formulated. Two statements of faith have been produced, one in 1935, and one in 1991, but these have been for educational purposes and to give guidance to the

---

[70] White, Article One.
[71] *Memorandum by Lord Sands on the Doctrinal Difficulty*, April 1918 (M) 8.
[72] *FR*, p. 66.
[73] John White, Article I (W) 40.

Church, and have not attempted to provide the kind of statement envisaged in this Article. Instead, when reference has been made to those doctrines which the Church considers to be essential to its life, reference has tended to be made to Article I, or to the statement in the Preamble used at services of ordination and induction and which is based upon that Article.[74] The declaration of faith in the Articles has thus come to serve a purpose for which it was not intended.

The second sentence of Article I also contained a reference to the Word of God contained in the scriptures as the supreme standard in all questions of faith and life. John White's first draft of the constitution declared that the Church's ultimate authority was the 'Holy Scriptures and the Holy Spirit'.[75] There was never any disagreement on this issue, but the preferred way of referring to the Bible was that which remained in the final version of Article I and which echoed previous statements on this issue in the documents forming the basis of the unions of 1847 and 1900:[76]

> The Church of Scotland ... receives the Word of God which is contained in the Scriptures of the Old and New Testaments as its supreme rule of faith and life ...

These in turn reflected the wording of the Westminster Shorter Catechism of 1648 which spoke of the Word of God being 'contained in the Scriptures'.[77] As far as the Westminster Divines were concerned, there would be no difference in the meaning of this statement from that in the Larger Catechism which said that 'The Holy Scriptures of the Old and New Testament are the Word of God'.[78] Yet the language of the Word of God being 'contained' in the scriptures allowed for a different interpretation to be given. An identification between the Bible and the Word of God was not being made, and the supreme standard was stated to be the Word of God, not the scriptures as such. In the earlier discussions, Cooper and Wotherspoon had suggested that a simple identification be made and that the Church's supreme standard should be said to be 'the Holy Scriptures of the Old and New Testaments',[79] but their proposal was not accepted. According to Archibald Henderson, the view that all parts of scripture are not alike binding on faith was a 'thoroughly Protestant doctrine'.[80]

---

[74] See, for example, *FR*, pp. 136-7.
[75] *JW*, p. 469.
[76] Cox, pp. 437, 443.
[77] The Shorter Catechism Q2, in Thomas F. Torrance, ed., *The School of Faith* (London, 1959), p. 263.
[78] The Larger Catechism Q3, in ibid., p. 185.
[79] Minutes of the Joint Committee, 15.9.10 (M) 1. Cf. *FR*, p. 44.
[80] A. Henderson to A. Martin, 6.9.10 (M) 17.5/45.

The final wording of the Article means that the Church of Scotland does not hold a fundamentalist view of scripture since it makes a distinction between the Word of God and the words of the Bible, while maintaining that the Word of God is contained in the scriptures.[81]

It should also be noted that this second sentence of Article I said that the Church of Scotland 'adheres to the Scottish Reformation'. This statement is capable of a variety of different meanings, but was intended to provide a reference to the nature of the Church as Protestant and Reformed. In Sands' view, this clause further emphasised the point that Article I was not to be taken as a definitive statement of fundamental doctrines.[82] If the doctrinal declaration and the reference to the fundamental doctrines stood alone there would be apt to be confusion and misunderstanding. This difficulty could be minimised, in his view, by also reserving other things such as Protestantism, or the principles of the Reformation, as well as the supreme authority of scripture. In the draft of 1914 it had been stated in Article II that the Church 'adheres to the principles of the Protestant Reformation'. The reference was thus made in the Article which dealt with the reformed standards of the Church, and that, indeed, was a logical place for it to be found. But while the standards of the Church could be changed, and thus could not be included in Article I, it was not intended that the Church should be free to go back upon the Scottish Reformation. The Church of Scotland was to be Protestant and that character would be part of its identity. One member of the minority in the United Free Church, John Willock, was anxious about this clause. The Church of Rome and the Church of Scotland were both branches of the Church of Christ. What right, he asked, has parliament 'to say that two branches of the Church of Christ must remain in perpetual feud?'[83] It could be argued, however, that if the Church of Scotland in the future considered that the Roman Catholic Church had come to adhere to the Scottish Reformation, then reunion would not be impossible.

The drafting of the first sentence of Article I containing the doctrinal testimony proved to be the most controversial.[84] Three distinct stages in the discussions can be identified. The first stage had already been reached in the preliminary discussions and had

---

[81] *FR*, p. 44.

[82] Memorandum by Lord Sands as to the Position of the Doctrinal Question.

[83] John Willock, in *Notes on Church Union*, No. 1, April 1925. Cf. J. Willock to A. Martin, 21.9.23 (M) 19.3/20.

[84] A full treatment of these discussions can be found in *FR*, especially ch. 3.

been mentioned in the joint report of 1911, that the constitution would have to contain some reference to doctrine. John White's draft constitution included a reference to the Westminster Confession of Faith as setting forth 'the sum and substance of the doctrine of the Reformed Churches'.[85] But a further draft in November 1913 simply stated that the Church held the faith 'which was once for all delivered to the saints'.[86] James Cooper objected that this did not contain the doctrinal reference which had been promised, and it was agreed that a fuller statement had to be made.[87]

Secondly, the question arose as to the nature of this statement. It could be in general terms, such as in the formula which had recently been agreed by the Church of Scotland in relation to the subscription of ministers to the Westminster Confession, which referred to the 'fundamental doctrines of the Christian faith' contained in the Confession. But what were those fundamental doctrines? James Cooper had at first supported the new formula at the assembly in 1909, but later had reservations and voted against it when it was considered by the presbytery of Glasgow later that year.[88] Those who want it, he said, refuse to define the fundamentals. He feared that the formula would be more of a snare than a help.[89] Thus when it came to consider the doctrinal statement in the Articles, Cooper was not prepared to be fobbed off this time with such a general reference, although such was the preferred solution of William Mair and Professor W. P. Paterson of Edinburgh.[90] The committee agreed that a statement of specific doctrines should be made and the third stage was therefore the drafting of this statement.

The first version of the doctrinal statement in 1914 failed to meet with the approval of Cooper and his colleagues who formed a minority on the committee. They produced a minority report and offered an alternative version of Article I which included what they considered to be a more adequate statement of the catholic doctrines of the trinity and the incarnation. It is important to realise their position regarding these two doctrines. In a pamphlet stating the minority position,[91] William Swan and

---

[85] *JW*, p. 469.
[86] Sketch Constitution C.
[87] *FR*, pp. 53–4.
[88] Murray, 'Scottish Church Society', p. 123.
[89] (JC) 31, 8 December 1909, p. 98.
[90] *FR*, pp. 39, 46, 58.
[91] Swan and Wotherspoon, *Nec Tamen Consumebatur*.

Arthur Wotherspoon said that they had realised that the statement in the Article would be brief. They recognised, too, 'that things fundamental are not all fundamental in the same sense'.[92] They continued:

> There are fundamentals of fundamentals, and the ultimate fundamentals are the doctrines of God and of Christ — the Doctrine of the Trinity and the Doctrine of the Incarnation: from these two all, even the Doctrine of the Atonement, are derivative.

For the minority members the Church had to remain openly and unambiguously committed to the catholic faith, the creeds of the undivided Church, otherwise it would be cut loose from the rest of Christendom and was in danger of becoming unitarian and apostate. They constantly had in mind the fact that Presbyterian Churches in England and Ireland had in previous centuries departed from the trinitarian faith.[93] The essence of the creeds, the basis upon which the whole framework of the faith rested, were the doctrines of the trinity and the incarnation.

The members of the minority did not just insist on those doctrines being stated in some form or other, but as formulated in the creeds. The Church had to be committed to the credal formulations of these otherwise it could not be said that the Church affirmed the catholic faith. Hence their desire for a statement of the Nicene-Constantinopolitan doctrine that the Son is of one substance with the Father, or as they wished to say, that the three persons are one God 'the same in substance, equal in power and glory'.[94] This phrase, beloved of Cooper, was found in both the Westminster Larger and Shorter Catechisms and would be well known to all those who had experienced a Scottish Presbyterian upbringing.[95] It was that formulation for which Cooper and his colleagues fought and which they eventually achieved. It was that definition which in their view was the most important in the history of Christian doctrine and was 'the very crux of orthodoxy and of Doctrinal Communion with the Universal Church'.[96] William Curtis would later point out that while the rest of the doctrinal content of Article I was couched in 'the vocabulary of religion' rather than the 'vocabulary of creeds and dogmatic systems', the use of these historical terms was an exception.[97] It

[92] Ibid., p. 9.
[93] James Cooper, 'The Present Call to Witness to the Fundamental Truths of the Gospel', in Scottish Church Society, *Conferences*, First Series (Edinburgh, 1894), p. 54.
[94] Swan and Wotherspoon, *Nec Tamen Consumebatur*, p. 10.
[95] Larger Catechism Q9, Shorter Catechism Q6, in Torrance, *School of Faith*, pp. 186, 261.
[96] Swan and Wotherspoon, *Nec Tamen Consumebatur*, p. 10.
[97] Curtis, 'Reunion in the Scottish Church', p. 252.

was also important for the high churchmen that the doctrine of the incarnation be stated in such a way that the one person and divine and human natures of Christ were clearly affirmed.

The work of the committee was suspended during most of the war years and the discussions on the Articles were not resumed until 1918. It seemed to John White that agreement on the content of Article I was as far away as ever, yet the whole movement towards reunion would be unable to proceed without some solution to the 'doctrinal difficulty'. He therefore decided on a bold measure which he later described as follows:[98]

> At one period of the negotiations there was such a constant endeavour on the part of one or two members to insert an elaborate catechetical statement of doctrine that it was moved and carried at a meeting of Committee, 5th March 1918, to eliminate from the Articles any reference to doctrine other than the general reference to the fundamental doctrines of the Christian Faith contained in the Confession. This was done with the simple object of ending an interminable discussion.

Cooper had left the meeting early and was reported later to be 'furiously angry' and to be threatening secession from the Kirk should the decision be implemented.[99] Not only were Cooper and the minority dismayed by this decision, but more moderate traditionalists like Lord Balfour of Burleigh also thought there should be some more definite doctrinal reference in the Article. But White's bold stroke had concentrated the minds. He had made it clear that the discussion could not go on for ever and that some compromise would have to be made. It was then that Lord Sands was asked to see if he could find a solution to the doctrinal question.

Sands drew up a Memorandum which provided a basis for an understanding.[100] The definition of the central doctrines requested by the minority would be accepted provided that the doctrinal Article would be taken as having been finalised as far as the committee was concerned. It would, of course, still have to be considered by the courts of the Church, and members of the committee would be free to consider changes in the light of the criticisms and suggestions made in the presbyteries and by the United Free Church. Nobody, he said, 'need be over-anxious at this stage because the Articles do not quite satisfy his ideal so long as they do not contain anything in which he can never acquiesce.'

[98] John White, Articles: Article I (W) 32.
[99] *FR*, p. 61.
[100] Memorandum by Lord Sands as to the Position of the Doctrinal Question.

The problem had arisen because the Church of Scotland would no longer be bound to the Westminster Confession of Faith by the Revolution Settlement of 1690:[101]

> Under the proposed Articles, the Church will no longer have the protection, or the fetter, whichever it be regarded, of the 1690 ratification, and will have express power to modify the Confession of Faith. This power is limited by the condition that any alteration must not be inconsistent with the fundamental doctrines of the Christian Faith contained in the Confession. These doctrines are not specified or defined, and as the Church is to be the sole judge of whether a change is consistent therewith, there is no legal restraint enforceable by any civil or other *ab extra* authority.

There were two possible views of this situation, either that the Church of the future must be trusted in this matter, or that legal restraints were a valuable safeguard against doctrinal defection, as seen in the history of the Presbyterian Church in England and in Ireland. If the second view was put into effect, it could be done in either of two ways. It could be left to the civil authority to decide when a proposed alteration was inconsistent with the fundamental doctrines of the faith, a view which would hardly be acceptable to the United Free Church in the light of its recent history. Or alternatively, certain doctrines could be defined as fundamental. This, then, brought them to their present problem of trying to define those doctrines, of deciding which were fundamental, which should be included and which left out, and how they should be stated. Would those who take the first view, that the Church be trusted in future, he asked, 'concede any doctrine as specifically reserved?' And would the other side 'accept anything less than an attempt to enumerate and define all fundamental doctrines?' Some of the minority, who took the latter view, had suggested that they would be content with the catholic doctrines of the trinity and the incarnation and Sands expounded the logic of this position:[102]

> The Catholic doctrine of the Incarnation in its relation to the doctrine of the Trinity is the Lynchpin of historical Christianity. Take it away and dogmatic christianity and supernatural christology fall together. Leave it, and you may have a dozen theories of the Atonement, you may accept or reject the confessional doctrines of Election and Justification by Faith; and historical christianity stands where it did.

[101] Ibid.
[102] Ibid.

Sands therefore proposed a version of the Article which would meet the concern of the high churchmen for these doctrines to be stated in a certain way, provided that they now accepted this as the final version. Cooper agreed to the terms of the Sands Memorandum since it embodied the main points for which he had been contending all along. Others in the minority, however, including his fellow high churchman Arthur Wotherspoon, were not so content with the proposal and would later resign from the committee.[103] For them, too, the position of the Church as an establishment was of concern.

The representatives of the United Free Church did not object to such a statement of doctrine being made in Article I, and said that, when it came to the actual union of the Churches, they too might have a statement of doctrine to submit.[104] The only further changes to the Article were made at their suggestion and were acceptable to the committee as a whole. They wished there to be a reference to the love of God, and thus the Church was described as 'worshipping one God, Almighty, all-wise and all-loving'. The first draft of the Articles had also not contained a reference to the doctrine of the atonement.[105] It had been the weakness of the stress of the creeds, from their point of view, that they did not take account of the controversies of the Reformation regarding the nature and scope of salvation. The final version thus also included a reference to Christ being made man 'for our salvation' and an explicit mention of 'His Cross and Resurrection'. The final version of this all-important first sentence of Article I was as follows:

> The Church of Scotland is part of the Holy Catholic or Universal Church; worshipping one God, Almighty, all-wise, and all-loving, in the Trinity of the Father, the Son, and the Holy Ghost, the same in substance, equal in power and glory; adoring the Father, infinite in Majesty, of whom are all things; confessing our Lord Jesus Christ, the Eternal Son, made very man for our salvation; glorying in His Cross and Resurrection, and owning obedience to Him as the Head over all things to His Church; trusting in the promised renewal and guidance of the Holy Spirit; proclaiming the forgiveness of sins and acceptance with God through faith in Christ, and the gift of Eternal Life; and labouring for the advancement of the Kingdom of God throughout the world.

[103] *FR*, pp. 65-6, and see below, p. 253.
[104] Memorandum of Meetings with Leaders of the United Free Church, 5 December 1918 (LS) 20.7.
[105] *FR*, p. 57.

The content of the Article was thus agreed but it had to have a different status within the Articles, an unchangeable character, otherwise it would be pointless. But could there be such an unalterable statement of fundamental doctrines? In the earlier discussions the distinction was made between the substance and the form of doctrinal statements. The content was not to be confused with the way in which that content was expressed. The Church could therefore change the forms of expression of its doctrinal statements 'without derogating from the essential meaning of the doctrines'.[106] The purpose of the Article was thus not to provide a definitive statement of these doctrines but to refer to the substance of the doctrines which would always remain. Thus Article VIII, which specified that the content of Article I was outwith the scope of change, spoke of the 'provisions' of the first Article being essential to the continuity and corporate life of the Church. This would imply that the words of the doctrinal reference could be changed provided its substance remained.[107] The final position, according to John White, was that Article I was not unalterable, but that the Church would unalterably adhere to the declaration contained in the Article. It was a subtle distinction, he admitted, between an unalterable Article, and an unalterable adherence to an Article. The declaration in Article I was not itself a statement or definition of the faith but a keynote or testimony. The final version, as Lord Sands admitted, was a compromise between 'the dogmatic claim of Church of Scotland High Churchmen and those who wished no doctrinal fixity at all'.[108] The UF committee also recognised that in future the Church would be committed to the substance, but not to the terms of the Article.[109]

Several voices from both Churches had been raised during the discussions about the dangers of making any statement unalterable and absolute.[110] Members of the UF minority thought that Article I would become a legally binding creed in the same way as the Westminster Confession had become for the Church of Scotland.[111] They were concerned that the Church was not free in doctrinal terms because of the permanent status of this Article.[112] Even if

[106] Minutes of the Joint Sub-Committee of Liberty in Relation to Creed, 22.7.10 (M) 6; *FR*, p. 45.

[107] *FR*, p. 72.

[108] Ibid.

[109] Draft Statement for consideration in Sub-Committee on Friday 6th July 1921 (UFC).

[110] *FR*, pp. 69-71.

[111] Barr, *Scottish Church Question*, pp. 150-1. Cf. *FR*, pp. 96-7.

[112] Ibid. Cf. 'A Convinced Voluntary' in *Notes on Church Union*, No.10, January 1926.

this creed was acceptable, they said, it was not right that a reformed Church should be tied to any human statement in this way. Language changed, and the Church should have the freedom to use different expressions in future years. The Article was said to be 'Trinitarian Protestantism' and as such was surely acceptable. But the minority argued that it was now a fixed creed, something that the reformers had always rejected. It contradicted the principle of *semper reformanda* laid down in the Preface to the Scots Confession of Faith.[113] However much the Church might interpret these words they had to remain 'as the fundamental part of the concordat with the State'.[114] The argument that the Church was only committed to the provisions of the Article did not impress the members of the minority: 'if it is necessary at so early a date to indulge in verbal subtleties,' they said, 'one may well ask why it is there at all.'[115] Why should there be such a permanent statement at all, they asked, if it were not to satisfy 'certain liturgically-minded individuals in the Auld Kirk' or 'to appease an Erastian Parliament by giving a promise of future orthodoxy so as to secure the teinds?' We as a Church, it was said in a leaflet published by the United Free Church Association, should have entire freedom 'to determine and to interpret our creed as the Spirit of God moves us without resort to any cosmopolitan parliament'.[116] The minority also did not accept the argument that Article I was not a creed but a keynote or testimony. Again some of those who spoke in parliament referred to this Article as the creed of the Church.[117] This, said James Barr, was 'elevating Article I into a leading instrument for determining the faith of the Church, and giving it a rigidity and a State-authority it should never possess'.[118] No matter how acceptable the content of Article I was at present, its permanent character meant that the State had to be brought in whenever the Church wished to make a change in its doctrinal position.[119]

Those in favour of union had to admit that a doctrinal limitation was being imposed in the Articles, but they also maintained that the doctrinal substance of the Article was 'Trinitarian and Protestant'. Was that a restraint upon the spiritual freedom of the

[113] UFCA, *The Proposed Union: Guide to Members of the United Free Church of Scotland*, August 1927, p. 3. Cf. A United Free Churchman (J. M. Macfie), *The Union of the Churches: A Plea for Readjustment* (Edinburgh, 1926), p. 6, and Barr, *Scottish Church Question*, p. 152.

[114] *UFC Rep.*, 1922, p. 10.

[115] Ibid., p. 8.

[116] UFCA, Leaflet No. 2, *Would Union be Strength?*

[117] *UFC Rep.*, 1922, p. 10; Draft Statement for consideration in Sub-Committee.

[118] Barr to Martin, 1.10.21.

[119] Letter to the Editor by A. Weir, *Scotsman*, 4.4.28.

Church? The UF Church did not possess the freedom as it stood to cease to be either one or other without parliamentary sanction.[120] To maintain its identity it must continue to be both Trinitarian and Protestant.[121] Archibald Henderson thought that Article I was unfortunate in its phrasing in several places but, in his view, it did not bind him to anything to which he did not wish to be bound.[122] The Trinitarian faith and Protestantism could not be regarded as a straightjacket. A Church which held property had to have some 'definition of its identity'. If the Church did not provide such a definition then the civil courts would do so instead. The intention of Article I, said James Denney, was to prevent any abuse of liberty in relation to doctrine. The Church claimed liberty as a Christian Church and in no other way.[123]

The advocates of union argued that the two Churches shared the same limitations with regard to spiritual freedom. Alexander Martin argued that, in presenting its claim to freedom, the Church had to present itself in a certain character, which it did as Trinitarian and Protestant.[124] If there was no objection to that character, then the apparent restraint on the freedom of the Church was merely apparent. 'Is it a spiritual hardship', he asked, 'that there should be a legal inhibition upon the abuse of funds — for is there any other way in which the question would arise? — bestowed upon her for properly evangelical ends?' The United Free Church, he said, was in essentially the same position, not under a special statute, but under the general law in which property was held. In other words, the Articles were no different from the constitution of any other Church, but had the advantage that the spiritual nature of the Church was thereby recognised by parliament. John White also thought that in this respect the two Churches were in the same position.[125] The UF minority seemed to think that a Christian Church should have the ability to alter the fundamental doctrines of the faith. They had difficulty joining with the Church of Scotland because they would not be able to depart from Article I. That is, said White, they would not have the liberty to dissociate themselves from the catholic Church. They would not have the liberty to become a Unitarian or a Roman Catholic, to question the Word of God contained in the scriptures, or to disavow the fundamental doctrines of the catholic faith.

[120] Draft Statement for consideration in Sub-Committee.
[121] Outline of Statement on the Prospect of Presbyterian Reunion in Scotland, 28th June 1923 (Draft) (UFC). Cf. UFC, Committee for Conference with the Church of Scotland on Union (M) 14.2.
[122] A. Henderson to A. Martin, 8.10.21 (M) 10.
[123] Dr Denney's Note on Articles I and VIII (M) 14.1.
[124] Alexander Martin, Memorandum on Minority Manifesto, June 1926 (M) 11.3.
[125] John White, A Halter Around its Neck (W) 97.

The Church would also have the freedom to interpret its own doctrine in relation to the needs of the age. Alexander Martin pointed out that the Church's continuing adherence to the provisions of Article I was to be 'interpreted by the Church'.[126] Thus Article VIII stated:

The Church has the right to interpret these Articles, and, subject to the safeguards for deliberate action and legislation provided by the Church itself, to modify or add to them; but always consistently with the provisions of the first Article hereof, adherence to which, as interpreted by the Church, is essential to its continuity and corporate life.

The question arose during the passage of the bill in parliament as to whether the Church was completely free in this power of interpretation, or whether an appeal could be made to the civil courts over a disputed interpretation.[127] The question had arisen because of remarks by the Solicitor General for Scotland, C. D. Murray, in the House of Commons, that the civil courts could intervene where the Church courts had made a misinterpretation or had failed to interpret the Articles.[128] Lord Sands, however, pointed out that while an absence of interpretation may be grounds for an appeal to the civil courts, a misinterpretation would not. The Church must be allowed to interpret the Articles even if its interpretation might not be agreed by the civil courts. It would only be if the Church abandoned the provisions of Article I, and interpreted the Articles so as to become, say, Unitarian or Roman Catholic, that the civil courts would have the right to interfere. In the debate in the Lords both Lord Finlay and Lord Haldane had spoken clearly of the Church's power of interpretation in which the civil authority could not interfere.[129] The minority in the UF Church made much of the Solicitor General's speech, and ignored the contributions to the debate in the Lords which had clarified this issue.[130] Bogle pointed out that the Solicitor General had been speaking, not of a misinterpretation, but of a failure by the Church to 'loyally and *bona fide* interpret its standard'.[131]

[126] Martin, *Church Union in Scotland: the first stage completed*, p. 18.
[127] See *FR*, pp. 85-8.
[128] Hansard HC, 143, 22 June 1921, Col. 1461.
[129] *FR*, pp. 87-8.
[130] Ibid. Cf. Barr to Martin, 1.10.21; W. McAlpine in *Notes on Church Union*, No. 1, April 1925.
[131] Bogle, 'Statement by the Minority Members', p. 9.

The Article as finally agreed had the effect of limiting the freedom of the Church in only one crucial respect. The Church did not have the freedom to cease to be the Church. Article I was intended to make clear, as Martin put it, that the Church 'has no desire, however high its claims to liberty be put, to claim the right to cease to be itself'.[132] All rights had limits. Just as the individual did not have a right to commit suicide, so the Church did not have the right to destroy itself. The limitation upon the Church's freedom was not dissimilar to that set out in the United Free Church's own Act anent Spiritual Independence of 1906. The UF Church, said Martin, also had 'no liberty within its constitution to become, say, Unitarian, not to speak of Buddhist or Mohammedan, nor does it desire such liberty.'[133] In this regard then the Articles and the Act of 1906 had a similar character. Article I was of the same character as the doctrinal references found in the UF Act of 1906 and served to indicate the identity of the Church.

Martin considered that the substance of the two documents was identical whereas Lord Sands seemed to imply that in adopting the Articles the doctrinal freedom of the united Church would be something less than it had been for the UF Church.[134] Sands' point was that the two documents would be seen differently from a theological than from a legal point of view. Martin, from a theological perspective, was no doubt right to regard the Articles as simply making explicit what was implicit in the Act of 1906, i.e. Trinitarian Protestantism. But from a legal perspective, while the Articles explicitly bound the Church to the doctrine of the trinity, the UF Act did not.[135] After all, it was because the UF Act was thought to be defective in this regard that the high churchmen in the Church of Scotland committee had fought to include a stronger doctrinal reference in Article I. Later, however, in a personal memorandum for the legal counsel who were being consulted by the UF Church, Sands put forward the view that Martin had expressed. He urged counsel to accept the argument that, as he put it, echoing the beloved phrase of James Cooper enshrined in Article I, the two documents were 'the same in substance, equal in power and glory'. If this view was not accepted, he gave notice that he would undertake, without transgressing in any way the letter of the Declaratory Act of 1906, 'to frame a definition of the Godhead not only inconsistent with Article I of the Church of Scotland Articles on any reasonable interpretation, but sufficient

[132] FR, p. 27.
[133] Martin, Church Union in Scotland: the first phase, p. 19.
[134] A. Martin to Lord Sands, 25.10.27 (M) 20.1/37.
[135] Lord Sands to A. Martin, 26.10.27 (M) 20.1/40.

to cause St. Athanasius, Luther and Dr. Cooper all to turn in their graves.'[136] In the event, the opinion of counsel would be that both the Articles and the Act were substantially the same.[137]

(c) the national recognition of religion

The principle of a national recognition of religion was, as we have seen, one point on which agreement had been reached in the earlier discussions. It was therefore not surprising that it gave rise to relatively little discussion in the framing of the Articles.

According to Alexander Martin, this principle was 'common to both Churches, and indeed to all branches of Scottish Presbyterianism'.[138] The United Free Church, he said, had always testified to this principle, and its definition in Article VI was acceptable to all.[139] In the first draft of the constitution Article III referred to the position of the Kirk as a national Church, and Article IV contained a reference to the divine calling of the civil magistrate and the nation.[140] This latter reference, however, was a preamble to a statement regarding the spiritual freedom of the Church with which Article IV was principally concerned. It was realised that a separate article on the subject of the national recognition of religion was required, and such was provided as a new Article VI in all subsequent versions. This Article, too, remained the same from the draft of 1918.

The first sentence of Article VI states:—

> This Church acknowledges the divine appointment and authority of the civil magistrate within his own sphere, and maintains its historic testimony to the duty of the nation acting in its corporate capacity to render homage to God, to acknowledge the Lord Jesus Christ to be King over the nations, to obey His laws, to reverence His ordinances, to honour His Church, and to promote in all appropriate ways the Kingdom of God.

The Article goes on to state that both Church and State 'owe mutual duties to each other, and acting within their respective spheres may signally promote each other's welfare.' Martin pointed out that these words had been borrowed from the much earlier 'Articles of Agreement as to National Religion' formulated

---

[136]Personal Memorandum by Lord Sands for the information of Mr H. P. Macmillan, K.C.

[137]See below, pp. 229–30.

[138]National Recognition of Religion (M) 14.4.

[139]Memorandum on the Church of Scotland and 'the Establishment Principle' (M) 12.1.

[140]See Appendix IV, pp. 295–6.

by the Free Church and the United Presbyterian Church during their discussions in 1869.[141] He contrasted the position in Scotland with that in the United States, where there was no visible connection between Church and State, yet where Christian values had a considerable influence on public life. In Scotland, on the other hand, a more visible connection had always been desired, and it was thought that the Church as a divine body was worthy of 'express acknowledgement and honour at the hands of the civil authority'. The Article also states that Church and State each have the right to determine 'all questions concerning the extent and the continuance of their mutual relations'. There was to be no dominion of the one over the other. According to John White, both the Roman Catholic view of the secular power being derived from the ecclesiastical power, and the Erastian view that spiritual power was derived from the civil power, were wrong since both powers were derived from Christ.[142]

There was much more discussion over the exact way in which the State should recognise the Church. This recognition was set out in Article III, the wording of which was changed slightly after the first draft but then remained the same in subsequent versions. In this Article the Church of Scotland was said to be 'a national Church representative of the Christian faith of the Scottish people', in continuity with the Church since the Reformation, and with an obligation to exercise a territorial ministry. Martin pointed out that the claim of the Kirk to be a national Church was exactly what had been claimed by the United Free Church, only this claim was now recognised by the State. The UF Church had also acknowledged its obligation to minister to all the people of Scotland.[143] In reply to one colleague who questioned him on this issue, he pointed out that, in the Article, national was spelt with a small 'n'. This was what their own Church claimed to be, he said, 'in virtue of the history behind us, the place we occupy today in the national life, and the work we have to do for the people'.[144]

It should be noted, too, that the Kirk was said to be 'a' national Church, not 'the' national Church. It was not an exclusive claim and did not detract from that role being carried out by other Churches, such as had been done by the UF Church. The Kirk was different in that it was recognised as such by the State whereas other Churches were not. It was, however, open for them to be so

---

[141] Martin, *Church Union in Scotland: the first stage completed*, p. 30. Articles of Agreement as to National Religion, p. 15. Conference with the C of S (M) 4, p. 3.
[142] John White, Establishment (W) 40.
[143] Martin, *Church Union in Scotland: the first stage completed*, p. 33.
[144] A. Martin to A. Scott, 8.10.25 (M) 19.6/4.

recognised. Following the passing of the Church of Scotland Act, other Churches could also obtain an improved legal status. Clause 2 stated that nothing 'shall prejudice the recognition of any other Church in Scotland as a Christian Church protected by law in the exercise of its spiritual functions.' This matter had been discussed by the joint conference of the Churches in 1919.[145] It was decided that formal proposals could not well be formulated except on the initiative of those Churches, but the Church of Scotland representatives undertook to ensure that those bodies would not be disadvantaged by the forthcoming legislation. In the view of John White a great deal had been won for these Churches should they choose to claim it.[146] Hence one of the questions raised by the United Free Church during the discussions, as to whether such a measure would give other Churches a similar position in the eye of the law as the Church of Scotland had, was answered in the affirmative.[147]

It was of vital importance to note that the State recognition in the Articles was not legal but factual. As Martin said, nothing legal was to be inferred from the Church of Scotland so describing itself.[148] Just as the Church's freedom was now recognised by parliament as something inherently belonging to the Church as part of the Church catholic, so, too, its role as a national Church was recognised in a similar way as already belonging to the Church. As Martin put it,[149]

> the 'national' character of the Church had been purged of those legal implications which had constituted it a 'branch of the institutions of the country', while retaining all that *de facto* connotation for which men really prize it.

John White was anxious to emphasise that in the Articles the State recognised a characteristic which already belonged to the Church and did not confer this national role upon it by statute. The Church was 'not made national by the State; it is the Church of the nation throughout a long history, it is national *de facto* and is recognised for what it is'.[150] Even a voluntary such as Professor James A. Paterson of New College could speak of the UF Church as being as much a *de facto* national Church as was the Church which was national *de jure*.[151] Before union could take place, in his

---

[145] The Position of Other Churches (M) 14.4. Reports of Joint Sub-Committee preparing for Meeting of Joint Sub-Committee (of 50) to be held 28th March 1919 (M) 13.1, and 10th March 1919 (M) 13.1.

[146] John White, Church and State (W) 40.

[147] Points in regard to National Recognition of Religion (M) 14.4.

[148] Ibid.

[149] Martin, *Church Union in Scotland: the first stage completed*, p. 36.

[150] John White, The Church National (W) 40.

[151] *UFC Proc.*, 1913, p. 264.

view, the Church which was national by law had to step down from its 'pedestal of privilege'. It was just that 'stepping down' from its legal position which the Church of Scotland was willing to do.

One feature of the Church of Scotland as a national Church was its historical role in the life of the nation. It was the Church, said Martin, 'which rocked the cradle of the nation at the beginning, and whose teaching and power have been so deeply interwoven with its life all down the centuries.'[152] Martin quoted his fellow churchman, the historian A. R. MacEwen, who had written: 'Scotland has no history apart from the history of the Scottish Church'.[153] This aspect was a fact of history, a description of the nature of the Kirk. Martin pointed out that the Church could, if it wished, take away this point from its constitution, since the reference to the national character of the Church was contained in Article III, not in the first of the Articles.[154] Being a national Church was a matter of history and was not part of the unchangeable identity of the Church, as were those doctrinal elements set out in Article I. But it was only right that an institution which had played such an important part in moulding the nation should still be recognised in such a way.

The Kirk also had a contemporary role as a national Church. It was said to be 'representative of the Christian faith of the Scottish people'. The united Church would have greater grounds for this claim since it would consist of a significant proportion of the population and would be by far the largest Church in Scotland. As John White said:[155]

> The united Church will be more representative of the national life. The various needs of the community should therefore receive a fuller expression. The variety and knowledge of the united Church should ensure that no aspects of the social question will be overlooked, and that no rash and one-sided views will prevail.

It was important for White, too, that a national Church should serve the nation as a whole regardless of church membership. The position of the Kirk was one of duty rather than of privilege. Only a national Church, in his view, could guarantee the universality of religious worship and teaching in all parts of the country. By its parochial system, he said, it 'not only gives every citizen a title to

[152] Martin, *Church Union in Scotland: the first stage completed*, p. 33.
[153] A. R. MacEwen, *A History of the Church in Scotland* (London, 1913), p. 1.
[154] Martin, *Church Union in Scotland: the first stage completed*, p. 34.
[155] White, The Church National.

the spiritual help of some minister of religion, but imposes upon some minister a responsibility for the spiritual welfare of every citizen.'[156] Under a voluntary system a Church necessarily gravitated towards people of more or less property. It was only a national Church which could ensure the presence of a minister in every parish however poor the people might be. White was thus anxious that Article III should refer to the Church's 'distinctive call and duty to bring the ordinances of religion to the people in every parish of Scotland through a territorial ministry.' In answer to a query from the UF side, too, it was made clear that the Church of Scotland wished to place a stress on the word 'distinctive' in this sentence.[157] The first draft of the Articles had described this call and duty as 'divine' rather than as 'distinctive'.[158] The call and duty to exercise a territorial ministry was one of the chief characteristics of being a national Church. The inclusion of this subject, however, did not prevent disagreement when it came to discuss the way in which this obligation was to be carried out.[159] An interesting suggestion regarding the wording of this Article had been considered by the Church of Scotland committee, that the Church should be said to be representative of the Christian faith *to* rather than *of* the Scottish people.[160] It was argued that the claim to be representative *of* the Christian faith of the Scottish people might offend other Christians. In addition, even if the people ceased to be Christian, and the Church thus no longer represented their faith, it would have an even greater obligation to acknowledge the 'call and duty' referred to in the Article.

The historical and contemporary character of the Church meant that it was to be seen as being in continuity with the Church of the past. This was stated in the first part of Article III:

> This Church is in historical continuity with the Church of Scotland which was reformed in 1560, whose liberties were ratified in 1592, and for whose security provision was made in the Treaty of Union of 1707.

This reference made the point that the Church which was now proposing to unite with the United Free Church, and the united Church which would emerge after the union, had the same identity as the Church which had been reformed in 1560 and had been recognised by the State at various times since then. The old

---

[156] White, A National Church.

[157] Memorandum of Meetings with Leaders of the United Free Church, 5 December 1918.

[158] See Appendix IV, p. 295.

[159] See below, pp. 187–9.

[160] Suggestions towards Amendment of the 'Articles Declaratory' 1918.

statutes were still valued and were not to be repealed in their entirety, even although they no longer restricted the Church in the exercise of its liberty. As Martin said, they 'restrain no liberty, they impose no claim, they confer no power or privilege.'[161] Both committees agreed that the statutes represented a symbol of continuity with the past. The Church would be recognised by statute in its proper spiritual character and, in accordance with the provisions of the Treaty of Union, the Protestant religion and Presbyterian Church government in Scotland would be protected.[162] John White agreed that the Articles had removed any of the ways in which these statutes might have impinged upon the liberty of the Church. But, he continued,[163]

> in so far as they secure the recognition of the Reformation by the State, the acceptance by the State of the Presbyterian Constitution which the Church has shaped for herself, and the recognition of orderly and friendly relations with the State, they will remain and we shall regard them with satisfaction.

It was important to notice that the two statutes referred to specifically in Article III were valued for a particular reason: the statute of 1592 had secured the liberties of the Church, and the Treaty of Union had made provision for the security of the Church. It was for these reasons that these statutes continued to be of relevance for the Kirk, not for any way in which they might restrict its life.

John White thought that a misunderstanding might have arisen because of the use of the word 'grantit' in the Act of 1592, whereby the liberties of the Church were said to have been 'grantit' by the king.[164] This word, he said, meant 'acknowledged', not 'bestowed'. 'In other words the civil power fully recognises, grants, acknowledges that the Church derives its powers and authority of government and jurisdiction in spiritual matters from a divine source alone.'[165] He said that the use of this term could also be seen in 1567 when the assembly approached parliament asking that the Church be 'grantit' freedom and authority as appertain to 'the true Kirk'. Clearly the Church did not ask parliament to confer anything on the Church but to recognise where spiritual authority now resided, with the Reformed Church rather than with the Roman Catholic Church.

---

[161] Martin, *Church Union in Scotland: the first stage completed*, p. 31.
[162] Memorandum on Agreement arrived at between C of S and the UFC of S and the legislation involved therein, February 1920 (M) 12.1.
[163] White, The Church National.
[164] Thomson, *Acts of Parliament*, III, p. 541.
[165] John White, Jurisdiction of Church Courts (W) 40.

White seemed to overlook the fact that the Act of 1592 said that the liberties of the Church were 'gevin and grantit' by the king. Even if 'grantit' meant 'acknowledged' in this case, the use of the verb 'gevin' was unambiguous. In the statute of 1567, too, the Church was said to be 'established', although its ecclesiastical jurisdiction was to be 'acknowledged'.[166]

White interpreted all the statutes in the sense of 'ratifying and confirming' the liberties of the Church rather than 'bestowing' them. He even referred to the Revolution Settlement of 1690 in this way, whereas by this act the Church was certainly 'by law established'.[167] In addition, White conveniently forgot about the Episcopalians who could not accept the terms of the Revolution Settlement and were deposed from the ministry of the Kirk. Did their successors in the Episcopal Church of Scotland not have a claim to be the national Church of Scotland? In historical terms the Presbyterian Church had never been the only form of church life in Scotland. White also made the point that the restrictive interpretation placed upon certain statutes by the civil courts prior to the Disruption had never been accepted by the Kirk as a true description of its constitution,[168] and that the Articles had removed any dubiety concerning the freedom of the Church. The Church had never accepted any interpretation of its constitution which made it a department of State.[169]

The statutes which might be interpreted as restricting the freedom of the Church were not repealed by the Church of Scotland Act, but Clause 1 contained a general repeal clause:

> The Declaratory Articles are lawful articles, and the constitution of the Church in matters spiritual is therein set forth, and no limitation of the liberty, rights, and powers in matters spiritual therein set forth shall be derived from any statute or law affecting the Church of Scotland in matters spiritual at present in force, it being hereby declared that in all questions of construction the Declaratory Articles shall prevail, and that all such statutes and laws shall be construed in conformity therewith and in subordination thereto, and all such statutes and laws in so far as they are inconsistent with the Declaratory Articles are hereby repealed and declared of no effect.

---

[166] Thomson, *Acts of Parliament*, III, pp. 24-5.
[167] John White, Speech on the Articles (W) 97.
[168] White, Church and State.
[169] White, Speech on the Articles.

Such statutes as the Act of Security, passed in relation to the Treaty of Union, would also be included in this clause. The validity of such a general clause was not challenged at the time, although doubt has been expressed more recently.[170] Such a clause had previously been found in Finlay's bill of 1886.[171] The effect of this clause has tended to be ignored by those, like James Barr of the UF minority, who have wished to argue for the continued state connection of the Kirk. Certainly a schedule of repeals would have made it clear exactly what the position was, but it was thought at the time to be too complicated and could have opened the door, as Lord Sands feared, for the statutes 'to be pulled apart'.[172] John White told the presbytery of Glasgow in 1913 that the committee was unanimous in holding that any attempt 'to cut and carve' at the ancient statutes, or to select certain statutes or passages for repeal, would be highly inexpedient.[173] At a meeting in 1918, the leaders of the Church of Scotland committee told their UF colleagues that any proposal to repeal the ancient statutes would make union 'an impossible endeavour'.[174]

The United Free Church committee, however, had assumed that there would be a repeal of the relevant statutes.[175] At one stage it looked as though the discussions on this issue had reached an impasse. It seemed to Lord Sands that, if the United Free Church were asking for a repeal of all the relevant statutes, it would amount to an end of the historical relations between Church and State. He drew up a memorandum for his own committee spelling out the seriousness of the position. The Articles had been prepared in order to remove the restraints upon freedom which were 'an incident of the historical relations of the Church of Scotland to the State'.[176] This would be wasted labour if the United Free Church were now to insist upon the termination of these historical relations as a condition of union. The issue of spiritual freedom was not separable from that of a national recognition of religion. Both were dealt with in the Articles, and the one was connected to the other. The UF Church could not say: 'You have met us with regard to freedom, now meet us with regard to national religion'. In other words, if a termination of relations between Church and State was a requirement for union, that should have made been clear in the first place. As Sands put it:

[170] *FR*, p. 91.
[171] *C of S Rep.*, 1887, p. 588.
[172] Lord Sands to Lord Balfour, 5.7.12 (BAL) 2.84. Cf. *FR*, p. 89 n. 61.
[173] Questions and Answers (W) 97.
[174] Memorandum of Meetings with Leaders of the United Free Church, 5 December 1918. Cf. An Informal Interview with Leaders of the United Free Church, December 1918 (W) 97.
[175] See above, p. 56.
[176] Union. Memorandum by Lord Sands (LS) 20/38.

The object of the Articles, as the United Free Church well know, was to reconcile the legal and historical position of the Church with the claim to freedom. It was folly to spend so much time and trouble in devising a hole for the kitten if nothing was to satisfy the United Free Church but a hole for the cat!

The leaders of the United Free Church committee, however, came to accept the situation.[177] At the assembly of the UF Church in 1919, Archibald Henderson argued that to dismantle all the statutes dealing with the Church of Scotland would not be practicable, and he commended the general repeal clause to his brethren.[178] The general clause was easier to frame, although it left open the exact way in which the statutes still affected the Church. The fact that certain statutes are still in existence means that reference can be made to them without also referring to the relevant clause in the Act of 1921. The general repeal clause was felt at the time to be a sufficient guarantee that the civil courts would not have the right to interfere in the spiritual freedom of the Church, otherwise stronger measures would have been proposed. As they stood the Articles stated clearly the separate spheres of Church and State and declared the right of the Church to 'adjudicate finally' in all matters of doctrine, worship, government, and discipline in the Church.[179]

The courts of the Church were thus no longer courts of the realm in any secular sense but only in a spiritual sense. The courts of the Church, said Lord Sands, are not courts of the realm in that they are not courts of the king, but they are courts of the realm in that they are recognised by the State as having certain functions within the realm.[180] And the only jurisdiction which remains to the church courts is in matters spiritual. John White said that the Church of Scotland was now autonomous in the regulation of its courts in the same way as the United Free Church.[181] The United Free Church representatives realised that, with the recognition of the Articles, the way in which the courts of the Church had been spoken of before and after the Disruption as of 'statutory creation', or as a 'creation of law', could no longer be maintained. The Church was stated in the Articles to be self-constitutive with an inherent jurisdiction. The State only recognised the Church and its courts for what they independently were.[182] The State had

[177] Conference with C of S (M) 4.
[178] UFC Proc., 1919, p. 249.
[179] A. Henderson to A. Martin, 12.9.26 (M) 19.8/18.
[180] Church Courts as Courts of the Realm. Memorandum by Lord Sands (M) 11.4.
[181] John White, Courts of the Church (W) 40.
[182] Memorandum on The Church of Scotland and 'the Establishment Principle'.

therefore recognised the courts of the Church as having a spiritual character and as having an independent jurisdiction, and had disclaimed the right of interference in them.

This recognition gave the Church courts a greater protection than the courts of other Churches since their status and independence were recognised by statute whereas those of other Churches were seen as voluntary associations. In the view of William Mair it was vital that Churches be recognised as having a different status from 'humanly created clubs that grow in a night and perish in a night'.[183] There was a distinction to be made between spiritual jurisdiction and independent jurisdiction. In Mair's view there was often confusion between these two. Speaking at the start of the discussions in 1909, he said with reference to the Church of Scotland:[184]

> The former the Church has not, but I hope soon will have in union with our friends; the latter the Church has, and our friends have not, but I hope soon will have in union with their friends.

It was this recognition of an independent as well as of a spiritual jurisdiction which appealed to many in the UF Church after the judgement in the Free Church Case in 1904. With the recognition of the Church as part of the catholic or universal Church, said Martin, it should be impossible for 1904 to happen again.[185] In answering questions at the presbytery of Glasgow in 1913, John White agreed that the Church could not be 'dragged into the Law Courts' as had happened in recent times.[186] Andrew Bogle argued forcibly at the UF assembly in 1912 that recognition of the Church by the State would give the Church greater rather than less protection.[187] And James Denney had said at the previous assembly that 'the law might provide an improved legal status for the Church as such — an improved status in which, just because it was legal, all branches of the Church would share alike.'[188]

It was therefore no longer the case that the Church of Scotland was 'established'. In the opinion of the United Free Church committee, still to describe the Church of Scotland as an 'established' Church, following upon the recognition of its spiritual independence, could only create misunderstanding: 'In existing conditions in Scotland the term is a misnomer, and its use should be foregone.'[189]

[183] *Jurisdiction* by Dr Mair. Spoken at the Conference, p. 3 (UFC).
[184] Ibid., p. 5.
[185] A. Martin to A. Scott, 8.10.25 (M) 19.6/4.
[186] Questions and Answers, 1913 (W) 97.
[187] *UFC Proc.*, 1912, p. 280; Reith, *Reminiscences*, p. 136.
[188] *UFC Proc.*, 1911, p. 276.
[189] Memorandum on the Church of Scotland and 'the Establishment Principle'. Cf. Memorandum on Agreement arrived at between C of S and the UFC of S, February 1920 (M) 12.1.

There was nothing in the Articles which made the establishment principle fundamental in its constitution.[190] As was the case in the United Free Church, and had been argued before the House of Lords, establishment would be an open question in the united Church.[191] The Church of Scotland was no longer concerned to stand for the 'establishment principle', and the opinion of counsel obtained by the UF Church in 1928 was that an establishment of religion was no longer an article of faith in the Church of Scotland.[192] The principle held by the Church was that of the national recognition of religion, now enshrined in Article VI, of which the 'establishment' of a Church was one application.

According to Alexander Martin, the adjective 'established' in relation to the Church could mean different things. But, he said, in Scotland it had until this point a definite meaning:[193]

> The 'establishment' of the Church in Scotland, as legally defined and given effect to, involved the adoption of a single Church into such a relation to the State that it acquired a civil or quasi-civil character, became invested with civil powers and privileges, and was restrained in the exercise of its proper rights and powers.

This 'fact' of establishment had now gone. In Martin's view, everything considered noxious in the relation of the Church to the State, everything, that is, that had given rise to the demand for disestablishment, had disappeared. It was still possible for someone to call the Kirk 'established' since it was a very elastic term. It had been pointed out that all Churches which hold property were to a certain extent 'established'. But he thought that to employ the term under existing conditions would breed confusion and that the term should be definitely dropped. Martin wrote to Lord Sands in 1919 on this matter and referred to some in the Church of Scotland who still spoke of the Kirk in terms of the Articles as 'established'.[194] As far as Martin was concerned, the terminology used mattered less than the actual arrangement between Church and State embodied in the Articles. He still considered three elements of the national role of the Church as important: the retention of the name, the retention of the statutes, as not absolutely repealed, and certain usages on which agreement would be reached. According to Bogle, the meaning of the term 'establishment' had to be taken from history.[195] In the past it had

---

[190] UFC of S, Committee for Conference with the C of S on Union (M) 14.2.
[191] Martin, *Church Union in Scotland: nearing the goal*, p. 12.
[192] *UFC Rep.*, 1928, p. 16. See further below, pp. 230–1.
[193] Martin, *Church Union in Scotland: the first stage completed*, p. 34.
[194] A. Martin to Lord Sands, 26.7.19 (LS) 23.
[195] *UFC Proc.*, 1919, p. 261.

meant several things: the control of the Church by the State, privilege granted by the State to one Church and denied to others, and financial support for the Church provided by the State. In none of these senses of the term was the Church of Scotland an 'established' Church according to the Articles.

It would also, in the view of the United Free Church committee, be offensive to speak of the Church as having been 'dis-established'. It would also be incorrect as suggesting (again in view of the past) a merely negative relation — or the absence of any relation — between the State and the Church.[196] This did not stop Martin from arguing at the presbytery of Edinburgh that the Church of Scotland was 'disestablished', but he had carefully defined establishment first in the same way as has been noted above.[197] John White, addressing a meeting in Hamilton in 1925, said that he would call himself a disestablisher.[198] The Church could no longer be regarded, as had been implied in some of the judicial findings before the Disruption, as some kind of 'department of state' or creature of the civil government.

The State would still recognise the Church of Scotland in various tangible ways, as, for example, in the presence of the Lord High Commissioner at the general assembly and by the use of the services of the Church on certain occasions. Both committees agreed that[199]

> The national character of the Church would be recognised by the civil authority in availing itself of the services of this Church (not necessarily to the exclusion of other Churches) on national occasions of special solemnity.

Such time-honoured usages, as in the recognition of the Church of Scotland by the crown and its servants, would be continued as might be agreed upon.[200] But such recognition would be the decision of the State and would be based on custom. The position of the Kirk rested not on law but on constitutional usage. The king would not transgress the law if he appointed Episcopalians as his chaplains in Scotland, or gave precedence to the bishop of Edinburgh over the moderator of the general assembly, but either proceeding would be unconstitutional. According to Sands, it was 'as the basis of this constitutional usage, rather than as containing any positive law' that the ancient statutes survived.[201]

[196] Memorandum on the Church of Scotland and 'the Establishment Principle'.

[197] A. Martin to A. Scott, 8.10.25 (M) 19.6/4.

[198] *Scotsman*, 20.10.25.

[199] Memorandum on Agreement arrived at between the C of S and the UFC of S and the legislation involved therein, February 1920 (M) 12.1.

[200] Churches Conference: Report of Joint Sub-Committee prepared for Meeting of Joint Conference, 2 April 1919 (UFC).

[201] Personal Memorandum by Lord Sands for the information of Mr H. P. Macmillan, K. C.

Such recognition by the State would be constitutional rather than legal, and would be dependent on the agreement of both parties. According to Article VI, Church and State both have the right to determine 'the extent and continuance' of their mutual relations. It is perhaps because such recognition by the State has continued to be given that it has been easy for some still to talk of the Church of Scotland as 'established' in a legal sense.

The minority in the United Free Church objected that there were residual elements of establishment which gave the Church of Scotland certain privileges and hence transgressed the principle of religious equality.[202] Certainly the Church of Scotland had not been deprived of its position as a Church recognised by the State as the historic national Church, representative of the religious faith of the Scottish people. But behind this objection, in Sands' view, was the fallacy that things which are equal should be treated alike:[203]

> The Church of Scotland is not recognised as holding a position to which other Churches have an equal claim any more than Edinburgh is recognised as possessing a position to which other cities have an equal claim.

Recognition as a national Church, he said, 'does not transgress any principle of equality if this recognition is not accompanied by the bestowal upon her of any tangible advantage inappropriate to a national Church.' Lord Sands, writing to John White, expressed the view that it was not spiritual freedom that was the main concern of the members of the UF minority but rather 'religious equality'.[204] They had wakened up to the fact that the Church of Scotland Act would result in much less of a disestablishment of the Kirk than they had thought. He continued: 'The privileged position as the national established Church remains just where it was. It would be injudicious to tell them this and it is best to let them talk.' It was indeed as well that this view was not expressed publicly. It would have caused considerable trouble to Alexander Martin and his colleagues in dealing with their minority.

Robertson Christie, the Church of Scotland elder and lawyer, agreed with Sands that the recognition of the Church by the State was a matter for the State. He told Martin:[205]

> Establishment really does not express a relation in which the Church places itself to the State; it is a position which arises

---

[202] *UFC Rep.*, 1922, p. 9. See further below, pp. 215–7.
[203] Personal Memorandum by Lord Sands for the information of Mr H. P. Macmillan, K. C.
[204] Lord Sands to J. White, 20.1.22 (W) 7.2.
[205] J. R. Christie to A. Martin, 25.1.28 (M) 20.3/6.

from the recognition of the State; and if—the Church always being recognised as independent and autonomous—the State chooses to confer a certain recognition upon it which does not interfere with these characteristics, isn't that after all more a matter for the State than the Church—and especially for the individual citizen rather than as Church member?

Recognition of one Church rather than another, he continued, was because that one Church 'does occupy in Scotland a position historically and practically that no other Church can', and thus it was difficult to see 'how the State can in some way or other avoid recognising this'. The way towards religious equality was not to take away such recognition as was given to that one Church, but to seek to extend the recognition of the State to all Christian Churches. It was a question of 'the extension of recognition rather than its repudiation and restriction'. The same held true of the courts of the Church as courts of the realm. They were only courts of the realm in that their spiritual function was recognised and assisted in appropriate ways. Again, this recognition was a matter for the State and did not interfere with the liberty of the Church. 'The Church Courts may not desire to avail themselves of the advantages which recognition as Courts of the Realm gives them,' he said, 'but they cannot prevent the State giving it to them.'

It became clear to Martin that there was 'very little if anything' between the Churches on this issue. It would be inappropriate for people in the United Free Church to speak of the Church of Scotland being 'dis-established' by the Act of 1921 and it would also be incorrect to do so.[206] It was only the extreme voluntaries of the minority who had stood for an entire absence of relationship between State and Church, while the rest of the Church had been willing that 'the former should at least "honour" the latter and further its work in all suitable ways'. On the other hand, for Church of Scotland people 'to make too much of their Church still being "established" might, in view of the past, breed trouble.' Martin recognised that they were entering a new chapter in the history of relations between Church and State in Scotland and that the old language was inappropriate.

(d) the approval of the Articles and the passing of the Act

When opinion in the Church was first tested concerning the Articles in 1918, replies were received from thirty-eight

[206] A. Martin to J. R. Christie, 26.1.28 (M) 20.3/11.

presbyteries, just less than half of the total number. Of those who replied, half passed the Articles with minor alterations while nine approved of them as they stood, six made no suggestions, and four rejected them on similar grounds to those contained in the minority report of 1914.[207] When the Articles were sent down for formal approval or disapproval in 1919, they were approved by seventy-four and rejected by only nine, and in one the voting was even.[208] The total number of votes was 992 in favour of the Articles and 273 against.[209] Those presbyteries which voted against the Articles were all in rural areas but were found in different parts of the country, from Stranraer in the south-west to Tain in the north-east, and included all three of the Shetland presbyteries. It should be noted, too, that the presbytery of Glasgow only approved of the Articles by the narrow margin of 48 votes to 46. Opposition to the policy of the committee had been vocal in Glasgow all along and had been led by the clerk of the presbytery, W. S. Provand. In 1913 John White had held a special question-and-answer session in the presbytery to seek to allay fears regarding the implications of the Memorandum.[210] Those of the minority who rejected the Articles did so because they felt the whole matter had been pushed through too quickly, and they suspected that the leaders of the union movement were prepared to destroy the Kirk as they knew it.[211] This suspicion was rejected outright by Wallace Williamson.

The next stage was an approach to parliament for legislation which would recognise the Articles Declaratory. The Church of Scotland committee made it clear that the Church desired, not the enactment of the Articles by parliament, 'but the removal of statutory obstacles to the adoption of these Articles by the Church itself, and recognition of them as lawful if and when so adopted by the Church.'[212] In making this approach, the committee had at its disposal the influential services of Lord Balfour of Burleigh, a former Scottish Secretary. Although the government at first talked in terms of the bill being a private members' bill, Lord Balfour strongly urged ministers to take up the measure in spite of a reluctance to deal in ecclesiastical matters.[213] He and Sir John M. MacLeod, the Scottish

---

[207] Abstract of replies from Presbyteries in reference to Draft Articles, December 1918 (LS)20; *PRS*, p. 307.

[208] *C of S Rep.*, 1920, p. 941.

[209] *Glasgow Herald*, 18.12.19.

[210] Questions and Answers (W) 97.

[211] *Glasgow Herald*, 18.12.19.

[212] Memorandum upon the Present Position of the Scottish Church Union Question, February 1920 (M) 14.2.

[213] *Scotsman*, 28.7.21.

Unionist MP and father of George MacLeod of the Iona Community, held a meeting of Scottish MPs after which fifty of the seventy-five Scottish members said that they were supportive of such a measure.[214] Disestablishment agitation in Scotland had died down, although parliament had recently dealt with the disestablishment of the Welsh Church.[215] Parliament was more concerned with problems concerning society as a whole, and was more concerned to seek the support of all the Churches in this enterprise, than with the older divisions between the Churches themselves. If there was a strong desire for union by the two main Presbyterian Churches in Scotland, then it was unlikely that parliament would object. Compared to the position at the end of the previous century, only six Scottish Liberal MPs were now prepared to vote for the disestablishment of the Church.[216]

In March 1920 a deputation from the Church of Scotland met with Lloyd George, the Prime Minister, Bonar Law, Leader of the House of Commons, and Robert Munro, the Scottish Secretary. Both Bonar Law and Robert Munro were the sons of Scottish Presbyterian ministers and Lloyd George had been concerned with ecclesiastical affairs in Wales.[217] It was not until May 1920, however, that the government announced that it would introduce legislation regarding the Articles.[218] It became clear, too, that two separate measures would be required, one dealing with the constitution, the other with the endowments, although many in the United Free Church had hoped that the two acts would be passed together. The UF Church sent a deputation to the government to make the point that the question of union would not be discussed between the Churches until both acts had been passed by parliament.[219] The UF leaders had been alarmed earlier by a circular sent by a majority of the Scottish members to the Prime Minister which spoke of the Articles as having been agreed to by their Church as a 'basis of union'.[220] As with many statements made by other parties during the union negotiations, they were concerned with the possible effect these pronouncements would have on the minority in their Church.

The two committees had to wait even longer for a draft bill to appear. It was eventually sent to them in March 1921.[221] After a

[214] *PRS* p. 310. Cf. J. M. MacLeod to J. Brown, 2.10.24 (W) 8.5.

[215] Machin, 'Voluntaryism and Reunion', p. 232.

[216] *PRS*, p. 312.

[217] *PRS*, p. 315.

[218] Hansard HC, 129, 18 May 1920, Col. 1226.

[219] UFC Min., 17.6.20; *PRS* p. 331.

[220] A. Martin to Lord Sands, 4.5.20 (LS) CH1/1/23. Cf. *PRS*, p. 327.

[221] Draft of a Bill to Declare the lawfulness of certain Articles declaratory of the Constitution of the Church of Scotland in matters spiritual (M) 10.

preamble setting out the reasons for the measure, the proposed bill contained four clauses. The first pronounced the Articles to be lawful and stated that no limitation upon the liberty of the Church as set out in the Articles was to be derived from any statute or law at present in force. It then contained the general repeal clause in relation to previous legislation affecting the Church.[222] The second clause referred to the position of other Churches, and stated that nothing in the Act would prejudice the recognition of any other Church 'as a Christian Church protected by law in the exercise of its spiritual functions'. The third clause said that nothing in the Act would affect or prejudice the civil courts in the exercise of their jurisdiction, and the fourth dealt with the operation of the Act by Order in Council following the Church's approval of the Articles under the Barrier Act.

We have already noted one of the objections made by the representatives of the United Free Church to this draft bill.[223] They were concerned with the reference in the preamble that the Act had been prepared with 'Presbyterian' reunion in view, and this restricting term was removed in order that the Church might be able to unite in future with non-Presbyterian denominations. Both committees had reservations about the reference to the civil courts in the third clause, and to avoid any misunderstanding an opening qualification was inserted which said that this provision was 'Subject to the recognition of the matters dealt with in the Declaratory Articles as matters spiritual'.[224] The UF leaders were also unhappy that the bill made no reference to the other parliamentary measure concerning the teinds. The Scottish Secretary repeated his assurance that, in introducing the bill, he would state that the endowments would require to be dealt with and that a small departmental committee would discuss the instructions for the executive commission which would be appointed by parliament.[225]

The bill was introduced in the House of Commons by Robert Munro on 28th April 1921 and given its second reading on 22nd June. Fears that there might be intervention from English MPs of either a nonconformist or establishment persuasion were unfounded.[226] No one objected to the measure on the grounds that considerably more freedom was being recognised for the Church of Scotland than was the case with the Church of England Enabling Act which parliament had recently passed. The debate was

[222] See above, p. 100.
[223] See above, p. 74.
[224] Munro to Martin, 18.4.21.
[225] Ibid.
[226] *PRS*, p. 345.

characterised by several features.[227] Almost all those who spoke were either Scotsmen or those who represented Scottish constituencies. Those who supported the bill placed it firmly in the context of the reunion of the Churches, and were prepared to recognise a completely new attitude to Church-State relationships in Scotland. This outlook was totally different from that which had been adopted by the civil courts prior to the Disruption in 1843. These features were seen in the speech of Robert Munro introducing the bill, and in the contributions to the debate by A. J. Balfour, the Lord President of the Council, and by Sir Arthur Steel-Maitland, who was a member of the Church of Scotland committee. Steel-Maitland spoke of the bill in terms of a new type of relationship between Church and State, not one in which the Church was set up or controlled by the State but one in which its independence was taken note of and recognised by the State.[228] Welcome support for the bill also came from James Brown, the Labour member and Kirk elder, who would later play a significant role in the passing of the property and endowments Act and would serve as Lord High Commissioner to the general assembly.[229] Opposition to the bill came from A. McCallum Scott, a member of the United Free Church and a supporter of disestablishment, and Joseph Johnstone, an elder who took a prominent part in the assembly of the UF Church. As well as echoing several of the criticisms of the Articles which had been made by the minority in the UF Church, they wished there to be a delay in passing the measure until the endowments of the Church could be dealt with.[230] The contribution which caused most problems for the Church committees was that by the Solicitor General, C. D. Murray, regarding the limits to the power of interpretation which the Church could exercise over the Articles.[231] As has been noted,[232] this point was taken up by Lord Sands, and Henderson and Martin from the UF committee also met with Lord Haldane prior to the bill coming before the upper chamber. In the debate in the House of Lords, general support was given to the bill, and both Lord Parmoor and Lord Haldane dealt with the question of interpretation in a way satisfactory to the Churches.[233] Lord Finlay dealt with this point but also argued that the powers of modification in Article VIII could not themselves be changed, a view which would give ammunition to the UF minority in coming years.[234]

[227] Ibid., p. 346.
[228] Hansard HC, 143, 22 June 1921, Col. 1446.
[229] Ibid., Cols. 1452-6.
[230] Ibid., Cols. 1406-16, 1416-28.
[231] Ibid., Col. 1461.
[232] See above, p. 92.
[233] Hansard HL, 45, 19 July 1921, Cols. 1149, 1164.
[234] Ibid., Col. 1162.

The Church of Scotland Act was passed without a division in either house and received the royal assent on 28th July 1921, but would only become effective by Order in Council when the Church of Scotland itself formally approved of the Articles. The general assembly still had to enact the Articles by using the Barrier Act procedure, and this did not take place until after the passing of the Act dealing with the property and endowments of the Church in 1925. Lord Sands was anxious that the Articles be approved by the Church of Scotland before union discussions as such got under way.[235] He did not want the Articles to become mixed up with the Basis of Union as he thought the UF committee members might set about having them altered. With both the teinds bill and the Articles in place the members of the Church of Scotland committee would be in a strong position if any difficulties should arise. They would be approaching the discussions on union with the constitutional framework of the Church fully in place.

It might have seemed that the enactment of the Articles under the Barrier Act would be a formality since the presbyteries had already approved the Articles by an overwhelming majority in 1919. But those who had misgivings about the Articles found a technicality on which to object to the procedure. The point was made that, in sending the Articles down to presbyteries for approval, the assembly had not framed the deliverance in the form of an act but had simply resolved to transmit the Articles 'as an Overture to Presbyteries for their consent under the Barrier Act'.[236] It was argued that the words 'the general assembly adopts', or 'the general assembly enacts and ordains', should have preceded the terms of the Articles.[237] One of the minority in the Church of Scotland, R. S. Kirkpatrick, raised this matter in the presbytery of Selkirk which then sent a memorial to the Procurator; and, according to Lord Sands, H. J. Wotherspoon caused trouble on this issue in the presbytery of Edinburgh.[238] The Procurator, William Chree, did not dispute the technical grounds on which the objection had been made, but he urged the presbytery of Selkirk still to approve the measure.[239] No objection was being made to the substance of the Articles and, in his view, any delay to the process of union would be most unfortunate.

---

[235] Lord Sands to J. White, 24.2.25 (W) 9.5.
[236] C of S Rep., 1925, p. 971.
[237] John White, The Articles (W) 97.
[238] Memo drawn up by R. S. Kirkpatrick re Barrier Act and Articles (W) 97; Lord Sands to J. White, 11.11.25 (W) 9.7.
[239] W. Chree to A. Sym, Clerk of the presbytery of Selkirk, 22.10.25 (W) 9.7.

Lord Sands was later horrified to discover that the Procurator was of the view that matters would have to be delayed for a year because of this objection.[240] He took it upon himself to examine every overture sent down under the Barrier Act since its introduction in 1697. He then informed John White that he had come across precedents which in his view would 'absolutely smash' the objection. Sands prepared a statement which White sent to the press containing these arguments.[241] White pointed out that two measures had been sent down under the Barrier Act in 1697 immediately after it had been passed, and that neither of them were in the form of a draft act. The more formal wording was used for the first time in 1736 and subsequently, but this was because the assembly recommended that the measure be observed as a rule until the following assembly. This precedent came to be followed when the assembly converted overtures into interim acts for a year, but not always in other cases. The most recent precedent for the sending down of an overture which was not in the form of a draft act was in 1901 and concerned the regulations of the curriculum of divinity students. White therefore concluded:

> An examination of the precedents makes it clear that the suggestion that the transmission of an Overture otherwise than as a formal draft Act with enacting words is contrary to the Barrier Act, as that Act has been interpreted for more than two centuries, is devoid even of plausibility.

In the event the Articles were approved by seventy-six presbyteries with four against, one being evenly divided and three not making a reply.[242] Edinburgh, while approving, doubted the correctness of the form in which the overture had been sent, and Peebles and Hamilton both held that since the Act under which it was proposed to adopt the Articles was not before the presbytery, they could not come to a decision on the matter.

Thus in spite of this technical objection which White thought had shown 'great ingenuity',[243] the assembly adopted the Articles by an overwhelming majority.[244] In commending the Articles to the assembly in 1926, White did not rehearse the arguments on this technical point but rather spoke about the importance of the step which was being taken. In his view the Articles were for the good of the Church even apart from union, since they were recognised 'to be the best and fullest

[240] Lord Sands to J. White, 8.11.25 (W) 9.7.
[241] J. White to Editors, 10.11.25 (W) 9.7.; *Glasgow Herald*, 11.11.25.
[242] *C of S Rep.*, 1926, pp. 1064-5.
[243] John White, Reply to Objection re Barrier Act and Articles (W) 97.
[244] *Glasgow Herald*, 5.6.26.

expression of the Spiritual Freedom of the Church to be found in any Church document.'[245] They also emphasised the historical continuity of the Church from the Reformation and from earliest times; and they made it clear that, while holding to the fundamental doctrines of the Christian faith, the Church should interpret theological truth for the present day. The Articles also declared the Church to be national, witnessing to the rule of Christ in the nation. These features were all maintained without prejudice to other Churches which might now claim to be recognised by the State as 'something more than voluntary associations'. With the passing of the Articles, the Church of Scotland had removed one of the two obstacles to union. We must now consider how the Church sought to remove the second obstacle, the way in which it held its property and endowments.

[245] White, The Articles.

Chapter 5

Removing the obstacles: property and endowments 1921–5

From the outset of the discussions on union it had been recognised that the property and endowments of the Church would have to be made over to the Church in accordance with the spiritual freedom which would be recognised by the State. The liberty set out in the Articles Declaratory had to be made effective in relation to the administration and temporal affairs of the Church.[1] It was also recognised by both Churches that this was a matter for parliament to decide.[2] The necessity for a further parliamentary measure was spelled out by the United Free Church committee in an internal memorandum.[3] As it was, the Teind Court, a part of the Court of Session, had jurisdiction over churches, manses, glebes, stipends, the membership of presbyteries, and the disjunction and union of parishes. This arose from the fact that stipends in the old parishes were paid in whole or in part by the heritors, the owners of land in the parish, who paid a teind, the equivalent of the English tithe, or 'tenth', of the annual produce of the land, in respect of their ownership. The Church of Scotland committee stated the position in this way:[4]

> In order that the liberty of the Church set forth in the Articles may be made effective, it is necessary to bring an end to the present system of paying stipend as a charge upon the produce of the land, and substitute a system which will be entirely under the control of the Church.

The committee recognised that Article IV in particular involved the power of the Church to alter the boundaries of existing parishes, and thus also made necessary some rearrangement of

[1] Martin, *Church Union in Scotland: the first stage completed*, p. 39; A. Henderson to A. Martin, 23.8.22 (M) 19.2/41.
[2] *C of S Rep.*, 1912, p. 1217; *UFC Rep.*, 1913, p. 9.
[3] UFC, Readjustment of Church of Scotland Temporalities (UFC).
[4] C of S, Memorandum as to Endowments, October 1921 (W) 98.

the existing law under which stipend was payable out of the teinds in the old parishes. It was recognised by the United Free Church leaders, however, that to place this matter in the hands of parliament, to be disposed of as parliament might decide, was a bold risk for the Kirk to take. It was, in the words of one of the popular *Papers for the People,* produced by the UF Church committee, 'a courageous and worthy act'.[5] As Alexander Martin put it, the Church of Scotland had appealed to Caesar, 'and by the award of Caesar she had no option but to abide'.[6] According to Adam Welch, the 'generous and courageous' action of the Church of Scotland with regard to the teinds had not always been fully recognised in the UF Church.[7]

The joint report of 1911 and the Memorandum of 1912 had both said that the teinds and the other endowments should be conserved for the use of the united Church and that they should not be secularised.[8] They were to be used in future for religious purposes, and in particular for the maintenance of a territorial ministry. The spiritual purpose of these material resources was emphasised. They should be recognised as belonging to the united Church, and not either shared with other Churches or put to other uses, because the Kirk was a national Church with a responsibility to serve the whole country. In the view of John White, disendowment would be justifiable if it could be shown that the possession of the endowments was injurious or 'without benefit to the nation'.[9] In any rearrangement of resources by parliament, he thought that the Kirk should receive at least as good terms as in the case of the disestablishment of both the Irish and Welsh Churches, which were not 'the Churches of the people as the Church of Scotland has always been'.[10] J. A. S. Millar, the convener of the Kirk's Special Committee on Property and Endowments, also thought that to take away such resources from the Church would be to remove them from public to private hands.[11] The property and endowments of the Church were held in trust for the people in every parish.

The Church of Scotland pointed out, too, that the united Church would have to have a common purse.[12] The Kirk would

---

[5] W. S. Matheson, 'What about the Teinds?' United Free Church of Scotland, *Papers for the People,* No. 8 (M) 5.

[6] Martin, *Church Union in Scotland: the first stage completed,* p. 43.

[7] *UFC Proc.,* 1924, p. 272.

[8] *C of S Rep.,* 1911, p. 942; *C of S Rep.,* 1912, p. 1217.

[9] Endowments (W) 97.

[10] Obiter Dicta (W) 99.

[11] *Scotsman,* 10.2.25.

[12] Memorandum on the Readjustment of Church of Scotland Finance with a View to Union, 1922 (M) 5.

thus have to be free to make arrangements with the UF Church regarding the best system of unified finance. No injury should be done to the framework of finance which the United Free Church had developed or to the spirit of liberality on which it was based. It was noted that the Church of Scotland increasingly depended on the liberality of its members and that the aim of any rearrangement of finance must be to encourage this liberality. On the other hand, Alexander Martin reminded a fellow member of the presbytery of Edinburgh that the United Free Church had very considerable endowments.[13] Between four and five hundred congregations had local endowments for stipend, ranging from small sums up to as much as four-fifths of the minimum stipend. It was also pointed out that the United Free Church was in receipt of support from the State in a variety of ways.[14] Annual grants had been made to support the foreign mission work of the Church which had also on occasion received grants of land. UF chaplains in the armed forces and in public institutions were supported from the public purse, and property and investments held by the Church were free of national and local taxation and local rates.

Apart from the question of reunion, it was thought that an adjustment of the endowments would be welcome as providing a simplification of the law which would be for the benefit of both the Church of Scotland and the landowners.[15] Archibald Henderson thought there was a desire 'all round' to deal with this matter once and for all.[16] He said that the heritors wished to see an end of it in case the price of corn should rise, the ministers lest the price should fall, and parliament 'because it can't understand about it and is sick of the business'. But it was also recognised on all sides that these matters were 'difficult and technical'. There had grown up such a complex mass of legislation and case law around the teinds that it was regarded even by lawyers 'as an obscure and highly specialised subject'.[17] In the view of Lord Haldane, the system in Scotland was more technical than the equivalent one in England.[18] According to John White, it had been said that only a famous teind clerk and Lucifer knew the subject: 'the former is dead, and the latter is too busy with international affairs to help'.[19]

---

[13] A. Martin to C. B. Davidson, 8.10.25 (M) 19.6/2.
[14] Hutchison Cockburn, Memorandum, 15.7.24 (W) 8.2.
[15] J. Robertson Christie, *Church of Scotland Endowments* (Edinburgh and Glasgow, 1923), pp. 4–5.
[16] A. Henderson to A. Martin, 19.8.22 (M) 19.2/39.
[17] Christie, *Endowments*, p. 10.
[18] Hansard HL, 57, 1 April 1924, Col. 8.
[19] Teind Clerk and the Devil (W) 100.

Since the stipend of parish ministers was paid out of the produce of the land, it was determined each year according to the value of the chalder, which was a measure of grain. This value was fixed by the sheriff in relation to the fiars or market prices in each county.[20] Thus the stipend not only varied from year to year according to the price of grain and the value of the chalder, but varied from county to county as well. In addition, where property had been subdivided, payment was due by a number of smaller landowners from whom the minister had to collect the amount himself. The system led to a large number of complications and these formed much of the business of the Teind Court. There had already been an attempt at reforming the system and a bill had been introduced in parliament in 1920. This measure had failed to win acceptance by the commission of assembly, largely because of the level of stipend which would have resulted.[21] The Church's failure to accept this measure, however, would lead to the landowners being less willing to accept the initial proposals in relation to Church union.

The payment of the stipend out of the teinds was also seen by many landowners as a tax levied on the land to support a Church to which they might not belong and of which they might not even approve. This, however, was a misapprehension according to the Church of Scotland. It was maintained that the Church's entitlement to a tenth or 'tithe' of the produce of the land had become part of the polity of western Christendom in the middle ages. Custom gradually became law and in Scotland the right of the Church to the teind or tenth came to be as distinct and fixed as the right of the landowner to the other nine-tenths. Confusion reigned after the Reformation, with some teinds being made over by the clergy to others while some were acquired by the nobility. During the reigns of James VI and Charles I, however, the stipend of the reformed clergy came to be provided out of the teinds, and the appropriation of the teind to a particular parish also came to be observed.[22] The payment of stipend to the minister, in the view of the Church, was thus not a tax upon the land but a recognition of the obligation, inherent in the ownership of the teind, of applying it to a religious purpose. Teinds were thus seen as a separate estate, and where the heritor had the title to the teinds, he was thought to be in right of two properties, the lands and the teinds. In paying out of the teinds he was therefore merely

[20] Hansard HL, 57, 1 April 1924, Col. 10.
[21] Christie, *Endowments*, p. 16; A. Menzies to J. White, 17.1.23 (W) 7.3.
[22] A. J. H. Gibson, *Stipend in the Church of Scotland* (Edinburgh and London, 1961), pp. 23–4.

fulfilling a condition inherent in his estate.[23] Whether or not the Church's arguments were accepted, it was undoubtedly true that all Scottish landowners either inherited or bought their land aware of these obligations in relation to the Established Church.

This view of the Church of Scotland would be refuted by those who were opposed to any form of religious establishment in Scotland, including those who had participated in the disestablishment campaign. They saw the teinds instead as the property of the State which had at one time been conferred by the State on the Church and which could thus be taken back again. And in taking this view, as Augustus Muir points out, they would have the support of the legal opinions of some eminent jurists.[24] According to this view, it was only after the Reformation that the State intervened to pay the stipend of the clergy out of funds which it chose to use for this purpose. One of the most vociferous opponents of the proposed arrangement with regard to the endowments of the Church was James Barr, the leader of the minority in the United Free Church. He would be elected as a Labour member of parliament for Motherwell in 1925 and took his opposition to the floor of the House of Commons. He had an extensive knowledge of the subject, although this could lead him on occasion to fail to distinguish between what was important and what was secondary in this matter. If it were true that the teinds had always belonged to the Church, he said, then it would be wrong to argue for their removal from the Church, and the whole disestablishment movement would have been 'most unworthy, vindictive, and unchristian'.[25] But he was in no doubt that the teinds belonged to the State and not to the Church. He said that the teinds had been regarded in this way by those in the former Free Church who had argued for disendowment. Even at the Disruption, he said, it was recognised that the temporalities of the Church were 'conferred by the State', as it was put in the Claim of Right.[26] It was against the voluntary principle for a Church to be supported by anything other than the voluntary giving of its members and thus any form of State aid was excluded.[27]

[23] Christie, *Endowments*, p. 14; Church of Scotland Union Committee, *The Endowments*, December 1918, p. 4 (W) 75.

[24] *JW*, p. 217.

[25] Barr, *United Free Church of Scotland*, p. 159.

[26] Ibid.; Claim, Declaration, and Protest anent the encroachments of the Court of Session, *AGA*, 1842, p. 47.

[27] Barr, *United Free Church of Scotland*, p. 158.

(a) the position of the Churches

Both Churches had set out prior conditions regarding the future settlement of the endowments. The Church of Scotland listed these in 1919 as follows:[28]

> That the endowments which have in the past been dedicated to religious purposes be retained for religious ordinances and uses;
> That all life interests be conserved;
> That the legitimate requirements of each parish to which endowments are at present attached be adequately met;
> That modern endowments ... do not come under review.

In its Report in the same year the United Free Church committee declared[29]

> that it could not accept or share endowments involving any State control or restraint of the Church's spiritual freedom, or continued dependence on statutory support. A union of the Churches would be possible only if such Funds and Properties as Parliament shall make over to the Church of Scotland are made its own, as the Funds and Properties of the United Free Church are its own.

The UF committee concluded that, while not identical, these positions were not mutually contradictory. The Church of Scotland was concerned about the future use of such funds, which was a matter which the UF Church thought parliament alone should decide. The UF Church, on the other hand, was concerned about the terms on which the Church would hold its property in the future. Union would not be possible if it involved a restriction on the freedom of the Church and a reliance by the Church on State support.[30]

Both Churches were agreed, however, that the initiative lay with parliament. No doubt wanting to avoid an unnecessary duplication of effort, the Scottish Secretary, Robert Munro, suggested that the Churches themselves come to an agreement regarding the endowments which the government could then consider. Archibald Henderson wrote to Alexander Martin to say that Munro seemed to be 'throwing on us what he should do himself'.[31] It was important that the ground between them should

[28] Church of Scotland, Statement of Position regarding Endowments, May 1919 (UFC).

[29] *UFC Rep.*, 1919, p. 9. Cf. Revised Report of Sub-committee on 'Matters still remaining to be dealt with — Temporalities etc.', 19 April 1922 (M) 5.

[30] UFC, Notes on Endowments and Properties of the Church of Scotland (M) 12.1.

[31] A. Henderson to A. Martin, 8.4.22 (M) 19.2.18.

be kept quite clear. This was all the more important in view of the fact that Munro was a member of the United Free Church. Martin would later write to the Liberal leader, Herbert H. Asquith, saying that his Church would 'stand aside' from the rearrangement of these matters other than to insist that the Church of Scotland should be free of restraint in regard to its property and finance.[32] It was important for the United Free Church representatives to be seen to be 'neutral', as Martin put it, since it was not their direct concern and they should not be seen to be taking sides. They had to avoid giving the impression to the minority in their Church that they were at all responsible for the settlement with the State.

Lord Sands also thought that the Churches should not be asked to take the initiative in this matter. He wrote to Munro to say that the position of the two Churches on the issue of the endowments was too general in nature to form the instructions to a parliamentary commission.[33] In addition, should the Churches put forward a definite scheme it would be difficult to modify these proposals without causing controversy. Sands thought, instead, that the Churches could offer elastic suggestions in conference with the commission. Final measures could then be offered in which the Churches would acquiesce, although not approving of them in every particular. In addition, Sands told White that it would be inappropriate for the Church to take a hand in adjusting a scheme with the commission before it reported to parliament.[34] It would be a different matter after the report was published, when the Church, along with others, could make representations to the government. Archibald Henderson agreed that the Churches should be free not to accept the results of a parliamentary commission.[35] Thus there were no differences between the Churches on this matter. Throughout the settlement of the question of the endowments, the Churches were usually of one mind in relation to the proposals. It was important for the UF representatives to know that their Church of Scotland colleagues were doing what they could to obtain a satisfactory measure. At the end of the day it was up to parliament to decide, and neither of them had the final say. What each Church had then to consider was whether this particular obstacle to reunion had been removed.

(b) the proposals of the Haldane committee

A departmental committee was finally appointed in April 1922 with Lord Haldane as chairman and four other members. Two

[32] A. Martin to H. Asquith, 2.10.23 (M) 9.3.35.
[33] Lord Sands to R. Munro, 20.12.21 (M) 19.1.24.
[34] Lord Sands to J. White, 15.5.22 (W) 7.2.
[35] A. Henderson to A. Martin, 14.12.21 (M) 19.1.48

members belonged to the United Free Church: Sir George Adam Smith, Principal of the University of Aberdeen, and Lord Maclay, the shipowner and social reformer, who was also known to be a warm supporter of union.[36] Two were members of the Church of Scotland: Mr John Prosser, the Crown Agent, and Sir James M. Dodds, a former Under-Secretary for Scotland.[37] Lord Haldane was not a member of the United Free Church, although he attended services and his family were members, but he had served as counsel for the Church in the celebrated Free Church Case and had previously campaigned for the disestablishment cause.[38] Some in the Church of Scotland were apprehensive lest there be a bias on the part of the committee towards disendowment, but Lord Sands thought that this fear was misplaced.[39]

The remit given to the committee was:[40]

> To enquire and report as to the existing law as affected by the Church of Scotland Act 1921, and as to what further legislative amendments or readjustments — particularly in relation to the tenure and enjoyment of the property and endowments of the Church of Scotland — are necessary or expedient in view of the coming into force of the said Act, in order to facilitate Church Union as contemplated therein.

Representatives of the two Churches duly met the committee and presented their views. The Church of Scotland members proceeded upon the footing that all of the endowments would be made over to the Church.[41] According to Lord Sands, no suggestion was made by the committee regarding partial disendowment. At one point in the discussions Lord Haldane had asked Sir George Adam Smith what he understood by the endowments not being secularised. Smith had replied that he had always taken it to mean that the endowments would be made over in full for the use of the united Church.[42] Sands met informally with the UF Church leaders after their meeting with the committee. They said that their discussions had been satisfactory and they had appreciated the way in which their Auld Kirk colleagues 'had opened up the matter'.[43]

[36] *LW*, June 1922, p. 124.
[37] Christie, *Endowments*, pp. 6–7. Cf. *JW*, p. 215, where Maclay is said to belong to the Church of Scotland, and Prosser to the UF Church.
[38] A. Henderson to A. Martin, 4.4.22 (M) 19.2.13; *JW*, p. 215.
[39] Lord Sands to J. White, 5.5.22.
[40] *JW*, p. 215. Report of the Committee on the Property and Endowments of the Church of Scotland, *C of S Rep.*, 1923, p. 68.
[41] Memorandum by Lord Sands re Conference with the Departmental committee, 2.5.22 (W) 7.2.
[42] Lord Sands to J. White, 27.4.22 (W) 7.2.
[43] Ibid.; Memorandum by Lord Sands, 2.5.22.

The committee published its report in April 1923 and both Churches gave a general welcome to the recommendations. The main provisions were with regard to the teinds. The general object of the proposals, it was stated, was

> to abolish the whole system of teinds, including the system by which stipend, varying annually in amount, is paid therefrom by the owners of land to the Ministers; and to substitute therefor a system under which the landowners will redeem the burden of teind, and the Ministers will receive stipends, fixed in amount, from a purely Ecclesiastical body.

This system could not be introduced immediately, but would be put into effect on the occurrence of a vacancy, or sooner if the minister wished, or if the general assembly agreed to provide him with the same stipend as before. The life interests of present incumbents would be preserved. The level of stipend to be redeemed would be ascertained by taking the average value of the chalder over the previous fifty years. The heritors would redeem the burden of the teinds either by a single capital payment, or by the payment of a terminable annuity made up of the stipend plus ten per cent, payable up to the point where it had produced the capital sum which would redeem the stipend. The capital sum should be that which, if invested in consols, would produce the same annual amount as the new level of stipend. The payments would be made to a body of Ecclesiastical Commissioners, such as the General Trustees of the Church, a body already set up by an act of parliament in 1921 as a holding body for properties and investments belonging to committees of the Church.[44] The General Trustees would then pay the stipends directly to the ministers. The payment of stipend would be the first call on the revenue of a parish, but other uses could be decided by the Church.

It was also proposed that churches, manses and glebes be vested in the General Trustees of the Church, in the case of burgh churches this being done by an Executive Commission since further detailed enquiry was necessary. Churchyards would become the property of Parish Councils. It followed, too, that landowners would no longer be required to pay Ecclesiastical Assessments for the provision and upkeep of churches and manses, subject to handing them over in a reasonable state of repair. The Church would in future be responsible for the maintenance of its buildings. Exchequer grants which were made for stipends in the parliamentary charges in the highlands would be commuted by the Treasury into a capital sum which would be

---

[44] A. W. Cowe, 'General Trustees', in *DSCHT*, p. 356.

capable of producing an equivalent income in the future. The Teind Court would in due course be abolished and the Church would itself have authority over the use of its property and regarding the disjunction and union of parishes.

The United Free Church committee concluded that, if these recommendations were carried out, the funds and property of the Church of Scotland would be its own in the same sense as the funds and property of the UF Church were its own. The general assembly thus 'cordially welcomed' the report as making 'an important further stage in the removal of the main obstacles keeping the Churches apart'.[45] The Church of Scotland's committee decided that the Haldane recommendations, 'when taken as a whole, and as embodying a considered scheme, be accepted in principle and agreed to by the Church'.[46] There were two matters of detail on which they wished to seek amendment, the value of the standard chalder and the upkeep of church buildings. It was felt that a fifty year average would be unfair to the Church since prices had been much lower in recent times.[47] They also wished to have definite provisions for the repair of buildings before they were handed over to the Church. The main criticisms of the proposals came from the Disestablishment Council for Scotland,[48] which said that the endowments were treated as if they belonged to the Church rather than to the State. The endowments should therefore not be made over to the Church of Scotland alone, but instead should be used to help the socially disadvantaged in society.

(c) the measures of the Novar bill

Lord Haldane later recalled that the report was 'without much delay embodied in a Statute',[49] but it was not until January of the following year that a bill was introduced by Viscount Novar, who was now the Secretary for Scotland, and the Act was not finally passed until 1925. Changes in government accounted in part for the delay. The Coalition government which had appointed the Haldane committee gave way to a Conservative cabinet which introduced the bill, but almost immediately a Labour administration came into power.[50] A further Conservative cabinet would oversee the final passage of the bill in 1925.

[45] *UFC Proc.*, 1923, p. 139.
[46] *C of S Rep.*, 1923, p. 46.
[47] Lord Sands to J. White, 15.7.23 and 27.7.23 (W) 7.4.
[48] The Disestablishment Council for Scotland, *The Haldane Report and the Haldane Declarations* (Dundee, 1924).
[49] R. B. Haldane, *Richard Burdon Haldane: An Autobiography* (London, 1929), p. 311.
[50] Fleming, *Story of Union*, p. 114.

John White and his colleagues found that their patience was severely tested as they waited for the bill to be published. They tried unsuccessfully to be given sight of the bill beforehand,[51] and they met with the Scottish Secretary and sought assurances regarding its contents. They feared that the measure would not be satisfactory and White thought that it could frustrate the union movement. In writing to Lord Sands he spoke of his dissatisfaction not only with Novar, but also with William Watson the Lord Advocate. He used an analogy with Rugby Union, a game which they both followed:[52]

> It will be a thousand pities if we do not score a try after our long years of scrummage. Novar is not proving much good behind the scrum, and Watson, his stand-off, is never in place, and does not seem to know what to do with the ball when he gets it. He is ignorant of the Union rules.

Novar tried to reassure White by saying that the bill would not deviate materially from the Haldane proposals except with regard to the redemption of the teinds by the purchase of consols.[53] But White pointed out that this was a serious difference and might well leave the Church much worse off than before.[54] Haldane, too, did not think the difference a serious one and considered that it would be 'easy to correct' in the committee stage.[55] It was thought by some observers that Novar, since he was the owner of 27,000 acres of land in Fife and Ross-shire, might well make changes to the proposals which would be more favourable to the landed interest.[56] In addition, like Haldane, he had previously supported disestablishment and disendowment.

The bill was introduced in the House of Lords on 15th January 1924. While in the main embodying the Haldane recommendations, the measure made significant changes to the method of redemption by the heritors. The departmental committee had proposed that a sufficient amount should be paid to purchase consols at the date of redemption in each parish, which would then provide the income necessary to meet the new stipend. The Novar bill proposed instead a fixed rate of redemption of twenty-two years purchase, that is twenty-two times the amount of the stipend to be redeemed. This change was welcomed in particular by the Scottish Land and Property Federation.[57] It met one of their objections to the Haldane

[51] J. White to Lord Novar, 15.12.23, and Lord Novar to J. White, 17.12.23 (W) 7.4.
[52] J. White to Lord Sands, undated, 12.23 (W) 7.4.
[53] Lord Novar to J. White, 21.12.23 (W) 7.4.
[54] J. White and J. Millar to Lord Novar, 28.12.23 (W) 7.4.
[55] Lord Haldane to J. White, 7.1.24 (W) 7.5.
[56] JW, p. 219.
[57] SLPF, Memorandum on the Church of Scotland (Property and Endowments) Bill, 4.2.24 (SLPF) 325/1/203.

scheme, that the price of redemption would vary according to the time when the vacancy occurred.[58] In the view of the Church of Scotland committee, this amount might or might not be sufficient to guarantee the stipend in the years to come. The equivalent of consols under the Haldane scheme was twenty-four years purchase.[59] Other changes were less important but still irksome to the Church. In particular, according to the Haldane recommendations, churches and manses were to be handed over to the Church 'in a reasonable state of repair', whereas in the bill the responsibility for seeing that the buildings were 'reasonably fit for occupation' was placed on the Church.[60] There would have to be an agreement with the heritors regarding any repairs that were to be carried out.

White and his colleagues were clear that the bill was unacceptable, but what could they do? As Sands pointed out, a defective bill was better than no bill, and the more they pressed for changes to be made 'the less atttractive to the Government becomes the proposal to proceed'.[61] In spite of being told by White that the bill in its present form would 'arouse strong opposition in the country and jeopardise the movement',[62] Lord Haldane urged the Church to support the measure. In his view there was the more serious matter of opposition from James Barr, who would try to stir up his fellow Labour MPs against the measure.[63] There was also a fear that the bill would be lost altogether because of the changes in government. John White sought to make sure that the bill would not be dropped. One of his London contacts, Lady Frances Balfour, had suggested a conference with the landowners, and White thought that the only body with which the Church could hold discussions was the Scottish Land and Property Federation. He considered that the heritors themselves would see that the terms of the bill were at least 'unintentionally unfair and based on financial ignorance'.[64] That, he said, was a charitable view, otherwise it would be 'another instance of the Lords of the Congregation helping themselves to the patrimony of the Kirk.'[65] He would soon discover that the landowners viewed even the Novar bill as quite unacceptable.

[58] SLPF, Interim Annual Report of the Committee, 1924, p. 13 (SLPF) 325/1/328.

[59] C of S Rep., 1924, p. 47.

[60] Ibid., pp. 49–50.

[61] Lord Sands to J. White, 31.1.24 (W) 7.6.

[62] J. White to Lord Haldane, 4.1.24 (W) 7.5.

[63] Lord Haldane to J. White, 5.2.24 (W) 7.6.

[64] J. White to Lady Frances Balfour 7.3.24 (W) 7.7.

[65] Ibid.; JW, p. 222.

The bill, however, was not lost and Haldane, now Lord Chancellor, moved the second reading in the Lords on 1st April 1924. He had drawn up a white paper drawing attention to the ways in which the provisions of the bill varied from the proposals in his report. But, as he made clear, amendments at the committee stage could not be taken until the assemblies of the Churches and the representatives of the landowners had pronounced upon the question.[66] The Duke of Buccleuch, however, moved the rejection of the bill. Both this bill and the Haldane recommendations were unacceptable to him and his fellow landowners. His main objection was to the compulsory redemption of the teinds. 'A very large number of heritors', he said, 'are hard hit. It will mean their ruin.'[67] Since this was a bill designed for purely Church purposes, it should not impose any burden on the landowners for which they were not already liable. If the Church for the sake of union desired a different method by which stipend was paid, such new arrangements ought not to be effected at the expense of the landowners. The redemption of the teinds was not sought by them and they could not pay it. He posed the question: 'Why should the heritors be asked to pay for Church union?'[68] He put forward the alternative proposal of a fixed charge on the land like a feu-duty. This was a preferable way of obtaining a fixed secure income to the purchase of consols. The Church had said that it was not concerned with capital value but with a certain and definite continuity of income. The fixed land charge, he said, would provide such an income. But he was not in favour of assessing this income from the average of fifty years. Some of these years were war years when there had been artificially high prices. In the light of this speech it became clear that the government would not proceed with the measure unless the Church could come to an agreement with the landowners. It had become apparent, too, that the Church was not going to find it easy to come to such an agreement.

(d) the position of the landowners

The Duke of Buccleuch had not been speaking in the debate in the Lords solely on his own behalf, but on behalf of the Scottish Land and Property Federation. The Federation later referred to his speech as both 'able and reasoned' and thought that it was responsible in no small degree for the subsequent settlement of

---

[66] Hansard HL, 57, 1 April 1924, Col. 4.
[67] Ibid., Col. 20.
[68] Ibid., Col. 21.

the issue.[69] The opposition of the heritors to the compulsory redemption of the teinds went back as far as the first publication of the Haldane Report, and thus did not date from the intervention of the Duke of Buccleuch in the debate in the Lords.[70] The objections of the Scottish Land and Property Federation to the Haldane proposals were sent to the Scottish Secretary in May 1923,[71] and their position was therefore known to the government from an early stage. They pointed out that the Haldane committee had not contained a representative of landed interests and had not asked for evidence from those interests. The committee had rightly been concerned to facilitate the union of the Churches, but had not taken into account the recent fluctuations in the stipends of ministers. In particular the heritors had experienced hardship during the war years when grain prices rose at an alarming rate. An emergency committee had been appointed by the Scottish Secretary in 1917 and ways were sought to relieve the situation facing the landowners, but the Church of Scotland opposed any such measures. It was in the light of this experience that discussions had been held which resulted in the publication of the teinds bill of 1920. The Federation regarded the provisions of this bill for the redemption of the teinds as less onerous than those of the Haldane proposals, and also approved of the fact that they would not be compulsory. But the Church of Scotland had not seen its way to supporting these proposals. Now there were new proposals as a result of the Church itself reopening the matter, not from the point of view of giving relief to the heritors, but to facilitate union between it and the United Free Church. It was understandable, therefore, that the landowners were not bending over backwards to agree to this bill.

They objected to two features of the Haldane report. First, they thought it unfair that the war years should be included in the calculation of the level at which stipends should be redeemed. They also thought that the average over a longer period should be taken, such as twenty-five years, instead of the twenty-two years in the Novar bill. Secondly, they objected to the redemption being compulsory. They found it intolerable that the landowners should be asked to meet these costs when they were not asking for the system to be changed. They instead proposed that redemption be

[69] SLPF, Interim Annual Report of the Committee, 1924, p. 10.
[70] Cf. Gavin White, 'Whose are the teinds? The Scottish union of 1929', in *The Church and Wealth*, Studies in Church History, 24, ed. W. J. Sheils and Diana Wood (Oxford, 1987), pp. 388–9.
[71] SLPF, Representations to the Right Hon. the Secretary for Scotland, 15th May 1923 (SLPF) 325/1/203.

voluntary and that it be carried out by a continuing land charge like a feu-duty rather than by a capital sum. The value of stipend would thus become a fixed burden upon the land rather than on the fruits of the land. As we have noted, the scheme of redemption of the teinds in the Novar bill was more favourable to the heritors, but they still objected that 'since redemption is solely in the interests of the Church, it seems neither logical nor equitable that Heritors should pay the entire cost'.[72] While the landowners thought that the abolition of the present obsolete system of fluctuating payments and stipends was in the interest of both the Church and the heritors, they were still opposed to compulsory redemption.

It appears that there were two underlying reasons for the opposition of the heritors to the scheme of redemption. The first, as John White had surmised, was the fear of a new tax on land. With their lands free from the burden of the teinds, there would be 'an open temptation to any Government on the outlook for a source of revenue'.[73] As long as the teinds or some similar levy was in place, the landowners felt reasonably secure against another financial obligation being made upon them. If land no longer had this burden, they said, it would only leave 'something more for the Land Taxers to expropriate'.[74] It would also, in the second place, make the nationalisation of land a more attractive prospect for a Labour Government. They were afraid that, 'in view of the trend of land legislation and the confiscatory aims of the Socialist Party', it was unwise to remove any of the burdens attaching to the land. These two reasons, allied to their reluctance to help the Church — since the Church had singularly failed to help them in either 1917 or 1920 — led the landowners to reject the compulsory redemption of the teinds in the way which was suggested. The legal adviser of the landowners, J. G. Scott, suggested that they should take a firm stand and 'decline to entertain any proposals based on compulsory redemption'.[75] It was also suggested, however, that should the Church meet the heritors on this point, they in turn should agree to the amount of stipend being calculated on the basis of the previous fifty years, including the war years. Buccleuch felt that by agreeing to this

[72] SLPF, Memorandum on the Church of Scotland (Property and Endowments) Bill.

[73] Speech by the Rev. Dr John White, 24th May 1924 (W) 75. Cf. Summary of Points dealt with at Conference in the Lord Advocate's Room (W) 98; JW, p. 224.

[74] SLPF, Church of Scotland (Property and Endowments) Bill: Some Criticisms from the Heritors' point of view (SLPF) 325/1/203.

[75] Memo by Mr J. G. Scott for the Federation committee dealing with the Church Endowments Bill (SLPF) 325/1/203.

average they had gone far enough, as he was sure prices would come down in the future. He thought the Church representatives could not see that, while they were entitled to an annual sum, they were not entitled to a capital sum.[76] Buccleuch thought that the Church was out to get all it could from the agreement. 'The Church', he said, 'will go on asking for more and more, and if you give way on one point, they will want you to give way on another.'[77] In this respect the Haldane report had done a great deal of damage as it had led the Church to think that it was entitled to a very favourable settlement.

(e) the agreement between the Church and the landowners

The idea of a permanent land charge instead of the compulsory redemption of the teinds had been mooted earlier by Viscount Novar when he met with representatives of the assembly's committee in July 1923, prior to the publication of the bill. Novar would already have known of the preference of the landowners for this alternative proposal. At that time the Church of Scotland representatives had said that such an arrangement would not facilitate the cause of Church reunion.[78] In their discussions with the Scottish Land and Property Federation, they maintained this view, although the heritors sought to assure them that the proposal would not be regarded unfavourably by the UF Church.

Members of the UF committee, however, thought that this alternative measure would create very real practical difficulties and might prove a hindrance to union.[79] Alexander Martin wrote to John White to say he very much hoped that it would not be necessary to surrender the idea of redemption. He and his colleagues felt under considerable pressure not to give 'further handle' to the opposition in their Church. If the minority could see not only the abolition of the teinds, but of all continued dependence on stipend from the land, this would remove one prejudice from their armoury.[80] White assured him that compulsory redemption was still the preferred option of the Kirk, but he pointed out that the heritors' proposals could not properly be called a 'dependence of stipend on the land' provided by statute.[81] At most, it would be a statute that recognised an antecedent obligation to pay stipend,

[76] Duke of Buccleuch to E. Jackson, 12.4.24 and 21.4.24 (SLPF) 325/1/305.
[77] Ibid., 2.5.24.
[78] C of S Rep., 1924 Special Joint-committee on Property and Endowments, p. 4.
[79] Ibid., p. 8. Cf. UFC Min., 24.4.24 (M) 5.
[80] A. Martin to J. White, 7.5.24 (M) 19.4.14.
[81] J. White to A. Martin, 8.5.24 (W) 7.9.

and altered the conditions and terms under which the obligation was fulfilled. White said that he had consulted several of the 'legal men' of the UF Church who had assured him that they could see no objection to the proposal as far as union was concerned, that is, as far as the free operation of the Articles Declaratory was concerned. Archibald Henderson thought that the new land charge would give more ammunition to Barr and the Disestablishment Council and start a new discussion which could not easily be stopped.[82] In particular, it would cause problems at the assemblies of both Churches. Henderson was pleased, however, with the stance of John White and the Church of Scotland committee. He wrote to Martin to say:[83]

> It not only puts the Church of Scotland altogether in the right in its attitude to the heritors but it puts us also in a thoroughly intimate union with them in their stand for the church's liberties as owner of its own Funds or Properties.

This assurance of the attitude on the side of the Auld Kirk no doubt enabled the UF leaders to support the settlement which was finally made with the heritors, even although it was less than satisfactory from their point of view. Henderson thought that the heritors were 'unreasonable men' who would find little support from the public when it was realised that they would in future be free from the annual cost of the building and repair of churches and manses. If the bill was lost the landowners would be saddled with both stipend and building costs *in perpetuum* 'by their own act', and they would not find building repairs as cheap in the future as in the past.

In this whole matter the Church was in a weak position. An agreement was necessary for union to proceed. The representatives of the landowners thought that the attitude of the Church leaders was 'stiff and difficult'. The churchmen did not appear to realise that unless an agreement was found the bill would be dropped.[84] The force of the question put by the Duke of Buccleuch in the debate in the Lords still remained: why should the landowners be asked to pay for something which the Church desired for the sake of union? Buccleuch was aware that it was far more important for the Church to get the bill than for the landowners, and that he and his colleagues could hold out knowing that the Church would have to come to an agreement.[85] He had earlier expressed the view

---

[82] A. Henderson to A. Martin, 8.5.24 (M) 19.4.16.
[83] A. Henderson to A. Martin, 10.5.24 (M) 19.4.23.
[84] SLPF, Meeting of South-Eastern District to consider Church Bill, 7 May 1924 (SLPF) 325/1/328.
[85] Duke of Buccleuch to E. Jackson, 7.5.24 (SLPF) 325/1/305.

that the Church should pay something for the new freedom it would enjoy.[86] If it was to be disestablished, it should give up a large amount of its funds.[87] Lord Sands had seen the force of an argument of this kind. He had doubted whether the Church would emerge with its favoured solution unless, as he put it to John White, 'Haldane and the government are prepared to tell the Duke of Buccleuch and Barr ... to go to the Devil and I doubt if they are strong enough for that.'[88]

White wrote to Buccleuch to say that, if the heritors were to agree to a percentage increase in the value of the stipend above the average of the previous fifty years, then the Church might well look favourably on the land-charge proposal. It would go some way to compensating the Kirk for the future cost of maintaining the buildings.[89] J. A. S. Millar, White's joint convener of the special committee, wrote to say that the Church should accept the permanent land charge provided ten per cent was added to the stipend.[90] He would later say that the Church should be prepared to accept a five or six per cent increase, otherwise the bill would be 'dead'.[91] The Federation representatives agreed in private that it might be politic for them to agree to five per cent on condition that they would not be liable to repair the buildings before they were handed over.[92]

With the assembly approaching in 1924, time was running out for the Church to reach an agreement with the landowners without waiting for yet another year before obtaining the assembly's approval. After a fruitless meeting between the representatives of the Church and the landowners chaired by Lord Haldane, when White had again tried to get the other side to see the merits of the compulsory redemption of the teinds, further meetings were agreed with just three representatives of each side.[93] These meetings would be chaired by the Lord Advocate, H. P. Macmillan. At what proved to be the decisive meeting, held during the assembly, White suggested that only two of them should seek to reach an agreement, himself for the Church, and

---

[86] Duke of Buccleuch to E. Jackson, 26.4.22 (SLPF) 325/1/327.
[87] Duke of Buccleuch to E. Jackson, 16.2.23 (SLPF) 325/1/327.
[88] Lord Sands to J. White, 22.3.24 (W) 7.7.
[89] J. White to Duke of Buccleuch, 19.4.24 (W) 7.8.
[90] J. A. S. Millar to J. White, 5.5.24 (W) 7.9.
[91] J. A. S. Millar to J. White, 15.5.24 (W) 7.9.
[92] SLPF, Meeting of the South-Eastern District to consider Church bill, 7 May 1924.
[93] Summary of Points; *JW*, pp. 225–31; Memorandum for the Right Hon. the Lord Chancellor on the Church of Scotland (Property and Endowments) Bill, Amendments agreed upon between Representatives of the Church and of the Scottish Land and Property Federation (W) 98.

Sir John Milne Home for the heritors. White had previously voiced the opinion that if the matter had been left to those who were not lawyers, a compromise could have been reached![94] White now realised that there was no alternative but to accept the landowners' proposal, and he announced right away that he would recommend to the assembly to accept the permanent land charge. While Milne Home was expressing his pleasure at this news, White said that the agreement would depend on how far the heritors would meet him on a number of other points. The main condition was the level of stipend. White said that the average of fifty years was not good enough in view of the concession that was being made by the Church and he demanded an increase of seven per cent. This led, as White recalled, to a 'stiff argument' until Sir John Milne Home eventually asked him how far he was willing to give way. White replied that, as a compromise, he would accept five per cent. That, he later said, 'was the critical moment of the interview'. When White's compromise was accepted, an agreement had been reached. The Lord Advocate rose and clasped White's hand and said: 'Within these last few minutes history has been made in Scotland.'[95] The agreement also included the measures of the Haldane committee for the putting of churches and manses into good repair. Each side had achieved an agreement in line with its own minimum conditions, except that the heritors were still liable for the repair of the buildings before they were handed over to the Church. In addition, small heritors were to be relieved of liability for stipend if the annual sum was one shilling or less, and where it did not exceed one pound the heritor was bound to redeem the annual payment outright, but could do so by a number of annual payments.

White's deal was received with acclaim at the assembly of the Church of Scotland. He announced the news at a private meeting of the assembly on the evening before he gave his report as convener, a practice he had found useful in explaining matters before the formality of a debate the next day.[96] White compared his role in the negotiations, where he was the only clergyman, the rest being lawyers, to that of Daniel in the lions' den. Some of the lions, however, had been on his side. Having explained the nature of the proposals, White was able to present his report the next day, as Norman Maclean put it, to an assembly 'already convinced'.[97]

---

[94] Summary of Points.

[95] Speech by Rev. Dr John White, 24th May 1924 (W) 75. Cf. Property and Endowments (W) 98; JW p. 228.

[96] Property and Endowments (W) 98.

[97] JW, p. 229.

White reminded the assembly of the necessity for the legislation. It would enable the Church to make the 'best and fullest use of its resources in the religious interests of the nation and in exercise of its powers and liberties declared in the Articles'.[98] So much time had been devoted to the question of the property and endowments of the Church, he said, that the great aim of the movement was in danger of being lost sight of. They now had an opportunity, however, to settle this issue. In the past the problems had been between the Churches, but today, he said, 'the difficulty lies not between Church and Church, but between Church and heritors'. He thus indicated the way in which both Churches had sought the same outcome from the discussions. The desired solution had not been found and a compromise had had to be made with the landowners. But White maintained that the proposed land-charge 'did not offend against the conditions stated as essential to Union'. The Church of Scotland's four conditions did not specify the way in which the endowments were to be made over to the Church, only that they were to be made freely available. For the United Free Church the endowments had to be held by the Church in a way consistent with the Articles. A careful examination of the heritors' scheme, he said, was not incompatible with that freedom. It should be noted, however, that the UF report of 1919 had said that the Church should be not involved in 'continued dependence on statutory support', and the agreement could be interpreted as involving that support. Alternatively, as White had said to Martin, it could be interpreted as making alternative provision by statute for the payment of an existing obligation.

White received the gratitude of the assembly and was congratulated by the Lord Advocate and by colleagues on the role he had played in reaching such an important agreement.[99] But he had taken a great risk. The Duke of Buccleuch thought that the Church had made a good bargain, but he realised that there would be strong objections on both sides.[100] He also thought that he and White should have discussed the idea of a 'feu-duty' at their first meeting and thus avoided the delay. White might have been accused of giving in to the heritors on the one issue where previously the Church had refused to compromise. He had gained an increase of five per cent, and he recalled that Lord Sands, on hearing the news, could not believe his ears since this was worth an additional £15,000 a year for the stipend fund.[101] The

[98] Speech by Rev. Dr John White, 24th May 1924 (W) 75.
[99] H. P. Macmillan to J. White, 28.5.24 (W) 98; T. B. S. Thomson to J. White, 2.5.24 (W) 7.9; J. A. S. Millar to J. White, 2.6.24 (W) 8.1; W. S. Provand to J. White, 5.6.24 (W) 8.1.
[100] Duke of Buccleuch to J. White, 3.5.24 (W) 7.9.
[101] Summary of Points.

dangers of a fixed stipend were realised at the time,[102] and the Church had always preferred the option of the Haldane report, which was not departed from in principle in the Novar bill. The purchase of consols would have ensured that the future stipend should keep pace with inflation. Certainly the value of the chalder was falling in 1924 and might keep on falling. But equally it could rise again. Should the stipend not be tied to the cost of living in some way? It should be said that the heritors did not anticipate that their scheme should turn out so much to the disadvantage of the Church. No one could foresee at that time that inflation would rise to the extent it has since then, especially during the second half of the twentieth century. It is always easy to be wise with hindsight. As John White realised at the time, the heritors had the upper hand. The Church required the measure, not only for the sake of union, but also to have freedom over its own affairs. He achieved what he considered to be the best deal possible for the Church in the circumstances, although the extra five per cent on the stipend of which he was so proud at the time now seems to be derisory.

Needless to say the arrangement was not received with the same enthusiasm in the United Free Church. One of the members of the Haldane committee, Sir George Adam Smith, had wished that the original scheme had been followed; any departures from it, he said, 'have not been calculated to promote a stable settlement and general content'.[103] The final agreement was not known when the UF assembly discussed this issue, since it met on the same day as White gave his report. Henderson restated the committee's view that the landowners' proposal for a land charge would 'create grave practical difficulties, and might prove a hindrance to union'.[104] But he also said that the need for union was as pressing as ever and that they should still seek that goal if at all possible.[105] An amendment by John Young proposed that the Church should withdraw from any involvement in the current legislation as it was contrary to their 'historic position and continuous testimony'.[106] Young's amendment was supported by 138 votes to 375 for the committee, which Martin thought was a 'considerable vote'.

According to Martin, most in the UF Church realised that the Church of Scotland was 'very far from getting everything' in relation to the teinds, and that they were making up their minds to be 'more or less content'.[107] He calculated that the Church of

[102] E.g. J. Mitchell to J. White, 2.5.23 (W) 7.3.
[103] G. A. Smith to A. Martin, 12.11.25 (M) 19.6.7.
[104] *UFC Proc.*, 1924, p. 255.
[105] Ibid., pp. 256–7.
[106] Ibid., p. 260.
[107] A. Martin to J. White, 14.6.24 (W) 8.1.

Scotland had 'lost heavily' over the agreement, one-sixth of all the annual revenues involved.[108] Martin, however, wondered whether some might be appeased if the Church gave up the Exchequer grants altogether. These grants related to the 'parliamentary Churches' set up to provide additional parishes in the highlands and islands in 1824. Both Lord Sands and W. P. Paterson thought they could be given up with life interests conserved, but White disagreed.[109] While Martin was concerned with the minority in his Church, White had to think of the minority in the Church of Scotland. In any case these grants were not a matter between the Church and the heritors but between the Church and the government. They were redeemed through negotiations with the Treasury and the Church thus derived some financial benefit.[110]

Another way of satisfying the UF minority was suggested by Henderson, that a purely civil body might be set up to deal with the income from the heritors, thus separating it from the money raised by voluntary contributions from church members.[111] A similar suggestion would later be made to appease the minority prior to union.[112] The Church would then, in Henderson's view, not be seen as an aggressive creditor in relation to landowners who did not pay their dues. Lord Sands appreciated the problem but agreed with Martin in thinking that 'the creation of a separate body would be only adding a fifth wheel to the cart'.[113] Having said that, Henderson also spoke of the problems of the agreement as practical in character and not as involving fundamental matters of principle. A sub-committee reported to the main UF committee that it was satisfied that the agreement, if carried out, would 'give over to the Church the funds and properties involved to be wholly its own, subject to no external control by the Court of Teinds or otherwise'.[114] The Church of Scotland had agreed, too, that there should be clauses in the Act dealing with *quoad sacra* churches, the ending of the Court of Teinds and its powers, and the linking of the Act with the previous legislation concerning the constitution.[115]

---

[108] Martin, *Church Union in Scotland: the first stage completed*, p. 43.

[109] A. Martin to J. White, 14.6.24 and Notes by John White (W) 8.1.

[110] Ibid.; Cf. *JW*, p. 234 and n.

[111] A. Henderson to J. White, 23.6.24 (W) 8.1. Cf. *JW*, pp. 233–4.

[112] See below, pp. 223–5.

[113] Lord Sands to J. White, 29.6.24 (W) 8.1.

[114] Report of Sub-committee appointed 'to consider carefully the proposals agreed to by the Church of Scotland with the Heritors etc.', as corrected by the Hundred, 19 July 1924 (M) 13.1. Cf. Report of Sub-committee on Church of Scotland (Property and Endowments) Bill (UFC).

[115] Church of Scotland Property and Endowments Bill, Informal Conference between United Free Church Conveners' Sub-committee and Representatives of the Church of Scotland, 13 March 1924 (W) 97.

It was to be expected that the minority in the United Free Church led by James Barr would reject the proposed legislation. Members of the minority organisation, the United Free Church Association, made representations to the Scottish Secretary in June 1924.[116] It was, they said, a perversion of history to regard the teinds as the property of the Church since these were public funds, the heritage of the people. By the Act this patrimony would be made over to the Church permanently through the fixed land charge, thus alienating the teinds from public use for all time. The legislation would not facilitate union since about one-third of the assembly of their Church had voted against the proposals. In the view of one member of the minority, the teinds were more secure than ever, confirmed by a new statute and guaranteeing the Church 'a very high rate of stipend indeed'.[117] Perhaps if this writer, and the rest of the minority, could have seen the way in which inflation has virtually destroyed the value of the fixed income of the Church from this source, they would not have been so opposed to the settlement. What they failed to do, inflation has achieved. But for them nothing less than the disendowment of the Church would suffice. In their view the teinds were not the property of the Church but rather belonged to the State and could be made over by the State to another purpose. The teinds and the other endowments were public funds and should be used for public purposes.[118] To make them over as an absolute gift to the Church was 'State-endowment, final and irretrievable'.[119] The funds should be made over for the good of the whole population and especially the common people. Not only was the Church retaining the bulk of the teinds on a permanent basis, but public control of these funds was also being withdrawn.[120] The continuing 'land tax', as the minority insisted on calling the new arrangement, perpetuated the element of compulsion in the support of religion: 'Men and women of every faith, and of no faith,' they said, 'are compelled to contribute to the maintenance of a particular Church.'[121] The Church would rely on the Sheriff Court to enforce payment of this charge.[122] Not only was this element of compulsion objectionable in itself, it meant that the Church would not be

---

[116] *Glasgow Herald*, 27.6.24.

[117] United Free Churchman, *Union of the Churches*, p. 10.

[118] UFCA, Leaflet No. 6, *"A State-Endowed Church"*, p. 5.

[119] *UFC Rep.*, 1922, p. 11.

[120] UFCA, *If the Proposals of the Haldane Report and the Novar Bill become Law — What Then?* 15 May 1924 (M) 12.1.

[121] UFCA, Edinburgh Branch, Letter of January 1927.

[122] UFCA, Leaflet No. 7, *Compulsion in Religion*.

totally reliant on voluntary giving, which was the only form of giving sanctioned in the New Testament.[123]

In reply Martin argued that the teinds had been given to the Church, although the present levels were only a fraction of the original gift.[124] The Church of Scotland would lose one-sixth of what it had previously received from the teinds, and this was comparable to the one-fifth lost by the Welsh Church under disestablishment, or the one half to three-quarters which the Disestablishment Council had proposed. The payment in future would be a feu-duty, not a land-tax, and could be redeemed or sold by the Church. A tax could not be bought or sold. As to the element of compulsion, it was simply the law of the land that those who owed an obligation should pay it.[125] The settlement of this issue had been made by the civil authority, the only authority competent to make it, and was it 'bad citizenship', Martin asked, to accept parliament's award? Adam Welch argued that there was no such thing as 'pure voluntaryism'.[126] The United Free Church held much of its present property as a result of an act of parliament following the ruling of the House of Lords in the Free Church Case. It could be said that the money had belonged to the Church, and that it was merely being returned by the State. But that was what the Church of Scotland argued in relation to the teinds. It was pointed out, too, that the UF Church also benefited from endowments. According to an editorial in the *Glasgow Herald*, only 'a casuist of Mr. Barr's extreme nicety' will be able to see any difference between the capital assets of the United Free Church and the endowments of the Church of Scotland following the Act of 1925.[127] As to the support from endowments throwing 'a blight upon the liberality of the people', as Barr had claimed,[128] it was said that the Church of Scotland itself had to rely to a large extent on the giving of its members to support *quoad sacra* parishes and the wider work of the Church. The bottom line for the minority, however, was that the Act of 1925 was not the disendowment of the Church and should be opposed for that reason alone.[129]

---

[123]UFCA, Leaflet No. 4, *Support of Church Ordinances in New Testament Times and Today.*

[124]Martin, Memorandum on Minority Manifesto, June 1926. Cf. A. Philip, 'Union: The First Stage Completed' in *Record*, December 1925, p. 563.

[125]Ibid.

[126]*Glasgow Herald*, 5.11.23.

[127]*Glasgow Herald*, 5.3.25.

[128]James Barr, *The Origin, Nature and Destination of the State Endowments of the Church of Scotland* (Dundee, 1924), p. 33.

[129]Ibid., p. 39.

The arguments of the minority were the same as those advanced by the Disestablishment Council for Scotland.[130] This should not surprise us since the president of the Council was James Barr! A deputation from the Council made points to the government similar to those made by the United Free Church Association. The Act would perpetuate the tax and divert it in future away from the purposes for which it had been intended, for the care of the poor and the sick and for education, responsibilities which were no longer laid upon the Church. The measures would mean the alienation of national property for the permanent endowment of a Church that did not represent the majority of the church-going people of Scotland.[131] Leading churchmen like John White feared that this viewpoint would be forcefully presented by James Barr in parliament. The final hurdle was still to be crossed.

(f) the passing of the Act

The problems of the Church were not over since it was highly desirable that the Act should be passed before the assembly in the following year. As it turned out this objective was only just achieved. John White wrote to Ramsay MacDonald, the Prime Minister, urging the speedy enactment of the legislation which had now received the support of the landowners and of both Churches.[132] The bill was read for the third time, uneventfully, in the Lords on 1st July 1924 and then went to the Commons. Norman Maclean prematurely wrote to White to say that after the safe passage of the bill through the Lords he must feel that he was 'seeing the port in sight' after his perilous voyage.[133] But White had been warned by the Labour MP and kirk elder James Brown that a tremendous effort would be made against the bill by its opponents in the Commons.[134]

The fate of the bill was made even more problematical when the Labour government fell, and following a general election Stanley Baldwin again became Prime Minister. According to Sands, however, the bill's progress would not necessarily be more difficult. With a change of government, he told White, we would have 'more friends but also probably more enemies'. If the Labour government had taken it up that would have had a restraining influence on a number of their supporters.[135] Pressure was kept up

---

[130] Disestablishment Council for Scotland, *Manifesto of the Proposals of the Heritors*, 20 June 1924 (M) 10.1.

[131] Ibid.

[132] J. White to R. MacDonald, 3.6.24 (W) 8.1; *JW*, p. 236.

[133] N. Maclean to J. White, 3.7.24 (W) 8.2.

[134] J. Brown to J. White, 27.6.24 (W) 8.1.

[135] Lord Sands to J. White, 11.11.24 (W) 8.5.

and letters written to various MPs and members of the House of
Lords, and White visited the Prime Minister and the new Secretary
for Scotland, Sir John Gilmour.[136] White was assured that the bill
would be passed before the next assembly, and he was pleased to
read in the King's Speech that it would come up in the next session
of parliament.[137]

The bill was debated in the Commons on 10th February 1925
and, as expected, was opposed by Barr and some of his fellow
Labour MPs. Barr's speech was by far the longest in the debate, in
spite of being his maiden speech, and although he was
congratulated by his colleagues, it was judged by Archibald
Fleming of St Columba's Church in London to have 'effectively
killed him in the House of Commons'.[138] His familiar arguments
were rehearsed before the house and, as White's biographer puts
it, he 'attacked Exchequer Grants, Burgh Grants, and teinds, as if
he were back in his pulpit attacking the works of the devil'.[139] He
showed his considerable knowledge of the subject and even
quoted Winston Churchill in favour of religious equality, but his
long tirade was not nearly so effective as the shorter speech in
favour of the measure by the more experienced member, James
Brown.[140] Earlier the Speaker had overruled attempts to question
the legality of the measure in that it went against the provisions
of the Treaty of Union which, it was claimed, parliament was
unable to change. The Speaker said that what parliament had
done, it could undo, that parliament was supreme.[141] The Scottish
Secretary argued that this point regarding the Treaty should have
been raised in relation to the Church of Scotland Act of 1921 which
had recognised the spiritual freedom of the Church.[142] This issue
had been discussed in the columns of the *Glasgow Herald* during
the previous year.[143] An editorial had pointed out that the teinds
were not mentioned in the Treaty of Union, and that in any case
the terms of the Treaty had already been altered by parliament
when the number of Scottish MPs had been increased and when
the professors of Scottish universities were no longer required to
subscribe to the Westminster Confession of Faith.

It became clear, however, that although the opposition failed
to win a majority of votes, the bill would be in for a stormy passage

[136] *JW*, p. 237; Letters to MPs (W) 8.6.
[137] Sir W. Lorne Mitchell to J. White, 19.11.24 (W) 8.7.; *JW*, p. 237.
[138] A. Fleming to J. White, 20.2.25 (W) 9.5.
[139] *JW*, p. 238.
[140] Hansard HC, 180, 10 February 1925, Cols. 69–86, 94–103.
[141] Ibid., Cols. 58, 59.
[142] Ibid., Col. 64.
[143] *Glasgow Herald*, 23.1.24.

at the Scottish Grand Committee. It was partly for that reason that John White was on hand with a desk beyond the bar in the Committee Room at Westminster so that he could answer questions on the teinds. White himself said that his knowledge had to be judged, not with reference to the thing itself, 'but by comparison with the ignorance of others'.[144] He found that he was consulted by those who were opposed, as well as by those who supported the bill. According to Norman Maclean, James Barr was even less impressive at the committee than he had been in the House, and although he would have been biased against Barr's position, his description nevertheless has a ring of truth:[145]

> Mr. Barr's oratory demands an audience continually cheering. Here there were no cheers. He couldn't soar uplifted by waves of applause. He was not sure of the forms of procedure. Self-consciousness held him, uncertain of himself, in its grip.

According to Maclean, Barr never quite recovered from an interruption by James Brown near the beginning of his speech. After twelve sessions the bill was passed back to the Commons to be debated on 12th May 1925. According to Archibald Fleming, the debate in the Commons on this occasion was 'quite the best of all the debates in parliament on this subject'.[146] Fleming's view was perhaps due in part to the fact that Barr on this occasion limited himself to two relatively short speeches,[147] while Brown said of Barr that his knowledge of church history was so great that 'he knows how to bring in points that have no point at all'.[148] The bill was passed by 274 votes to 117.[149]

The bill came before the Lords again on 19th May. Could it be passed in time for White's report to the assembly on 26th May? Lord Balfour of Burleigh took over the mantle of church affairs from his late father and ably introduced the bill. He pointed out that it had received majorites in the Commons of two to one. The measure was supported by the Duke of Buccleuch, and the Lords even agreed to the possibility of sitting on the Monday to enable it to be passed before the vital meeting of the assembly on the following day.[150] Thus the famous telegram allegedly sent by John White urging their lordships to sit on the Monday was perhaps not as crucial after all.[151]

---

[144] JW, p. 239 n.
[145] Scotsman, 6.3.25.
[146] A. Fleming to J. White, 15.5.25 (W) 9.7.
[147] Hansard HC, 183, 12 May 1925, Cols. 1696–1701, 1751–7.
[148] Ibid., Col. 1760.
[149] Ibid., Col. 1772.
[150] Hansard HL, 61, 19 May 1926, Col. 326.
[151] JW, p. 242; Text of broadcast talk by Robin Scott, 'John White' BBC Radio, 24.4.49 (W) 61.

White was thus able to report the final passage of the bill at the assembly in 1925 of which he was moderator. He could report that parliament had now passed the measure desired by the Church and the way was open for the Church now to ratify the Articles Declaratory. The delay in obtaining the measure could be regretted, but it had meant at least that there had been the fullest opportunities for arriving at a carefully considered settlement.[152] The bill had reformed the system by which stipends were paid and, he said, would be an advantage to both ministers and heritors. It would also remove the irksome matter of ecclesiastical assessments from the heritors. The churches and manses were now the property of the Church. This meant that the Church had the responsibility for their upkeep and he pointed out that membership of the Church implied obligations. With the passing of the Articles, the way would be open for them to realise the great object which they had had in view all along, the more effective service of the nation by a united Church. This last point was emphasised by James Brown, who said that the object of the bill was to help the Church to meet the ends of the people.[153]

The motion was opposed by one of the leading members of the minority, Gordon Mitchell of Killearn. He said that the bill was not a boon to the Church but 'materially and seriously crippled the Church in the prosecution of its spirtual and national work'.[154] It was unconstitutional since it was in violation of the Treaty of Union, a point which, as we have noted, had been made unsuccessfully in the Commons. With the concessions made to the heritors over the teinds, it had divided up the ancient patrimony of the Church unevenly between heritors and the Church. In addition, manses and glebes, which were the property of ministers, were transferred to the General Trustees. At the end of the debate, however, the opposition only received seven votes. With the adoption of the Articles Declaratory by the Church, what had been seen as the two main obstacles to union would be finally removed. As it was stated in *Life and Work*:[155]

> the two matters that were regarded as stumbling blocks to union with the United Free Church — the question of spiritual freedom and the question of temporalities or endowments — will be removed, and the way made clear for considering with the United Free Church the terms and the basis of Union.

[152] *Glasgow Herald*, 27.5.25.
[153] Ibid.
[154] Ibid.
[155] *LW*, July 1925, p. 149. Cf. Martin, *Church Union in Scotland: the first stage completed*, p. 48.

Chapter 6

Laying the foundations: the Basis of Union 1926–9

(a) the decision to proceed with union

Following the passing of the Church of Scotland (Property and Endowments) Act in 1925, and the subsequent adoption of the Articles Declaratory by the Barrier Act in 1926, the way was clear for the Churches to begin discussions regarding the Basis and Plan of Union. As Alexander Martin put it, the question before the Churches at this point was not whether to unite, but whether the way was clear for attempting the task.[1] Adam Welch said that the only reason for not going forward to union would be if the two Acts of 1921 and 1925 had not achieved their object.[2]

The Churches now faced a new phase of the movement. Up to this point the onus, and most of the work, had fallen on the representatives of the Church of Scotland, since they had had to seek the removal by parliament of the two obstacles to union. Throughout this process they had consulted with the representatives of the United Free Church, but the responsibility had been theirs alone. For example, the UF Church had declined to make a joint approach to parliament about the recognition of the Articles Declaratory. The Articles were, in the first instance, a new statement of the constitution of the Church of Scotland, not of the united Church. Yet it was important for parliament to know, in passing the Act in 1921, that this document would indeed be an acceptable constitution from the point of view of the United Free Church. This assurance was given, but the approach to parliament was made by the Kirk alone.

With the removal of the two obstacles to union, the situation was different. John White referred to the members of the United Free Church committee in his address as moderator in 1925:[3]

[1] *Record,* October 1925, p. 425.
[2] *Record,* November 1925, p. 491.
[3] White, *Efficiency,* p. 38.

> Up to the present, while loyally co-operating with us, they have held, as it were, a watching brief. The duty of action was ours alone. It is for them now to share with us the burden and responsibility of a further advance.

Until now the UF side had not been directly involved and had not been forced to make irrevocable decisions. The moment had come, and those in the minority, who had all along opposed the policy of the committee, would have to be reckoned with. In the event, a minority would remain out of the united Church, although its size would be reduced as a result of various measures. When the agreement on the teinds had been reached with the heritors, W. S. Provand, clerk to the presbytery of Glasgow, had written to John White saying that for the first time they 'had got the weather berth of the UFs ... *and they know it.*' As another Auld Kirk minister put it in a letter to John White, 'The rails for the union train are now laid as far as the Church in Scotland is concerned; it remains with the U. F. C. to say whether the train is to run or not.'[4] The Church of Scotland leaders would also find that the leaders and the majority of members of the United Free Church committee were ready to meet this challenge. It was now their turn to work hard in order to accommodate the members of the minority and if possible to include them within the united Church. Alexander Martin told the members of his church in the pages of *The Record* that, since the representatives of the Church of Scotland had met their objections and views by obtaining two parliamentary measures, they now deserved a positive response.[5]

Before negotiations could get under way both Churches were asked to approve the decision to go ahead with the process of union. The committees issued statements setting out the history and aims of the movement and arguing that talks on union should now begin as the obstacles had been removed. The United Free Church committee's statement was sent down to presbyteries, kirk sessions and congregations.[6] It argued that the Church of Scotland was now in a similar position to other Churches, since, according to Article IV of the Articles Declaratory, it had the 'right and power subject to no civil authority to legislate, and adjudicate finally, in all matters of doctrine, worship, government, and discipline'. Its funds were also under its own control and it had the right to unite with any other Church without loss of its identity

---

[4] J. N. Ogilvie to J. White, 4.6.24 (W) 8.1.
[5] *Record*, October 1925, p. 425.
[6] *UFC Rep.*, 1926, pp. 8–11.

on terms which it found to be consistent with the Articles. This position, it was claimed, was the same as that of the UF Church. The time had therefore come for the two Churches to frame a basis on which to unite. The Church of Scotland statement[7] emphasised the need for union in view of the unnecessary duplication of effort in so many parishes and the need for greater efforts to be made to meet the needs of both the rural and industrial areas of Scotland. The movement for reunion was not a new development without foundation in the history and traditions of the Kirk. Division had been deprecated and reunion had been sought for many years.

In the Church of Scotland an overwhelming majority of presbyteries had approved of the Articles Declaratory, and the assembly in 1926 decided almost unanimously that a new committee should be appointed to discuss a Basis and Plan of Union with the representatives of the other Church.[8] In the United Free Church kirk sessions and congregations as well as presbyteries were consulted. They were asked to respond to the question as to whether, by the passing of the Acts of 1921 and 1925, the main causes of separation between the Churches had been removed, and the way was open for the consideration by the Churches themselves of an incorporating union. Of the sixty-three home presbyteries, all but one, the presbytery of Islay, answered in the affirmative, the presbytery of Uist declining to make a decision. Of these, twenty-three were unanimous in their reply, while three of the thirty-eight which voted by a majority, Galashiels, Paisley, and Dunfermline and Kinross, entered some qualifications.[9] Of the larger presbyteries, Edinburgh voted by 88 to 22 in favour, Glasgow by 273 to 116, and Hamilton by 85 to 18. Of the overseas presbyteries, all who replied were in favour with the exception of Calabar. There was greater opposition, however, among the kirk sessions and congregations. Of the kirk sessions voting, 1159 were in favour of negotiations for union continuing (820 by a majority and 339 unanimously), while 235 were against (100 unanimously and 135 by a majority). In eighteen cases the voting was equal and four asked for delay. Of the congregations voting, 1126 were in favour (651 unanimously and 475 by a majority), while 285 were against (49 unanimously and 236 by a majority).

The number of congregations which had voted against talks proceeding was of concern to the leaders of the movement. The results, said Alexander Martin in presenting the report to the assembly in 1926, were disappointing. In his view they represented

[7] Church Union in Scotland, 1926 (M) 5.
[8] Glasgow Herald, 5.6.26.
[9] UFC Min., 17.3.26; UFC Rep., 1926, pp. 12–15.

apathy rather than opposition since the number of members voting was only a fraction of the total.[10] In the cases where a majority was against, it was probable that the activities of the United Free Church Association had been responsible for the dissentients polling their full strength. According to one observer, the alleged apathy was due to many members feeling that the outcome was inevitable.[11] Many congregations who voted against at this stage would later change their minds at better attended meetings when a final decision regarding union had to be made. In view of the difficulties which had had to be faced in the movement thus far, Martin thought it surprising that the opposition had not been greater.[12] The number of congregations voting against was made much of by the minority and it led to the committee issuing a series of fourteen *Papers for the People*, short tracts dealing with the question of union, and in particular with the Acts of 1921 and 1925.[13]

In the light of these decisions both assemblies formed new committees with the remit 'to prepare a provisional Basis of Union between the Churches'.[14] Two committees of around one hundred members each were again appointed. On the UF side the joint conveners were Alexander Martin and Robert J. Drummond, minister of Lothian Road Church in Edinburgh, while Andrew N. Bogle, secretary to the Home Department of the Church, acted as clerk. Archibald Henderson had been forced to resign from the committee because of ill health and he died in the following year. The Church of Scotland committee was led by John White and Lord Sands with Hutchison Cockburn, minister of Dunblane Cathedral, as clerk. Henderson had earlier written to Martin to say that the discussions on union as such would be a completely new situation, and that he would not be a party to 'raking over the ashes of 1921'.[15] The position of the Articles, and indeed of the UF Act of 1906, would be one of the major items of discussion in the committee, although it was only the minority in the UF Church who insisted on 'raking over the ashes'. Lord Sands was dismayed to find that he had been appointed, with John White, as joint convener of the sub-committee dealing with the Basis of Union: 'I had thought', he said, 'that some younger or less tired men should take this up. Oh dear, am I to be up against Article I again?'[16]

---

[10] Reith, *Reminiscences*, p. 296. *UFC Proc.*, 1926, p. 199. A. Martin to J. White, 29.9.25 (W) 9.7.

[11] Reith, *Reminiscences*, p. 296.

[12] Ibid.

[13] United Free Church of Scotland, *Papers for the People*, Nos. 1–14 (M) 5.

[14] *UFC Proc.*, 1926, pp. 202–3; *C of S Rep.*, 1926, p. 1055.

[15] A. Henderson to A. Martin, 8.11.24 (M) 19.4/90.

[16] Lord Sands to J. White, 4.7.26 (W) 10.3. Cf. *JW*, p. 252 n.

The previous committees had already met during the winter to discuss the matters which would have to be dealt with when discussions began. Thus the conveners of the new committees could meet early after the assemblies in 1926 with the suggestion that seven sub-committees be appointed to deal with the various matters which had to be discussed with a view to union. These were as follows:

1. Basis of Union.
2. Constitution and Powers of Courts, with Rearrangement of Presbyteries.
3. Training of the Ministry; and Relation of Divinity Halls to the Universities.
4. Property and Finance.
5. Rules and Forms of Procedure.
6. Arrangement of Standing Committees—Foreign Missions, Home Missions.
7. Relations with other Churches.

Not all of these topics were of equal status. Clearly the most important issue was the Basis of Union. The other subjects would form the Plan of Union, the means by which the decision to unite would be put into effect. Many of these questions could be decided by the united Church, but certain items had to be settled to enable the Church to begin its work. For example, the composition of the courts of the Church had to be settled so that they could begin to meet, and the rules and forms of procedure had to be decided so that business could be transacted right away. Thus the rearrangement of presbyteries had to be agreed in advance, but this was a matter which could be adjusted at any future stage, and was not, in any case, a matter for Barrier Act procedure. It would also be desirable for questions of property and finance to be settled so that the Church could begin to use its resources. The arrangements of the assembly's standing committees, and issues such as the admission of ministers of other Churches, could be readjusted by the united Church in the light of experience. The training of the ministry and the relationship between the universities and the theological colleges were recognised as matters which would have to be decided finally by the united Church. While preliminary discussions with the universities could be held, the process was likely to be prolonged and the universities would only approach parliament for the necessary legislation once the union had taken place.

As will be seen in what follows, the two committees tended to leave matters for the united Church to decide if they could be left over until after the union. Apart from the Basis of Union, only those issues which were non-controversial, or were essential arrangements for the Church to begin its work, were dealt with in the Plan of Union. This procedure left a legacy of different traditions and practices on various matters continuing to exist side by side in the united Church. At the local level, for example, different congregational constitutions continued, as did different ways of electing elders. The two Churches also represented different traditions regarding the office of the elder, the United Free Church holding a 'high' view, and the Auld Kirk taking a 'low' view. While this policy of leaving over such matters to be decided by the united Church meant that the union could be finalised more quickly, it has led to other consequences in the long term.[17]

Of all the matters to be discussed the essential one was that of the Basis of Union, and the sub-committee dealing with this subject was chaired by the joint conveners of the committees, thus showing the importance of the issue. There was to be no escape for Lord Sands from Article I!

(b) the nature of the uniting Act

When they came to discuss the Act by which the two Churches would unite, the committees had a precedent in the Act by which the Free Church and the United Presbyterian Church had united in 1900. It was also important that the uniting Act should show continuity with the United Free Church which had been formed in 1900. It was vital that there should be no legal loophole by which it could be claimed that the UF Church had changed its identity by uniting with the Church of Scotland. It was agreed at the first meeting of the sub-committee on 18th October that the Act of 1900 should be taken as the model in drafting the Basis of Union between the Churches.[18] This act consisted, in the first place, of a preamble giving the history of the movement for union which led up to the decision of the Churches to unite. There was then a series of four declarations in view of which the Churches agreed to unite. These covered matters such as the liberty of the Church to determine its own constitution, the place of the Catechisms, the liberty of judgement of members of the Churches, and the obligation of members to contribute to the work of the Church.

At the first meeting, too, Lord Sands submitted a paper of notes regarding the framing of a Basis of Union.[19] In Sands' view, it was

---

[17] See below, pp. 274–6.
[18] Church of Scotland Committee on Union, Sub–Committee upon a 'Basis of Union', Notes by Special Sub-Committee re Framing a Basis of Union (M) 5.
[19] Ibid.

most important that the union be seen as the coming together of 'two branches of one historic Church', rather than the merger of two Churches of 'separate and independent origin'. Each Church must be viewed as belonging to the one tradition in spite of the differences which had led to separation in the past. Sands told John White that, in an interview, Martin had been anxious to emphasise the idea of reunion, not as two rivers joining, but as 'one river which has been flowing in two channels gathering itself into one channel again'.[20] They were thus keen to include a historical preamble setting out the background to the movement for reunion. This was, said Sands, the old Scottish idea of 'testimony'.[21]

Lord Sands also referred to the doctrinal and other standards of the Churches. These would now be the common standards of the united Church, and in his view it was unnecessary to make any 'definitions or elaborate restatements in regard to these documents'.[22] There was no divergence between the Churches with regard to the standards, although in the future the united Church could deal with any questions which might arise about their position. Such differences of view or tendency as might exist were to be found within both Churches, not between the Churches. In relation to constitutional matters, the Churches were on a similar footing. Neither Church could unite except under the powers of its own constitution. In the case of the Church of Scotland these powers were set out in the Articles Declaratory. The Articles contained powers for their alteration, but it would be impracticable, in his opinion, for these powers to be exercised as part of a scheme of union. In other words, the union had to be agreed on the basis of the constitutions as they stood at present. Even if the Churches were in a position to frame a new constitution, said Sands, 'the experience of the Church of Scotland in regard to the framing of the Articles confirms the view that any attempt to do so would be inexpedient, and might indefinitely delay Union.' Sands therefore concluded that the 'operative enacting provision of any Act of Union should be short and simple'. According to Sands, Martin had previously indicated that he was at one with him as to 'the undesirability of attempting to formulate a new constitution of a comprehensive character'.[23] Henderson had advised Martin: 'Keep everything out of the Basis but what ought to go in'.[24] He thought that only general principles should be

---

[20] Lord Sands to J. White, 5.10.26 (W) 10.3.
[21] Ibid.
[22] Notes by Special Sub-Committee re Framing a Basis of Union.
[23] Sands to White, 5.10.26.
[24] A. Henderson to A. Martin, 9.7.26 (M) 19.8/11.

included, setting forth the present position of the Churches and the powers that were claimed to deal with doctrinal and other matters.[25] Martin was thus able to report after the first meeting that 'no difficulties of principle emerged' in the discussions regarding this uniting act,[26] and the minimalist approach of Sands was the one adopted by the committee. The uniting Act would be as brief as possible and would seek to avoid any unnecessary complications. A rough draft was then prepared by the conveners and presented to the sub-committee by John White.[27]

There were two alternative proposals made at the meeting of the sub-committee on 15th November and they were considered at the following meeting in December.[28] One was suggested by Thomas Wardrop, of Stonelaw Church in Rutherglen, a member of the UF minority, that the Act take the form of a fresh declaration of 'the faith once delivered to the saints'. He said that the uniting Act should contain a 'simple, brief, elemental statement' of the central place which Jesus Christ held in their thoughts and lives.[29] Martin thought that this suggestion amounted to the formulation of a new and rather indefinite doctrinal statement.[30] He sympathised with what was being aimed at, but said that it would be the task of the newly united Church to prepare a fresh statement of fundamental doctrines, and that it was not acceptable 'to make union wait until that has been done'.[31] Both Lord Sands and W. P. Paterson pointed out the difficulties involved 'in attempting to formulate doctrine before Union was consummated'.[32] It was left to the conveners to take Wardrop's draft into account as they revised the uniting Act.

The motive behind Wardrop's proposal seems to have been an attempt to diminish the importance of the Articles Declaratory in the Basis of Union and hence, too, in the constitution of the united Church. As Adam Renwick, one of the leading members of the UF minority, put it, the amendment was 'an effort to state in a "foreword" the essential doctrine of the united Church, and to have the Articles relegated to "an appendix" where they would cease troubling anybody.'[33] Although he would have been in favour of thus banishing the Articles, Renwick thought that they

---

[25] A. Henderson to A. Martin, 17.8.26 (M) 19. 8/5.
[26] Martin, Notebook, 15.11.26 (M) 2.5.
[27] Minutes of the Sub-Committee on the Basis of Union, 15.11.26 (M) 13.2.
[28] Ibid. 15.11.26 and 6.12.26.
[29] T. Wardrop to A. Martin, 26.11.26 (M) 19.8/60.
[30] A. Martin to T. Wardrop 25.11.26 (M) 19.8/58.
[31] A. Martin to T. Wardrop, 29.11.26 (M) 19.8/61.
[32] Minutes of the Sub-Committee, 5.12.26.
[33] A. Renwick to A. Martin, 8.12.26 (M) 19.8/62.

could not be treated in that way. If Wardrop's proposal was of that nature, in Martin's view, then it would have overridden both the Articles and the standards of the UF Church and become a new doctrinal constitution framed prior to union. This, he thought, was too much to ask for.[34] The UF minority were thus faced with the Articles as a major element in the Basis of Union and hence, too, in the constitution of the united Church.

The other suggestion was made by P. D. Thomson of Kelvinside UF Church in Glasgow. He felt that the Act should be much fuller than was being proposed, and that 'the governing principles of National Recognition of Religion and Spiritual Freedom should be set forth *in extenso*'.[35] It was a plea for the uniting Act to be framed on more popular lines.[36] It was pointed out that the document was of an essentially constitutional character, but that it could be accompanied by a more popular explanatory statement for the use of presbyteries, kirk sessions and congregations. It was agreed, however, that a reference should be made to the need for union 'in order to meet the practical requirements of the religious situation in Scotland'.[37] Both Lord Sands and Sir George Adam Smith thought that such a reference would be appropriate as representing a strong reason for union.

The objections of the minority to the Articles, in particular to Articles I and VIII, surfaced again at the meeting of the UF 'hundred' and the Church of Scotland representatives were asked to comment on whether the Church was free to unite with the UF Church.[38] Lord Sands spoke to this subject at the meeting of the sub-committee in January 1927.[39] The UF majority also pointed out that the two issues could be separated. Under the Articles, the Church of Scotland was as free as the United Free Church to enter into union. That was a different matter from the objections which they still might have to the contents of the Articles. However objectionable they might be, in Martin's view, they did not constitute an obstacle to union.[40]

(c) the narrative of reunion and the name of the Church

Following, then, the precedent of the uniting Act of 1900, the document began with a preamble narrating the background to the present Act of union.[41] The narrative began with a theological

[34] Ibid., note by A. Martin.
[35] Minutes of the Sub-Committee, 5.12.26.
[36] Martin, Notebook, 22.11.26 (M) 2.5.
[37] Minutes of the Sub-Committee, 5.12.26.
[38] UFC Min., 22 December 1926.
[39] Martin, Notebook, 10.1.27 (M) 2.5.
[40] Ibid.
[41] Basis and Plan of Union, May 1927 (W) 76.

statement which included a reference to the high priestly prayer of Christ recorded in John's Gospel chapter 17. Both Churches thus acknowledged that it was the will and prayer of their Lord that his disciples 'all may be one ... that the world may believe that Thou hast sent Me'. The witness of the Churches was obscured when their work was 'hindered by divisions and separations'.

The narrative then recounted the historical background to reunion, that the Church of Scotland had been reformed in 1560 and had continued for some time unbroken until divisions took place among those who 'alike claimed to share in the common heritage and adhered to the common traditions and standards'. The various separations were then listed, beginning in 1690 with the Reformed Presbyterian Church which arose out of disagreement with the Revolution Settlement, continuing with the Secession of 1733, the formation of the Relief Church in 1761, and concluding with the Disruption in 1843. It was the view of the Scottish Church Society that a friendly reference should have been made to the Episcopal Church which had been treated harshly at the Revolution in 1690.[42] In the view of John White, dissent from the Church of Scotland had 'not been out of disloyalty to her traditions and principles', but from the belief that it had not been 'loyal enough'.[43] The divisions, it was stated, had taken place 'with profound reluctance and in hope of ultimate reunion'. The various reunions which had already taken place were also mentioned. The United Presbyterian Church had been formed in 1843, the Reformed Presbyterian Church had joined the Free Church in 1876, and finally the Free Church had united with the United Presbyterian Church to form the United Free Church in 1900.

The narrative continued with an account of the movement for reunion between the Church of Scotland and the United Free Church, beginning with the opening of discussions in 1909. The two obstacles to union had been identified, the differences which had arisen concerning the principles, common to both Churches, of the national recognition of religion, and the spiritual freedom of the Church. These principles were now said to be 'reaffirmed and set forth in a manner which is in accordance with the convictions of both Churches' in the Articles Declaratory and the United Free Church Act of 1906. John White noted that the national recognition of religion was reaffirmed in Article VI and that the spiritual freedom of the Church was affirmed both in the 1906 Act and by Articles IV and V.[44]

---

[42] SCS, Memorandum on the Basis and Plan of Union, p. 7.
[43] Marginal Notes by John White on the Basis of Union, May 1927 (W) 76.
[44] Ibid.

The next paragraph referred to the need for reunion 'to meet more adequately the religious requirement of the land', the point which was included in response to the suggestions of P. D. Thomson. White thought that the members of the committees had taken the greatest step forward when they had considered the religious situation in Scotland. He recalled the effect of Archibald Henderson's map showing the density of population on the one hand and the major presence of the Churches on the other.[45] 'We then took courage', he said, 'to set every sectional principle in the light of the greatest principle of all—the will of Christ that we should have fellowship with each other.'[46] He felt that in the large cities and industrial centres a united Church would have a much greater appeal than the two Churches working separately.

The document then referred to the substantial agreement which existed between the Churches regarding doctrine, worship, government, and discipline, and said that further necessary adjustment of a practical nature had been made. As a result, it continued, the two general assemblies 'ENACT AND DECLARE that these Churches, representing historic branches of the Presbyterian Church in Scotland, do and shall henceforth constitute one united Church, and that the name of the united Church shall be THE CHURCH OF SCOTLAND.' It was perhaps surprising that there was so little problem about agreeing to the name of the united Church. Alternatives had been discussed widely throughout both Churches, such as 'The Free United Church of Scotland', or 'The United Church of Scotland'. For members of the Church of Scotland, however, there was only one name which would express the continuity of the united Church with the historic Kirk in Scotland. One of the many tales about John White's role in the negotiations is that he pre-empted discussion on this topic at one meeting by saying:[47]

> Well, gentlemen, in this very difficult matter, those of us in the Church of Scotland have decided that it would be only right to admit a claim that the United Free Church has always made. She has always claimed, has she not, to be the Church of Scotland? Very well. The united Church will be known under that name. Surely nobody could disapprove of our giving way to our brethren! Since that is settled, let us take up the next item on the agenda.

If this story is true—and it is certainly in character—White would have found little opposition to this suggestion on the part of

---

[45] See above, p. 39.
[46] Marginal Notes by John White.
[47] *JW*, p. 254.

Alexander Martin. Yet White and Martin had different reasons for wishing the name of the united Church to be the Church of Scotland.

Martin, speaking at his Church's assembly in 1927, defended the choice of name in an eloquent way.[48] He had, he said, never taken himself out of the Church of Scotland. But the true character of the Church of Scotland had little to do with its relation to that outside body, the State. The traditions of the Kirk were those of Knox and Melville, of the Covenanters, of Erskine and Gillespie, as well as of those who had remained within the Kirk 'in the same spirit'. If it had been suggested that the name should be 'The Church of Scotland by law established' that would have been a different matter. But since the suffix had been removed, there was no need to keep the prefix, 'United Free', either. The one name included them all. In his notes on the Basis of Union, on the other hand, John White spoke of the importance of the name of the Church of Scotland because of its historic links with the nation.[49] The Church of Scotland was 'rooted in the history, in the life, in the very soil of Scotland'. For him the Church of Scotland was the 'natural and spontaneous expression of the religious life of Scotland'; it still held the hearts of the Scottish people and was 'the chief symbol of Scottish nationality'. Since the Reformation it had been the most truly popular institution in the country because it had consistently been the representative of 'the convictions, the independence, and the patriotism of the people'. It had been the chief factor in moulding the national character. These two reasons for the continuation of the old name were not, however, incompatible. As will be seen, the Basis of Union allowed such different views to be held within the one Church.

(d) the declaration of liberty

Following an enactment recognising the authority of the first united general assembly of the Church, there followed a series of declarations in view of which the Churches entered into union, based upon the uniting Act of 1900. The first of these related to the 'inherent liberty of the united Church as a branch of the Church of God to determine and regulate her own constitution and laws as duty may require, in dependence on the grace of God and under the guidance of His Word and Spirit.' The question arose as to the relation of this declaration of liberty to both the Articles

[48] Alexander Martin, *Church Union, The Proposed Uniting Act*: Speech by Rev. Principal Martin D.D. at the General Assembly of the United Free Church of Scotland, 27th May 1927, p. 9.
[49] Marginal Notes by John White.

Declaratory and the UF Act anent the Spiritual Independence of the Church. Both documents had been mentioned in the historical preamble of the uniting Act, but how did they relate to this additional affirmation of the Church's freedom, and what was the relationship of all three documents to the constitution of the Church?

The Church of Scotland committee members were not against making such an affirmation regarding the liberty of the Church. As Henderson had thought, the Church of Scotland representatives were only too willing to state the freedom of the Church 'in large letters'.[50] He had written to Martin to say that one of the committee members of the other Church had been 'crowing about their power to consider whether any parish Church, as it fell vacant, should be continued!' He advised his colleague: 'Keep quietly along the line of their being free to act, and they won't quarrel much'. Lord Sands, however, thought that the statement in the declaration was too sweeping as it stood. It was attempting to state the constitutional powers of the Church apart from its constitution. It seemed to be setting itself up as an alternative to the Articles and to the UF Act of 1906. The Church did have liberty over its constitution, but not in an absolute way. He wrote to Martin:[51]

> The Church you say cannot cease to be itself. But when any body of men are united for any purpose sacred or secular what they are as a corporate body depends upon the constitution of that body. Without a constitution there is no 'it'. This Church is Trinitarian is just as much an article of its constitution as This Church is Presbyterian. If as you concede there are certain things which you cannot alter then these things are part of your constitution and an unqualified power to alter your constitution is too wide a claim. The constitution is not a body of rules tacked on to an entity which is capable of definition in propositions which do not form part of its constitution.

Sands' point had been one of the main issues in the debate over the drafting of the Articles and was the reason why the minority in the UF Church was unhappy with Articles I and VIII. Hence, in his view, this declaration could not stand alone without some reference to the Articles and the Act of 1906.

In response to Sands' view, Martin referred to the opinion of Lord Lindley in the Free Church Case of 1904, that a Church could

---

[50] A. Henderson to A. Martin, 9.7.26 (M) 19.8/11.
[51] Lord Sands to A. Martin, 13.1.27 (M) 19.9/12.

not have an unlimited right to change its constitution. The Church had to remain a Christian Church and a Reformed Protestant Church.[52] The proposed declaration was, in Martin's view, very like that opinion. Its claim to liberty was qualified by relation to the dependence on the grace of God and the guidance of his Word. Speaking at the assembly in 1927, he would say that there was no such thing as an unlimited freedom:[53]

> The freedom of the Church ... was not freedom to be or to do anything it liked. The Christian conscience rejected such 'unchartered liberty'—it was an un-Christian thing. Christian liberty was liberty in the Lord. The freedom of a Christian man was freedom to be Jesus Christ's man; the freedom of a Christian man was freedom to be all that Jesus Christ, the King and Head of the same, desired the Church which was His Body to be.

With regard to the freedom of the Church, the declaration was no more *ultra vires* of the Articles than of the Act of 1906. He was strenuously opposed to any suggestion that there was a difference between the Articles and the Act. But the declaration, said Martin, was not in conflict with either:

> All it says is that the Church, in investing itself in the constitutional character indicated in the documents after named, retains, nevertheless, the 'inherent liberty of a Church of Christ to determine and regulate its own constitution and laws ... under the guidance of His Word and Spirit.' Is any Church really autonomous which does not possess this power? And, again, is not just this power definitely claimed in the Act and the Articles alike?

In his later correspondence with Sands in relation to the opinion of counsel sought by the UF committee, Martin also found himself at variance with Sands on this issue.[54] In Martin's view the Articles appeared to be taking precedence over the Act.[55]

According to Lord Sands, however, when the two documents were put together, as they were in the Basis of Union, then the particular overrode the general. The only way by which the two documents could be taken together was by treating the specific provisions as special qualifications of the general ones.[56] Thus

[52] A. Martin to Members of Conveners' Sub-Committee 15.1.27 (M) 19.9/13. Robert Low Orr, *The Free Church of Scotland Appeals 1903–4* (Edinburgh, 1904), p. 606.
[53] Martin, *Church Union: The Proposed Uniting Act*, pp. 9–10.
[54] See above, p. 93.
[55] A. Martin to Lord Sands, 27.10.27 (M) 20.3/1.
[56] Lord Sands to A. Martin, 27.10.27 (M) 20.1/45.

because of their nature the Articles could be said to supersede the Act. The Act stressed the power of change whereas the Articles set out what could not be changed. Sands' original suggestion in drafting the Basis of Union was to say expressly that the two documents were to be read and construed together so that 'it might not appear that two inconsistent documents had been heedlessly incorporated in the Act of Union'.[57] As it was, the provision of the Articles in relation to the Act had to be seen in the nature of a proviso, 'a particular limitation of the general power'. If they were both embodied in one Act, the 'particular detail would form an exception to the general rule'.[58] In Sands' view, in any case, there had to be an irreducible creed for which the Church stood and which formed part of its constitution. This had been the concern of the high churchmen, as well as of Lord Balfour of Burleigh, in the drafting of the Articles; the Church could not have the freedom to become Unitarian as had happened to the Presbyterian Church in England in the seventeenth century. He told Martin:[59]

> There are I fancy some who think that the most vital article of your creed is that you may alter it. But it sometimes seems to me that they are more apostolic in spirit who are able to say of their creed: 'This is the truth of God. Anyone who may seek to alter this must be in deadly error.'

He could not imagine a martyr going to the scaffold saying: 'This doctrine is my belief. I die for it but it gives me much consolation to think that the Church may alter it.'

The discussion between two of the leading exponents of union illustrates the essence of the doctrinal issue with which they had wrestled all along. At the end of the day, while they had come to an agreement, their understanding of that agreement was still rather different. As in the Basis of Union, so in the united Church, there would continue to be two different emphases, on the need for a minimum requirement of belief, and on the freedom of the Church and of the individual minister to restate that faith in other terms. Ministers would have 'liberty of opinion' on such points of doctrine as did not enter into the substance of the faith, but to some it seemed that this liberty of opinion had become the only fundamental doctrine which ministers were required to believe.[60]

[57] Personal Memorandum by Lord Sands (W) 10.6.
[58] Ibid.
[59] Lord Sands to A. Martin, 16.11.27 (M) 20.2/6.
[60] See *FR*, pp. 119–20.

Various experts were consulted with regard to the inclusion of a declaration of freedom. The UF elder and lawyer, A. H. MacLean, pointed out that in 1900 legal opinion was sought by both the uniting Churches about the advisability of inserting such a declaration in the uniting Act.[61] Counsel for the Free Church felt that legal problems would arise from what was included as well as what was excluded. Counsel for the United Presbyterian Church, on the other hand, thought it advisable that such an express statement of liberty should be made since such had been approved by both Churches. To consent to its deletion might have serious consequences. Although different opinions had been given, the process had at least enabled the Churches to consider the matter in an informed way. MacLean suggested that the same course might be followed by the committees. It was an important legal point and should be cleared up before the Basis of Union was sent down to presbyteries.

According to Professor Robert Candlish Henderson, the son of Archibald Henderson, the dilemma facing the Churches in 1926 was similar to that in 1900.[62] He set out the problem in this way. If such a statement was made, Lord Sands had feared that it would go beyond what was said in the Articles. On the other hand, if the statement was not made, James Barr would say that the United Free Church had adopted the 1921 Act and had given up its liberty as a Church. It could therefore be claimed in a court of law that the United Free Church did not stand in continuity with the Church of 1900 since the Basis of Union did not contain a comparable clause regarding liberty as did the uniting Act in 1900. In the view of Alexander Martin,[63] it would not do simply to state explicitly that Article I was a fundamental part of the constitution of the united Church. Certainly the Articles would become part of the Church's constitution, but the United Free Church had maintained all along that it imported nothing new that was not already contained in the 1906 Act. If Article I was adopted as fundamental, he said, they would be admitting that there was a difference between the Articles and the Act and inviting the minority to turn round and say, 'We told you so!'

Sheriff J. L. Wark agreed with Martin that the Articles and the Act said the same thing:[64]

However wide the words of 1906 — and they are very wide — they must have some limitation. The power to alter and

[61] A. H. MacLean to A. Martin, 15.1.27 (M) 19.9/15.
[62] R. C. Henderson to A. Martin, 29.1.27 (M) 19.9/20.
[63] A. Martin to J. P. Watson, 2.2.27 (M) 19.9/26.
[64] J. L. Wark to A. Martin, 22.1.27 (M) 19.9/18.

> modify the constitution cannot be construed, and would
> not be construed in my opinion, in any court as a power to
> destroy the Church as a Christian Church and a Protestant
> Church—and these limits which I think the law would
> imply in the declaration of 1906 are precisely the limits
> which are expressed in Article I of the Schedule.

He made the same point which Sands would later make in his informal submission to the learned counsel consulted by the UF Church. Because the Articles were more limiting the Act of 1906 had to be interpreted in the light of the Articles and not the other way round.[65] In Wark's view it would thus be desirable for there to be something in the uniting Act to show that the matter had been considered, and that the substantial identity of the Articles and the 1906 Act had been accepted by both Churches. He suggested that each Church might formally adopt the other's document before union and declare that they are to be construed together. Lord Sands had suggested, as had A. H. MacLean, that the declaration might be joined to the Articles and the Act of 1906. Lord Constable, who had served as Solicitor-General in 1922, agreed and thought that it might end with the words, 'which liberty is more particularly set forth in Act 1906 and Articles, 1926'.[66] This suggestion was accepted by the conveners' sub-committee,[67] and later by the sub-committee as a whole.[68] This meant that the united Church would have three declarations of spiritual freedom in its constitution, all of which were held to be in agreement: the Articles, the 1906 Act, and the declaration. It also meant that, not only did the uniting Act take the 1900 Act as its model, but it made a similar affirmation of the liberty of the Church as a Church of God.

There is thus, within the uniting Act itself, an unequivocal statement of the freedom of the Church to change its constitution. Those who would maintain that the Articles Declaratory do not declare this freedom have to contend with this statement, which not only maintains such liberty but explicitly says that both the Articles and the Act of 1906 say the same thing. On the other hand, James Barr and the members of the UF minority were afraid that the Articles would come to dominate the constitution of the united Church since they were recognised by an act of parliament. The 1906 Act, they said, would have 'no operative validity in the new Church'.[69] While the latter opinion could be challenged, in

[65] See above, p. 90.
[66] Martin, Notebook, 3.2.27 (M) 2.5.
[67] Ibid., 9.2.27.
[68] Ibid., 21.2.27.
[69] Ibid., 3.3.27.

practical terms this has often been the case. In interpreting the Articles, attention has very rarely been paid to the Act of 1906.[70]

(e) the leading documents and the other declarations

The status of the Articles Declaratory and of the Act of 1906 was also an issue when it came to the second declaration which listed the 'leading documents setting forth the existing constitution, standards, rules, and methods of the united Church'. The word 'constitution' had been added to an earlier draft since it was realised that both of the key documents should be included. But where should they be placed? It was vital that the leading documents should be detailed since, as Alexander Martin would say, this was something which should not be left in doubt.[71] The Church's constitutional position had evolved and had not been defined. But in order to avoid the danger of being 'at the mercy of lawyers who looked everywhere for the material they wanted, as in moderators' addresses', these documents had now to be listed for the first time since the seventeenth century. He was referring, of course, to the judgement in the Free Church Case when several references were made to the moderatorial address of Thomas Chalmers in 1843 as setting out the 'prospectus' of the Free Church, instead of simply his own views, regarding the establishment of religion.[72]

The standards of both Churches were therefore identified, beginning appropriately with those concerning doctrine. Along with the Westminster Confession of Faith, the Declaratory Acts passed by the United Presbyterian Church in 1879 and by the Free Church in 1892 and 1894 were also included. It was in addition proposed that the Church of Scotland Declaratory Act of 1889 and the Act on the Formula be added to show that the Auld Kirk 'had, at an early date, claimed liberty on the doctrinal question'.[73] In the end the Act on the Formula of 1910 was listed by itself. The general assembly in 1889 had departed from its own strict formula of subscription of 1711 and had restored the less stringent formula of 1693. It had also declared in 1903 that the Westminster Confession was 'to be regarded as an infallible rule of faith and worship only in so far as it accords with Holy Scripture interpreted by the Holy Spirit'.[74] The UP Act of 1879 had been followed closely in terms of content and expression by the Free Church in 1892. Both acts

---

[70] See *FR*, ch. 6.
[71] Martin, *Church Union: The Proposed Uniting Act*, p. 10.
[72] Orr, *Free Church of Scotland Appeals*, pp. 566, 581, 587, 594, 612–13.
[73] J. White to A. Martin, 8.3.27 (M) 19.9/32.
[74] Sands, *Archibald Scott*, p. 124.

declared the sense in which the Church understood the Confession of Faith. It was thus important that both these acts be included in the uniting Act. The united Church was not to lose the understanding of the Confession which these documents represented. The teaching of the Confession had been qualified in certain very important respects and this interpretation was to be continued in the future. The statement in Article II of the Articles Declaratory, that the Church's principal subordinate standard was the Westminster Confession, thus had to be taken along with this declaration of leading documents. The three acts qualifying the Church's adherence to the Confession were listed along with the Confession itself as of equal standing. In terms of government, worship and discipline, the same standards were listed as in Article II, the Westminster Form of Presbyterial Church Government, the Westminster Directory of Public Worship, and the Form of Process of 1707. In that these had not been qualified in a similar way to the Confession, it was added that these were to be regarded 'as generally regulative and as of validity, as these have been or may be hereafter interpreted or modified by Acts of General Assembly or by consuetude.'

The original draft then listed the Articles and the Act of 1906 last of all, under the heading 'The Spirituality and Freedom of the Church and the National Recognition of Religion.' Lord Sands, however, was not sure about the place assigned to these constitutional documents, which was in fifth place, especially when the Church's power to alter them had just been asserted.[75] He thought that the Church's powers in relation to its constitution should be mentioned in second place, after the Church's doctrinal standards.[76] John White, however, pointed out that both documents referred to all the matters listed, including doctrine.[77] In the end it was agreed that they should be placed first under the heading 'General Constitution, including the Principles of the Spirituality and Freedom of the Church, and the National Recognition of Religion'. The two documents were again treated as of equal status, as in the first declaration, and of the first importance in relation, not just to the Church's constitution, but also in relation to the doctrine, worship, government and discipline of the Church.

The third declaration included a list of the Articles and Acts whereby previous unions had taken place and by which the United Free Church had reached its present form. The general principles of these documents were to be conserved in the united

---

[75] Lord Sands to A. Martin, 11.1.27 (M) 19.9/9.
[76] Lord Sands to A. Martin, 11.1.27 (M) 19.9/9.
[77] White to Martin, 8.3.27.

Church. The next declaration contained documents which had an important place in the history of Scottish Presbyterianism, and continued to be held in honour in the Church. These were the Scots Confession of 1560, the First and Second Books of Discipline, the Book of Common Order of 1564, and the Westminster Larger and Shorter Catechisms. These documents, said Martin, no longer had constitutional validity but were still entitled to a place of honour. Some, he said, preferred the Scots Confession to that of Westminster; the Books of Discipline set out the programmes of the first and second generation of reformers; while the Book of Common Order had been the recognised authority in matters of worship from 1560 to 1645.[78] The committee had considered a short paper outlining the official position of 'Knox's Liturgy'.[79] According to White, some in the Church of Scotland, including those who belonged to the Scottish Church Society,[80] wished to delete the reference to the First Book of Discipline, but the Church of Scotland committee wished it retained.[81]

The most persistent suggestion, however, was for a more important position to be assigned to the two Catechisms. Cromarty Smith, minister of Coatdyke Church, Coatbridge, and a leading high churchman, suggested during the following year that the Catechisms should be listed as 'leading documents' in a separate section after discipline headed 'Directory for Catechising'.[82] He felt that many people in the presbyteries objected to their being placed 'on the shelf with those other documents which are now out of date'.[83] The Catechisms were in regular use by ministers, particularly in the training of young communicants. In making this point he was following the policy of the Scottish Church Society which said that the Catechisms had always been regarded as 'standards' in the Kirk.[84] If the proposal of the committee was followed, the Society said, the Church would be left without a standard of doctrinal instruction. In addition, the Shorter Catechism provided the Kirk with an official witness to the Apostles' Creed since the Creed formed a constituent element of its teaching. The Catechisms were not just to be held in honour in the Church, they were 'the authorised manuals of religious instruction'. The assembly in 1928 received several overtures which asked for the position of the Catechisms to be reconsidered,[85] and the final version of the Basis of

---

[78] Martin, *Church Union: The Proposed Uniting Act*, p. 10.
[79] Relation of the General Assembly to Knox's Liturgy (M) 5.
[80] Scottish Church Society, *Notes on the Revised Basis and Plan of Union* (Edinburgh, 1928), p. 16.
[81] White to Martin, 8.3.27.
[82] J. C. Smith to J. White, 23.6.28 and 23.7.28 (W) 11.4.
[83] J. C. Smith to J. White, 19.7.28 (W) 11.4.
[84] SCS, *Notes*, p. 15.
[85] See below, p. 262.

Union went some way to meeting this point, although not as far as had been wished. The Catechisms were not included among the doctrinal and other standards of the Church, but in a separate declaration which came immediately before the other documents 'held in honour' in the Church. It was stated that the Catechisms had been for long approved as manuals of instruction and that they continued to be held in honour in the united Church. The fifth declaration thus contained the four documents from the sixteenth century, the Scots Confession, the First and Second Books of Discipline, and the Book of Common Order.

The final two declarations echoed similar statements contained in the uniting Act of 1900. They reflected two of the central concerns of the former United Presbyterian Church. One concerned liberty of individual conscience. It was declared that the union took place 'on the footing of maintaining the liberty of judgment and action heretofore recognised in either of the Churches uniting'. Members would have the full right 'to assert and maintain the views of truth and duty which they had liberty to maintain in the said Churches'. This proviso had a long history, as Martin reminded the UF assembly.[86] It had first appeared in 1820 when it enabled 'the Breach' over the Burgher Oath to be healed with the formation of the United Secession Church. In a similar way, it had allowed the Seceders and the Relief Church to come together in 1847. The history of their Church, he said, 'was one of the broadening of the area of open questions, or "matters of forbearance" as they were termed, among Christian brethren'. They now had the opportunity to broaden the area still further. The united Church, with this declaration, could even include 'Mr. Barr … along with the entire Disestablishment Council if they could find in the Church of the future anything on which to operate!' In other words, the issues of establishment and disestablishment were to be treated as 'open questions' in the united Church. Those who held such views would be welcome, provided they accorded the same liberty of opinion to those who did not share their view. John White also emphasised this point at the other assembly.[87]

Lord Sands had previously pointed out to the committee that in the Free Church Case several legal opinions had agreed in saying that neither establishment nor voluntaryism were fundamental principles in the United Free Church and that both were to be open questions.[88] Similarly, in the Church of Scotland,

[86] Martin, *Church Union: The Proposed Uniting Act*, p. 11.
[87] Basis and Plan of Union, 1927 (W) 97.
[88] Lord Sands, Objections taken to Draft Uniting Act: Memorandum of Replies to the above (M) 14.2. Orr, *Free Church of Scotland Appeals*, p. 589 (Lord James), cf. p. 571 (Lord Chancellor) and p. 584 (Lord Davey).

the establishment of religion was no longer to be regarded as a fundamental principle of the constitution of the Church. Articles II and VI showed that there was nothing to support the contention 'that the principle in question is a fundamental part of the constitution of the Church of Scotland—any more than the Voluntary principle is a fundamental part of the constitution of the United Free Church'. A similar opinion would be given by the counsel consulted by the United Free Church as part of the attempt to include the minority in the united Church.[89]

The final declaration reflected another central concern of the former United Presbyterian Church, the importance of voluntary giving. It spoke of the obligation resting upon members of the Church 'to contribute, according to their ability, for the support of the ordinances of religion and the extension of the Kingdom of Christ throughout the world.' As we have seen, it had been recognised by the leaders of the Church of Scotland that the Church in future would have to rely increasingly on the freewill offerings of its members. Indeed, according to Martin, the only criticism of this clause from the Church of Scotland side had been that the obligation 'might have been stressed more strongly'.[90] To begin with the Church would be able to count on income from 'public sources' to the extent of one-eighth or one-ninth. It would be the duty of members, said Martin, to make this proportion less and less as the years went by. Those who belonged to the former UP tradition must have rejoiced over this inclusion of the principle of voluntary giving in the uniting Act with the Auld Kirk.

[89] See below, pp. 230–1.
[90] Martin, *Church Union: The Proposed Uniting Act*, p. 11.

Chapter 7

Building the structure: the Plan of Union 1926–9

According to John White, while the Basis of Union dealt with the principles on which the two Churches agreed to unite, the Plan dealt with matters which had to be adjusted before union could be effectively carried out.[1] While there was in his view a great measure of community, each of the Churches was, nevertheless, 'a complex organisation with rules, methods, practices, and business arrangements of its own, and union without adjustment of these would lead to confusion.' Not everything, however, had to be 'definitely and finally fixed', and White thought that there could be a transition period during which the status quo as regards certain matters of detail in organisation and arrangement could be maintained. Some matters could be left over for the united Church to deal with, but the Plan of Union should be as complete as possible. In discussing these more practical matters it had to be realised that each side could not have everything its own way, and compromise would be as necessary in making these arrangements as had been the case with regard to the basic principles of union. It would thus be possible, as White pointed out, for some matters to be left undecided until after the union had taken place, and there could also be a difference of opinion as to what these might be. It was a temptation, not always resisted by the two committees, to leave to be decided by the united Church certain more controversial matters which would have benefited from being dealt with beforehand. But this could well have meant delaying union even further, and this was something which the leaders on both sides were anxious not to do. The arrangements concerning the merging of the committee structures of the two Churches, and questions of property and finance, presented practical problems but did not create controversy. The areas which proved to be more controversial will be examined in turn.

[1] Marginal Notes by John White on the Plan of Union (W) 76.

(a) the ordination of ministers

The first section of the Plan of Union consisted of the Preamble, Questions, and Formula for use at the ordination of a minister. The pattern of these documents was again taken from the uniting Act of 1900 and thus a Preamble was adopted although there was a 'narrative' in the ordination service of the Church of Scotland.[2] The Preamble was fuller than that of the United Free Church and reflected the understanding which had now been reached between the two Churches. As Alexander Martin reported, there was remarkably little discussion over the drafts of these statements when they were first brought before the UF committee.[3] This was the case despite the fact that the Declaratory Acts in relation to the Confession of Faith were not mentioned in the Preamble, and that the question to the minister regarding the spiritual freedom of the Church had been omitted.

The Preamble was agreed with the inclusion of a reference to the doctrine of ordination, an addition which had been suggested by the high churchman, Cromarty Smith. Thus the opening words reflected Ephesians 4:

> In the name of the Lord Jesus Christ, the King and Head of the Church, Who, being ascended on high, hath given gifts unto men for the perfecting of the saints, for the work of the Ministry, for the edifying of the body of Christ, we are met here as a Presbytery to ordain A. B. to the office of the Holy Ministry by prayer and the laying on of hands by the Presbyters to whom it doth belong ...

The issue about the laying on of hands at ordination belonging to ministers rather than elders was made later in the Plan of Union when it dealt with the Rules and Forms of Procedure relating to the ordination of ministers.[4] This became a controversial matter in the course of the discussions. It had become the practice in the United Free Church, in some instances, for elders to take part in the laying on of hands at the ordination of ministers. The question had been raised in the United Presbyterian Church, but its synod had decided to maintain the traditional practice of the Presbyterian Church.[5] The standard of the Churches in this matter, the Westminster Form of Presbyterial Church Government, said that the laying on of hands was to be by 'the preaching presbyters to

---

[2] Marginal Notes by John White. Cf. William Mair, *A Digest of Laws and Decisions Ecclesiastical and Civil* 2nd edn. (Edinburgh and London, 1895). pp. 262–4.

[3] Martin, Notebook, 3.3.27 (M) 2.

[4] Plan of Union, p. 32 (W) 76.

[5] Woodside, *Soul of a Scottish Church*, p. 245.

whom it doth belong', and it was this authority which was quoted almost exactly in the Preamble.[6] As John White made clear at the assembly in 1927, the participation of elders did not invalidate the ordination. He said this, not to justify the interference of ruling elders, but to emphasise the validity of the ordination despite such interference.[7]

There was no disagreement over this issue in the committee, but the UF minority made the following comment in a leaflet issued on the Basis and Plan:[8]

> henceforward ordination is to be by the laying on of hands by ministers only. Elders are expressly debarred from taking part, a disability not formally recognised in the United Free Church, and a step in the direction of priestism.

John White told the Synod of Glasgow and Ayr, meeting in Hamilton in April 1927, that he had read that statement 'with some considerable amazement'.[9] This view, he said, must have been thoughtlessly made and gave a false representation of the position both of the Church of Scotland and of the UF Church. The words 'step in the direction of priestism' were 'wild words'. For White the statement in the Preamble was 'a simple restatement of the doctrine of ordination set forth in the standards of the Churches'. He quoted not only from the Westminster Form of Church Government, but also from the *Manual of Practice and Procedure in the United Free Church of Scotland* of 1905 which had just been revised and reissued and said:[10]

> the minister-elect kneels and the moderator by prayer, with the imposition of hands in which all the ministers present join, ordains to the office of the Holy Ministry.

Elders were a distinctive feature of Presbyterianism, he said, and had a significant role to play in the life of the Church, and 'nothing but harm would follow the confusing of their function with that of the ministry'. In presenting the report to the assembly in 1928, White said that 'Our United Free Church brethren are, with very few exceptions, quite as sound on Ordination as any in the Church of Scotland, and are just a little sensitive at the frequent suspicion that they are not.'[11] He emphasised that ordination in the united

[6] The Form of Presbyterial Church Government, 'Touching the Doctrine of Ordination'.

[7] Marginal Notes by John White.

[8] UFCA, *The Proposed Union. Guide to Members of the United Free Church of Scotland*, August 1927, p. 5 (UFCA).

[9] John White, Hamilton — Ordination (W) 97.

[10] United Free Church of Scotland, *Manual of Practice and Procedure in the United Free Church of Scotland*, (Edinburgh, 1905), pp. 49–50; 2nd edn. (Edinburgh, 1927), p. 53.

[11] John White, Speech to General Assembly, May 1928 (W) 98.

Church would be according to the standards of the Church. He thought that the Plan of Union gave a more definite statement of the position than did the present Church of Scotland Order of Service.

The statement about the place of ministers in the act of ordination was later changed, and this alteration was opposed by high churchmen in the Church of Scotland minority. Not only were ministers described as 'teaching elders', a description to which they took strong exception, but the statement did not unmistakably confine the act of ordination to ministers.[12] Had the original statement not been included in the first place, they might not have been uneasy; but the fact that it had been included but was now omitted gave cause for concern. Ministers should be assured about the transmission of the ministry. The phrase 'teaching elders' was, however, changed to 'Presbyters' in the final version of the document. White also made the point that elders and people were not simply spectators at the service. Ordination was by prayer — in which elders and people join — as well as by the laying on of hands. It was the symbolic act alone that pertained to ministers. The high churchmen also made the point, which was reflected by changes in the final wording of the Preamble, that while induction was carried out by the presbytery, the act of ordination was carried out by presbyters. Thus while the presbytery directed the ordination, it did not as a court ordain.[13]

Lord Sands thought that the controversy over this issue was the result of a 'difference of atmosphere between the Churches'.[14] It came down, in his view, to a difference about Presbyterianism. The divergence had resulted because the 'free' Presbyterian Churches in Scotland had developed links with the dissenters in England, whereas the Church of Scotland had usually allied itself with the Church of England. In particular, the high church grouping in the Auld Kirk was suspicious of the union and would have wished the Episcopal Church to be included.

(b) the Preamble, the Questions and the Formula

The United Free Church Preamble had contained references to the Word of God as the supreme standard and the Westminster Confession as its subordinate standard in matters of the faith, qualified by the Declaratory Acts and with the liberty of the Church to 'interpret, add to, modify, or change' its subordinate

---

[12] SCS, *Notes*, p. 21.
[13] SCS, Memorandum on the Basis and Plan of Union, pp. 9–10 (SCS).
[14] Lord Sands to A. Martin, 8.4.27 (M) 19.9/41.

standards. The proposed Preamble for the united Church of Scotland was longer in that, following the statement about ordination, it set out the faith of the Church. This paragraph was a remarkable composition, remarkable because it seems to have been accepted without demur, but also for the apparent ease with which it had been composed. The reason for both circumstances is that it was modelled closely on Article I of the Articles Declaratory. It stated:

> In this act of ordination the Church of Scotland, as part of the Holy Catholic or Universal Church worshipping one God—Father, Son, and Holy Spirit—affirms anew its belief in the Gospel of the sovereign grace and love of God, wherein through Jesus Christ, His only Son, our Lord, Incarnate, Crucified, and Risen, He freely offers to all men, upon repentance and faith, the forgiveness of sins, renewal by the Holy Spirit, and eternal life, and calls them to labour in the fellowship of faith for the advancement of the Kingdom of God throughout the world.

This Preamble was the essence of Article I, only in the form of an affirmation rather than a declaration, and without the theological elaboration of the doctrines of the trinity and the incarnation. John White thought it was a clear statement of the fundamentals but still thought there was a need for a fuller statement of these doctrines for the members of the Church.[15] He also thought that the Preamble could be used for specific religious purposes, to inform people about the act of ordination and to give a simple summary of the faith of the Church. It was quoted in full in the Brief Statement on the Basis and Plan of Union for Congregations, issued by the Church of Scotland in 1927, since it was said to set forth in brief compass 'the fundamental doctrines of the Christian faith'.[16] Since the Church of Scotland has yet to produce a statement of the fundamental doctrines of the faith, the Preamble has served that purpose on occasions. For example, the remit given to the Panel on Doctrine by the general assembly of 1987, regarding the relationship of the Church to Freemasonry, referred to the Preamble as giving the reference point for the faith of the Church.[17]

The Preamble concluded with similar references to those in the United Free Church statement regarding the Church's standards and its freedom in relation to them:

[15] Marginal Notes, pp, 15, 16.
[16] C of S, A Brief Statement on the Basis and Plan of Union for Congregations, 1927, p. 7.
[17] *C of S Rep.*, 1989, p. 182.

The Church of Scotland, with the Churches of the Reformation, acknowledges the Word of God which is contained in the Scriptures of the Old and New Testaments to be the supreme rule of faith and life. The Church of Scotland holds as its Subordinate Standard the Westminster Confession of Faith, recognising liberty of opinion on such points of doctrine as do not enter into the substance of the Faith, and claiming the right, in dependence on the promised guidance of the Holy Spirit, to formulate, interpret, or modify its subordinate standards: but always in agreement with the Word of God and the fundamental doctrines of the Christian Faith contained in the said Confession — of which agreement the Church itself shall be sole judge.

This statement reflected the affirmation concerning the Word of God in Article I and the Church's relationship to its subordinate standards in Article V. The Formula to be signed by ordinands was worded in a similar way: 'I believe the fundamental doctrines of the Christian faith contained in the Confession of Faith of this Church.'

In the Formula the ordinand also acknowledged 'Presbyterian Church government as agreeable to the Word of God', and promised to 'submit thereto and concur therewith'. A similar affirmation was made in answer to the third of the Questions put to ordinands. In the light of replies from presbyteries, both the Formula and the Question were strengthened and made explicitly to refer to the government of the Church of Scotland being Presbyterian. The Formula now read: 'I acknowledge the Presbyterian Government of this Church to be agreeable to the Word of God ...' There had been no desire to avoid such an assertion in the original draft since, as John White pointed out, the Articles declare the government of the Church to be Presbyterian. In addition, by the terms of Article VIII, Presbyterianism could only be altered with the consent of two-thirds of the presbyteries of the Church in two successive years.[18] There could be no change to the government of the Church without a general demand for such change. He also noted that among the leading documents listed in the Basis of Union was the Form of Presbyterial Church Government.

The Questions to the ordinand were similar to those used by the United Free Church, except for the omission of the one regarding the liberty of the Church. In reply to that Question, the minister affirmed that the Church derived from Christ 'a government

---

[18] White, Speech to General Assembly, May 1928.

distinct from civil government' and that civil rulers possess 'no jurisdiction in her spiritual affairs'. While these statements could still be made in the united Church they were capable of a one-sided interpretation. Also, the Questions regarding the faith of the ordinand in the trinity and the gospel were not included in the first draft. The Questions thus began with affirmations of the Word of God contained in the scriptures and the fundamental doctrines of the Christian faith contained in the Confession of Faith of the Church. Thus the draft followed the practice of the Church of Scotland. The first Question regarding the ordinand's faith in the trinity and in the Lordship of Christ was, however, later included. The Question regarding Presbyterian government was also followed by a separate one whereby the ordinand promised to 'seek the unity and peace of this Church; to uphold the doctrine, worship, government, and discipline thereof; and to cherish a spirit of brotherhood towards all the faithful followers of the Lord'. A challenging Question was also put, similar to one used in the ordination service of the United Free Church:[19]

> Are not zeal for the glory of God, love to the Lord Jesus Christ, and a desire for the salvation of men, so far as you know your own heart, your great motives and chief inducements to enter into the office of the Holy Ministry?

(c) the general assembly

When it came to the constitution and powers of the general assembly of the united Church, it might have appeared that there was little difference between the Churches, except that the assembly of the Church of Scotland was attended by a Lord High Commissioner. For both Churches, the assembly was the supreme court, and this could be stated unequivocally in the Plan of Union.[20] It was also stated that the decisions of the assembly were final and were not 'subject to review by any Civil Court'. In the view of the members of the Scottish Church Society, however, the assembly should be described as the 'highest' and not as the 'supreme' court of the Church.[21] This term to them smacked of the authority of the Wesleyan Conference. In addition, there was no reference to the Barrier Act which was a check on the 'supremacy' of the assembly. The order in which the courts were described, starting with the general assembly, was an inversion of the Presbyterian system:

[19] *Manual of the United Free Church* (1927), p. 172.
[20] Plan of Union, p. 18.
[21] SCS, Memorandum, p. 11.

> In Presbyterian Church Government, the system of Ecclesiastical Courts rises as a fabric from the foundation upwards. It does not descend from above. Church Courts, as regards membership, are constituted, not by themselves, nor from above, but from beneath.

The one court which did perpetuate itself, and which was thus an exception to this rule, was the kirk session. In this they had a point, that, while the assembly is the highest of the courts, it is made up of those commissioned by presbyteries.

The composition of the assemblies of the two Churches, however, was quite different. The Church of Scotland assembly did not just draw its membership from the presbyteries of the Church as did that of the United Free Church. Each presbytery sent one out of four of its ministers, and one out of six of its elders. Each of the four universities sent an elder, the city of Edinburgh sent two elders, and the remaining sixty-nine royal burghs sent one elder each. This meant, too, that there were not equal numbers of ministers and elders. The representation worked out at 371 ministers and 333 elders.[22] While the universities and the burghs could send only elders, their presence was a reminder of the national representation of the assembly of the Established Church. In the United Free Church, however, only presbyteries sent commissioners and there were equal numbers of ministers and elders in attendance. The assembly was composed of 'a number of ministers equal to one-third of the sanctioned congregations and professorial charges within the bounds of each Presbytery, and the same number of elders.'[23] This also meant that the assembly was much larger, 1100 members compared to just over 700 in the Auld Kirk. For the united Church, the model of the UF assembly was taken. Only presbyteries would send commissioners, and theological professors would be eligible to attend in their own right and not just as representing the universities or as elders. There would be an equal number of ministers and elders, each presbytery sending one in four of its ministers and an equal number of elders, making a court of 1500 members.

Such a large body in which equality was important reflected a different ethos from that of the Church of Scotland and was criticised by members of the high church minority as a revolutionary proposal. In their view strict equality had never been insisted upon in the past. Indeed, since the assembly would

---

[22] David Hunter, 'Presbyterianism in the Church of Scotland', in *Historical Papers submitted to the Christian Unity Association* (Edinburgh, 1914), p. 8.

[23] 'Notes on Dr. Hunter's Paper by Professor MacEwen', in ibid., p. 10.

deal with matters 'which transcend the sphere of discipline and government, the power of determination should, in the last resort, rest with those to whom responsible stewardship of the Word and Sacraments directly belongs.'[24] The classical Presbyterian position was that, while ministers were 'standing members' of presbyteries, elders were 'simply delegates from the congregations who hold office for a given period'. Thus a presbytery could meet without elders being present, but 'no number of ruling elders could of themselves constitute a meeting of presbytery'. They felt that the way this matter had been arranged was one-sided and not a compromise. In this regard, certainly, the stress of the UF Church upon equality of representation between ministers and elders has continued to be the pattern in the Church of Scotland. The size of the assembly was also of concern to the members of the Scottish Church Society. They thought that an assembly, which was double the size of the Kirk's assembly, could not function properly. In order to work efficiently it would have to be drastically reduced in size and organised in smaller committees; or some of its functions might be delegated to synods. At any rate they considered that a judicial court of that size would be a 'monstrosity'.[25]

(d) the Lord High Commissioner

If the composition of the assembly was based more on UF than on Auld Kirk custom, then the continuing presence of the Lord High Commissioner was a concession to the practice of the Church of Scotland. The Plan of Union stated that

> The General Assembly will loyally welcome the Sovereign should it be the royal pleasure to attend in person: or, failing the Sovereign, a Lord High Commissioner as the royal representative. Neither the Sovereign nor the Lord High Commissioner as such is a constituent member of the Assembly.

It should be noted that the attendance of the sovereign or of a royal representative was a matter for the monarch to decide. But if the sovereign wished to attend the assembly or to send a Lord High Commissioner, then it was both loyal and courteous of the Church to welcome him. The attendance of the Lord High Commissioner was thus not part of the constitution of the Church; and the decision to attend lay with the civil power. The assembly could

---

[24] SCS, *Notes*, p. 7.
[25] SCS, Memorandum, p. 11.

meet without the Lord High Commissioner, and had indeed done
so on occasions in the past, mostly during the troubles of the
seventeenth century.[26] Since 1911, the United Free Church assembly
had also been in the habit of welcoming a brief visit by the Lord
High Commissioner.[27]

Both John White and Lord Sands were aware of the troubled
history of the relations between the monarch and the assembly
and knew that the continuation of the office of Lord High
Commissioner only served to remind some in the United Free
Church of previous difficulties. Archibald Henderson thought
that many in his Church would desire the entire disappearance of
the office, but he was also sure that this would be resolutely
opposed by the other Church.[28] Lord Sands sent a memorandum
on the subject to Alexander Martin. He pointed out that the
'Golden Act' of 1592 provided that the assembly should meet at
least once a year, and that if the king or his commissioner was
present at the close of the assembly, he should appoint the time
and place for the next meeting. Should he be absent, the assembly
could decide this by themselves.[29] Subsequently, however, trouble
arose because the king 'took to dissolving assemblies without
calling another and failed to call annual assemblies'.[30] In particular,
in 1638 and in 1692, the commissioner dissolved the assembly
without fixing a date for the next assembly. The assembly, however,
on both occasions 'refused to treat itself as dissolved and in
dissolving itself fixed a day for its next meeting'.[31] In 1703 there
was a repetition of what happened in 1692 when the assembly
was abruptly dissolved by the commissioner.[32] Since then,
however, controversy had been avoided by what John White
called an 'ingenious device':[33]

> The Assembly passes an Act fixing the date of the meeting
> of the next Assembly. The Moderator then in the name of

---

[26] Lord Sands, The Lord High Commissioner (April 1926) (M) 11.4.

[27] Reith, *Reminiscences*, p. 127.

[28] A. Henderson to A. Martin, 22.6.26 (M) 19.8/10.

[29] Sands, Lord High Commissioner. Cf. Thomson, *Acts of the Parliament of Scotland*, III, p. 541; Stewart Mechie, *The Office of Lord High Commissioner* (Edinburgh, 1957), p. 11.

[30] Sands, Lord High Commissioner.

[31] Memorandum with reference to the Dissolution of the General Assembly and the Appointment of the Date of the next General Assembly by the Lord High Commissioner, 1927 (W) 98. Cf. Mechie, *Lord High Commissioner*, pp. 16, 22–3; *LW*, October 1924, p. 228.

[32] Mechie, *Lord High Commissioner*, pp. 28–31.

[33] Memorandum with reference to the Dissolution of the General Assembly. Cf. Mechie, *Lord High Commissioner*, pp. 31–2.

the Lord Jesus Christ, sole King and Head of the Church, dissolves the Assembly. Thereafter, after an exchange of courtesies, the Commissioner delivers a short address and concludes by dissolving the Assembly in the King's name and appointing the next Assembly to meet on the same day which the Assembly has already fixed in its own Act.

This ceremony, according to White, was a reminder of the historical controversy but occasioned no dissatisfaction in the Kirk. As recently as 1912 the Lord High Commissioner had inadvertently closed his speech without the usual formula appointing the next meeting, but 'of course the Assembly met as usual in the following year on the day fixed by its own Act'. According to Henderson, this incident showed that the office could not be treated as a matter of essential importance.[34] Sands also referred to this incident and pointed out, too, that there was no reference in the minutes of the assembly, or in any other record, to the appointment by the crown of a date.[35] Sands also pointed out that all doubt about the assembly's right to fix the place and date of its meetings had been removed by the Articles Declaratory.[36] This point was not accepted by James Barr and the minority in the United Free Church. For Barr the Articles of 1921 did not overturn the Act of 1592 which established the office by statute.[37]

White was aware, however, that many of the pro-union majority of the United Free Church committee were not prepared to accept the customary device by which the assembly was dissolved.[38] It suggested a claim by the State to control the Church in the arrangement of the meetings of its own courts. In addition, this was felt so strongly by a section of the UF Church that some alteration would have to be made in order that the presence of the Lord High Commissioner at the assembly was at all acceptable. It would be preferable, too, that such a change be agreed privately with the crown rather than being made the subject of public discussion. It would also be better if it were made prior to the union as resulting from the Church of Scotland Act, which recognised the autonomy of the Church, rather than be made later at the insistence of the United Free Church as a condition of union. If the change was to be made it had to be done at the assembly of 1927, said White, 'otherwise the opportunity will pass of treating the matter as consequential upon the Act of 1921, with the consequent

---

34 Henderson to Martin, 22.6.26.
35 Lord Sands, Lord High Commissioner.
36 Cf. Mechie, *Lord High Commissioner*, pp. 47–9.
37 Barr, *United Free Church of Scotland*, p. 129.
38 Memorandum with reference to the Dissolution of the General Assembly.

risk of the Crown being involved in the Union negotiations.'[39] It should be noted that the Church of Scotland Act, while it had been passed in 1921, only became effective by Order of Council in 1926 following the adoption of the Articles Declaratory by the Church of Scotland.

Instead of simply dropping the formula, White proposed devising a new one which would be acceptable to the crown and to the Church. The existing arrangement by which the moderator dissolved the assembly and then proceeded to address the commissioner was somewhat incongruous. The dissolution by the moderator should be the final step. White therefore suggested that after the assembly had passed the act of dissolution, the moderator should address the commissioner who would then reply, concluding with these words:[40]

> Right Reverend and well beloved, your labours are now at an end, and I shall inform His Majesty that, having concluded the business for which you were assembled, you have passed an Act appointing the next meeting of General Assembly to be held upon ..., and now in the King's name I bid you farewell.

The moderator would then dissolve the assembly. The advantage of this formula, from White's point of view, was that it gave away very little. The commissioner would simply report to the sovereign, who would then be free to recognise the meeting thus fixed by act of assembly by sending a commissioner to it. According to Henderson, such an arrangement, which he had suggested previously to Martin, would not be interference on the part of the sovereign but a way of keeping him informed.[41]

Lord Sands was told by the Scottish Office prior to the meeting of the assembly in 1927 that the king had agreed to the proposed new formula of dissolution. He then wrote to Alexander Martin to assure him that the assembly would not be dissolved in the king's name.[42] But it was not only the closing ceremony that had to be altered. The opening words spoken by the commissioner could also be interpreted as a claim by the crown to some measure of control over the Church, although Henderson did not himself think that there was anything in the form of constituting the assembly which called for change.[43] The words in question were:

[39] Ibid.
[40] Ibid.
[41] Henderson to Martin, 22.6.26.
[42] J. Lamb to Lord Sands, 16.4.27 (W) 10.4; Lord Sands to A. Martin, 21.5.27 (M) 19.2/38.
[43] Henderson to Martin, 22.6.26.

> In the name of His Majesty, I now invite you to proceed to the business for which you are assembled, and I most earnestly commend your labours to the blessing and guidance of Almighty God.

As it happened these words continued to be used by the Lord High Commissioner, the Earl of Stair, at the opening of the assembly in 1927, and John White was worried in case the more significant words at the closing ceremony should also not be used as had been agreed.[44] Accordingly he contacted the Solicitor General and urged in the strongest possible terms that the customary formula be not used on this occasion. When Lord Stair realised that the new arrangement had the approval of the king, he agreed to follow it.[45]

It had been hoped that King George V would himself be present at the union assembly in October 1929. The presence of the king in person would obviate the need for the appointment of a Lord High Commissioner and would thus go some way towards silencing criticism of the office. Some in the UF Church, such as David Cairns, wished the king to be present at the first assembly and then 'withdraw for good'.[46] Lord Sands wrote to the Scottish Office to say that, if the king could not be present, it would be a catastrophe if His Royal Highness the Duke of York was not appointed as his representative.[47] The Duke of York, the future King George VI, acted as Lord High Commissioner at the last pre-union assembly of the Church of Scotland. Even if the king were to be present for some of the time, say the opening ceremony, but was unable to be present throughout, it would not mean that the presence of the Lord High Commissioner would be superfluous. It was the desire of the Kirk, and he believed also of many in the United Free Church, that

> the historical continuity of the relations of the Church to the Crown should be maintained by a Court at Holyrood and the presence of His Majesty's representative during the sittings of the Assembly.

If this continuity was to be maintained, then it was important that, at the first assembly of the united Church, there should be more than just a 'complimentary visit' by the king or his representative. If a commissioner was present throughout then the way would be clear for the appointment of a commissioner in the usual way for the general assembly in 1930.

---

[44] *JW*, pp. 260–1.
[45] Mechie, *Lord High Commissioner*, pp. 51–2.
[46] D. S. Cairns to A. Martin, 29.9.25 (M) 19.5/20.
[47] Lord Sands to the Scottish Office, 4.5.29 (W) 12.8.

The Church was gratified that, although the king would not be present in person at the union assembly, the Duke of York was appointed to act as Lord High Commissioner during the entire assembly. A problem arose, however, over the entrance of the Lord High Commissioner to the assembly hall. The first joint meeting of the assembly was to be held in the only building found to be capable of accommodating such a large gathering, the Industrial Hall in Annandale Street. As was the case in the Church of Scotland assembly hall in the Lawnmarket, the throne gallery, where the monarch or his representative sat, was separated by a low partition from the rest of the hall. This arrangement indicated that the commissioner was not a member of the assembly and symbolised the separation of civil and spiritual authority. In addition the commissioner entered the hall by a separate entrance which led directly to the throne gallery. Arrangements were made at the Industrial Hall for a special entrance to be made to the throne gallery at the side of the hall but, as John White thought, 'everything was done for comfort and for fitness of appearance'.[48] The throne was in fact the minister's chair from behind the communion table at Kippen Parish Church, a fine piece of furniture by John Annand of Whytock and Reid in Edinburgh.[49] It was borrowed for the occasion by the artist Sir D. Y. Cameron, an elder at Kippen, who was in charge of decorating the hall for the occasion, and its use represented an interesting conflation of the secular and spiritual spheres!

Before the assembly the Purse-Bearer, who waits upon the Lord High Commissioner, was in touch with Mr J. J. Herdman, the convener of the General Committee, regarding the arrangements for the attendance of the Duke of York. It appeared that the Royal Guard had been having a rehearsal and that it had been decided that His Royal Highness should enter the hall by the front door and thus pass through the assembly hall to the throne gallery. A military band would also be outside the hall. On being informed of these arrangements, John White was vehement in his disapproval. He disliked the military band and told the Purse-Bearer that the Lord High Commissioner could not pass through the hall, since 'a Lord High Commissioner had never passed through the General Assembly for three hundred years and was not going to commence in Dr White's Moderatorial year.'[50]

[48] John White, The High Commissioner and the Hall of Assembly (W) 14.1.
[49] R. W. A. Begg, *The Renovation of Kippen Parish Church 1924–1991*, 6th edn. (Kippen, 1991), pp. 8–9.
[50] White, The High Commissioner.

The matter seemed to be settled until a few days before the assembly when Mr Herdman was summoned to Holyrood Palace to meet Rear Admiral Basil Vernon Brooke, Comptroller and Equerry to the Duke of York. Admiral Brooke said that he was sorry to insist upon any arrangements the Church was making, but that 'he must take the final say'.[51] He insisted that His Royal Highness enter the hall by the front door on this first occasion, but that when there was no guard of honour the other entrance could be used. Herdman tried in vain to maintain adherence to the original arrangements. He immediately reported to John White that in his view it was useless to attempt to argue further and that he would assume that the moderator would acquiesce, however unwillingly, in 'the front door arrangement'. White had no intention of arguing further, but he had no intention, either, of agreeing to the new proposal by Admiral Brooke. He instructed Herdman to inform the Admiral 'that the last word was with the Church and that he, Dr White, had spoken it'.[52] He arranged to meet with Herdman, the Purse-Bearer and Admiral Brooke 'to hear definitely from him that the Lord High Commissioner must enter by the doorway arranged, and that otherwise they could have no Lord High Commissioner present'.[53] As it was, the Duke of York himself was informed of the position and at once agreed to the Church's arrangements.[54] John White later commented:[55]

No one could have been more considerate and sympathetic than the Duke of York the moment it was explained to him what it all meant. We are fortunate in having had as Lord High Commissioner a man of that quick intuition and courtesy that the Duke always shows.

Thus it was that the principle of the separation of the spiritual and civil authorities was recognised symbolically by the presence of the Lord High Commissioner at the union assembly. White was aware of the objections of some, and the reservations of others, in the United Free Church to the continuation of the office, and it was therefore of the utmost importance that the procedures which illustrated the true nature of the relationship between Church and State be observed. He had therefore had no alternative but to say that there would be no Lord High Commissioner if these arrangements would not be carried out. If the Lord High Commissioner had

---

[51] J. J. Herdman to J. White, 30.9.29 (W) 14.1.
[52] White, The High Commissioner.
[53] Ibid.
[54] Mechie, *Lord High Commissioner*, p. 50.
[55] Ibid. Cf. *JW*, p. 263.

entered through the hall it would have cast a shadow over the whole proceedings. It seemed most unfortunate to him that 'the whole question should be raised in this acute form'.[56]

For James Barr and the UF minority, however, the office of itself was unacceptable because of its statutory basis and the terms of the king's commission. Barr had a point in that following the union the commission continued to refer to the Church of Scotland by law established.[57] Even if these words were removed, and they were said to be a mistake, the sovereign still took the coronation oath to 'maintain and preserve' the settlement of the Church of Scotland as established by the Revolution Settlement of 1690. It was this obligation which was referred to by the terms of the commission to the assembly. For Barr this still represented an establishment of religion which had remained unaffected by the Church of Scotland Act of 1921. Barr all along refused to give weight to the general repeal clause of that act which gave precedence to the Articles in any conflict with previous legislation.

(e) synods and presbyteries

An appendix to the draft Basis and Plan of Union contained a scheme of synods and presbyteries for the united Church, and this scheme was altered in the light of comments from presbyteries before reaching its final form. The position was, as John White put it, that the creation of synods and presbyteries was a function of the general assembly and was not subject to the Barrier Act.[58] The new arrangements for these courts would therefore be decided by the first united assembly of the Church. The discussion of the scheme by the union committees, and by the present presbyteries and synods of the two Churches, must therefore be regarded as a preparation for the business of that first assembly. It followed, too, that the scheme could be changed by that assembly and by subsequent ones.

The main change in the scheme between the proposals of 1927 and 1928 concerned the composition of the presbyteries. While the total number of presbyteries was reduced by only one, from sixty-eight to sixty-seven, the distribution was rather different. Four extra presbyteries were created in rural areas in both the highlands and lowlands, while there were five fewer urban presbyteries. Perhaps the most radical suggestion in the committee's first proposals, which bear the marks of John White's

---

[56] Ibid.
[57] Barr, *United Free Church*, pp. 135–6.
[58] John White, Note referred to (W)97.

creative mind, was that the three largest presbyteries be subdivided. Glasgow was to be divided into five presbyteries (St Mungo, centred on the Cathedral; Shettleston in the east; Kelvinside in the north-west; Cathcart in the south; and Govan in the south-west), while Edinburgh would have two (north and south), and the presbytery of Monklands would be created out of the presbytery of Hamilton.[59] It would appear that these suggestions were rejected by the presbyteries concerned in both Churches, and the committee had no alternative but to suggest instead that there be single large presbyteries in each of these three urban areas.[60] The opportunity was missed to create much more workable city presbyteries. It was pointed out by W. S. Provand, clerk to the Church of Scotland's presbytery of Glasgow, that with five presbyteries in the city, there would be a need for a synod of Glasgow in order to oversee the work of the Church in the city.[61] In addition four extra rural presbyteries were created in the scheme of 1928: Penpont was created out of Dumfries, Arbroath out of Forfar, Ross was divided in two (Chanonry and Dingwall, and Easter Ross), and Lochalsh was divided into Lochcarron and Skye. The final scheme was thus inconsistent, in creating smaller units in the country but not in the cities. It also meant that in terms of the Barrier Act the large cities of Glasgow and Edinburgh each counted as one vote in the same way as any of the much smaller rural presbyteries.

One matter, however, did appear within the Plan of Union, and that concerned the membership of synods and presbyteries. As with the general assembly, it was proposed that there be equal numbers of elders and ministers, again something which had not been the case in the Church of Scotland. In addition all the theological professors were to be members of presbyteries, which also reflected the practice in the United Free Church. In the Church of Scotland, only the professors of Divinity, of whom there was one at each of Glasgow, Edinburgh and St Andrews, and two at Aberdeen, were members of presbyteries.[62]

[59] Draft Plan of Union 1927 and 1928 (M) 6.

[60] SRO, CH2/121/38–9, Minutes of the Presbytery of Edinburgh, 19 October, 2 and 9 November 1927, and 27 June 1928; CH3/111/50, Minutes of the United Free Church Presbytery of Edinburgh, 1 November 1927; CH3/171/23 Minutes of the United Free Church Presbytery of Hamilton, 13 December 1927; Glasgow City Archives, CH2/171/30, Minutes of the Presbytery of Glasgow 8 December 1927. The minutes of the Church of Scotland Presbytery of Hamilton simply refer to the Basis and Plan of Union in general terms (Office of the Clerk of the Presbytery of Hamilton, Hamilton, Minutes of the Presbytery of Hamilton, 6 and 13 December 1927). It has not been possible to locate the Minutes of the United Free Church Presbytery of Glasgow 1924–9.

[61] W. S. Provand to J. White, 13.4.27 (W)10.4.

[62] Mair, *Digest*, p. 131.

Most controversy in the Church of Scotland, however, was occasioned by the proposal that retired ministers were to continue to have a seat in both presbyteries and synods, and that additional elders be elected to these courts to maintain equal numbers. In the Established Church, ministers who had demitted their charge, or who had assistants and successors, were no longer members of presbytery.[63] This proposal was objected to by many presbyteries in the Church of Scotland. According to Cromarty Smith,[64] very few retired ministers in the Church of Scotland would wish to have a seat in presbytery, and, if this were rejected, there would be no reason for additional elders to be co-opted in order to balance the numbers. He thought, too, that the presence of retired ministers was not popular at present among the younger UF ministers. A compromise in his view would be to give them consultative status.

These proposals met with outright rejection by the members of the Scottish Church Society. They regarded both measures, that retired ministers should continue as members of presbyteries, and that presbyteries could co-opt additional elders who did not therefore have a commission from a kirk session, as fundamental changes in Presbyterianism. Presbyteries were courts, and thus should only be composed of those who exercise rule in the Church. Retired ministers no longer exercised such responsibility and the introduction of their membership of presbyteries, and hence also of synods and assemblies, would be an alteration of 'the very nature of the constitution of these courts'.[65] Since the higher courts were a gathering of the jurisdiction of the lower courts, this was the intrusion into these courts of those without such authority. Retired ministers, it was said, 'have no jurisdiction, they have laid it down, they are not in exercise of it. They are not, therefore, qualified to intromit with the jurisdiction which belongs to others.'[66] Their continuing membership was also not just, in that they would have the same say in the framing of a presbytery's decisions as those who had the responsibility of carrying them out.

The opposition of the high churchmen to the co-option of additional elders was based on similar grounds. This measure, in their view, was the introduction of a 'radical novelty' since, according to the previous practice of the Church of Scotland, elders sat in presbyteries as the commissioned representatives of

[63] Ibid.
[64] J. C. Smith to J. White, 23.6.28 (W) 11.4.
[65] SCS, *Notes*, p. 9.
[66] Ibid., p. 10.

kirk sessions and in no other way. It would also inflict an injustice since those co-opted elders would give a greater representation to certain kirk sessions. Another consideration was that the jurisdiction of kirk sessions was invaded, since they would have no say over the election of one of their number to sit in the presbytery.

According to John White, the Church of Scotland committee had much sympathy with the comments of presbyteries, if not with all the arguments advanced by the Scottish Church Society, and had originally planned to suggest that both professors and retired ministers should not have seats in presbytery.[67] Lord Sands, however, could not understand the fuss over retired ministers being allowed to continue as members of presbytery since it had long been in operation in the United Free Church.[68] In order for the united Church to begin its work immediately, a temporary scheme was proposed which would then be reconsidered after two years under the Barrier Act. In the meantime, then, the retired ministers of the Church of Scotland would be in the same position as those of the UF Church.[69] If this was not done, as White pointed out, there would be more former UF ministers in the presbyteries of the Church. It was a matter which could be changed by the united Church, but as with so many of those compromises it has stood the test of time, and it is only in recent years that the situation has changed. Ministers who have retired since 1985 can continue to retain a seat in presbytery only until the age of 75.[70]

The result of these proposals was to increase the size of presbyteries, particularly those with large numbers of retired ministers, since additional elders also had to be elected to preserve equality of numbers. It also had the effect of increasing the overall age of members and the number of those who did not exercise the active pastoral charge of a congregation. Since the union of 1929, and the growth of other non-parochial appointments, the number of ministers without a pastoral charge who are also members of presbyteries has increased rather than diminished. The opposition in the Auld Kirk to this development would have been more muted if this had not also meant an increase in the number of elected elders to preserve what they saw as an unnecessary feature, that of equality between ministers and elders. It could be argued that the practice of both Churches prior to the union

[67] John White, Speech to the General Assembly, May 1928, p. 21 (W) 98.
[68] Lord Sands to J. White, 20.6.28 (W) 11.4.
[69] White, Speech to the General Assembly, May 1928, p. 21.
[70] Andrew Herron, *The Law and Practice of the Kirk* (Glasgow, 1995), pp. 174–5.

contained an element of clericalism. In the Church of Scotland there were always more ministers than elders in presbyteries, while in the United Free Church there were a greater number of ministers present by virtue of their ordination than because of the responsibility they exercised within the bounds.

Another issue in the first draft of the Plan of Union, on which several Church of Scotland presbyteries had commented adversely, was the respective powers of presbyteries in relation to committees of the general assembly.[71] The issue arose in relation to stipend arrangements and contributions by congregations to the Maintenance of the Ministry Fund, and with regard to the amalgamation of congregations to secure greater efficiency in the work of the Church. As John White said at the assembly in May 1928, presbyteries had disapproved of any reference which seemed to empower standing committees of the assembly to interfere with and supersede the constitutional functions of presbyteries.[72] Changes were made to remove such fears, and further changes were carried out before the final version was approved.

With regard to the contributions of congregations to the Maintenance of the Ministry Fund, for example, the document stated that it would be the duty of the presbytery and the committee 'acting in concert' to take appropriate measures to ensure that payments were made.[73] It was changed to say that the presbytery would act 'in consultation with' the committee. White was anxious to make it clear that no committee of the assembly could interfere with the constitutional functions of presbyteries. On the other hand he thought that presbyteries would welcome the assistance of a committee when dealing with the amalgamation of parishes or with delicate matters of finance. In such cases he thought that presbyteries 'may be only too glad to welcome the assistance of a Committee to carry the onus and the odium of responsibility'.[74] With these proposals the Scottish Church Society detected a move towards a centralised bureaucratic Church and away from the traditional Presbyterian system.[75] Even with the changes in the wording of the Plan, the Society felt that it still was not clear which of the parties, the presbytery or the committee, would have the final say when a dispute arose. The answer, of course, is that the final decision would rest with the assembly.

[71] White, Speech to the General Assembly, May 1928, p. 24.
[72] Ibid.
[73] Ibid., pp. 11–12.
[74] Ibid., p. 24.
[75] SCS, Notes, pp. 13–15.

(f) kirk sessions

Very little was said regarding kirk sessions since it was agreed that the method of election of elders, and the powers and duties of these courts, should continue as before and follow the regulations previously applicable within each Church. The only change mentioned in the Plan was that the Formula to be signed by elders would be the same as that which had now been agreed for ministers. With regard to the election of elders there were differences between the two Churches. In the Church of Scotland it was clear that election was a matter for the kirk session, but in recent years sessions had increasingly adopted the practice of consulting the congregation. In the United Free Church election was by the congregation, but the session was the final judge of those selected. Both methods of election have continued to be valid within the Church of Scotland and kirk sessions are at liberty to adopt either method plus the method of 'signed lists' by congregations.[76] A dual practice concerning the election of elders would thus continue, and the opportunity was not taken of trying to come to a common mind on this subject.

The financial affairs of congregations would also continue to be administered in different ways. The attempt was not made to find a uniform method of government at the local level, and the appeal of one elder of the United Free Church that this should be done was not heard.[77] If the present methods continued, in his view, union might take place in name, but the old rivalry would continue. Thus it was stated in the Plan that Deacons' Courts, Committees of Management, and Congregational Boards should also continue to elect members and operate as before. At the union of 1900 the two different systems of dealing with congregational finance and property of the former UP constitution, with the Board of Management and directly elected office-bearers, and that of the Deacons' Court of the Free Church, were continued. In some cases a former Free Church had replaced the Deacons' Court with a Congregational Board. To this would now be added the historic *quoad omnia* constitutions of the old parishes plus the congregational boards of the more recently constituted *quoad sacra* parishes of the Church of Scotland. In the view of the legal agents of the Auld Kirk, there was much to be said for a uniform constitution to be agreed for all the congregations of the united Church.[78] A more recent commentator has also said that there

---

[76] Herron, *Law and Practice*, pp. 282–5.
[77] *Record*, April 1923, p. 166.
[78] Menzies & Thomson WS to J. White, 22.3.26 (W) 10.2.

would be clear advantages in adopting a uniform system.[79] The issue had been glossed over when the unions took place in 1900 and 1929 in the hope that once united the two bodies would grow together. Instead, as the different types of congregational constitutions have been allowed to survive, new generations are brought up in their separate traditions and become proud of their distinctive way of doing things. It has been impracticable to insist on uniformity but congregations have been encouraged to adopt the Model Deed of Constitution as *quoad sacra* parishes with congregational boards to administer their temporal affairs.

The one real difficulty for White and his colleagues was that of the function of kirk sessions. According to the *Manual of Practice and Procedure in the United Free Church,* it belonged to the session not only to regulate the hours of worship but also its 'forms and modes' while for its proper conduct the minister was responsible to the presbytery.[80] He understood that in practice the UF Church did not differ from the Church of Scotland in that ministers were held to be responsible, subject to the presbytery, for the 'forms and modes' of worship, and the *Manual* did not thus reflect the true position. To make the matter clear, a further sentence was added in the final draft of the Plan when dealing with the 'Function, Ordination, and Induction of Ministers'. This sentence stated that 'The ministry of the Word, the conduct of Public Worship, and the dispensing of the Sacraments belong to the Minister, subject to the control and direction of the Presbytery.'[81] It was thus made clear that all matters regarding the content and conduct of worship pertained to the teaching rather than the ruling eldership. Such a statement had been urged by the Scottish Church Society.[82] It was pointed out that, according to the UF *Manual,* the session made provision for special services and for the celebration of the Lord's Supper. A quorum of the session had to be present at the dispensation of communion, which included its celebration in the homes of the sick and aged members of the Church. John White had originally thought of a compromise proposal whereby it would be recognised that the administration of the sacraments belonged to the minister, but that there should normally be two elders at least in attendance when the sacraments were celebrated.[83] Joseph Mitchell pointed out, however, that it

---

[79] Herron, *Law and Practice*, p. 21.

[80] White, Speech to the General Assembly, May 1928, p. 23. *Manual of the United Free Church* (1927), p. 4.

[81] Cox, p. 413. John White, Speech to the General Assembly, 21 November 1928, pp. 9–10 (W) 99.

[82] SCS, *Notes*, pp. 4–5.

[83] J. White to Lord Sands, 3.5.28 (W) 11.3.

was not the practice in either Church for there to be two elders present at every baptism, and that it would be difficult to advance grounds on which elders had to be present at one sacrament and not the other.[84] In this regard the final decision was more in line with previous Church of Scotland than with United Free Church practice. The minister was said to be responsible for the way in which the sacraments were celebrated; the session did not have to be constituted, and elders were not required to distribute the elements. In the Church of Scotland elders thus take part by invitation of the minister who may invite others to assist in this way.[85]

(g) congregations and parishes

John White agreed with many of the presbyteries of his own Church that some reference should be made to the territorial system of parishes in the Plan of Union.[86] There should be some way of indicating that, as stated in Article III, the Church had a distinctive call and duty 'to bring the ordinances of religion to the people in every parish of Scotland through a territorial ministry'. It was, of course, as he recognised at the assembly in May 1928, the responsibility of presbyteries to frame schemes for the ministerial oversight of defined areas, but it should be made clear that the territorial principle should govern. There was a great need to meet the unsatisfactory religious condition of a vast portion of the population. It was thus the first duty of presbyteries after the union 'to make systematic provision by mapping the country out into ecclesiastical districts for bringing the Gospel to the doors of the entire population.' This obligation was written into the final version of the Plan under the heading 'Sundry Matters', where it was said to be an early duty of presbyteries to readjust parochial and other areas where necessary, and to assign spheres of pastoral labour and responsibility to the ministers of particular charges. Until this had been done the previous churches of the Church of Scotland would remain in use for the purposes of the proclamation of banns. The Scottish Church Society welcomed this new clause, but it was not thought to be definite enough. The ultimate aim should be the re-emergence of the ancient parochial system.[87]

[84] J. Mitchell to J. White, 3.5.28 (W) 11.3.

[85] Cf. Herron, *Law and Practice*, p. 159: 'It is a custom of long standing that the Elders assist the Minister in the distribution of the elements, but there is no law requiring this to be so. At, say, a Dedication Service for the Woman's Guild it would be fitting and perfectly in order that Guild members should render this service.'

[86] White, Speech to the General Assembly, May 1928, pp. 12–13.

[87] SCS, *Notes*, p. 20.

It proved to be difficult, however, to introduce the concept of a parish church to the former congregations of the United Free Church. This problem showed itself prior to union when churches had to be renamed to distinguish them from their neighbouring congregations. What name should be chosen? Should the word 'parish' occur in every title or in none? One of the difficulties was pointed out to John White by W. H. Harrowes, minister of St Enoch's United Free Church in Glasgow.[88] It had been assumed by many in his Church that, just as the title 'United Free' would be dropped from the nomenclature of their churches, so the name of 'parish' would no longer be used by those belonging to the pre-union Church of Scotland. In the United Free Church the term 'parish' meant 'Established Church', as used by the historic *quoad omnia* parishes which had civil functions, whereas in the Church of Scotland it was taken to mean a *quoad sacra* parish which had purely spiritual and ecclesiastical functions. Lord Sands appreciated the difficulty which arose from the popular use of the term 'parish' to distinguish the Established Church from the United Free or some other Church.[89] He felt that until a new sub-division of the country into ecclesiastical parishes had been carried out, no particular church could officially call itself 'the parish Church'.

According to John White, it was often the little things which gave rise to the most discussion and bother, and the use or disuse of the term 'parish' was an instance.[90] It was clear, in his view, that the territorial reference in the Articles Declaratory was to an ecclesiastical and not a civil parish and hence the term could only refer to a parish *quoad sacra*. White agreed with Sands that the key to the issue of nomenclature was that of territorial division, but the names were being decided before parish boundaries were drawn up and this was a large part of the problem. Another factor was that this matter was being discussed prior to the union so that the names of churches would be agreed as soon as possible thereafter. White agreed with one correspondent that the members of the new presbyteries were not being given a chance to gain confidence in each other before settling this controversial question.[91]

It fell to the first commission of assembly, meeting on 20th November 1929, to receive a memorandum on this matter from

---

[88] W. H. Harrowes to J. White, 28.5.29 (W) 12.9.
[89] Lord Sands to J. White, 1.6.29 (W) 13.1.
[90] John White, Parish (W) 49.
[91] F. C. Donald to J. White, 1.7.29 (W) 13.4; J. White to F. C. Donald, 19.8.29 (W) 13.6.

the Continuing Union Committee.[92] The memorandum suggested that as few changes as possible were to be made in nomenclature, and the principle was laid down that all churches in a parish were of equal standing. No name or part of a name should convey any suggestion of inequality. It was clearly stated, too, that all charges within a parish 'are obviously parish churches *quoad sacra'*. No congregation should be pressurised into adopting the term 'parish' in its name, but equally no congregation should be prevented from using that word. The statement also urged presbyteries to proceed with the task of renaming churches as soon as possible and to carry out immediately the assignment of spheres of pastoral labour and responsibility to ministers. In spite of this memorandum, the presbytery of Linlithgow and Falkirk decided by a narrow margin, on the motion of T. Alexander of Bo'ness, that the term parish should not be used by any church within the bounds.[93] On the other hand, the presbytery of Glasgow was told at its February meeting that all the names had been agreed with only one exception.[94] In this respect the official usage of the united Church has come to approximate to that of the former Church of Scotland rather than that of the United Free Church. In 1961 the general assembly quoted the authorisation of the word 'parish' by the commission of 1929, but then went on to urge the use of the word 'parish' in the naming of all Churches.[95]

(h) the training of the ministry

The way by which ministers would be trained in the united Church was set out in the Plan of Union, but the final arrangements would have to wait until after the union and would involve an act of parliament and agreements with each of the universities. The training of ministers was a clear example of the different character of the two Churches, and neither body had expressed dissatisfaction with its own procedures. Ministers of the Church of Scotland were trained in the divinity faculties of the universities whose professors were drawn from its ministry and subscribed to the Westminster Confession of Faith. Although only one of the chairs, that of Systematic Theology at Aberdeen, was a church appointment, the patronage of the other chairs was usually exercised after unofficial consultation with the Church.[96] In

---

[92] Memorandum anent Naming of Charges and Delimitation of Areas (W) 14.4; *Scotsman*, 21.11.29.

[93] *Scotsman*, 11.12.29.

[94] *Scotsman*, 12.2.30.

[95] Herron, *Law and Practice*, p. 5.

[96] Hugh Watt, *New College, Edinburgh: A Centenary History* (Edinburgh, 1946), p. 131.

addition the Church had been seeking to improve the practical training of its ministers by the development of Pastoral Institutes in connection with the divinity faculties. The wide-ranging Committee on Legislation and Church Reform made this proposal as early as 1897 in order to supplement the special lectures which had been given by visiting ministers since 1870.[97] By 1929 there were Pastoral Institutes in Edinburgh, Glasgow and St Andrews, while short courses of lectures were given to students at Aberdeen.[98] Ministers of the United Free Church were trained in the Church's own colleges in Edinburgh, Glasgow and Aberdeen. The professors were appointed by the general assembly and their stipends were wholly derived from Church sources. The Church thus exercised direct and sole supervision of the training of its ministers through its committees and courts.

As Hugh Watt put it,[99] while there were those in the Church of Scotland who simply wished the faculties to be enlarged, and those in the United Free Church who argued for augmented colleges, the majority came to the view that some form of amalgamation was necessary. In addition, the union was seen more positively by some as an opportunity to develop the study and teaching of theology in Scotland. The question of tests for the theological chairs had previously been examined in 1890 by the Scottish Universities Commission.[100] The general assembly had expressed itself willing to look at any measures which would broaden the scope of theological education while guaranteeing the Christian faith of professors of theology. It was important that a close relationship be maintained between the Church and the Divinity Halls. One way forward might be for the colleges of other Churches to form part of the universities where appropriate.[101]

The issue was examined by a committee of the General Council of the University of Glasgow, which presented a report on the relationship of the universities and the theological colleges in 1907.[102] The report spoke of the possibility of the faculties being enlarged by the Churches founding chairs in the universities. The patronage of such chairs could be vested in a board of curators drawn from the Churches thus involved, and professors would not be subject to doctrinal or ecclesiastical tests. Information

---

[97] Stewart Mechie, 'Education for the Ministry since the Reformation II', in *RSCHS*, 14 (1962), pp. 174–6.

[98] Ibid., pp. 177–8.

[99] Watt, *New College*, p. 131.

[100] *C of S Rep.*, 1890, p. 1075.

[101] John White, The Universities and Theological Colleges (W) 99.

[102] Glasgow University Archives, DC 183/1/4, Minutes of Half-Yearly Meetings of the University of Glasgow General Council, 18 October 1907, p. 116.

about the different relationships between universities and theological colleges in the United States and in England was sought, and copies of the report were sent to the Scottish universities and to the Churches. While the universities expressed some interest in the proposals, no action was taken.[103] None of the non-established Churches gave an unequivocal welcome to the proposals, as one result would be that the Churches would not have direct control over the training of their students. Discussions were also held under the auspices of the Church Union Association to seek ways by which the theological education offered by all the Protestant Churches in Scotland could be rationalised and shared.[104] One proposal argued that the study and teaching of theology should be removed from the universities and all the colleges combined into one national college for the Churches in Scotland. A conference on this subject in 1912 called for greater co-operation between the various theological institutions.[105] One area of partnership was in the field of postgraduate studies, as at Edinburgh where a postgraduate school of theology was set up by the university faculty and New College just after the First World War.[106]

It was the prospect of union that focused the issue for the two Churches and gave the necessary impetus for a solution to be found. The third of the sub-committees dealing with the Basis and Plan of Union was concerned with the training of the ministry. At an early meeting of this sub-committee, the Church of Scotland members laid stress on the desirability of the faculties of theology remaining within the university system. The UF representatives, on the other hand, spoke of the difficulties connected with the questions of patronage, tests and control, arising from the relationship of the chairs of theology to the State and to the universities.[107] This was the problem in a nutshell. The United Free Church disapproved of the special arrangement whereby only Church of Scotland ministers could be appointed to theological chairs, and of the statutory tests which were applied to these chairs. It felt that the present arrangements in the faculties were in conflict with the new position of the Church in the light of the Church of Scotland

---

[103] Ibid., 17 October 1908, pp. 161–5. Cf. Glasgow University Archives, C/1/1/15, Minutes of the University Court, p. 74.

[104] Church Union Association, *Report of Conference on the Union of the Theological Colleges*, held on 7 March 1912.

[105] Ibid., p. 6.

[106] Sir Alfred Ewing, 'The Scottish Universities: The Effect of a United National Church', in *Scots Observer*, 3 October 1929; A. C. Cheyne, *Studies in Scottish Church History* (Edinburgh, 1999), p. 297.

[107] Minutes of Sub-Committee III, 22 September 1926 (PGA) 1.

Act of 1921. Such arrangements gave a privileged position to one Church and limited the choice of the universities as to who could teach theology. Thus the status of the professors of the Church within the universities would have to be one which was within the reach of any other Church which desired it and which met the requirements of the universities.[108] In other words, this matter was one in which the position of other Churches had to be safeguarded as set out in the Act of 1921. On the other hand, the UF Church wished more control over the teaching of its students than could exist in the universities which were autonomous bodies supported by the State. If the first condition was met, and professors need not belong to the united Church, then it was difficult to see how the second condition, adequate supervision by the Church, could also be fulfilled. Some kind of compromise would be necessary if a combination of the two systems was to be acceptable. The first draft of the Plan of Union recognised that two such systems could not simply be amalgamated, and that a large amount of adjustment would be necessary.[109]

An early suggestion discussed in the United Free Church committee was one that sought to combine the resources of the faculties and the colleges with the 'least possible interference' to existing arrangements.[110] It envisaged the continuation of the present provision of academic theology in the faculties, but free from tests. The existing chairs would be retained and would cover the following subjects: Hebrew and Semitics, Church History, Divinity (transformed into a chair of Comparative Religion, or of the Philosophy and History of Religion), and Hellenistic Greek. These chairs would provide training for the students of all Churches who might wish to avail themselves of it. Instruction in further theological subjects would be provided by the united Church in colleges supported and controlled by the Church itself. These professors, however, along with those occupying the existing chairs, would constitute the university faculty of theology. It would be open to any other Church to claim a similar recognition and status within the university, provided it met the necessary academic requirements.

This scheme preserved far more independence to the continuing Church colleges, although it also envisaged the professors becoming part of the university. Such an arrangement would not have been so readily accepted by the universities, which might not recognise professors appointed by, and under the control of,

---

[108] UFC, Sub-Committee on Amalgamation of Theological Faculties, etc., Interim Report, 17 March 1926 (UFC).

[109] Plan of Union, p. 21 (W) 76.

[110] UFC, Draft Statement re University Divinity Chairs (UFC) and (M) 12.1.

an outside body. It also envisaged a division in theological study and education between that offered by the university and that provided by the Church. This division could be described as one between the purely academic study of religion, and the confessional and vocational study of Christian theology. Hence the chair of Divinity was to be concerned with the study of Comparative Religion. The point was made by Sir Alfred Ewing, the principal of Edinburgh University, however, that the faculty of divinity within a university also served a vocational purpose in a similar way to the faculties of law and medicine. He said:[111]

> It does not treat theology as a mere subject of general culture. It is a training school for the Presbyterian ministry, providing ordinands of the Church of Scotland with that special knowledge which is required to qualify them for admission to the pastorate.

The professors of the United Free Church colleges considered alternative schemes of amalgamation which were broadly similar to the one outlined by the committee. One proposal envisaged the universities' own faculties ceasing to exist once life-interests had expired and then recognising the church colleges as forming the faculties of theology.[112] In another scheme, the existing chairs in the divinity faculties would become chairs in the faculties of arts. The chair of Hebrew would be part of a department of Semitic languages, Ecclesiastical History part of the History department, New Testament Greek part of Classics, and Philosophy of Religion would belong to the Philosophy department. This would leave the colleges teaching theology as affiliated institutions, in which task they could be joined by the colleges of other Churches.[113]

In the event a far more integrated approach was the one favoured by the joint sub-committee. While the UF members favoured affiliation, the Church of Scotland members wished incorporation.[114] Three general principles came to form the basis on which an agreement could be reached:[115]

[111] Ewing, 'Scottish Universities'.

[112] New College Library, Edinburgh, New College Archives and Edinburgh University Faculty of Divinity Archives, Amalgamation of Theological Faculties: A. Outline of alternative scheme, AA.1.5.22.

[113] New College Library, Edinburgh, New College Archives and Edinburgh University Faculy of Divinity Archives, Amalgamation of Theological Faculties: B. Draft Scheme of Affiliation, AA.1.5.22.

[114] C of S, Union Committee, Report of Sub-Committee No. III, 10 February 1927 (PGA) 4.

[115] Ibid. Cf. UFC, Supplementary Joint Report on Training of the Ministry: and relation of Divinity Halls to the Universities, (PGA) 4; Churches Conference, Union Committees, Report by Sub-Committees No. III, (PGA) 4.

The *first* is that the existing University Theological Chairs, while they should be freed from the statutory tests now imposed upon the holders of such Chairs, should be continued in some form in which they would still be serviceable for the instruction of the students of the Church. The *second* is that the relations between the Theological Colleges and the Universities should be as close as possible. The *third* is that the Church must retain effective control over those to whom the doctrinal instruction of its Ministry is to be entrusted.

The difficulties of the United Free Church over tests would be met, and the Church would no longer occupy a privileged position in that respect. But in order that the future occupants of the chairs would not be repugnant to the Church, it would have a say in the appointments to chairs in the enlarged faculties in the universities. The sub-committee thus had to ask the universities whether they would agree to appointment boards being constituted for these chairs, and to the Church having a preponderant voice in these boards.[116] They also had to know how far the universities would be prepared to accept chairs, the occupants of which would be appointed solely by the Church. These chairs would be for the existing professors of the church colleges and their successors. In addition there was the question as to how far independent colleges would be regarded as forming part of the university system. A further provision of the scheme was that the universities would agree to frame the theological curriculum so as to suit the instruction prescribed by the Church for candidates for the ministry.[117]

Discussions were held with the universities as to how these proposals might be implemented. The principals of the four universities approved generally of the plan to enlarge the faculties of divinity by the addition of the professors of the United Free Church colleges. Sir James Irvine of St Andrews said that his university would have a strong claim to an increase in the size of its divinity faculty to correspond with these accessions to the faculties in the other universities.[118] The principals were agreed that the universities should retain the right of appointment to chairs, and that the proposed new boards should have the power of nomination rather than of appointment. There were several

---

[116] Minutes of Sub-Committee III, 2 February 1927 (PGA) 1.

[117] C of S, Union Committee, Report of Sub-Committee III, 10 February 1927.

[118] Précis of the Reports of the Deputations to the Principals of the four Universities with regard to the teaching of Theology after the contemplated Union of the Churches (IRV).

precedents for such joint boards, including the arrangements made for filling chairs in agriculture and medicine.

The basis for an agreement was reached at a conference of representatives of the Church committee and of the four Scottish university courts in July 1927.[119] It was agreed that the closest possible relation should be maintained between the united Church and the university with regard to theological teaching. The existing theological chairs would be retained but free from their present statutory tests. The Church would retain control of the course of training prescribed for its students, but facilities should also be made available for the training of students of other Churches. In view of the increase in the number of students, the faculties of divinity should be enlarged. Arrangements would be made for the existing professors of the United Free Church college to be associated with the university.

With regard to the university chairs, it was agreed that the crown and the university would relinquish their respective rights of patronage and that appointments in future would be made by an electoral board consisting of equal numbers of representatives appointed by the university court and by the united Church. Any appointment would have to be approved by at least two-thirds of the whole members of the board. The University of Glasgow proposed that the board should have a majority of Church representatives, and there was thus no need for the reference to a two-thirds majority in making an appointment.[120] It was also stated that, should other Churches wish to participate in the scheme, powers would be taken to enlarge the membership of the board. This clause met the desire of the United Free Church that the arrangements would not be seen as giving an exclusive privilege to the united Church.

With regard to the chairs in the United Free Church college, those holding such appointments at the date of the union would become professors in the university provided the Church guaranteed their present stipend. When the chair fell vacant, an advisory committee, consisting of representatives of the Church and the university, would report as to whether the chair should be continued with or without modification of subject matter or other conditions. It would also be open to the advisory committee to recommend the substitution of a lectureship. In the final

[119]C of S, Union Committee, Report of Sub-Committee III, 23 July 1927. (GUC) 9 and 12 October 1927, p. 146.

[120]University of Glasgow, Memorandum of points for consideration by the University Court, suggested by the Joint Sub-Committee of the Church of Scotland and the United Free Church, 20 April 1927 (W) 99.

arrangements, the board of nomination would also serve as the advisory committee to avoid the creation of yet another body. Nomination to these chairs would be made by the Church, subject to confirmation by the university court. A condition of appointment would be that the professor should be, and continue to be, an ordinand or ordained minister of the Church. The senate of Edinburgh University wished the church chairs to be appointed in the same way as the university chairs, or, if still nominated by the Church, by a board rather than by the assembly as a whole.[121] Both Edinburgh and Glasgow thought that at least one university representative should be a member of the nominating board.[122] These suggestions were not reflected in the agreements following the passing of the Act in 1932, but a significant change was made by new arrangements between the Church and the university courts in 1950. The appointment to 'church chairs' would in future be by the same board of nomination as for university chairs, and the appointment would thus no longer be restricted to ministers of the Kirk.[123] The Church would meet the salaries and superannuation provision of these chairs and the university would, in turn, remit to the Church a proportion of students' fees. Further clauses made provision for the college buildings to be made available for the use of the enlarged faculties, for the university professors to be 'associated in the closest possible way' with the governing body of the colleges, and for the appointment of a principal or other administrative head of each college. All students training for the ministry of the Church would be required to become matriculated students of the university.

The scheme was sent down to presbyteries in the Church of Scotland for comment, but only twenty-four made returns. Of these twelve expressed complete approval while the others were concerned with certain aspects of the scheme.[124] Five presbyteries wished the tests for professors to remain, while two thought that all divinity professors should continue to be ministers of the Kirk. One presbytery thought that the appointment of a professor should require a majority of the representatives of both the Church and the university instead of a two-thirds majority of the whole board. One spoke in favour of students being integrated into the life of the university rather than being separated in church colleges. Sufficient support had been received, however, to proceed with the scheme. Professor D. M. Kay of St Andrews proposed

---

[121] Prospective Church Union (EUD) 1VA.
[122] W. A. Curtis to Principal of the University, 12.7.30 (EUD) 1VA.
[123] C of S Rep., 1950, pp. 488–93.
[124] Minutes of the C of S Sub-Committeee, 14 March 1928 (PGA) 1.

unsuccessfully that the electoral boards should adhere to the usage 'that those who prepare divinity students should themselves be ordained'.[125] He had previously proposed a similar motion at a meeting of the faculty of divinity at St Andrews.[126] Principal Galloway of St Mary's College had pointed out, however, that such would amount to the imposition of a test, and would therefore reopen a question that had already been settled in the discussions. The faculty agreed instead that in most cases it would be desirable that the chairs should be filled 'by those who were ministers of the Church of Scotland or some other Christian Church'. This motion was subsequently agreed by the university court.[127] At the assembly that year Kay put forward this suggestion and it was accepted by John White.[128] Its terms, however, were not reflected in any of the agreements which were later made with the universities. The fact that the Church had an equal representation on the boards of nomination, and that any nomination had to secure a two-thirds majority, was regarded as satisfying the interests of the Church. Attempts in the sub-committee by Professors Kay and Curtis to have the patronage of the chair of Systematic Theology at Aberdeen retained by the synod of Aberdeen were also unsuccessful.[129] In both the Act, and in the subsequent agreement between the Church and the university court, however, the previous method of appointment to this chair was to be continued.

When it came to discussing the legislation which would be required, it became clear that the universities, while agreeing with the broad principles involved, faced different circumstances in the way in which the new arrangements would work. The way forward was thus for the Act to contain the minimum necessary in order that each university might enter into an agreement with the Church. Further discussions on the terms of the legislation did not take place until a year after the union of the Churches when a joint conference of the university courts took place at Perth.[130] A draft bill had been drawn up by the court of St Andrews University as a basis for discussion. One matter of principle on which the universities were not in agreement was the abolition of tests.

[125] Ibid.
[126] St Andrews University Library, Special Collections, UY 408, Minutes of the Faculty of Divinity, St Mary's College, 5.3.28.
[127] (StAUC) 16.3.28, p. 57.
[128] *Glasgow Herald*, 26.5.28.
[129] Minutes of the C of S Sub-Committee, 14 March and 10 October 1928; Minutes of Sub-Committee III, 14 March 1928.
[130] (GUC) 13 November 1930; Minute of Conference of Representatives of the Four Scottish University Courts, 17 October 1930 (GUC) 517752.

Aberdeen had favoured their retention, in that both the former Church professors and the holders of the university chairs should be ministers of the Church. The universities agreed, however, that, as far as legislation was concerned, the statutory tests should be abolished. The point was raised as to whether a university could make a separate ordinance in agreement with the Church for the holder of a chair to be a minister of the Church of Scotland, but this was not felt to be a matter for the legislation. The conference then discussed whether the appointment should be made by an electoral board, as in the original proposal, or whether a board of nomination should have the power to make a nomination to the university court which would then make the appointment. Electoral boards were favoured by Aberdeen,[131] but it was agreed, by only ten votes to eight, that the appointment should be made through a board of nomination, and that patronage should be vested in the university courts. The boards of nomination would contain equal numbers of both Church and university representatives and a nomination would have to receive the support of two-thirds of the members. If a nomination was not made within six months, the right of appointment reverted to the university court. This time limit was subsequently increased to twelve months. The size of each board was to be left to the agreements between the Church and each university. In the event each board would consist of six representatives from each body. The way by which the former United Free Church colleges would be incorporated into the universities did not need to be included in the Act and would be the subject of separate arrangements. A further conference was held later that year when Aberdeen again proposed that electoral boards should be preferred, but this motion was not supported.[132]

The conference then met with the Church representatives who indicated that the draft bill had been approved in principle by the committee and by the commission of assembly.[133] The Church had approved the change from electoral boards to boards of nomination, although it would mean that the university courts would possess the power of veto. It was pointed out, however, that neither the university nor the Church could appoint anyone to a chair 'who was obnoxious to either', and 'practically no one

---

[131] (AUC) 11 October 1927, p. 501.

[132] (GUC) 8 January 1931; Minute of Conference of Representatives of the Four Scottish University Courts, 13 December 1930 (GUC) 51754.

[133] Minute of Conference between Representatives of the four Scottish University Courts and Representatives of the Committee of the Church of Scotland on the Training for the Ministry, 13 December 1930 (GUC) 51754.

would be nominated by the boards of nomination whom the university court would not appoint'. The universities had also been in favour of dropping the reference to the possibility of similar agreements being made with other Churches, whereby their teachers of theology might become university professors. This provision was retained at the request of the Church, it being an important aspect of the former United Free Church view relating to religious equality. A further consultation took place with representatives of the United Free Church (Continuing) which resulted in their students being eligible for bursaries.[134]

The Universities (Scotland) Act was passed on 16th June 1932.[135] It made over the patronage of the theological chairs to the university courts and gave powers to the courts to establish boards of nomination consisting of equal numbers of university and church representatives and to found 'church chairs'. Provisions were also made to separate the principalship of St Mary's College in St Andrews from the chair of Divinity and allowing Aberdeen, in filling the chair of Systematic Theology, to follow the existing procedure involving the synod of Aberdeen. In addition, university courts were free to enter into similar arrangements with other Churches. The tests relating to theological chairs were abolished.

Agreements were then made by each of the universities with the Church. St Andrews was in a different position from the other centres since no college had been established there by the Free or United Free Church of Scotland. The point regarding the need to strengthen the faculty at St Andrews had been made in the early discussions and had been agreed in principle by the Church representatives.[136] The university court of St Andrews wrote to the other universities making the point that the faculty in St Andrews could only compare with the other faculties after the union of the Churches if it received some accession of strength from the teaching resources of the Church Colleges.[137] In particular, if the doctrinal and practical religious teaching would be in the hands of church professors in the other faculties, a difficulty would arise if the faculty in St Andrews was not strengthened by professors who were ministers of the Church. In the view of the staff of the college in Glasgow, however, it would be invidious for

[134] (GUC) 14 May 1931; (EUC) 17 April 1931.
[135] Cox, (1935), pp. 479–82.
[136] Memorandum of Conference of Representatives of the Joint Committee of the Church of Scotland and the United Free Church and Representatives of the University Court, 21 April 1927 (IRV).
[137] (StAUC) 18.11.27, pp. 16–17; The Secretary of the University Court, St Andrews to the Secretary of the University Court, Edinburgh, 22.11.27 (EUD); (AUC) 13 December 1927, p. 524; (GUC) 8 December 1927.

them to name one of their number who would be transferred to St Andrews.[138] In any case, since the teaching of Practical Theology was required in all of the faculties, there would not be a spare teacher of that subject available. It became clear that the best way to meet the situation at St Andrews was for the Church to agree to pay the salaries of the extra professors. According to the Minute of Agreement, there would be chairs in St Mary's College of Systematic Theology and of Practical Theology and Christian Ethics.[139]

At Glasgow, three chairs were transferred from the church college to the university, those of Systematic Theology, Old Testament Language and Literature and New Testament Language and Literature. The chair of Church History in the college was suppressed.[140] The university court did not agree to a chair in Practical Theology, although such was recommended by the faculty of divinity.[141] This meant that the professor at Glasgow did not hold a university chair and was a professor in the church college alone. This position would change in 1939 when the occupant of the chair, Arthur J. Gossip, became a university professor.[142] On his retiral in 1945, however, the university chair was again suppressed, the Church having expressed itself in favour of the professor devoting himself to the practical training of candidates for the ministry.[143] The former church college in Lynedoch Place became known as Trinity College, and the buildings were used for some of the classes of the divinity faculty. The independence of the principal of the College was also emphasised. It was stated that 'The Head of the College, unless otherwise qualified, shall not be a member of the Senate or of the Faculty of Theology, and the duties and powers of the Dean of the Faculty of Theology shall not be affected by any duties or powers assigned by the Church to the Head of the College.'[144]

Aberdeen had all along been out of step with the others. From an early stage in the discussions, the university court had expressed the view that professors should be ordained ministers of the Kirk, and that the patronage of the chair of Systematic Theology should remain with the synod of Aberdeen.[145] It was later agreed that a

[138]Glasgow University Archives, DC84/1/2/3, Minutes of the Senate of Trinity College Glasgow, 26 February 1932, p. 90.
[139]C of S Rep. 1933, pp. 1205–8.
[140]Stewart Mechie, Trinity College Glasgow 1856–1956 (Glasgow, 1956), p. 43.
[141](GUC) 14 April 1932, pp. 347–8.
[142]Mechie, Trinity College, pp. 37, 43.
[143]Ibid., p. 44. AGA, 1945, pp. 401–2.
[144]C of S Rep., 1933, p. 1218.
[145](AUC) 12 July 1927, p. 482, 29 July 1927, p. 496; 11 October 1927, p. 501.

separate arrangement might be made with regard to this chair[146] and this was reflected in the Act and in the Minute of Agreement drawn up between the Church and the university.[147] The university court had also thought that the nomination of professors to both university and church chairs should be by the boards of nomination. It also wished to see the amalgamation of the theological colleges with the faculties so that the colleges would not continue as distinct institutions with separate governing bodies.[148] It would not be necessary, therefore, for there to be a separate administrative head of the college. The UF College in Aberdeen, however, indicated its wish to remain as a separate body within the university as Christ's College.[149] The university court had also wished that all the teaching of theology should be carried out at King's College,[150] but in the event it was decided that the Church college buildings be used subject to their refurbishment.[151] It was also agreed that there be six professors in the new faculty, four university and two church, one of which would be in Practical Theology and the other in Christian Dogmatics.[152]

One factor which may have influenced the view of the university in Aberdeen was that there were fewer students attending the church college than was the case at either Edinburgh or Glasgow. In addition the college buildings in Alford Place were at a much greater distance from the main university campus than was the case in the other two cities. At the Aberdeen college in session 1925–6, there only eleven students, of whom seven were candidates for the ministry of the Church, while at Edinburgh there were seventy-eight students, of whom thirty-two were candidates, and at Glasgow there were fifty-two, of whom forty-three were training for the ministry.[153] The corresponding figures for the four divinity faculties in that session were: Edinburgh 79 students (20 candidates); Glasgow 49 (25); St Andrews 11 (6); Aberdeen 20 (17).[154] Church candidates thus did not make up the whole of the student body in any of the centres and at Edinburgh, in both college and university, they were in a minority. The largest

[146] Ibid., 30 January 1930, p. 185.
[147] C of S Rep., 1933, p.1222.
[148] (AUC) 9 January 1928, p. 533; 3 December 1929, p. 147.
[149] (AUC) 17 January 1928, p. 536.
[150] (AUC) 3 December 1929, p. 147.
[151] (AUC) 8 December 1931, p. 458.
[152] C of S Rep., 1933, p. 1222.
[153] UFC, Memorandum on the Financial Provisions made by the UFC of S for the payment of Theological Professors, 16 February 1927, (PGA) 4.
[154] Endowments of Theological Chairs in the Scottish Universities (PGA) 4.

number of candidates in both Churches studied in Glasgow. It is interesting to note, too, that while each Church before the union spoke in terms of having a deficit of candidates in training for the ministry, following the union there was an increase. The total number of candidates went up from 244 in 1929–30 to as high as 367 in 1936–7.[155]

At Edinburgh some controversy was aroused by the proposal from the university that the Dean of the faculty of divinity and the Principal of New College should be the same person. From the point of view of the university it was 'the only tolerable solution if a cleavage within the combined Faculty … is to be avoided'.[156] What may seem from a later perspective to have been a concession by the university to the Church[157] was at the time demanded by the university. One reason for this demand was that the buildings of New College at the top of the Mound would be the seat of the faculty. It was thought that if the principalship and the deanship were retained in separate individuals, 'their authority will inevitably clash'.[158] There would be a problem for the Dean carrying out his duties in the building of the college and the Principal would be at a disadvantage in the university where the Dean had precedence. There would be potential conflict over who should preside at public functions, as well as meetings relating to teaching and administration. David Frew, the secretary of the Church's committee on education for the ministry, thought the proposal was an excellent one. In his view it was a 'generous concession on the part of the University' which the Church should welcome, although he had not been able to get his committee to see it in the same light.[159]

There was also resistance on the part of the staff at New College itself, with which the Dean, Professor Curtis, could not disguise his frustration in a confidential memorandum.[160] He suspected that an attempt was being made to annex the faculty to the Church, not merging 'but submerging the aim under a variety of incompatible pleas'. He thought that the aim of the Church was to have the best of both worlds, to be dominant in the faculty 'and at the same time to operate through a Faculty or Senate of its own,

---

[155]Stewart Mechie, 'Education for the Ministry in Scotland since the Reformation, III' in *RSCHS*, 15 (1965), pp. 13–14.

[156]T. H. Holland to D. Frew, 3.2.33 (EUD) 1VA.

[157]D. W. D. Shaw, 'Dual Identity: Church College and University Faculty', in David F. Wright and Gary D. Badcock, eds., *Disruption to Diversity: Edinburgh Divinity 1846–1996* (Edinburgh, 1996), p. 176.

[158]Holland to Frew, 3.2.33.

[159]D. Frew to T. H. Holland, 6.2.33 (EUD) 1VA.

[160]Note on the Edinburgh Draft Agreement: March 30th, 1933 (EUD) 1VA.

on the strength of contributing the College Building and a majority of teaching staff'. In the end it was agreed that the two posts should be held by the same person on the retiral of the present Principal, Alexander Martin. The board of nomination would nominate someone who was both a member of the faculty and a minister of the Church of Scotland as both Dean and Principal. As a concession to the Church, a provision was included for this arrangement to be reviewed after ten years. This arrangement continued until 1984 when Professor James P. Mackey, a laicised Roman Catholic priest, became Dean and Professor Alec C. Cheyne was appointed as Principal.[161] This meant, too, that the senate of the college and the faculty were in effect one body although they each retained their constitutional identity.[162] Four church chairs were transferred from the college, in Christian Dogmatics, Old Testament Language Literature and Theology, New Testament Language Literature and Theology, and Church History, and they joined the four professors in the divinity faculty. This made Edinburgh the strongest faculty in terms of personnel. The university court also agreed to establish a 'church chair' of Practical Theology and Christian Ethics in 1934, but the filling of the post was delayed until the similar post in Glasgow was agreed.[163]

The arrangements were thus made for the coming together of the faculties of divinity and the church colleges in Glasgow, Aberdeen and Edinburgh, and for the strengthening of the faculty at St Andrews. These measures have continued in being with some modifications. In 1950, as has been noted, the church chairs came to be filled in the same way as the university chairs and were therefore open to those who were not ministers of the Church of Scotland. In recent years developments in the universities have overtaken the original agreements in many respects. The nature of the student body has changed following the expansion of higher education in recent decades. The number of candidates for the ministry of the Church of Scotland has also declined and consists of a decided minority of the total student body. More lectureships in theology were created by the universities in the post-war period and appointments to these posts have been a matter for the university alone without reference to the Church of Scotland. Most of the church chairs have gone, and with cutbacks in university finance fewer chairs have been filled in any case. There have thus been fewer appointments involving the boards of

---

[161] Shaw, 'Dual Identity', p. 180.
[162] Ibid., pp. 176, 179.
[163] David Lyall, 'Christian Ethics and Practical Theology' in Wright and Badcock, *Disruption to Diversity*, pp. 144–5.

nomination.[164] It has ceased to be the case, too, that such appointments will tend to be of those who are ministers of the Church of Scotland. In one celebrated case—the appointment of James Mackey, a Roman Catholic theologian, to the renamed Thomas Chalmers Chair at Edinburgh—the decision of the board of nomination created a storm of controversy in the general assembly and far beyond.[165] The debate which had been ignited by this appointment led to a discussion on the training of the ministry for the Church of Scotland, and the idea of a separate church college was raised once more.[166] It was generally recognised that in many ways the balance in the relationship had shifted in favour of the universities. In addition the college buildings in Glasgow and Aberdeen have been sold, thus ending the physical presence of the Church within the academic community. New College remains but the buildings were made over to the university in the 1960s, with the proviso that should the faculty cease to provide suitable courses for candidates for the ministry the buildings would revert to Church ownership.[167] The Church has, however, maintained the view that candidates should receive their education for the ministry within the faculties of divinity. A special assembly committee reported in 1991 that the agreement reached with the universities following 1929 was still advantageous to the Church.[168] Recent proposals for a vocational degree which combines academic study and assessed practical placements have had to be abandoned, but the Church of Scotland continues to seek ways of making better provision for the training of its ministers in collaboration with the faculties of divinity. These discussions have renewed the close relationship between the Church of Scotland and the universities which was formed at the time of the union.

[164] Cheyne, *Studies*, p. 306.
[165] *C of S Rep.*, 1980, pp. 372–6; Cheyne, *Studies*, pp. 306–7.
[166] Jock Stein, ed., *Ministry for the 1980s* (Edinburgh, 1980).
[167] Cheyne, *Studies*, p. 302.
[168] Ibid., p. 307; *C of S Rep.*, 1991, pp. 550–2.

Chapter 8

Dealing with difficulties: the minority in the United Free Church

From the beginning of the discussions on union there were those
in both Churches who had serious reservations about the prospect
of union unless it preserved the principles of their Church in a
clear and unambiguous way. Thus in the United Free Church
there were those who remained firmly of the voluntary position
and would not enter a Church which retained any relationship
with the State, however much it was modified by act of parliament.
In other words, union would only be accepted on the basis of
disestablishment. Equally in the Church of Scotland there were
those who wished the Kirk to retain its position as an established
Church without any modification as might be carried out to meet
the difficulties of the other Church. Thus the middle way which
had been sought by the union committees was unacceptable to
both minorities. It is significant that organisations representing
the minority positions were formed in both Churches following
the general assemblies in 1919 when the Articles Declaratory had
been framed as the *via media* on which union could be achieved.
The United Free Church Association was formed in June 1919 and
the National Church Defence Association was formed in the
Church of Scotland later that same year.[1]

It was the new constitution of the Church of Scotland as set out
in the Articles, and the subsequent settlement concerning the
teinds, which remained the chief problems for both minorities
and this continued to be the case right up to the union in 1929. The
Act of 1921 which recognised the Articles as 'lawful', supplemented
by the property and endowments Act of 1925, had not removed
the obstacles to union as far as the UF minority were concerned
and they remained outside of the united Church as the United
Free Church (Continuing). In this connection, it is worth noting
that the two efforts by the UF committee to accommodate the
views of the minority, the obtaining of a legal opinion regarding

---

[1] Barr, *United Free Church*, p. 192; *Glasgow Herald* 15.10.19; *PRS*, p. 316.

the constitutional question, and the permission for congregations to opt out of the new financial arrangements, were designed to meet the objections to the two Acts of 1921 and 1925. Similarly, in the Church of Scotland, the two Acts were the chief reasons why the members of the minority remained against the union, although in their case there was no real option to continue as a separate denomination since they could not continue as an established Church. Thus although both minorities might object to various aspects of the Basis and Plan of Union, they remained unhappy with the underlying constitutional settlement.

(a) the emergence of the minority

Although the decision to begin talks with the Church of Scotland had been a unanimous decision of the general assembly of the UF Church in 1909, criticism of the committee's policy emerged in the following year. Four members of the committee dissented from the report including Benjamin Martin of Leslie in Fife and Professor James A. Paterson of New College, both well known as champions of disestablishment.[2] Although they criticised the report during the debate for not tackling the issues, they did not formally oppose the committee's deliverance. At the assembly of 1911, however, the first motion in direct opposition to the policy of union was proposed by Alexander Weir of Coatbridge, who would remain opposed to the union to the very end.[3] He proposed that the discussions be broken off until the Church of Scotland was disestablished and disendowed. This in effect would remain the outlook of the more extreme members of the minority, and would mean that they would be unable to enter the united Church. The committee's deliverance, however, was passed by an overwhelming majority.[4] A similar motion by Robert Watson of Dundee at the assembly in the following year, when the Memorandum was being considered, only attracted thirteen votes.[5] Some of the minority supported an amendment by Professor James Orr of Glasgow, which was accepted by the committee, and instructed it, in considering the Memorandum, to regard as a primary question how far agreement was possible between the Churches on the question of the relationship to the State.[6] At the assembly in 1913 the United Free Church had to come to a

---

[2] *UFC Proc.*, 1910, p. 250; Reith, *Reminiscences*, p. 116.
[3] *UFC Proc.*, 1911, pp. 273–4.
[4] Ibid., p. 278.
[5] *UFC Proc.*, 1912, pp. 276, 285.
[6] Ibid., pp. 271–2, 278, 285; Reith, *Reminiscences*, p. 137.

decision regarding the invitation from the Church of Scotland to assist in the framing of its new constitution. Amendments were proposed by Benjamin Martin and by Thomas Whitelaw of Kilmarnock, both of whom were concerned that the new constitution would retain a statutory connection with the State.[7] Martin withdrew his amendment in favour of that by Whitelaw, who later withdrew his amendment when the instructions to the committee were amended slightly.[8] Thus although the assembly came to a unanimous decision, and Whitelaw had not wished his amendment to be regarded as hostile to the committee, contributions to the debate by James Barr and J. A. Paterson showed that the Church was still deeply divided on the issue.[9] Perhaps regretting that he had withdrawn his amendment in the previous year, Whitelaw at the assembly of 1914 refused to withdraw another amendment in spite of being pressed by many of his supporters to do so.[10] The motion was to the effect that the constitution of the Church of Scotland should provide, not only for spiritual independence, but also for 'the equality of all Churches before the civil law'.[11] Thus another of the main concerns of the minority was flagged up, that of religious equality. A speech by James Denney on this occasion, which would later be quoted with approval by A. N. Bogle at a future assembly, spoke of those who had not got beyond 'the barren logomachy of talking about establishment and disestablishment'.[12] In his view, the relationship between Church and State was a complicated historical question, and it could not be described in abstract terms. The UF Church had to deal with the present situation, not with a mathematical puzzle which could be solved in terms of black and white. When discussions resumed after the war, however, there was again an attempt, this time by W. D. Miller of Ruchill in Glasgow, a staunch campaigner for disestablishment who remained opposed to the Articles Declaratory,[13] to have the committee deal with the issue of Church and State.[14] The committee, of course, had been dealing with this issue all along, but not in the way desired by Miller and the other members of the minority.

The emergence of a more sizeable support for the minority can be seen for the first time at the assembly in 1919 when the Church

[7] *UFC Proc.*, 1913, pp. 249–50, 255.
[8] Ibid., pp. 268–9.
[9] Reith, *Reminiscences*, p. 145.
[10] Ibid., p. 155.
[11] *UFC Proc.*, 1914, pp. 286–7.
[12] Ibid., p. 291. Cf. *UFC Proc.*, 1919, p. 259.
[13] J. Sommerville Smith, *Miller of Ruchill* (Glasgow, n.d.), pp. 158–62.
[14] *UFC Proc.*, 1918, pp. 237–8.

faced what Archibald Henderson called 'the valley of decision' with regard to the Articles Declaratory.[15] James Barr objected to support being given to the Articles Declaratory since the Church of Scotland would still be established, the question of the endowments still had to be settled, and the Church would be committed to union before it had been submitted to the presbyteries and membership of the Church.[16] His motion was seconded by Alexander Weir and attracted the support of about sixty-five commissioners. Barr and thirty-six others entered their dissent.[17] Significantly, too, at this assembly, the annual remit of the Church and State Committee, which in the past had pursued an active policy of disestablishment, was changed so that, in the words of George Reith, a 'once bellicose committee was thus deprived of its weapons and handed a watching brief'.[18] This change could be seen as the final disentanglement of the assembly from the disestablishment campaign, which in any case had been dead for some time. Following the assembly's decision to approve the Articles Declaratory, steps were taken which led to the formation of the United Free Church Association. This organisation would campaign for the position of the minority for the next ten years.

At the assemblies of 1920 and 1921 opposition to the Articles, led by W. D. Miller and James Barr, continued and attracted around fifty or sixty votes in support.[19] The first significant sign of disagreement in the UF committee was the resignation of John Young as vice-convener in 1922. He gave the reasons for his resignation in a speech at the assembly that year, and George Reith thought that they were 'neither convincing nor even plausible'.[20] He spoke about the difficulties involved in the union discussions being concealed by the committee, and of the need to preserve the unity of the Church.[21] It is likely, as Reith suggests, that he was afraid that the Church was heading for another schism. The minority had been growing in size, and it was looking increasingly unlikely that union could be brought about without division. Following the passing of the Church of Scotland Act in 1921, Young proposed that discussions take place with the Church of Scotland committee regarding the implications of the Articles. Henderson argued that the UF committee had no mandate to enter into such discussions and that they were in any case

[15] *UFC Proc.*, 1919, p. 247.
[16] *UFC Proc.*, 1919, pp. 247, 257.
[17] *UFC Proc.*, 1919, p. 263.
[18] Reith, *Reminiscences*, p. 215.
[19] *UFC Proc.*, 1920, p. 246; 1921, p. 227.
[20] Reith, *Reminiscences*, p. 247.
[21] *UFC Proc.*, 1922, p. 170.

premature and unnecessary.[22] 'Can we,' he asked, 'till we have proved the full effects or defects of the Articles in working out the practical details of a union, know wherein the Articles may need to be "modified or added to"?' He pointed out that the Articles were not unalterable. If changes were thought to be required, the Church could carry them out itself: 'If it sought parliament's intervention parliament would reply "Do your own business and don't trouble us with it".' James Barr made a statement to the committee early in 1922 containing many of the arguments of the minority against acceptance of the Articles, but Henderson thought that it contained nothing which the committee had not considered before.[23] Nevertheless the minority were allowed to present a statement to the assembly in 1922 for the first time.[24] It was supported by five ministers and five elders. At the assembly Barr moved against the committee, saying that the Articles Declaratory had made no fundamental change in the relationship between the Church of Scotland and the State.[25] Barr's motion received 101 votes and, as Reith pointed out, the opposition vote had thus increased significantly since 1919.[26] The activities of the United Free Church Association were certainly one factor in this increase.

Young proposed another delay following the publication of the Haldane report on the teinds in 1923.[27] Another minority amendment by Robert Small of North Berwick, which was seconded by James Barr, was said by its mover to breathe the spirit of 'strong and consistent voluntaryism' and was in favour of strict religious equality.[28] In replying to these motions, Alexander Martin referred to the work of the United Free Church Association.[29] He raised some laughter when he said that he had never been asked to become a member, and that he had not the time to belong to societies, 'antiquarian or others', that were looking out for members. While Small's motion found little support, Young's appeal for delay received 127 votes. Archibald Henderson felt that the proposal for delay was 'quite out of court'.[30] The UF Church was in a perfectly good position to comment on the contents of the report without waiting to see how it worked in practice. In any case the report called for the Church

[22] A. Henderson to A. Martin, 20.1.22 (M) 19. 2/4.
[23] A. Henderson to A. Martin, 23.1.22 (M) 19. 2/8.
[24] *UFC Rep.*, 1922, pp. 8–12.
[25] *UFC Proc.*, 1922, p. 162.
[26] Reith, *Reminiscences*, p. 247.
[27] Ibid., p. 256; *UFC Proc.*, 1923, p. 140.
[28] *UFC Proc.*, 1923, pp. 143–4, 145–7.
[29] Ibid., p. 148.
[30] A. Henderson to A. Martin, 6.8.23 (M) 19. 3/7.

to have an absolute control of its temporalities. Any doubt regarding the outworking of the proposals would, in effect, cast doubt on the Church itself in its use of this responsibility. Henderson was not inclined to humour the minority, especially those like Barr whom he considered to be against union on any terms other than disestablishment. There was a difference, in Henderson's view, between consistency and persistency: 'The former makes for union, the latter refuses it thoroughly.'[31]

The committee, however, would come to adopt a more conciliatory approach to the minority position in view of the growing support it received in the Church. One member of the minority, William McAlpine of Langside in Glasgow, pointed out to Alexander Martin that the number of those voting against the report of the union committee had increased from sixty in 1921 to about 150 in 1923.[32] In view of the growing extent of the opposition to union he urged that the procedures be sisted until a greater degree of approval could be given throughout the Church. The Church would be split in two if the committee pursued its course towards union with an established Church.[33] It may also have been the case, as John Cullen, a retired minister, suggested to Martin,[34] that the minority had received greater support because their views had received coverage in the newspapers.

The high-water mark of the opposition vote was in 1924 when the assembly was again discussing the proposed property and endowments bill. This time a motion by Young received 138 votes over against 375 for the committee.[35] A motion was also proposed at this assembly by D. J. Ross of Stirling who was unhappy with the name of the Church being used by the United Free Church Association.[36] In his view it caused confusion among church members when the official name of the Church was used by an unofficial organisation. The activities of the Association were defended by A. M. Smith of Moffat and by James Barr, and Ross withdrew his motion when the principal clerk, James Harvey, said the assembly should not take notice of such a group. He did agree that it was calculated to cause confusion when the Association stated that it was opposed to union on the basis of civil establishment, which implied that such was indeed the policy of the Church.[37] At the following assembly the minority

31 A. Henderson to A. Martin, 13.10.23 (M) 19. 3/48.
32 W. McAlpine to A. Martin, 23.10.23 (M) 19. 3/58.
33 W. McAlpine to A. Martin, 30.10.23 (M) 19. 3/61.
34 J. Cullen to A. Martin, 6.6.24 (M) 19. 4/28.
35 *UFC Proc.*, 1924, p. 266. See above, p. 135.
36 Ibid., p. 279.
37 Ibid., p. 280.

vote had gone down to 104.[38] The assembly that year decided to ask presbyteries, kirk sessions and congregations whether the time was now right, with the passing of the two Acts of 1921 and 1925, for discussions on union to begin. It was to be the result of that consultation process which would lead the committee into more strenuous efforts to conciliate the minority.

(b) the position of the minority

At this point some account needs to be taken of the organisation and views of the minority which would lead to the formation of the United Free Church (Continuing). Following the approval of the Articles Declaratory of the Church of Scotland in 1919 the United Free Church Association was formally launched in Glasgow on 4th September at a meeting of twenty-two ministers and fifteen elders presided over by James Barr.[39] The object of the Association was 'strenuously to oppose all proposals for Church reunion that are based on Civil Establishment, or involve the continuance in any form of the statutory connection of Church and State.'[40] In many of its publications the aim 'to oppose Church Union on the basis of civil establishment' was stated below the name of the organisation. Another two objects were later listed as: 'To promote Church Union in Scotland on the Basis of complete Spiritual Freedom, perfect Religious Equality, and full National Justice', and 'To safeguard the interests of the United Free Church at a critical juncture'.[41] Thus only the disestablishment of the Church of Scotland would suffice, and clearly the Articles Declaratory were not intended to achieve that result. It is significant that three of the office-bearers of the Association also held office in the Disestablishment Council for Scotland. James Barr was president of both organisations, Charles Jerdan was an honorary president of both, and J. Sommerville Smith of North Woodside Church in Glasgow, the indefatigable secretary of the Association, was a member of the Executive of the Council.[42] On at least one occasion the Association approached the Council about the possibility of financial support for the holding of a conference.[43] Not all those in the minority belonged to the Association, but many of those who

[38] *UFC Proc.*, 1925, p. 212.

[39] J. Sommerville Smith, 'Our Ten Years' Conflict', in *UFC Handbook*, 1931, p. 40.

[40] Ibid.; UFCA, Constitution (M) 14.3.

[41] UFCA, *Annual Report and Statement on Report of Lord Haldane's Committee on the Property and Endowments of the Church of Scotland.*

[42] UFCA, Constitution; Disestablishment Council for Scotland, Manifesto on the Proposals for the Heritors, 20 June 1924 (M) 10.1.

[43] UFCA Min., 2 May 1923.

in the end refused to enter the union were its members. At the first annual meeting of the Association in June 1920 there were 194 members but, according to the secretary, the size of the Association increased until between 4,000 and 5,000 had enrolled as subscribing members.[44] The Association sought to further its aims by producing literature and by holding public meetings. Many pamphlets and leaflets were published. One leaflet had to be reprinted several times during the winter of 1925-6 when the Church was being consulted as to whether the obstacles to union had been removed.[45] The meetings organised by the Association could attract large numbers, as when 800 were present at a gathering in the Assembly Hall in Edinburgh in February 1927.[46] Another method was also adopted, that of writing letters to the correspondence columns of the press. At one meeting of the Association, it was noted that newspaper correspondence was 'a good means to secure greater publicity to our cause'.[47] The columns of *The Scotsman* and the *Glasgow Herald* regularly contained letters from the minority, and chief among those correspondents was James Barr.

For Barr, as for others in the minority, the prospect of union with the Church of Scotland was bound up with the kind of Church they wished to see. They wished to see a Church which took a progressive stance on social and moral issues and which, for example, campaigned enthusiastically for the temperance cause. If the union went ahead there would no longer be a non-established liberal Presbyterian Church in Scotland which accepted 'the light of modern knowledge and Biblical scholarship' and which gave an independent witness on moral issues.[48] In one pamphlet Rutherford Hill, a leading lay member of the Association, said:[49]

> We are progressives. We look forward to that widening and development and adaptation to changing conditions which is possible only to a Free and Independent Church, delivered from all State connection, and relying wholly on the free-will offerings of the members thereof, and on the sustaining grace of Christ, her only King and Head.

In another pamphlet Hill made it clear that it was establishment which kept the Churches apart, and only establishment.[50] Unity of

---

[44]   Smith, 'Our Ten Years' Conflict', p. 43.
[45]   UFCA Min., 13 January 1926.
[46]   *Scotsman*, 8.2.27.
[47]   UFCA Min., 11 June 1924.
[48]   *Notes on Church Union*, No. 4, July 1925.
[49]   J. Rutherford Hill, *A Frankly Critical Commentary* (n.d.), pp. 9–10.
[50]   W. Brown and J. Rutherford Hill, *Church and State in Scotland: where are we today?* (Edinburgh, 1925), p. 9.

spirit and ideals must be present before any ecclesiastical union could take place. Because of the relationship between Church and State, the two Churches were still poles apart politically. It did not help that the two most prominent advocates of union in the Church of Scotland, John White and Lord Sands, were staunch Tories. Lord Sands, said Hill, was essentially a 'Church and State man'.[51] The difference was also seen in the approach of the Churches to the issue of temperance. In 1925, whereas the Temperance Committee's deliverance was passed unanimously by the UF assembly, in the Church of Scotland eighty-four voted in favour while sixty-six voted against the equivalent deliverance.[52]

In their arguments against the proposals for union, Barr and his colleagues never wavered, and indeed their arguments rarely varied either. The same points were repeated time and again right up to 1929. No matter what the majority might say, they held to their view. Several of the arguments of the minority have already been described when dealing with the issues. It may be helpful, however, to summarise their main concerns. These can be identified from the statements and reports of the minority on the committee, the official publications of the Association, and the writings of some of the members of the minority. In addition, an anti-union monthly leaflet started to appear in April 1925 entitled *Notes on Church Union* and was 'published for a Committee'. Several of the contributors were prominent members of the minority and included John Willock of Lerwick and Charles Jerdan.

As might be expected, almost all of those who took a leading role in supporting the minority position came from a background in the former United Presbyterian Church with its strong voluntary tradition. There were several notable exceptions however. We have already noted[53] that James Barr had been brought up in the Free Church, but later changed his mind on the issue of establishment, and the same was true of W. D. Miller and of Adam Renwick of Motherwell. Miller died before 1929, but Renwick became the leader of those of the minority who agreed to accept the compromise measures offered by the committee and who went into the union. In addition, one of the younger members of the minority, W. R. Forrester of Roslin, had been trained for the ministry since 1900 within the United Free Church.

---

[51] Hill, *Frankly Critical Commentary*, pp. 8–9.
[52] Ibid., p. 11. Cf. *Notes on Church Union*, No. 4, July 1925. *UFC Proc.*, 1925, pp. 337–49; *C of S Rep.*, 1925, p. 868.
[53] See above, p. 45.

(i) a return to the establishment

The basic argument of the minority was that union with the Church of Scotland would mean a return to the establishment.[54] Notwithstanding the passing of the Church of Scotland Act, 1921, it was said that the Church of Scotland still occupied 'a special and exclusive position through her continued statutory connection with the State'.[55] A statement in 1927, authorised by the minority members of the committee and by the executive of the Association, said that they could not unite with an established Church, even if its position could be described as 'establishment with freedom'.[56] One area of concern in this regard was that the ancient statutes were not repealed under the terms of the Church of Scotland Act of 1921. They were repealed in so far as they were inconsistent with the provisions of the Articles Declaratory, but not in so far as they conferred a privileged status on the Church of Scotland that was denied to other Churches. James Barr, in a statement to the UF committee in 1922, said that the statutes were still the operative instrument by which national preference and material privilege were given to one Church. Thus claims could still be made upon this Church, not only as a spiritual, but also as a 'National Institution'.[57] The statutes remained which stated that the Kirk is 'by law established'. The minority argued that it was not the time for the UF Church to abandon the voluntary principle and to forsake its friends in English Nonconformity with whom the battle against establishment had been fought both north and south of the Border.[58]

The minority also did not accept that the Articles would prevent a repetition of the House of Lords decision of 1904. That decision, in their view, was due to the existence of an established Church. The judges had looked at the ancient statutes to determine what powers a Church could have, and which rights the Free Church had carried over from the establishment into its position of freedom. The judgement was made in the light of the historical relationship of Church and State in Scotland. As long as there was an established Church, other Churches would not be fully free. The answer to the verdict of the Free Church Case was therefore,

[54] UFCA, Leaflet No. 1, *Back to Establishment.* Cf. Barr, *Scottish Church Question*, ch. 15.

[55] Statement by the Minority, *UFC Rep.*, 1922, p. 8.

[56] Statement authorised by the Minority members of the Conference Committee and also by the Executive of the United Free Church Association, 29 January 1927 (M) 14.3

[57] Draft Statement by Mr. James Barr on the Present Position in light of the passing of the Church of Scotland Act 1921 (M) 13.1.

[58] UFCA, *Back to Establishment.*

not a new concordat with the State as set out in the Articles, but disestablishment.[59] In addition, it was clear, in Barr's view, that had the Church's constitution contained the right and power of making the changes in question, the case would have been decided otherwise.[60]

Three instances of the continuing establishment of the Church were of particular concern to the minority. In the first place there was the reservation to Church of Scotland ministers of appointment as royal chaplains, as chaplains in the Indian Establishment, and as theological professors. The later agreement with the universities would remove the last of these restrictions, however, and the others would remain only in terms of custom rather than by statute. Secondly, it was argued that the courts of the Church would remain courts of the realm, and this status could only be changed by an act of disestablishment.[61] As Lord Sands had pointed out,[62] the courts of the Church would indeed be courts of the realm, but only in spiritual matters, and in this regard they would be recognised by the civil authority as having an independent jurisdiction. And finally, the minority were concerned that the office of Lord High Commissioner would remain untouched and that it likewise could only be altered by an act of parliament. The majority pointed out, however, that the power to convene and dissolve assemblies had been given up in practice. For the members of the minority what mattered in the end was the practice of establishment, even if they were to accept the arguments that its statutory basis was no more, which they were not prepared to do. In practice the Church of Scotland would be recognised in various ways by the State, ways which were privileged and preferential. The outward appearances of establishment have remained, such as the royal chaplains and the presence of the Lord High Commissioner at the assembly and the court at Holyrood. Such manifestations have led many to assume that the Kirk is still the Established Church, and it can often be referred to in that way.

(ii) religious equality and the nature of the Church
The underlying objection of the minority was the continuing recognition of the Church of Scotland as a national Church in a way different from that of other Churches. The minority wished to see complete religious equality and could not support a Church

---

[59] UFCA, Leaflet No. 5, *"Establishment with Freedom"*.
[60] Barr, Draft Statement. Cf. Orr, *Free Church Appeals*, p. 580.
[61] Cf. *UFC Rep.*, 1922, p. 9.
[62] See above, p. 102.

'that stands in a position before the law and the country in any wise different from that of the other Christian Churches in the land'.[63] In spite of the clause in the Act of 1921 which allowed a similar recognition to be given to other Churches, nothing less than disestablishment and the creation of a level playing field for all the Churches would have satisfied the minority. The theme of religious equality was stated forcibly in a manifesto issued by the executive of the Association:[64]

> We are prepared to consider and work for union or federation with Christians of any denomination 'who heartily hold the evangelical view of JESUS CHRIST, GOD's only Son, and of His redeeming work; and who also stand on an equal footing with all other Churches in regard to the State and to the law'.

They objected to any Church being given preferential treatment at the hands of the State and held that the only true establishment of the Church was 'at the hands of her Divine Lord alone'. For the minority, however, the concern for equality was not an abstract matter but was linked to their concern for evangelism. This was made clear by the minority committee members in 1922 when they stated: 'We share with our brethren the eager desire to make a united appeal in the effort to win the masses; but it is from the platform of religious equality alone that this appeal can be effectively made in our time.'[65] For the Church to share in the state privileges and state endowments, against which protest had been made for so long, would be to drive away the masses not to win them.

W. R. Forrester argued that the day of national Churches was over.[66] Society was now heterogeneous in terms of its religious beliefs and lack of them. Only a comparatively small proportion of the community had more than a nominal Church connection and thus any claim to be a national Church was empty of meaning. In addition, a national Church tended to sink to the religious level of the community rather than raising it. Its desire to be comprehensive had usually led to compromise. It must choose whether to speak for the nation or to speak for God. One of the statements issued by the Association also spoke of the day of State Churches being over.[67] What was needed was rather the Church

---

[63] Statement authorised by the Minority, 29 January 1927. Cf. *UFC Rep.*, 1922, p. 9.

[64] Manifesto by the Executive of the United Free Church Association (M) 15.1.

[65] *UFC Rep.*, 1922, p. 12.

[66] W. R. Forrester, *Christian Unity and Church Union, A plea for federation* (Edinburgh, 1925), pp. 13–14.

[67] Reasons against Union on the basis of the Articles, Issued by the United Free Church Association (M) 12.1.

everywhere freed from the State and organised according to spiritual necessities, thus forming a spiritual unity worldwide, a confederation of Churches in all countries. One writer in *Notes on Church Union* spoke of the true nature of the Church being invisible rather than visible.[68] Unity could not be achieved by simply uniting the visible Churches in each country. A far better way of union, said William Morison of Rosehall Church in Edinburgh, would be one which sprang out of unity of the Spirit, a federation of all the Churches, 'in which they recognise each other's equal standing in the Church catholic, and maintain the fullest and freest communion and co-operation with one another'.[69] From these comments it is apparent that at the root of the minority's position was the doctrine of the Church. To be the Church in a spiritual and catholic sense, the Church could not be connected in any official way to the State. For the minority in the Church of Scotland, too, the basic issue was one of catholicity, in terms of doctrine and practice. But in their view such catholicity was to be found in relation to the State, where the Church was recognised as being part of the Church catholic and not just one denomination among many others.

(iii) the Basis and Plan of Union
The objections of the minority to the Articles Declaratory and the parliamentary Acts of 1921 and 1925 have already been noted in relation to these subjects.[70] For the minority, the Articles were a fixed constitution with a fixed creed and did not adequately provide for the spiritual freedom of the Church. In addition the Church would still receive state support through the continuing charge on land and would not be wholly dependent on the voluntary giving of its members. The minority members were also concerned about certain aspects of the Basis and Plan of Union. We have noted their objection to elders not being permitted to lay on hands at the ordination of ministers, and they were unhappy with the election, functions and powers of kirk sessions being defined in terms of Church of Scotland rather than UF practice.[71] They objected, too, to the continuing presence of the Lord High Commissioner at the assembly and to the proposed arrangements for the training of ministers.[72] It was not for the Church to seek a role in the appointment of university professors. Theological teachers should be appointed

---

[68] *Notes on Church Union*, No. 10, January 1926.
[69] UFCA, Edinburgh Branch Letter, January 1927 (M) 14.3.
[70] See above, pp. 76–7, 89–90, 106, 137–8.
[71] See above, p. 167; Barr, *United Free Church*, pp. 220–6.
[72] UFCA, *Proposed Union*, p. 6.

and paid for by the Church. They were also against the new arrangements for vacancies. If a congregation failed to obtain a minister within nine months, the presbytery could intervene. This was based upon the Church of Scotland practice and was 'entirely alien to the spirit of a Free Church'.

In addition the minority was concerned that many country churches formerly of the United Free Church would close following reunion as a result of the policy of readjustment. There were 262 congregations with fewer than 100 members in the UF Church compared to 207 in the Church of Scotland.[73] There were, however, almost twice the number of such UF congregations in rural areas outside the highlands: 162 compared to 85. The former UF congregations would be at a disadvantage financially compared to the former parish kirks which would still receive money from the land charge.[74] This concern was also voiced in an issue of *Notes on Church Union*.[75] It was, however, a basic misunderstanding of what the position would be following the union. In any local readjustment the continuing land charge would be for the benefit of the united charge and the main question to be decided would be about the building to be used. Former parish churches would thus not be at an advantage, except that, as part of the agreement with the landowners, they were to be put into good repair before being transferred to the General Trustees of the Church.[76] The editor of *Life and Work* also made the point that readjustment would not be carried out solely on the basis of a congregation's size; a consideration of major importance would be whether it was required for the needs of the parish or area in which it was set.[77]

Two other concerns were expressed by W. R. Forrester. One was the territorial principle as found in the Articles which implied a parish ministry based on the pattern of the Church of Scotland. This, in his view, was less flexible than the UF approach.[78] In the UF Church the territorial unit was the presbytery, within which congregations had no definitely assigned boundaries. In the Church of Scotland the parish was the territorial unit and the waste was greater since the Church had to provide ordinances in every parish no matter how numerous the other Churches and how scanty the population. He did admit, however, that the UF

---

[73] Small Charges in the Two Churches (M) 14.3.
[74] UFCA, Leaflet No. 3, *Country Kirks and Union*.
[75] *Notes on Church Union*, January 1926.
[76] See above, p. 133.
[77] *LW*, March 1926, p. 54.
[78] Forrester, *Christian Unity and Church Union*, pp. 7–8.

system was partly territorial and partly congregational since the Church followed the people—and by this he meant not the population as a whole, but the church membership. His argument, however, did have the advantage of flexibility. In his view the parish system had broken down due to the movement of population. In the united Church, however, the Church itself would be able to make any changes in the extent and size of its parishes without reference to the civil courts, and hence there need be no less flexibility. The problem would remain of making changes which had the agreement of all the local parties concerned, congregations and presbytery, and this would be true under the alternative system as well. It could be argued, however, that his identification of the presbytery rather than the parish as the primary territorial unit at the local level is a more faithful reflection of the original proposals of the Second Book of Discipline in the late sixteenth century. This book spoke of 'elderships', a grouping of kirk sessions, as the focal point of local ministry, and envisaged a reduction in the number of parishes.[79]

Forrester's other concern was one shared by the minority in the Church of Scotland and concerned the size and centralising tendencies of the united Church.[80] He saw the trend towards church union as reflecting the tendencies in industry and commerce towards large international groupings, which might lead to greater efficiency for the organisation, but did not necessarily work for the benefit of the industry as a whole or for the common good. He also viewed the movement for union as a belated expression of the age of imperialism in Britain and of Prussianism in Germany. In particular the leaders of church union were men who had been trained in Hegelian idealism, which was the philosophical justification of imperialism in all its forms. This philosophy lay behind Karl Marx's *Das Capital*. It had now been discredited, he said, for not giving sufficient room for the development of the individual personality and for degenerating into materialism. Since the Great War, too, the emphasis had changed from Empire to Commonwealth, a federation of free peoples. The union was thus a belated application of a discredited philosophy. The federation rather than the union of Churches should be the ideal. 'I can well imagine', he said, 'the United Church admirably organised, splendidly efficient, wealthy, influential—and incapable of revival.'[81] Humility was a more vital characteristic of

---

[79] Kirk, *Second Book of Discipline*, VII.14. p. 199.
[80] Forrester, *Christian Unity and Church Union*, pp. 9–11.
[81] Ibid., p. 11.

a Christian Church than efficiency: 'God is not always on the side of the big battalions, because they are seldom fighting for God.'[82] He detected a desire among some in the Church of Scotland to create a central executive, 'sufficiently strong to coerce presbyteries, parishes, and congregations, and to direct religious operations on a national scale with adequate resources for all emergencies'.[83] A Church dominated by its headquarters would be the enemy of religious liberty and would destroy the autonomy of congregations. It is interesting that the other minority were afraid of the very same result after the union but accused the United Free Church of having such centralising tendencies.[84] It should be noted that it was at the insistence of the Church of Scotland that the Plan of Union was changed to ensure that the central committee on the maintenance of the ministry would not be able to override the wishes of presbyteries. It should be pointed out, too, that for the leaders of the union, efficiency was always seen as but a prelude to evangelism.

(c) the accommodation with the minority

In both Churches prominent members of the minority had been included on the union committee so that their point of view could be expressed within the discussions. There had been no attempt to prevent such discussion or to include only those favourable to union. This policy was particularly noticeable in 1926 when new committees were appointed to negotiate the Basis and Plan of Union. The UF committee contained several prominent members of the minority. They opposed the Basis and Plan of Union, but it became clear that only an abandonment of the acts of 1921 and 1925 by the Church of Scotland would fully meet their demands. A statement to this effect was made by the minority at the end of the committee's report in 1927.[85] The statement did refer, however, to two proposals. One concerned the consulting of counsel for a legal opinion prior to the union, and the other involved the creation of a voluntary synod for those congregations which did not wish to benefit from money which came from the endowments and the continuing land charge. These proposals were pursued patiently by the committee and in the following year it was clear that they had been successful in reducing the number of those who would not join the united Church. A minority report by the remaining members was presented in 1928.

[82] Ibid., p. 12.
[83] Ibid.
[84] See below, p. 261.
[85] *UFC Rep.*, 1927, pp. 5–7.

The significance of the developments in the two years before the union, however, was that Alexander Martin and his colleagues sought ways by which the views of the minority might be met, and the measures which were taken reduced the size of the minority considerably. Some were reassured by the legal opinion and by the provisions which enabled some congregations not to participate in the continuing endowments of the Kirk. Others were not so reassured by these measures but nevertheless did not feel the situation demanded the setting up of another Church in Scotland. Barr and the leaders of the United Free Church Association, however, remained unwilling to enter the union with what they considered to be an established Church.

The policy of accommodation with the minority was favoured by Professor David Cairns of Aberdeen, someone from the old UP tradition who was in favour of union. He had told Bogle in November 1923 that he did not want to lose Barr or Young or the other prominent members of the minority.[86] It would be a tragedy if bitterness and division were perpetuated in local situations; and it would be likewise tragic if there was 'the slow withering out of congregations with an honourable history and a big power for good.' The real danger to the union was from the UF Church, not the Church of Scotland, and he was therefore in favour of discussions with representatives of the minority, as he put it, 'before the crack becomes a gulf'. The minority, he said, 'think they have been tactically manoeuvred into a situation which is difficult, and they resent it.' They were angry and would become more so. He therefore asked what could be done, short of wrecking the union, to meet them.

Alexander Martin and David Cairns were good friends, and Martin was grateful for what he called a clear exposition of the views of the minority which he thought was 'very much better than their own'.[87] He felt, however, that since it was axiomatic that the union was to be achieved 'not by violent "Disestablishment" and "Disendowment", but by way of accommodation', it obliged all parties to recognise when the substance of their claims had been satisfied, albeit in a new form and by a new way. 'Is it uncharitable', he asked, 'to consider the minority as failing here?' The members of the minority had, in Martin's view, allowed their prejudice to blind them to the true character of the new situation. In addition, *animus*, which was understandable, 'but a good deal of it dubiously — or defectively! — Christian', did the rest. They suffered from an 'inelasticity of mind' and a consequent

---

[86] D. S. Cairns to A. N. Bogle, 30.10.23 (copy), (M) 19.3/62.
[87] A. Martin to D. S. Cairns, 14.7.24 (M) 19.4/46.

'unreasonableness' when a 'new but genuine solution of an old problem is before them'. They continued to refer to the Church of Scotland as an 'established' Church but did not define this term and did not specify the ways in which establishment remained. He asked: 'Have they recognised the undoubted alteration made in the status of the Established Church by 1921, or the serious endeavours publicly made by responsible people —without any demur from the Established Church side — to shew that the act means nothing less than a self-disestablished Church?' Martin could not adopt such an understanding and sympathetic attitude to the minority as his friend, although he was grateful for Cairns acting as a kind of link between the committee and the minority. A meeting was to be arranged during the winter of 1924–5 between the two sides. Cairns, however, was not prepared to try and get the minority members to 'back down' from their position without some indication from the committee as to what new measures they were prepared to offer to meet their views.[88] For Martin it was for the other side to make proposals and say what would content them, and the majority could then judge to what extent or in what way these could be met.[89] No record of the meeting survives, if it took place.

A significant change in the situation came about after the passing of the property and endowments Act of 1925 and the testing of opinion in the United Free Church regarding the next stage in the movement towards union. As has been noted,[90] a large number of members failed to vote on the issue and there were a significant number of kirk sessions and congregations opposed to going further. This result, too, was probably due in part to the active campaign carried out by the United Free Church Association.[91] In April 1926 it was reported that more than 250 members had been added to the ranks of the Association since the previous assembly.[92] Later that year the Association saw significant increases in its membership. In the north-west 200 new members were recruited, and in Perth and Alloa the roll of members more than trebled.[93] It was clear to the committee that, even if the minority did not have the active support of many ministers and elders of the Church, there was sufficient apathy and misunderstanding to influence the way in which

---

[88] D. S. Cairns to A. Martin, 19.10.24 (M) 19.4/80.
[89] A. Martin to D. S. Cairns, 21.10.24 (M) 19.4/82.
[90] See above, pp. 145–6.
[91] Smith, 'Our Ten Years' Conflict', p. 47.
[92] UFCA Min., 7 April 1926.
[93] UFCA Min., 23 September and 17 December 1926.

union would be decided. In the UF committee therefore discussions took place as to what measures, if any, could be obtained which would satisfy some of the concerns of the minority.

Martin reported to the committee in March 1927 that informal discussions had been held with representatives of those who felt serious difficulty in connection with the Church's union policy.[94] The ministers in this group with whom Martin discussed these matters were Adam Renwick and W. R. Forrester. Thomas Wardrop of Rutherglen was another prominent member of the minority which was prepared to come to an agreement. It was of the utmost concern to Forrester that there be no 'continuing' Church after the union. He would not be a party 'to the planting of a new root of bitterness in Scotland'.[95] Two long meetings took place in a spirit of 'complete frankness and friendliness'.[96] The committee was then informed of two proposals which might meet the difficulties of the minority. The two measures concerned the financial settlement and the constitution of the Church. These proposals were referred to in the report to the assembly in 1927 and during the debate which followed.[97] The opposition at the assembly of 1927 proposed delay, as it had done the previous year, and while the number voting for the minority had gone up by 11 votes to 126, those voting for the committee had also increased, only by a larger amount, by 44, to 675.[98] The minority motions were proposed by A. M. Smith in 1926 and by Charles Robson of Alloa and J. M. Macfie of Bowden in 1927.

(i) the voluntary synod.
In order to meet the conscientious objections of those who were against the Church receiving support from the new form of the endowments, it was proposed that congregations would be able to opt out of any financial support from that source and be entirely reliant on the voluntary giving of members. At first the suggestion was that such congregations might form a separate synod within the Church, a 'voluntary synod', and it was on that basis that discussions at first took place within the United Free Church committee.[99] The first outline of the proposal was that such congregations would contract out of the general arrangements for the payment of stipend, and would constitute a court of the

---

[94] UFC Min, 3 March 1927.
[95] W. R. Forrester to A. Martin, 25.4.27 (M) 19.9/51.
[96] UFC Min., 3 March 1927.
[97] *UFC Rep.*, 1927, p. 3; *UFC Proc.*, 1927, pp. 174–5.
[98] *UFC Proc.*, 1926, p. 217; 1927, p. 182.
[99] UFC Min., 31 March 1927. UFC Committee, Proposed Basis for the Constitution of a Voluntary Synod H.1 (M) 14.3.

Church taking responsibility for the raising and distributing of a Central Fund of its own.[100] Along with this synodical court *quoad stipendia*, there would be formed an 'Association for the Voluntary Support of the Ministry' of which ministers and others within the voluntary synod would be members, but which would not have the status of a church court.

It soon became clear that such a proposal would not be acceptable to the Church of Scotland and that, in any case, such a body would only serve to perpetuate a major source of division within what was supposed to be a united Church. It might well become, in effect, a Church within a Church. The proposal then became one of providing a mechanism by which those congregations, while not forming a separate synod, might yet be able to opt out of the centralised maintenance of the ministry fund and rely solely on local or other congregational giving. This modified proposal was put to the committee in October 1927.[101] Congregations could declare their conscientious objection to participating in standardised stipend and be formed into a group. Congregations in the group would not share in any local or national allocation of standardised stipend, which would be administered by a separate committee.[102] Membership of the group would be taken into account by the Readjustment of Agencies Committee.[103] The final section of the Plan of Union reflected these suggestions, except that the administration of the scheme was altered. Instead of separate committees, the Maintenance of the Ministry Committee would keep two separate accounts, one derived from endowments, and one derived solely from the freewill offerings of the people. Congregations belonging to the 'voluntary group' would only benefit from the second fund and the auditors of the committee's accounts would make certification to that effect each year.[104] Consultation was held with representatives of the Church of Scotland committee who approved of the proposal in principle and it was remitted to the joint conference for possible inclusion in the Plan of Union.

As Martin pointed out to one correspondent, however, the effect of this measure would be to militate against the creation of a strong centralised system of ministerial support.[105] The Church of Scotland had suffered, in his view, from 'the congregational system of finance which was implied in its possession of the old

[100] UFC Min., 27 April 1927
[101] UFC Min.,12 October 1927.
[102] UFC Committee, H.14 (M) 14.3.
[103] UFC Committee, H.19 and H.20 (M) 14.3.
[104] Cox, p. 409.
[105] A. Martin to T. E. Sandeman, 25.10.27 (M) 20.1/38.

parochial endowments'. The union gave the opportunity to break down that system and 'produce the real unification of Church life towards which unity of organisation is little more than a means.' The setting up of a voluntary maintenance of the ministry fund would inevitably retard that process, but it was necessary in order to 'avert a still greater evil'. Lord Sands, when first consulted about the proposal, did not think that any obstacle should be put in the way of this measure from the point of view of the Church of Scotland.[106] His main concern, voiced to Martin, was that ministers would have an exaggerated idea as to the amount of surplus available for stipend in the united Church and thus feel inclined to vote against the proposal.[107] He did not think there would be much of a surplus and in the Plan of Union such surplus was not designated specifically for the maintenance of the ministry. John White did not see any reason to object to the proposal since it would apply to a distinct group of congregations in terms of financial matters only.[108] He also felt it less objectionable if those contracting out of moneys from endowments did so from all endowments and not just from the former teinds of the Church of Scotland.[109] In this way no distinction was being made between the ancient endowments, *quoad sacra* endowments, and UF endowments. This in the end was what was agreed.

The voluntary scheme did not meet the requirements of the hardline members of the minority who produced a paper setting out their views.[110] They objected to the proposal for two main reasons. In the first place the voluntary fund and congregations would still be under the control of a body which accepted state endowments. 'To convinced "voluntaries"', they said, 'Union on such terms would be merely absorption camouflaged by a subtle piece of book-keeping.' Secondly, any scheme must allow the minority members to enter the united Church as a body where they could act together and where their distinctive principles would be recognised. It was clear that this measure, along with the other dealing with the constitutional position, was designed to divide the minority.

(ii) the legal opinion and the declaration
The other measure proposed following the informal conference

[106] Lord Sands to J. White, 13.10.27 (W) 10.5.
[107] Lord Sands to A. Martin, 14.10.27 (M) 20.1/30.
[108] Presbyteries to be kept in touch with all that is being proposed; also references to certain "Provisional Proposals" to meet objectors to Endowments (W) 97.
[109] In the General Assembly Dr White referred to 'Provisional Proposals' affecting Stipend of a few conscientious objectors (W) 97.
[110] UFC Committee, H.12 (M) 14.3.

held with members of the minority of the committee early in 1927 was that an approach be made to the Church of Scotland committee with a view to obtaining 'a reasoned opinion from the most eminent Counsel upon the questions in dispute.'[111] It became clear, however, that the Church of Scotland saw this matter as an internal one for the United Free Church.[112] At the next meeting it was intimated, too, that the executive of the United Free Church Association did not wish to be parties to any such approach in the meantime.[113]

It did not prove possible, however, to come to an agreement with members of the minority as to the questions to be put to counsel. It was suggested that the committee simply seek the opinion of counsel on the uniting Act as effecting union and maintaining the continuity and identity of the United Free Church in the united Church. It was, in any case, the Law Committee of the Church which would be responsible for submitting the memorial and queries to counsel. The obtaining of a legal opinion was something which the committee would have considered in any event. It was a sensible precaution in view of a possible challenge to the legality of the union as had happened after 1900. But it was also seen as a way of dealing with the difficulties of the minority members of the committee. The legal opinion was thus seen as serving two different but related purposes.

Points made by the minority would be taken into consideration in the framing of the memorial, and they were given the opportunity of presenting their views separately to counsel.[114] The minority wished to ask whether the two statutes of 1921 and 1925 affected the position of the United Free Church as set out in its Act anent Spiritual Independence of 1906. They wished to know also whether any statutory privilege still attached to the Church of Scotland in view of the Act of 1921, and whether the united Church would enjoy the same doctrinal freedom as declared in the UF Act of 1906. Finally they wished to ask counsel whether the union would break the continuity or identity of the UF Church.[115] Martin felt that some of the questions could be allowed to stand if seen in the light of the memorial which would precede them,[116] but one member of the Law Committee at least felt that the second group of questions were clearly designed to cause trouble.[117] For example, if the opinion

[111] UFC Min., 31 March 1927.
[112] UFC Min., 27 April 1927.
[113] Ibid.
[114] UFC Min., 12 October 1927.
[115] Ibid. UFC Committee, H.22 (M) 14.2.
[116] A. Martin to Lord Constable, 24.9.27 (M) 20.1/8.
[117] T. S. Brown to A. H. McLean, 6.1.28 (M) 20.3/1.

were to say that the relations between the Church of Scotland and the State no longer constituted an establishment, it would cause trouble in the Church of Scotland. On the other hand, if the opinion concluded that such a relationship continued, then there would be more trouble in the UF Church. This point continued to be the difficulty for the Church of Scotland side. They were anxious lest a legal opinion created new problems with their own minority. In seeking to satisfy one minority, the other could be alienated. They would have preferred the UF committee not to make an approach to counsel as the procedure involved considerable risk. Lord Sands told Martin in a typically graphic way:[118]

> I do not like the idea of an opinion of Counsel. Law, particularly this branch of it, is not an exact science any more than theology, and no matter how eminent a lawyer may be his opinion is not the law but just his opinion. Lord Finlay is a very eminent lawyer but you know the trouble caused by an opinion expressed by him which other lawyers do not agree with. I am satisfied that I am validly a communicant of the Church. I am satisfied with the advice I have had in the matter. I am not going to enter into an agreement with Bishop Walpole to take the opinion of some eminent theologian on the understanding that if it is adverse I shall allow the Bishop to admit me by confirmation.

Lord Constable also thought it would be impossible to obtain a legal opinion that would satisfy the minority.[119] In particular the doctrinal issue was, in his view, 'not for a lawyer but for a theologian'. Should a dispute arise over the funds and property of the UF Church, as had happened following the union of 1900, the burden of proof would be placed on the minority. In that case he thought that the legal opinion, should it be obtained, should be sought in that form.

In spite of his misgivings, Lord Sands agreed to assist in the process and prepared an informal memorandum for H. P. Macmillan, K. C., one of the learned counsel whose opinion was sought.[120] The establishment principle in the Church of Scotland, in his view, could be placed no higher than adherence to the present status quo as created by the statutes of 1921 and 1925 and accepted by the Church. In agreeing to union, the UF Church would also accept that status quo. In the Articles the Church of Scotland had set out its understanding of the rights and duties of Church and State in

[118] Lord Sands to A. Martin, 1.10.27 (M) 20.1/22.
[119] Lord Constable to A. Martin, 1.10.27 (M) 20.1/21.
[120] Personal Memorandum by Lord Sands (W) 10.6.

relation to each other. Article VI was 'wholly incompatible' with the establishment principle held as a matter of faith, i.e. that it is the duty of the State, under all circumstances, to maintain an established Church. The difficulties of the UF minority, he thought, were not difficulties round which a way must be found but difficulties round which 'no way can be found under existing conditions'. Nothing would satisfy the minority except the equivalent of the dis-establishment and disendowment of the Church of Scotland. In addition, the minority said that the inclusion of the Articles in the schedule of an act of parliament meant that there was a legal barrier to the alteration of the constitution of the Kirk. But this, according to Sands, would be true of the Articles were they the constitution of a voluntary Church or of a corporation.

The memorial for the opinion of counsel presented by the Law Committee gave an account of the union of 1900 and quoted opinions from the House of Lords in the Free Church Case. According to these opinions, both establishment and voluntaryism were open questions in the United Free Church.[121] Reference was also made to the UF Act of 1906 and the Church of Scotland Acts of 1921 and 1925. In view of the passing of these measures, the United Free Church had come to the view that the main causes of separation between the Churches had been removed. The Basis of Union was then described and objections made to the draft uniting Act by the minority were listed and answered in a way which would have satisfied Lord Sands! These objections were contained in a representation made by certain minority members of the committee to counsel.[122] The minority argued that, by the 1921 Act, the Church of Scotland had a 'State-fixed Constitution' whereas the voluntary principle was a fundamental doctrine or principle of the UF Church. According to this view, too, the Church of Scotland still held the establishment principle, and the ancient statutes, which had not been repealed, gave the Church of Scotland special privileges. In addition, the UF Act of 1906 was inconsistent with the permanent status of Article I, and the mechanism for change in Article VIII was not alterable by the Church itself. The minority members concluded that the constitutions of the two Churches could not be reconciled, and that the relationship between Church and State constituted an establishment. The union would therefore involve acceptance by the UF Church of that establishment and the abandonment of its identity, freedom and property. Counsel was therefore asked: would the United Free Church, by uniting with the Church of

---

[121] *UFC Rep.*, May 1928, Appendix, p. 3.
[122] Ibid., pp. 20–22.

Scotland, carry with it into the union its whole rights and property? Counsel were also asked if they had any suggestions to make with regard to revision of the proposed Act or the procedure to be adopted, and the most appropriate means of vesting in the united Church the funds, properties, rights, and privileges belonging to the two separate Churches.

The opinion of counsel[123] proved to be most satisfactory to the majority of the UF committee and vindicated the measures by which union had been prepared. In Martin's view it was an historic opinion by which the main contentions of the minority were 'blown out of the water'.[124] Counsel began by referring to the Free Church Case and its aftermath in the Churches (Scotland) Act of 1905. The property of the UF Church was now held for the purpose and in accordance with its constitution. They then considered the UF Act of 1906 and the Church of Scotland Act of 1921. They concluded that they were in a different position from the courts which considered the Free Church Case, since they had before them two documents which enunciated the essential tenets and principles of the Churches. According to its Articles, the Church of Scotland possessed 'a wide, though not entirely unlimited, power of modifying its own Constitution.'[125] The provisions of Article I, which could be described as 'the doctrines of Protestantism and Trinitarianism', were essential to the identity of the Church.[126] The UF Act of 1906 did not contain any such express restrictions as did the Articles. In the view of counsel, the doctrinal content of Article I was 'substantially consistent' with the 'doctrines at present accepted and professed by the United Free Church'. Was there a distinction, however, in that the Church of Scotland had express restrictions upon its powers of alteration while the UF Church had 'unlimited and uncontrolled powers of alteration'? According to counsel, this involved a 'fallacy':[127]

> The United Free Church, although its Constitution contains no express limitation on its powers of alteration, is in law no less subject to restriction than the Church of Scotland. There cannot in law be a trust for purposes at large. There must in every case be an ascertainable and fundamental trust purpose to be served, however wide may be the ambit of the permissible methods of attaining it. To borrow an expression from a different branch of law, a church, like a company,

[123] Ibid., pp. 1–22.
[124] A. Martin, Notebook, 5.3.28 (M) 2.6.
[125] *UFC Rep.*, May 1928, Appendix, p. 14.
[126] Ibid.
[127] Ibid., p. 15.

must have a permanent substratum. Its identity cannot be in solution. The law will not support a trust for objects changeable at will. A declaration by the United Free Church that it no longer adhered to the doctrine of the Trinity would in our opinion be as fatal to its legal identity as a similar declaration would be in the case of the Church of Scotland, and would as inevitably lead to the loss of all the assets at present held in trust for it. In the case of the Church of Scotland the nucleus of fundamental doctrine is an expressed term of its Constitution; in the case of the United Free Church a similar nucleus is implied. We are of opinion that for the present purpose this is a distinction without a difference, and that accordingly there is between the two Churches the substantial identity of doctrine which is essential for the valid amalgamation of the trusts on which their properties are held.

There was no difference between the Churches, either, in that the constitution of one Church was a schedule in an act of parliament. In each case the law would not 'go behind' the constitutions which the Churches had lawfully adopted.

Counsel also dealt with the question of the relationship between Church and State which was, they said, the 'rock' upon which the union of 1900 was wrecked.[128] Could it be said that it was an article of faith of the Church of Scotland that the State had the right and duty to support an establishment of religion? The Articles, they said, nowhere so declared. Instead they referred to the recognition by the civil authority of the separate government and jurisdiction of the Church. Not only so, but clause two of the statute opened the way for other Churches to be similarly recognised in their spiritual functions. Equally, by the statute of 1925, the Church of Scotland had absolved the State from any obligation for its support or maintenance. They thus came to the conclusion that the establishment principle was no longer an article of 'religious belief and obligation' in the Church of Scotland.[129] There remained some 'vestiges' of its former relation to the State. The courts of the Church were one instance of this, since they did not depend entirely on contract, as did the courts of other Churches. They formed part of the official judicatories of Scotland but they were 'spiritual, not secular' courts, and according to Article IV were subject to 'no civil authority'. With regard to the mechanism for changing the Articles, they did not think that the Barrier Act and

[128] Ibid., p. 16.
[129] Ibid., p. 17.

the enhanced procedures contained in Article VIII were 'necessarily incompatible'. The existence of these two systems was a purely procedural matter, which could not affect the validity of the proposed union.

Counsel therefore came to the conclusion that, while only an act of parliament would preclude a successful challenge by any minority against the validity of the proposed union, they felt that such a challenge would be attended by far greater difficulty than in 1900. Every means should be taken, however, to minimise the risk. They thought that any risk would be materially reduced if the United Free Church were to pass an act which stated 'that there is in the relations of the Church of Scotland to the State nothing which is inconsistent with the Constitution and Principles of the United Free Church of Scotland.'[130] Thus while they answered the main query in the affirmative they suggested this measure in answer to the other questions.

Although John White was alarmed at this opinion, especially in view of what it said on the subject of establishment, Lord Sands did not think there was cause for concern.[131] If the establishment principle was an article of faith in the Church of Scotland, then, said Sands, the whole union movement had been a hypocrisy, 'for we knew that the UFs did not hold it as an article of faith', and they would be unlikely to enter a Church where it was held in that way. Sands, however, did not have the same attitude to the proposed declaration that was suggested in the opinion. Although Martin thought that a statement might be made by the joint conference that neither establishment nor voluntaryism were articles of faith and obligation, it was clear that both White and Sands thought that to say anything on this issue could cause trouble on their side.[132] As with the opinion, so with the declaration, it was left to the United Free Church leaders to go it alone; their minority was, after all, their problem. As Sands pointed out: 'our people do not look upon your minority in so brotherly a way as you do: and certain misgivings might be caused by proposals that we should do anything to meet not *you*, but *them*.'[133] According to Sands the issue of voluntaryism was part of the history of the UF Church and they had to deal with it. For their part they would have preferred 'to let sleeping dogs lie'. It was the description of these matters as 'principles' which disturbed Sands, as it seemed to call up the unfortunate periods of the Disruption judgements and the

[130] Ibid., p. 19.
[131] Lord Sands to J. White, 17.3.28 (W) 11.2.
[132] A. Martin to J. White, 7.4.28 and 11.4.28 (W) 11.2.
[133] Lord Sands to A. Martin, 9.4.28 (M) 20.4/8.

disestablishment campaign. There was no divergence over what was a matter of religious faith and obligation. He saw that the difficulty would be to frame any pronouncement which would not cause misunderstanding. John White was clear that neither establishment nor disestablishment was a principle, and that the union negotiations had proceeded on that understanding. He told Martin:[134]

> Our Conferences proceeded on the understanding that there would be no proposal to insert new propositions in regard to the relation of Church and State as an article of faith, or to annul the relation of Church and State. The policy, as frequently stated, was that on condition of Spiritual Independence being recognised and the position of other Churches as Churches of Christ acknowledged, those who held negative views on the state relationship would be expected to acquiesce in the alliance between Church and State indicated in the ancient statutes so far as not modified or repealed by the Articles and as sanctioned by the usage of many generations.

In his view it would be a disastrous step 'to endeavour to interpret the Uniting Act in terms of establishment or of voluntaryism.'

The minority members who had taken part in the approach to counsel indicated that they would be willing to reconsider their position in the light of the opinion and in view of the declaration. Again it proved difficult to reach an agreement over the form of words in the declaration. The minority wished the principle of religious equality to be clearly stated.[135] In the end it was agreed that the majority would draft the declaration and that the minority could make a statement setting out its position. Only the official declaration would, of course, become part of the 'binding laws and constitutions' of the Church which would be taken into the union.[136] The minority had wished that the declaration form part of the Basis of Union itself, a position which could not be maintained unless it was a joint declaration of the two Churches.[137]

The form of the declaration suggested by counsel, that there was nothing in the relations of the Church of Scotland to the State which was inconsistent with the constitution and principles of the

[134] J. White to A. Martin, 9.4.28 (M) 20.4/5.

[135] Draft Declaration H.31; Declaration suggested by Minority H.29 (M) 11.3.

[136] A. Martin to J. White, 21.4.28 (W) 11.2; A. Martin to A. Renwick, 16.4.28 (M) 20.4/12.

[137] Memo on Counsel's Opinion, and the Declaration (M) 14.3.

United Free Church, was straightforward enough; it was the preceding preamble which was controversial. The proposed preamble first of all referred to the United Free Church's principles of spiritual freedom and its well-known position as to any branch of the Church being placed in a position of privilege by enactment of the State. It also referred to the position taken in 1909 by the UF assembly when negotiations began. It then said that the Articles of the Church of Scotland, in particular Article VI, did not make it an article of faith and obligation that the State should support an establishment of religion. It concluded with the view that any special relations of the Church of Scotland with the State were not among the essential principles of the Church.

John White sympathised with the object of the declaration but did not like the form which it took.[138] He thought it might be fatal. The extract from the report of 1909 was incomplete and was, after all, only the starting position of one of the parties. A fuller reference to the points of agreement was made in the joint report of 1911. What was sought was 'a modification of the historical relations of the Church to the State, not on the lines of a rupture of these relations, followed by a building upon new foundations.' The reference to the Articles did not refer to the recognition by the civil courts of the independent character of the courts of the Church, or imply that such recognition could be extended to other Churches. The inference from the declaration was that the voluntary principle was to be regarded as an article of religious belief and obligation whereas neither establishment nor voluntaryism was to be regarded in that way; both rather were to be left as open questions. This position, White felt, was altered by the declaration. White thought it would be a 'disastrous step' to try to interpret the uniting Act in terms of either principle. While the declaration was 'a UF affair' it might necessitate a declaration from his side which 'would bring forward neglected aspects' and would not be for amity. Lord Sands also wrote to Martin in an official capacity as joint convener of the Church of Scotland committee to say why he and his colleagues did not like the proposed declaration.[139] He said that there were elements of continuity in the Church's relations with the State, not matters of privilege, but rather of constitutional usage. The UF minority wished to think otherwise, that the Church of Scotland was in the same position as the Episcopal Church in Ireland or Wales, which had been disestablished:

[138] J. White to A. Martin, 24.4.28 (M) 20.4/18.
[139] Lord Sands to A. Martin, 28.4.28 (M) 20.4/24.

Now the minority are quite at liberty to think this: it does not matter if it pleases them. But it is a different and more serious matter if the United Free Church as a whole takes formal action which may seem to bear the construction that it disavows the view of the constitutional position as I have tried to explain it. That is why we do not like this proposed Act.

What White and Sands were concerned about was not so much the declaration itself but what their own side might make of it.

Martin was anxious to let them know that he realised their difficulties.[140] All reference to these matters was delicate, and he thought that the wording of the declaration must try the patience of the other Church 'pretty high'. He agreed that the document was a one-sided reading of the arrangement reached between the Churches, and that it would be important for the UF Church not to go further in any formal way. He had wished that such a statement had not been necessary, but, he said, 'we are in a situation upon which varying interpretations are bound to be put on both sides'. Just as the declaration said that the establishment principle was no longer part of the constitution of the Church of Scotland, so it could also be said that the voluntary theory was no part of the constitution of the UF Church.[141] The declaration did not give the voluntaries all that they wished, but rather all they required in order to enter the union. The important thing was that they united on the uniting Act, and that the declaration was not included in the Basis and Plan of Union. At the assembly of the Church of Scotland, White referred to the declaration as a matter for the United Free Church alone and pointed out that it did not form part of the Basis of Union.[142]

While the declaration created problems for the Church of Scotland, it did serve to meet the difficulties of some of the minority who now agreed to enter the united Church in view of both it and the financial arrangements regarding stipend. Of the eleven ministers and seven elders belonging to the minority in the committee, eight ministers, including Adam Renwick, W. R. Forrester and Thomas Wardrop, signed a statement which was appended to the committee's report to the assembly in 1928. Three ministers and six elders, however, produced a minority report which continued the opposition to the union. The mollified members of the minority said in their statement:[143]

[140] A. Martin to Lord Sands, 30.4.28 (M) 20.4/27.
[141] Memo on Accommodation reached with certain Minority members of the United Free Committee (M) 14.3.
[142] White, Speech to the General Assembly, May 1928.
[143] UFC Rep., 1928, p. 9.

We consider that the proposed Declaration — reasserting as it does our Church's historic testimony on behalf of spiritual freedom and religious equality—enables us to enter the Union on the understanding that these principles are being safeguarded and maintained, the vestiges of the old relation of State privilege, State control, and State maintenance which still remain being non-essential, and no such special relation being any longer claimed or admitted by the State, or implied in the constitution of the Church of Scotland, or in that of the united Church.

They now felt able to enter the union, the only other requirement being that, in relation to those of the minority who could not accept the declaration, steps would be taken to prevent litigation and to secure a just and amicable settlement. Renwick seconded the adoption of the committee's report at the assembly in 1928, and Forrester also spoke in favour.[144] According to Forrester, the declaration meant that no one could say that the union would be on the basis of civil establishment. But needless to say James Barr still spoke in those terms and moved against the committee, saying that a bill was required stating that the Church of Scotland was no longer by law established.[145] Barr's speech was thought by *The Scots Observer* to be less militant in tone than on former occasions,[146] but his motion only received 53 votes and only twenty-three joined him in entering their dissent.[147] An editorial in *The Scotsman* pointed out that this vote was less than half the minority vote of a year ago, and that the remaining dissidents should take the view of those who had accepted the declaration as meeting their difficulties.[148]

(d) the continuing minority and the continuing Church

The continuing minority members of the committee presented a minority report to the assembly in 1928 which followed the statement by those who accepted the declaration. For them the basic position of the Church of Scotland remained unchanged. The fact remained beyond dispute, they said, that the Church of Scotland 'continues to have a special statutory relation to the State, and in that position no other branch of Christ's Church in Scotland shares or can share.'[149] The declaration was entirely

---

[144] *UFC Proc.*, 1928, pp. 178–81, 192–3.
[145] Ibid., p. 186.
[146] *The Scots Observer*, 2.6.28.
[147] *UFC Proc.*, p. 198.
[148] *Scotsman*, 26.5.28
[149] *Record*, January 1928, p. 11. Cf. *Scotsman*, 30.3.28 and 15.5.28, and The Minority's opinion on the Opinion of Counsel (UFCA).

negative in character and in no way committed the Church of Scotland. It was based on the assumption that the Church would remain established. The issue of doctrinal freedom had not been addressed and the relationship between Church and State was still ambiguous. The plans for a voluntary synod and a voluntary central fund had also been set aside and those congregations who wished to remain voluntary would face extinction. According to the United Free Church Association, the declaration did not change the situation since the Church of Scotland remained established, and reference was made to the remarks by John White distancing his Church from its terms.[150]

It became clear to Renwick that the executive of the United Free Church Association favoured a continuing Church. He and his colleagues failed to get from them a statement of the terms on which they would enter the union, but all indications pointed to 'the old Disestablishment and Disendowment position'.[151] The leaders of the Association wanted a delay, but there would be a delay of six months before the assembly in November considered the Basis and Plan of Union again, and in that time they could state their position. If it was in favour of disestablishment then they should say so. The executive of the Association refused permission to Renwick and Wardrop to put forward a motion at the annual meeting in 1928 in favour of the declaration, since it would not be in order to allow a motion which contradicted the fundamental positions of the Association.[152] The annual report of the Association for 1928 spoke of the two proposals as 'dangerous and delusive'.[153] The opinion of counsel and the declaration settled nothing and sought to give comfort to those who entered the united Church with the assurance 'that they can hold good Voluntary Principles inside an Established Church'. They were designed to make absorption as 'painless, as unconscious and as complete as possible'. At the annual meeting an amendment by Wardrop was ruled out of order, but he and Forrester were allowed to speak in support of a direct negative against the main resolution. The resolution said that no substantial change in the position had been made by the declaration and that the Church of Scotland was still 'by law established'. In his speech Wardrop maintained that the declaration, by saying that the establishment principle was no longer held in the Church of Scotland, was a vindication of the

---

[150] UFCA, *The United Free Church Declaration: a delusive safeguard* (M) 3. Cf. Letter to the Editor by James Barr, in *Scotsman*, 30.8.28.
[151] A. Renwick to A. Martin, 20.4.28 (M) 20.4/23.
[152] UFCA Min., 18.5.28.
[153] Ibid.

stance of the Association, and should be seen as a victory for their campaign.[154] Wardrop and Forrester, however, were only supported by four others and the resolution against the declaration was carried by a large majority.

Sommerville Smith described this parting of the ways as a 'momentous breach'.[155] In view of the position of Wardrop and the others, a declaration was framed stating the 'root principles' of the Association. This statement, as Renwick had suspected, was in favour of disestablishment and disendowment. The points had all been made before. According to the Association, the Church of Scotland was still established, was shackled by an unalterable doctrinal statement, could not accept any other constitution than that to which it was bound by parliament, accepted public money, and stood in a different position to the State from other Churches.[156] Smith regretted the loss to the 'pro-Union' position of his colleagues, some of whom had been the most outspoken in favour of the minority and who had campaigned for kirk sessions and congregations to reject the terms of the Basis and Plan of Union.[157] He thought that their departure was a setting aside of their own consciences and of the fellowship of their brethren. However it could not prevent disruption, only reduce the number of those who stayed out of the union.

The Association sent its conditions for union to the UF committee: that the united Church renounce the ancient statutes, renounce all aid from funds derived from public sources, and put Article I on the same footing as the other Articles, by making it alterable in the same way.[158] The committee replied that these were 'in direct opposition to those on which the negotiations for re-union between the Churches have proceeded from the first', and as such they would be rejected by the Church of Scotland.[159] On the other hand, the Association said that the original basis for the discussions had been unrestricted, and the Church of Scotland had therefore abandoned establishment as a basis for union.[160] In addition the UF Church, through its Church and State Committee, had repeatedly sought the disestablishment and disendowment of the Church of Scotland.

---

[154] *Glasgow Herald*, 24.5.28.
[155] Smith, 'Our Ten Years' Conflict', p. 49.
[156] Ibid., pp. 50–1.
[157] Ibid. Cf. UFCA Min., 18.5.28.
[158] UFC Min., 23 October 1928; *Record*, November 1928, pp. 2–3.
[159] A. Martin and R. J. Drummond to J. S. Smith, 23.10.28 (M) 20.6/5.
[160] J. S. Smith to A. Martin, 14.11.28 (M) 20.6/30.

The Association issued a statement, approved at a convention held in Glasgow on 27th June 1928, which was later published in the *Record*.[161] The members proposed to remain in the United Free Church, a Church that had kept, and was to keep, the fullest control of its doctrine, government, discipline and worship. It was also a Church which held its properties under the common law of the land, and which was placed alongside all other branches of the Church 'on the footing of the equality of all forms of religion before the law'. They would also rely solely on the giving of their members. Instead of a recourse to law, they suggested a friendly arbitration by a joint commission. They wished to see a Church which was 'enlightened and progressive' and which worked for the building up of Christ's kingdom in all places of the earth. While they recognised that the Church of Scotland would also share most of these ideals, they wanted to be part of a Church which was 'simpler and directer in its appeal, more compact, less clerical and official'. In their view the state connection tended to 'formalism and indifference on the part of church members, and towards ritualism and priestism on the part of its ministers.' Christian progress in regard to many social reforms would be grievously retarded. They thought, too, that the amalgamating or dissolving of congregations rarely led to church extension. In the view of *The Scotsman*, it was useless to try and accommodate the remnant minority since they continued to make arrogant assertions as if they were based on fact.[162] It asked: 'Is it possible that the Acts of 1921 and 1925 have made no difference? Only those who are determined not to be convinced can believe so.' At the convention, however, John Macfie of Bowden and Alexander Bain of North Queensferry moved unsuccessfully that the Association 'deeply conscious of the harm that would result from a disruption ... resolves to make no arrangement for a continuing Church'.[163] Not all in the Association would follow the leadership into the continuing Church.

Martin and Drummond prepared a reply to the minority statement, which was also published in the *Record*, entitled 'Is Separation Called For?' One more schism, they said, was the last thing to be desired in view of the wasteful duplication of resources which was already present within the Scottish Church. They rehearsed the familiar arguments over establishment and the

[161] UFCA, To the Members and Adherents, Office-bearers, Students and Probationers, Missionaries and Ministers of the United Free Church of Scotland, 27 June 1928 (M) 14.2; *Record*, September 1928, pp. 360–1. Cf. *Scotsman*, 28.6.28.
[162] *Scotsman*, 28.6.28.
[163] UFCA Min., 27.6.28.

endowments and pointed to the provisions for voluntary congregations and the content of the declaration. They concluded by asking: '…why disrupt the United Free Church? Or, to put it differently, on what ground is it proposed to build the "continuing" Church…?' They answered their own question by saying: 'Surely it is narrowest.' The minority were agreed that 'the grand essentials' of church life were shared by those who proposed to enter the united Church. The only difference was with regard to 'their application to a new solution of the old Church problem in Scotland'. Could it really be said that this of itself was enough to justify separation? They held out the hope that separation might still be avoided.

The declaration proved to be of help to all but the determined minority of those who adhered to the disestablishment position. Renwick suggested to Martin that the speeches in favour of union given at the assembly in 1928 should be circulated to members and those on the fringes of the Association.[164] Forrester was of the opinion that the move for a continuing Church was especially strong in the west among laymen, and that some in the west had always wanted a Church of their own with its H. Q. in Glasgow.[165] When it emerged, the United Free Church (Continuing) would be far stronger in the west central belt than elsewhere and would have its offices in Glasgow. According to Renwick, the problem in areas such as Greenock, Ayr, Rothesay, and in certain parts of Ayrshire and Dumfriesshire, was not the matters of principle or the land charges, but rather the unsatisfactory life of some of the parish ministers in those areas. It would be important to seek to reassure members that the UF colleges would be in the position of supplying the whole Church with the best possible ministry.[166]

The debate at the meeting of the assembly in November 1928, which finally considered the Basis and Plan of Union before it went down to presbyteries under the Barrier Act, was one of the shortest in the history of such discussions. The only speeches were those of Martin and Drummond, who moved the committee's deliverance, and those of Barr and Forrester Paton, an elder from Alloa and an honorary president of the UFCA, who moved against. The arguments on both sides had been well rehearsed and were familiar to all in the assembly hall. Martin challenged the view of the minority that they were the ones who were safeguarding the principles of the United Free Church. According to Martin, the Church was entering the union with its principles

[164] A. Renwick to A. Martin, 6.6.28 (M) 20.5/1.
[165] W. R. Forrester to A. Martin, 25.4.27 (M) 19.9/51 and 1.5.28 (M) 20.4/29.
[166] A. Renwick to A. Martin, 29.8.28 (M) 20.5/13.

intact. Singling out one of the minority, Alexander Weir, he said that Mr Weir need not think he would carry the principles of the Church away with him like another Samson carrying off the doors and posts of the city. He then quoted the relevant passage of scripture to long and loud laughter:[167]

> And he arose at midnight and took the doors of the gate of the city, and the two posts with them, *bar and all*, and put them upon his shoulders, and carried them up to the top of an hill that is before Hebron.

The minority, he said, would be left with the ghost of the United Free Church sitting on the grave of the Disestablishment Council. Barr however did gain some sympathy from the assembly when he complained about a piece in the Gaelic supplement of the *Record* which had tried to frighten highland church people against the minority by saying that they would depart from the fundamentals of the faith.[168] The end result of the debate was never in doubt and Barr's motion received only 48 votes and he and twenty-seven others registered their dissent.[169] A motion by Weir to instruct the committee to draw up proposals regarding an equitable division of property and funds between the majority and the minority was rejected as being premature.[170]

A similar motion was, however, accepted by the convener at the following assembly in May 1929.[171] At this assembly the results of the various overtures sent down under the Barrier Act were announced.[172] The campaign by the minority did not have such an impact as on the previous occasion when the opinion of the lower courts of the Church and congregations had been consulted regarding the discussions on union. During this campaign Martin thought that, while Barr was addressing meetings of sympathisers, he was making little impact and the coverage in the press was not as it once was.[173] As Martin put it, his stuff had ceased to be good copy. Many people whose sympathies were with Barr shrank from the prospect of a continuing Church. The declaration was approved by 63 home and 10 overseas presbyteries, while only one home presbytery disapproved. Only 46 kirk sessions disapproved. All the presbyteries which made returns approved of the Basis and of the

---

[167] *UFC Proc.*, 1929, p. 11; Reith, *Reminiscences*, p. 325. Judges 16: 3.
[168] *UFC Proc.*, 1929, p. 17.
[169] Ibid., pp. 23, 24.
[170] Ibid., p. 26.
[171] Ibid., pp. 190–1.
[172] Ibid., p. 165.
[173] A. Martin to J. White, September 1928 (W) 11.5.

Plan of Union. Of the kirk sessions, 88 disapproved of the Basis and Plan and 1301 approved. Of the congregations, while 1298 approved, 101 disapproved and four were equally divided. The voting at the assembly itself was equally emphatic with only 39 supporting the minority motion which was moved by D. M. Forrester of Broughton and seconded by James Barr.[174] A total of seventeen entered their dissent. In his speech, Forrester referred to what he considered to be a significant number of congregations that had voted against the union, and argued that the present proposals would therefore cause cleavage in the Church.[175] Barr's speech was familiar to the assembly both in terms of its content and its length. It greatly exceeded the time limits but he was allowed to continue since, as he said, it was likely to be the last speech he made there.[176] This speech by Barr prompted George Reith to recount a story which was then current in the Church. The story was about a minister, eager for the union but doubtful of his congregation's attitude, who was inspired to read one of Barr's anti-union speeches at the decisive congregational meeting, and thereby secured a unanimous vote in favour of union.[177]

In his speech Drummond said that a vote by a congregation against the Basis and Plan of Union did not mean a vote to stay out of the union.[178] He referred to a statement made by eight ministers who belonged to the minority but who had nevertheless decided to enter the union. They were not associated with Renwick and the others who were satisfied with the declaration and the arrangements for the voluntary congregations. They retained their principled objection to the union but had decided not to stay out and perpetuate division in the Church. This group included John Willock of Lerwick and both John Macfie and Alexander Bain, who had moved the motion in those terms in the Association. They had issued a statement in December 1928 saying that, while they were not in agreement with the Basis and Plan of Union, it was not their duty 'to carry opposition to the point that would cause a disruption in the Church'.[179] They suggested that those congregations which may have voted against union might nevertheless wish to pass a resolution stating that they 'do not consider the situation to be such as would justify them in taking the grave step of separating themselves from the majority of their

---

[174] *UFC Proc.*, p. 188.
[175] Ibid., p. 177.
[176] Ibid., p. 183; Reith, *Reminiscences*, pp. 333–4.
[177] Reith, *Reminiscences*, p. 334 n.1.
[178] Ibid., p. 167.
[179] *Record*, January 1929, p. 10.

brethren.' The minority was thus weakened even further by those who were unwilling to join a continuing Church. It was reported in *The British Weekly* that there were ministers who had voted for the minority right up to the end but who would not go as far as secession.[180] According to this source, too, there were congregations who had voted against the terms of union but, on finding themselves vacant, reversed the decision in order to call a minister.

The question troubling many was whether the continuing minority would make an appeal to the civil courts. This had been explicitly discounted in the statement of June 1928, and had been earlier rejected by a leading member of the Association, Alexander Weir. Renwick thought, however, there were others who did not agree with this position.[181] As was pointed out in the columns of the Church of Scotland's magazine, *Life and Work*, to go to the civil courts would be a strange threat from those who held voluntary principles.[182] Barr later spoke of the division of opinion among the minority on this issue.[183] The view prevailed among the continuing minority, however, that it would ill become them 'to prove in the Law Courts that the powers of the United Free Church were limited, even though she had used those powers unlawfully and disastrously in uniting with a Church by law established.'[184] Both sides made assurances that litigation would be avoided, and only in the case of one congregation was there a necessity to take action in the civil courts.[185]

Congregations who wished to do so could hold a ballot on whether or not to enter the union. Out of 1,441 congregations, 108 asked for voting papers. Of these, 64 voted 'yes' to the union, 33 voted 'no', while in one the voting was equal.[186] It was the view of Sommerville Smith that the voting should have been held in all congregations. Some members, he said, were denied the right to hold a ballot by their ministers or kirk sessions.[187] With regard to church buildings, even where a congregation had voted to stay out of the union, and the minister was also of that mind, it could happen that the building stayed in the Church of Scotland because of the terms of the title deeds or of the constitution.[188] According to D. M. Forrester, almost all the cases of local properties had to

[180] *The British Weekly*, 20.6.29.
[181] A. Renwick to A. Martin, 6.6.28 (M) 20.5/1.
[182] *LW*, August 1928, p. 185.
[183] Barr, *United Free Church*, p. 202.
[184] Ibid.
[185] Ibid.
[186] *UFC Handbook*, 1931, p. 35.
[187] Ibid., p. 52.
[188] Ibid., p. 207.

be argued over. While the joint negotiating sub-committee was reasonable, he felt that the courts of the Church of Scotland were not, and in 1931 the continuing Church still waited for a fair division of 'the family possessions'.[189] As part of the arrangement whereby the civil courts would not be reverted to by either side, a sum of £25,000 was made available to the minority by the United Free Church. This was raised separately and was thus not a call on those funds which the UF Church took into the union. This sum was to cover the interest of the minority in the offices, theological colleges and other heritable property and assets of the UF Church.[190] It was thought by outside observers to be an example of 'generosity unparalleled in ecclesiastical history'.[191] John White was able to announce at the meeting of the commission of assembly of the united Church in November 1929 that the funds had been raised to make this payment.[192]

The name of the continuing Church was a contentious issue. Martin felt that the use of the name of the United Free Church might give legitimacy to the claim that the continuing Church was the true successor of the Church. It was important that the UF Church carried both its name and property into the union. Other names were suggested to the minority, such as the 'United Free Presbyterian Church of Scotland', but they refused to consider any other name than that of their present Church.[193] They considered that they were not founding a new Church but continuing an old one. In addition it would be far more difficult to recruit members and ministers to a new Church than to a continuing one. The name was accepted by the majority on two conditions. The use of the name was not to be taken to imply any claim in law to the property of the United Free Church, and, to avoid misunderstanding, the Church should be known as the United Free Church of Scotland (Continuing) for the first five years.[194]

The first assembly of the continuing Church was held on 2nd October, the day of the union, in St Andrew's Halls in Glasgow, and James Barr was elected as the first moderator.[195] He would be succeeded in subsequent years by Charles Robson, Sommerville Smith, and D. M. Forrester, the leading ministers involved in the United Free Church Association. The continuing Church began its life with 92 congregations, which had risen to 114 by the end of

---

[189] Ibid., p. 210.
[190] Barr, *United Free Church*, p. 205.
[191] *The British Weekly*, 3.10.29. Cf. *Scotsman*, 26.9.29.
[192] *Glasgow Herald*, 21.11.29.
[193] Barr, *United Free Church*, pp. 189–90.
[194] Ibid., p. 191.
[195] Ibid., p. 183.

the year.[196] There were 37 ministers and 13,791 members. By the end of ten years of their separate existence the Church had grown to 125 congregations with 23,328 members and 75 ministers.[197] The fear had been expressed before the final break that the continuing Church would have insufficient numbers of ministers for the number of congregations, and while this was the case the shortfall was not as high as had been predicted.[198] The main strength was in the west central belt of Scotland: forty-nine congregations, over half of the total number, were in the presbytery of Glasgow and the south-west of Scotland.

While not large, and not as large as had been feared by the UF majority, the continuing UF Church still survived and increased in size in the coming years. After a few years Barr could claim that, although it was a small Church, it was making great progress.[199] The prediction by some that it would only continue for a few years proved unfounded.[200] It did not catch the popular imagination or appeal to the working classes in the way in which Barr had envisaged. It remained, however, as a living testimony to the principles of voluntaryism and religious equality. Barr was correct in saying that theirs was the only Presbyterian Church in Scotland fully to accept the principle of religious equality.[201] The Free Church and Free Presbyterian Church, for example, believed in the principle of an establishment of religion. It was also a progressive Church. From the beginning it admitted members as well as elders to the membership of committees, elders were able to take part with ministers in ordinations, and women were admitted to office on the same terms as men.[202] The first women to be ordained to the ministry were Elizabeth Barr, a daughter of James Barr, and Edith Martin, in 1935.[203] The United Free Church thus was over thirty years in advance of the Church of Scotland with regard to the ordination of women. In addition the Church did not hesitate, in Barr's words, 'to call for a new and better order of Society'.[204] The social policy of the Church continued to be liberal and compared markedly with the far more conservative social policy of the Church of Scotland in the 1930s.[205]

[196] Ibid., pp. 57, 168.

[197] *UFC Handbook*, 1940, p. 9.

[198] Letters to the Editor, *Glasgow Herald*, 12.10.28 and *Scotsman*, 9.1.29; Cf. *The British Weekly*, 20.6.29.

[199] Barr, *United Free Church*, p. 191.

[200] Ibid., pp. 182–3.

[201] *UFC Handbook*, 1931, p. 60.

[202] United Free Church of Scotland, *Supplement to the Manual of Practice and Procedure in the United Free Church of Scotland*, containing changes adopted from 1929 to 1935 (Glasgow, 1936), p. 5.

[203] *DSCHT*, p. 886.

[204] *UFC Handbook*, 1931, pp. 63–4.

[205] See below, pp. 272–3.

Alexander Martin and his colleagues, who led the vast majority of the United Free Church into the union, could be satisfied that the minority had been considerably reduced in size as a result of the two measures which had been taken. The breach, while still to be bitterly regretted, was relatively small. Martin considered that, in spite of the satisfactory agreement with the continuing minority, the committee had still failed in two respects. Union had been achieved, but at the price of disunion, and the right of a Church to unite with another body without loss of its identity had not been vindicated in the absolute way that had been wished.[206]

[206] A. Martin, Notebook, 25.9.29 (M) 2.7.

Chapter 9

Dealing with difficulties: the minority in the Church of Scotland

Since the minority in the Church of Scotland did not form a continuing Church as did the minority in the United Free Church, its presence and influence upon the union can be underestimated. The Auld Kirk minority was the upholder of establishment and endowment, and in its view these had been altered irrevocably by the Acts of 1921 and 1925. Thus it could not have continued in an established Church in the way in which the other minority would continue in a voluntary Church. It would have been possible for it to have continued as a separate Church holding to the establishment principle in a similar way to the Free Church of Scotland. But that prospect did not appeal to the members of the minority who were not as large or as united as their UF counterparts. Like their opposite numbers in the other Church, it was the fact of establishment, rather than the principle, which mattered in the end, and the united Church was still the nearest thing to a religious establishment in Scotland. Although they disapproved of the changes which had taken place in the constitution of the Kirk, they decided to stay within it and make the best of it.

As was pointed out at the time, the arguments of each minority were the mirror image of the other. At the assembly in 1912, Lord Balfour of Burleigh said that they could not both be right: 'The one says we have gone too far; the other, that we have given up nothing at all.'[1] If the UF minority said that the Church of Scotland was still established, the Church of Scotland minority said that it was no longer established. If the one said that the spiritual freedom of the Church had not been stated strongly enough, the other said that this claim was excessive and dangerous. If the one said that the Church would still depend upon income from public sources in the form of the ancient endowments, the other regretted that this was no longer the case. If the one criticised the Articles

[1] *Layman's Book*, 1912, p. 99. Cf. *PRS*, p. 320.

because they contained a fixed creed, the other side disapproved of what it saw as unhealthy fluidity of doctrine in the constitution of the Church. If the one thought that the constitution was unchangeable because it was embodied in an act of parliament, the other thought that the constitution was too flexible and lacked the stability which establishment had provided. If the one thought that change to the constitution was almost impossible because of the inclusion of the enhanced Barrier Act procedure in Article VIII, the other thought that this provision allowed far too much scope for change to take place. Both were agreed that the *via media* sought by the union committee was unacceptable. The only possibilities were either establishment or disestablishment. This point was made by a leading figure of the minority in the Church of Scotland, A. Gordon Mitchell of Killearn, in a letter printed in the anti-union publication of the UF minority, *Notes on Church Union,* in May 1925.[2] It was somewhat surprising that he should have tried to make common cause with the other side. He somewhat optimistically thought that he could remove the distance between them by showing that a State Church did not mean that privilege or status was granted to the Church as an institution, but rather that honour was being given to the Lord of the Church. He did think, however, that there were only two alternatives: 'Either there must be a State Church or what is called "religious equality".' There was, he said, 'no halting ground, no *via media,* no half-way house between the two.' The union committee had devised a 'chimerical compromise', an 'impracticable and impossible groove', and was doomed to failure. The two minorities were at one in rejecting the middle way of the union committees.

(a) the minority and the drafting of the Articles Declaratory

Two different positions can be identified among those who opposed the policy of the committee at various stages of the discussions on union. One outlook was that of the high church group, whose most prominent figure was James Cooper, and whose views were embodied in the programme of the Scottish Church Society. The main concerns of the high churchmen were set out before the start of the discussions in a memorial sent to the conveners of the Church of Scotland committee. The three conditions which they wished to be met in any reunion were:[3]

---

[2] *Notes on Church Union,* No. 1, May 1925.
[3] (JC) 31, 22 June 1909. Cf. *FR,* p. 34.

I. Fundamentals—Trinity, Incarnation. II. Ministry and Sacraments. III. Establishment and Endowments.

The primary requirement in any reunion was security for the catholic faith. For Cooper the faith was always more important than reunion. It was for this reason that he held out for what he considered to be a satisfactory statement of the doctrines of the trinity and the incarnation in Article I. It was for this reason that he threatened to secede from the Kirk should the committee sanction what he considered to be a 'creedless Church'. At the end of the day he achieved what he wished and he agreed with the final version of the Articles. It cannot be said, however, that the high churchmen succeeded in securing their other requirements, although they did have some success regarding the role of the minister in relation to the sacraments in the drafting of the Plan of Union. Unlike Cooper, others of the high church minority were unhappy about the doctrinal content of the Articles and about the position of the establishment and the endowments resulting from the Acts of 1921 and 1925. The aim of this group, and of the Scottish Church Society in its publications in the 1920s, was not to oppose the union as such but to seek to improve its conditions, and in this they achieved some success. The minority included also those who did not belong to the high church group and who were mainly concerned with the issue of establishment. The formation of the National Church Defence Association in 1919 illustrates the fact that opposition to the union was not confined to the high church group. A broader organisation was needed to include those for whom establishment was the primary issue. Gordon Mitchell would emerge as the leader of this latter group which, unlike the high churchmen, would remain opposed to the union right up to 1929.

The two different outlooks of the minority were first seen at the assembly of 1912. The two high churchmen, Cooper and Wotherspoon, were the sole signatories of a minority report on the subject of the Memorandum.[4] For them it was necessary to consider the nature and contents of the constitution rather than the method by which it was to be prepared. The Church might find itself committed to union in advance without knowing on what terms it was to be agreed. It seemed to them 'illogical and hazardous' to arrange the method of union before the terms of union were determined or their acceptability ascertained. They argued that the endowments should not be alienated from the parish for which they had been given, and that Church-State

---

[4] C of S. Rep., 1912, pp. 1225–30.

relations were being attenuated 'almost to vanishing point' and would become 'a mere shadow without substance'. In their view there was no recognition of the Christian faith in the Memorandum. This was vital, not only for the Church itself, but for the State which could not establish a Church which gave no guarantee that it was a true branch of the catholic Church and would remain as such. In view of the explanations and assurances given by Lord Sands at the assembly, however, Cooper withdrew his motion and the committee's deliverance was accepted unopposed.

The other minority position was represented by Malcolm McCallum of Muckairn. He proposed an amendment, which was later withdrawn, to the effect that the committee had exceeded its remit. McCallum would become a regular opponent of union, but his stance was very different from that of the high churchmen. He thought that union should be carried out on the basis of what he called 'the creedless Apostolic Church'.[5] In his view the emphasis of the Articles was on 'Creed and Church' instead of 'conduct and conscience'. In his concern for social issues he was much closer in outlook to the minority of the other Church. He contested Argyllshire for the Labour Party at the general election of 1920,[6] and in his book, *Religion as Social Justice*, published in 1915, he argued that the task of a reunited Church must be to turn the nation away from the sins of industrial capitalism toward the justice of the Kingdom of God.[7] Unlike the UF minority, however, he believed that a closer relationship between Church and State, rather than a divorce, was the way to achieve social justice.[8]

The opposition to the policy of the union committee emerged more vocally in the Kirk earlier than in the UF Church because significant changes to the position of the Church of Scotland were proposed before the other Church was committed to union. A series of four tracts entitled *Plain Words on Church Union* was published after the Memorandum of 1912 had set out the course which the Church would follow. In the first of the tracts it was made clear that the guarantees of the Church's status in the ancient statutes were to be erased from the statute book and the different status of non-established Churches would be removed.[9] The Church would be 'national', but in a new sense, and deprived of the things which really made it so. The teinds would be 'pooled'

---

[5] *Layman's Book*, 1918, p. 136.

[6] Hew Scott, ed., *Fasti Ecclesiae Scoticanae*, 4 (Edinburgh, 1915), p. 101.

[7] S. J. Brown, 'Reform, Reconstruction, Reaction: the social vision of Scottish Presbyterianism c.1830–c.1930', in *Scottish Journal of Theology*, 44 (1991), p. 503.

[8] *Layman's Book*, 1914, p. 120.

[9] *Plain Words on Church Union*, Tract No. 1.

and the resources centralised rather than used for the benefit of the parish. Both 'spiritual freedom' and 'religious equality', the two cherished ideals of the United Free Church, were enshrined in the proposals, and the result would be a centralised Church. The theme of spiritual independence was the subject of the second tract. The outcome of the Free Church Case had shown there was no such thing as spiritual freedom outside of a relationship with the State in which the Church would be protected. The UF Act anent Spiritual Independence of 1906 made extensive claims but had yet to be tested in the courts of the land. The Church of Scotland, especially after the Act concerning the new formula for subscription, was free in all that mattered. The absolute claim to spiritual freedom made by the UF Church was similar to that made by the Church of Rome. Was that the kind of claim which the Kirk wished to make? Instead of unity between Church and State there would be separation.

These tracts spelled out the underlying reasons why some of the minority in the Church of Scotland opposed the first draft of the Articles in the minority report of 1914.[10] This report was signed by fifteen members of the committee, nine of whom were ministers, and included Cooper and Wotherspoon along with Donald Macmillan of Kelvinhaugh in Glasgow, Professor H. M. B. Reid of Glasgow University, William Swan of South Leith and Alfred Warr of Rosneath. Apart from Cooper and Wotherspoon, the only other signatory who was a member of the Scottish Church Society was David Milligan, an Aberdeen lawyer and the son of Professor William Milligan, the founder of the Society. It should be noted, too, that two other committee members who were also members of the Society, Samuel M. Dill of Alloway and J. Montgomery Campbell of Dumfries, did not join the minority. Not all members were thus in favour of the stance taken by their two prominent colleagues. It is also worth noting that, while the Scottish Church Society had set out the basic principles it wished to see conserved in a united Church when discussions began in 1909,[11] it did not thereafter issue an official statement on the proposals until 1928 when it published *Notes on the Basis and Plan of Union*.[12]

The Church of Scotland minority cannot therefore be identified with the high churchmen, neither can the Scottish Church Society always be identified with the stance taken by some of its members, although these men played a leading role in opposing the policy

---

[10] *C of S Rep.*, 1914, pp. 27–8.
[11] Scottish Church Society, *Reunion: the necessary requirements of the Church of Scotland*, Conferences, Fourth Series (Edinburgh, 1909).
[12] See above, pp. 182–3, 184, 186, 187, and below, pp. 261–2.

of the committee at various stages. The supporters of the minority report wished to see a differently worded doctrinal article which would contain the doctrines of the trinity and the incarnation in what they considered to be more satisfactory terms. In addition this doctrinal confession should be stated to be unalterable.[13] They also wished to see a stronger statement about national religion, that the Church should seek the support and aid of the State and that it values and maintains the ancient statutory connection. The outlook of the minority was given fuller expression in a pamphlet published later that year and written by Swan and Wotherspoon.[14] In their view the Articles would introduce an ambiguity and fluidity into the constitution of the Church, both in terms of doctrine and in terms of its relationship with the State. The contribution by Alfred Warr in the assembly debate made it clear that for him at least it was the position of the Church as an establishment which was of paramount importance.[15]

Since the committee had agreed that the minority report should also be sent down to presbyteries for discussion along with its own report, those who had signed it did not oppose the committee at the assembly. There were two motions against the committee's deliverance, but one of them was procedural in character. J. D. McCallum of Larkhall, a member of the Scottish Church Society, wished the draft Articles to be sent back to the committee for further revision before being sent down to presbyteries.[16] The only hostile motion was once again made by Malcolm McCallum and he was seconded by Gordon Mitchell.[17] McCallum wished the Articles to be revised but laid down the lines on which they were to be altered. An additional article was to be drawn up referring among other things to 'the priesthood of the people and the divine sonship of the nation' and 'the amelioration of social conditions'. The committee's deliverance, however, was carried by an overwhelming majority.[18]

When the assembly resumed consideration of the Articles in 1918, there was still opposition from some of the minority even although the doctrinal content of Article I had been strengthened to meet the views of James Cooper. McCallum this time moved that the committee be discharged and that steps be taken for the reconstruction of the Church on a truly national basis and with a

---

[13] *FR*, p. 69.
[14] Swan and Wotherspoon, *Nec Tamen Consumebatur*.
[15] *Layman's Book*, 1914, pp. 124–5.
[16] Ibid., pp. 121–2.
[17] Ibid., pp. 119–20.
[18] Ibid., p. 129.

much wider union involving all the Churches in Scotland. He also felt that there should be a recognised spokesman of organised labour on the committee.[19] Gordon Mitchell failed to find a seconder for a motion which called for a complete recasting of the Articles to stress the duty of the nation to establish the Church of Christ.[20] Donald Macmillan, however, proposed an amendment which was seconded by W. S. Provand, clerk of the presbytery of Glasgow, which reflected one of Mitchell's concerns. He wished to curb what he considered to be the absolute freedom of the Church as expressed in the Articles. In particular, the Church should not have the power to interpret its Articles or to be 'sole judge' with regard to its doctrinal standards.[21] At the end of the debate, a motion by Joseph Mitchell of Mauchline to delete all the doctrinal references from Article I was withdrawn, and only three supported McCallum's motion and five Macmillan's amendment.[22] Mitchell and McCallum dissented from the decision of the assembly.[23]

The support for the minority at the assembly of 1919 was also small in number and could be counted on the fingers of both hands. An editorial in the *Glasgow Herald* thought that complete unanimity at the assembly would not have been half so impressive as the feeble display, both in terms of argument and content, which had been mounted by the minority.[24] A motion, which proposed that the replies of presbyteries concerning the Articles should go to the next assembly rather than a commission of assembly, was later withdrawn. Two other proposals, that kirk sessions should also be consulted, and that the United Free Church should give an undertaking to join them in the approach to parliament for legislation, received only a few votes. Cooper gave enthusiastic support to the committee since 'the things he had asked for in former Assemblies had been granted in these articles'.[25] Following the acceptance of the Articles by the assembly, the National Church Defence Association was formed to represent the minority position. At the meeting of the commission in December 1919, when the Articles had received the approval of the overwhelming majority of presbyteries, Macmillan's motion for a delay in seeking parliamentary legislation was defeated by 219 votes to thirty-six.[26]

[19] *Layman's Book*, 1918, pp. 135–6.
[20] Ibid., p. 136.
[21] Ibid., pp. 137–9.
[22] Ibid., p. 143.
[23] *C of S Rep.*, 1918, p. 442.
[24] *Glasgow Herald*, 28.5.19.
[25] Ibid.
[26] *Glasgow Herald*, 18.12.19.

For Cooper doctrine was the main concern, but it became clear that for other members of the Scottish Church Society, and for others in the minority not of the high church grouping, the establishment issue was just as important. While Cooper considered that Article I now contained a satisfactory statement of the doctrines of the trinity and the incarnation, other members of the minority, such as Wotherspoon and Provand, thought he was wavering![27] Both these members, along with Donald Macmillan, R. S. Kirkpatrick, formerly minister of Govan, J. MacGilchrist, his successor, and Professor H. M. B. Reid, resigned from the committee in January 1920.[28] Wotherspoon requested that his reasons for resignation be recorded in the minutes:[29]

> While thankful for the wording of the First of the Articles declaratory of the Constitution, I believe that the larger Church-union we hope for (apart from the coming together of Presbyterians) must base itself on the Nicene Symbol — every word of which has a place in the Westminster Confession, but of which Article I comes short. Farther, the claim made in other Articles to spiritual independence is excessive — to the extent (I hold) of being unspiritual and un-Catholic.

In addition to the doctrinal issue and the claim of spiritual independence, another concern of high churchmen can be detected in this statement. For them Presbyterian reunion was not an end in itself. Cooper's great dream had been the reunion of the two national Churches north and south of the Border, a 'United Church for the British Empire', and a merely Presbyterian reunion had been a danger which he had dreaded for some time.[30] Such a union would not be safe in the interests of catholic truth and would 'deepen the ditch' between the Episcopal Church and the Church of Scotland. He had wished to include the Episcopal Church in the talks on reunion at an early stage and had been supported by John White.[31] Yet for Cooper and the others this desire did not mean that Presbyterian reunion should not be promoted if it was a possibility. It was on offer, a reunion with the Episcopal Church was not.

At the assembly of 1920 McCallum and Mitchell continued their outright opposition to the Articles, but their motion, along with others critical of the committee's policy, was heavily defeated. Mitchell and nine others registered their dissent.[32] At the assembly

---

[27] *FR*, p. 65.
[28] C of S Min., 21.1.20 (W) 106. Cf. *FR*, p. 66; *PRS*, p. 316.
[29] Ibid.
[30] Wotherspoon, *James Cooper*, p. 246; Murray, 'James Cooper at Glasgow', p. 70.
[31] See above, pp. 32–3, 44–5.
[32] *C of S. Rep.*, 1920, pp. 936–7.

in 1921, while some of the minority, including the high churchmen Henry J. Wotherspoon and James F. Leishman, and Donald Macmillan, had reservations about the Articles, they did not move against the committee. Wotherspoon thought that the provisions of Article VIII should themselves be unalterable. We can note that the UF minority was against these provisions because it was thought that they were unalterable! Henry Wotherspoon also wished that references be made to the doctrines of the sacraments and the ministry, two of the other concerns of the Scottish Church Society which had been expressed at the beginning of the discussions.[33] The only hostile motion was McCallum's last one before he retired from the parish ministry. In his view the policy of the committee would mean the disestablishment of the Church of Scotland, which was again the exact opposite of the position of the minority in the other Church which held that the Church of Scotland was still 'by law established'.[34] McCallum's motion was defeated by 292 votes to fourteen and he entered his dissent along with three others including James Landreth, minister of Logie-Pert, and his brother Peter, minister of the West Church in Perth.[35] Peter Landreth, unlike his brother James, was not a member of the Scottish Church Society, and would continue to oppose the policy of the committee. Following the retirement of Malcolm McCallum, the leading role of the opposition to the policy of the union committee was taken by Gordon Mitchell. At the assembly in 1922 he proposed that the Church of Scotland Act, which recognised the Articles, be repealed, but the motion received the support of only two votes, that of himself and his seconder.[36] This motion reflected the views of the executive committee of the National Church Defence Association which had previously expressed its disapproval of the legislation and the content of the Articles.[37]

(b) the position of the continuing minority

The finalisation of the Articles in 1919 led not only to the formation of the National Church Defence Association, but also to the publication of a number of articles and pamphlets in which the continuing minority position was set out. J. Hay Thorburn, an elder and one of the founders of the Laymen's League, which had helped to defend the Church during the disestablishment

[33] *Layman's Book*, 1921, pp. 118–9. Cf. *FR*, pp. 99–100.
[34] Ibid., p. 118.
[35] Ibid., p. 121; *C of S Rep.*, 1921, p. 744.
[36] *C of S Rep.*, 1922, p. 653; *Glasgow Herald*, 27.5.22.
[37] *Scotsman*, 27.5.21.

campaign, wrote a pamphlet which was published by the Association entitled *Gold may be Bought too Dear: An Appeal to the People of Scotland and a Challenge to the Promoters of the Draft Articles of Union*. J. M. Finlayson of Lonmay wrote in 1919 *The Church of Scotland in Danger: Objections to the Policy of the Union Committee*. And 'A Parish Minister' wrote an anonymous pamphlet arguing against acceptance of the Articles entitled *Article VIII: Its Provisions and Safeguards*. This pamphlet was published in Paisley, most probably in 1920 since it refers to the final version of Article VIII.

Several themes can be identified in these pamphlets. In terms of procedure, the Articles were seen themselves as forming the basis of union, as was indicated in the title of Hay Thorburn's pamphlet. In this the minority members agreed with their counterparts in the other Church who also saw the Articles as the basis on which the Churches would unite rather than as a constitution for the Church of Scotland. The Articles were seen, too, as making concessions by the Church of Scotland side without the United Free Church having to make any alterations to its position. The sacrifice was all one way. But this was the nature of the exercise since the Church of Scotland had to take the initiative in seeking to remove the obstacles to union. The UF Church would then be involved in 'giving up' something when it came to accepting the Articles as part of the constitution of the united Church. The Articles involved compromise by both sides, although not yet formally by the UF Church.

With regard to the substance of the Articles, all the authors were concerned in the first place about the unchecked claim to spiritual freedom being made by the Church. The Established Church was not absolutely free in its own sphere; there were limitations to its exercise of freedom, and there was always the possibility of an appeal to the civil courts. The authors saw this as an advantage since it prevented the tyranny of the majority in the general assembly which would otherwise act as 'pope' in all matters. Under the Articles, there would an absence of control of any kind and the Kirk would be making the same claims as the Roman Catholic Church. It would be above the laws of any and every country and even be free to unite with that Church.[38] This claim to freedom, especially the claim to alter the doctrine, worship, government and discipline of the Church stated in Article IV, was incompatible with a relationship to the State. The Church could not have that freedom and also be established or 'national' in any

---

[38] J. Hay Thorburn, *Gold May be Bought too Dear: An Appeal to the People of Scotland and a Challenge to the Promoters of the Draft Articles of Union* (National Church Defence Association), p. 7.

meaningful sense.[39] According to Finlayson, Article IV went 'a very long way indeed towards the severance of the connection between Church and State'.[40] It would in effect be disestablishment from within.

Secondly, the authors said that the Church of Scotland would no longer be established but the same as any other Church in the land. It would be said to be 'national' but only because of its size, not because of its relationship with the State. If another Church became the largest body numerically, then it could claim to be the National Church.[41] Indeed it was one of the features of the Act of 1921 that other Churches could claim to be recognised in a similar way. Article III, after all, only stated that the Church of Scotland was 'a' national Church, not 'the' national Church.

In the third place, the authors thought that the Articles introduced a fluidity of doctrine into the Church. The Confession of Faith could be altered and the Church could formulate new statements. There was no guarantee that it would remain faithful to reformed doctrine. None of them thought that Article I was satisfactory as a doctrinal statement. The anonymous author of *Article VIII: Its Provisions and Safeguards* was the most eloquent on this subject. To begin with, he said, the Church claimed the right to interpret its Articles, including Article I.[42] This introduced an element of ambiguity because the Articles were very much in need of interpretation. In recent theological debate, too, interpretation had come to include the right to treat something symbolically instead of in a literal sense. This meant that there was a dangerous elasticity in the Articles. The only arbiter of interpretation was the Church itself, and this meant the general assembly which would assume an absolute power. Not only was Article I subject to interpretation by the Church, but also it only contained four statements. These were that the Church of Scotland is part of the catholic Church, that it adheres to the Scottish Reformation, that it receives the Word of God as its supreme rule of faith and life, and that it avows the fundamental doctrines of the Christian faith. The doctrinal content of Article I was not couched in terms of a statement but consisted of a collection of participial clauses of a quasi-credal character, which were however 'destitute of categorical authority'.[43] None of the four statements were as firm

---

[39] J. M. Finlayson, *The Church of Scotland in Danger: Objections to the Policy of the Union Committee* (Peterhead, 1919), pp. 9–10.

[40] Ibid., p. 10.

[41] Ibid., p. 9.

[42] *Article VIII: Its Provisions and Safeguards*, by a Parish Minister (Paisley, n.d.), pp. 6–8.

[43] Ibid., p. 10.

as they at first might seem as their meaning was deliberately ambiguous. There was also the ability of the Church to change its constitution as set out in the provisions of Article VIII which had given rise to the pamphlet by the 'Parish Minister'. The enhanced Barrier Act procedure was no consolation to him as the Church still had boundless possibilities for change, with of course the exception of Article I. But since Article I was unsatisfactory, the sovereignty of Article VIII was unlimited. Thorburn, too, was anxious in view of the whole trend of German theology and biblical criticism which was evident in the United Free Church. The Word of God was said in Article I to be 'contained' in the scriptures and was not identified with them.[44] In this respect the establishment minority completely disagreed with the members of the UF minority who criticised Article I as being a fixed creed and Article VIII as setting 'a five-barred gate' against any change in the constitution. They did not think that the mechanism for change in Article VIII could be changed except by act of parliament and they quoted Lord Finlay to this effect. It was one the great weaknesses of Article VIII for 'Parish Minister', however, that it could be changed by using its own procedures. For him, this was 'the *reductio ad absurdum* of the whole protean constitution.'[45]

One of the leading minority members, Donald Macmillan, wrote an article in the *Hibbert Journal*[46] which provoked a response both from a United Free Church minister, W. R. Thomson of Bellshill,[47] and from Professor W. A. Curtis, one of the strongest proponents of union on the Church of Scotland side.[48] Like the minority in the other Church, Macmillan objected to the legislation on the constitution and on the endowments of the Church being separated. It would be a mistake to hand over to parliament the disposal of the endowments; the Church should have a say in what happened to them.[49] The claim in the Articles to 'absolute spiritual independence' was quite unacceptable. There would be no protection for minorities in the Church if the majority of the assembly held sway, since there could be no appeal to the civil courts. Both Thomson and Curtis criticised Macmillan for seeing the State as a guardian of the Church's freedom and a kind of

[44] Thorburn, *Gold may be Bought too Dear*, p. 12.

[45] Ibid., p. 15.

[46] Donald Macmillan, 'Presbyterian Reunion in Scotland: The Draft Articles', in *The Hibbert Journal*, 17 (1918–19), pp. 309–18.

[47] W. R. Thomson, 'Presbyterian Reunion in Scotland', in *The Hibbert Journal*, 17 (1918–19), pp. 449–57.

[48] William A. Curtis, 'Reunion in the Scottish Church and the proposed Articles', in *The Hibbert Journal*, 18 (1919–20), pp. 240–58.

[49] Macmillan, 'Presbyterian Reunion', p. 311.

referee in ecclesiastical matters.[50] Curtis saw an inconsistency in his wishing to accept parliament as an arbiter in spiritual matters and as a protector of minority interests while being unwilling to entrust it with the disposal of the endowments: 'In one breath Parliament is the champion of the distressed minorities and the dispenser of ideal justice; in the next it is not to be trusted with the disposal of the Church's possessions.'[51] Parliament, said Thomson, could surely be relied upon to make a national settlement of what was a national issue.[52]

Gordon Mitchell, who had become one of the secretaries of the National Church Defence Association, also contributed to the debate in the press. He sent copies of correspondence between himself and Lord Balfour of Burleigh to the editor of *The Scotsman*, which were then published.[53] In these letters Mitchell appealed to Lord Balfour to prevent the Kirk becoming a voluntary sect and to stand up for its position as he had done during the disestablishment campaign. Mitchell also wrote a letter which was published in *The Spectator* and which provoked a debate in the correspondence columns of the magazine, in which he was supported by Andrew Haldane of Inverkeilor[54] and opposed by Archibald Fleming and a member of the committee who signed himself 'Unionist'.[55] To attract the attention of English readers, Mitchell referred to the forthcoming legislation incorporating the Articles Declaratory as the Scottish 'Enabling Bill', since such a bill in relation to the Church of England was then being considered by parliament. The Scottish measure, he said, would lead to 'the complete separation between Church and State' and would result in disestablishment and probable disendowment.[56] The crucial point for him was that the two Churches were divided by matters of principle which could not be reconciled. The scheme in the Articles was, he said, a 'ramshackle make-believe of union which brings together antagonistic and irreconcilable principles of sectarianism and national religion on a footing of voluntaryism.'[57] In reply, Fleming pointed out that James Barr, the leader of the minority in the other Church, did not agree with Mitchell, since he considered that with this act the establishment and endowment of the Church of Scotland would be more entrenched than ever.[58] He referred to the

50 Cf. *PRS*, p. 318.
51 Curtis, 'Reunion in the Scottish Church', p. 241.
52 Thomson, 'Presbyterian Reunion', p. 455.
53 *Scotsman*, 29.10.19. Cf *PRS*, p. 318.
54 *The Spectator*, 23.8.19, pp. 242–3; 11.10.19, p. 471; 18.10.19, p 502.
55 *The Spectator*, 30.8.19, pp. 275–6; 8.11.19, pp. 613–4.
56 *The Spectator*, 23.8.19, pp. 242, 243.
57 Ibid., p. 243.
58 *The Spectator*, 8.11.19, pp. 613–4.

terms of Article III, which listed the various acts of parliament by which the Church's position had been recognised, and to the provisions of Article I, which in his view comprised a meticulous summary of the Christian faith in its time-honoured essentials. What more, he asked, could Mitchell and 'his little band of stalwarts' want?[59] The minority lost the argument over the content of the Articles in the Church, but, as we have seen, there was an ingenious attempt by some high churchmen to object to their passing under the Barrier Act on procedural grounds.[60] It was claimed that the Articles should have been preceded by words of enactment. This ploy was successfully countered by the leaders of the union committee.

When it came to discussing the proposals of the Haldane committee concerning the property and endowments of the Church, there was much less in the way of opposition than there had been over the framing of the Articles. At the assembly in 1923 J. M. Finlayson moved that the assembly express disapproval of the Haldane report, but this motion only attracted the support of himself and his seconder.[61] Another amendment critical of the Haldane recommendations had the same fate. There was little opposition to the final settlement which John White announced to the assembly in 1924. A motion supported by Peter Landreth, that the proposals should go down to the presbyteries of the Church, was withdrawn and the assembly came to a unanimous finding in support of the agreement. Notable at this assembly, as Archibald Fleming pointed out in an article in the *Glasgow Herald*, was the support given to the measure by W. S. Provand, for long an opponent of the union policy of the Church.[62] At the assembly of 1925, however, Mitchell proposed a motion deploring the passing of the property and endowments bill in parliament, but it attracted only seven votes. One of Mitchell's arguments was that the bill was a violation of the terms of the Treaty of Union of 1707, an argument which had been put forward and answered during the parliamentary debate.[63] Mitchell would also later move against the continuance of the committee on union but he attracted only five votes in support of his motion.[64]

(c) the minority and the Basis and Plan of Union

With the publication of the Basis and Plan of Union the council of the Scottish Church Society at first issued a Memorandum for

[59] Ibid., p. 614.
[60] See above, pp. 112–3.
[61] *C of S Rep.*, 1923, p. 49; *Glasgow Herald*, 26.5.23.
[62] *Glasgow Herald*, 28.5.24.
[63] *C of S Rep.*, 1925, p. 615; *Glasgow Herald*, 27.5.25.
[64] *C of S Rep.*, 1925, p. 973.

members and later published *Notes on the Revised Basis and Plan of Union* for the wider public. Their policy was not one of outright opposition to the union but of seeking improvements to the proposals in the Basis and Plan. Some of the issues which concerned them, regarding the role of elders at ordinations, the authority of the minister in relation to the sacrament, and the place of the Catechisms, have been noted in relation to the drafting of the document.[65] The high churchmen, however, shared an underlying unease about the proposals. The council of the Society made it clear that its Memorandum had been motivated, not by a spirit of hostility to union, but by a desire that the union might be as satisfactory as possible, 'a union consonant with Church principles and really conducive towards Catholic unity'.[66] For the members of the Society, the Basis and Plan were equally important as the one presupposed the other. They therefore rejected one of the basic premises of the committee, that the Basis was foundational and had to be agreed prior to union, while the Plan was not as important and could be altered later. They were also anxious about the timescale involved and wished for a further year of deliberation before the final step was taken. Discussion of such a momentous and complex matter would be restricted by the tight timetable and the Plan was still quite incomplete. In this respect they had a point since, as we have seen, some matters of considerable importance were left to be decided later by the united Church. While this was of itself not a bad thing, it could mean that some issues were simply left in abeyance to be decided by use and wont rather than by considered reflection. The documents, however, had several general characteristics which gave cause for concern to the high churchmen.

The first feature they identified was 'a bias that cannot be regarded as Catholic'. Although the Church of Scotland was spoken of throughout the Basis and Plan of Union as a 'part' or 'branch' of the Catholic Church, it was treated as 'an isolated ecclesiastical state, self-contained, sovereign, entirely independent, acknowledging allegiance to no ecclesiastical authority more august than its own.'[67] The Church was expected to fraternise 'not with the Catholic but with the non-Catholic elements of Christendom'. This concern was based on their misgivings regarding the absolute claim to spiritual independence made in the Articles and in the Basis of Union. Any one branch of the Catholic Church did not have an absolute freedom but belonged

---

[65] See above, pp. 168, 186–7, 162–3.
[66] SCS, Memorandum, p. 1.
[67] Ibid., p. 3.

to the Catholic Church as a whole, and must remain bound to it in terms of doctrine and practice. They also thought that the union was being seen 'less as the repairing of age-long breaches in the walls of a National Church, than as the amalgamation of two Scottish Presbyterian Sects, and the creation thereby of one comprehensive Presbyterian Sect of much more impressive and even of National dimensions.'[68]

The other concerns of the members of the Scottish Church Society related to the organisation of the Church. In agreement with the minority in the United Free Church, they objected to the 'excessive centralisation of authority' in the proposals.[69] Centralisation was essential to efficient organisation, but it must be 'constitutional' rather than 'excessive'.[70] This tendency was seen especially in terms of finance but it infected the entire system. They criticised the way in which the courts of the Church below the assembly would be 'depressed and their functions more or less evacuated'. The size of the assembly, too, would become the instrument of the 'leaders' who also controlled the permanent machinery of the committees and their officials. Power would be concentrated in the hands of the few for the sake of bureaucratic management. They felt, too, that the need for finance was stated in a 'commercial, a compulsory and dictatorial tone which belongs rather to a business concern than to the Church'.[71] The scheme was 'revolutionary' and much more sweeping than had been anticipated. The face of the Church was entirely remodelled and, while the name remained, the content had changed. In most respects the practice chosen for the future was not that of the Church of Scotland. The one exception was with regard to the appointment of ministers where the system of 'naked election' in the Church of Scotland had been chosen rather than the 'superior tradition' of the United Free Church. This tradition retained 'some face of spiritual responsibility and motion in the Church, as instituting, and in the Flock, as seeking,' and the emphasis was upon the call rather than upon election.[72] The more specific concerns of the Scottish Church Society were published in 1928 as *Notes on the Revised Basis and Plan of Union* which was circulated widely to members of presbyteries as they considered the document before the assembly meeting in November of that year. These concerns have already been noted when discussing

---

[68] Ibid., pp. 3–4.
[69] See above, pp. 219–20.
[70] SCS, Memorandum, p. 4.
[71] Ibid., p. 5.
[72] Ibid., pp. 5, 17.

the content of the Basis and Plan, and related to the functions and powers of kirk sessions in relation to those of the minister, the inclusion of retired ministers and co-opted elders in the courts of the Church, the extensive powers given to committees, and the absence of a definite territorial system of parish organisation.[73]

When the Basis and Plan first came before the assembly in 1927, there was only one critical motion. Alexander Spark of Blythswood in Glasgow moved that the assembly send the report to presbyteries without an expression of welcome being given to the proposals, but this motion received only seven votes.[74] John White was able to accept another amendment which encouraged ministers and kirk sessions to bring this matter before their congregations. The influence of the Scottish Church Society could be seen at the following assembly in May 1928. Overtures, 'bearing a strong family likeness',[75] were sent up from ten presbyteries and from the synod of Lothian and Tweeddale seeking consideration of some of the main concerns of the Society. One correspondent, writing to *The Scotsman*, pointed out that while the Scottish Church Society complained about the proposed 'invasion' of presbyteries by assembly committees, this was an 'invasion' of overtures by presbyteries where the Society had representatives.[76] On the other hand, the fact that the members of the Society were able to persuade these courts to support the overtures shows that their concerns were more widely shared in the Church. The assembly agreed by 192 votes to 172 on a motion by H. J. Wotherspoon to remit these overtures to the union committee in order if possible to secure the desired amendments.[77] In the event the points concerning the relation of minister and kirk session and the relation of presbyteries to the assembly committees were met to some extent. The concerns regarding the composition of the courts of the Church and parish structure were not changed. It could be said, however, that in a very important area, the authority of the minister in relation to the conduct of worship and the sacraments, the Society had achieved a notable success and one which would have far-reaching effects in the united Church. It could not be said, at the end of the day, that the Plan of Union simply reflected the practice of the United Free Church. Two other motions, however, were not accepted by the assembly.[78] A

---

[73] Fleming, *The Story of Union*, p. 135.
[74] *Scotsman*, 28.5.27.
[75] Ibid.
[76] *Scotsman*, 9.5.28.
[77] *C of S Rep.*, 1927, pp. 855–7; Fleming, *The Story of Union*, p. 138.
[78] *C of S Rep.*, 1927, pp. 857–8.

motion by Provand asked the committee to examine the bearing of the opinion of counsel and the declaration of the United Free Church on the proposed Act of union. And a motion by Mitchell proposed that the committee draw up a statement on the way in which the Articles had altered the relationship between Church and State.[79]

At the adjourned meeting of the assembly in November 1928, Cromarty Smith and H. J. Wotherspoon put forward an amendment seeking the postponement of a decision on the Basis and Plan of Union. They wished further conference be held with the United Free Church regarding the composition of church courts and the relations between the assembly committees and the presbyteries of the Church.[80] These were two of the matters which had been the subject of the earlier overtures but which had not been agreed by the joint committee. When it was pointed out that this proposal was 'wholly impracticable', Smith withdrew the motion. The only motion to disapprove of the Basis and Plan of Union was made by Gordon Mitchell and seconded by E. E. Williamson of Shurrery and received only seven votes. Mitchell and Williamson entered their dissent.[81] At the final assembly before the union in May 1929 Mitchell had given up the unequal fight and the only opposition came from Peter Landreth whose motion was seconded by John L. McPhee of Orkney. Landreth said that he represented a considerable minority of the presbytery of Perth and a very large majority of his own congregation.[82] He maintained that people in the Church had not had an opportunity to express their views on the question of union. In addition the assembly and courts of the united Church would be 'afflicted by senility' in view of the decision to admit retired ministers as members. Only three voted for this motion and Landreth and McPhee dissented from the decision.[83] Thus at the end the minority at the assembly had shrunk to a very small number. Most of the minority, such as the members of the Scottish Church Society, had attempted to improve the Basis and Plan of Union rather than to oppose the committee directly, and their policy had met with some success. It had been left to Mitchell and one or two others to fight a lonely and doomed battle against the inevitable outcome.

[79] *Glasgow Herald*, 26.5.28.
[80] *C of S Rep.*, November 1928, pp. 5–6.
[81] Ibid., p. 6; *Glasgow Herald*, 22.11.28.
[82] *Glasgow Herald*, 25.5.29.
[83] *C of S Rep.*, 1929, p. 899.

Chapter 10

Assessing the outcome: the promise fulfilled?

When the union of the Churches took place on 2nd October 1929 there was an atmosphere of expectation as well as of gratitude, and even of relief, that the long process had finally come to an end. In both assemblies there were regrets as well as anticipation. The Church of Scotland assembly would not meet again in the hall at the top of the Lawnmarket, while the United Free Church would not enter the union with 'ranks unbroken'.[1] There also appeared to be a lack of enthusiasm among the membership of the Church at large, something which was recognised by both John White and Alexander Martin. They pointed out, however, that this reaction had been observed at previous unions. Martin himself could remember the union of 1900 and that of 1876 when the Cameronians had joined forces with the Free Church. On neither of these occasions, he recalled, 'did the achievement come about in that atmosphere of high exhilaration which might have been expected'.[2] Although he hoped that they would not see this apathy once more, he recognised that, while they might look for the whole membership 'to furnish the driving-power to carry the project through', it might be that they would have to do without it. One minister reminded Martin that 1901, the year after the previous union, had been a 'flat year'.[3] The Church began to face 'the difficult questions that rise everywhere in the practical working out of union.' John White referred to what Professor David W. Forrest, who had moved the resolution for union at the UP assembly in 1900, had to say on this subject.[4] Forrest had thought it unfair to compare the union to the Disruption. There had been no popular excitement in 1900 as there had been in 1843. At a secession, there was inevitably excitement; there would not have

---

[1] *JW*, p. 264.

[2] A. Martin and R. J. Drummond, *Church Union*, Speeches delivered at the adjourned meeting of the General Assembly of the United Free Church of Scotland, on 21st November 1928 (Edinburgh, 1928), p. 7.

[3] A. Philip to A. Martin, 25.10.28 (M) 20. 6/8.

[4] John White, Absence of Enthusiasm (W) 99.

been such an event unless people had felt called to make a stand on principle and something vital was at stake. When two Churches united, he said, there was not the same sense of crisis. There was not the same pressure with regard to time: 'If it has been postponed so long, why not delay it a few years more?' Thus when a union took place it was due rather to 'a quiet, serious consciousness of duty, than to the excited feelings that are natural when a conscientious protest has to be made, and made at once.' In spite of Martin's hope, some detected apathy rather than enthusiasm in 1929.[5]

The apparent apathy of the membership could not be laid at the door of the press. Throughout the process of reunion the Scottish press had given very full coverage to the debates and discussions, including the publication of a generous number of letters in the correspondence columns. The two leading quality newspapers in Scotland, *The Scotsman* and the *Glasgow Herald* had both been supportive of union, the religious affairs correspondent of the former being none other than Norman Maclean. For example, when the Basis and Plan of Union was finally sent down to presbyteries in November 1928, *The Scotsman* said that the decision 'will issue in the realisation of a lofty ideal and in the fulfilment of a dream cherished by our forefathers'.[6] The article also spoke of the benefits flowing from the union being for the 'abiding good of Scotland'. The *Glasgow Herald* on the same day called for consideration to be given to the principles rather than the details of the proposals.[7] Not everyone would agree with every point in the Plan of Union, but none of these matters, it was argued, was important enough to justify delay. Sacrifices of this kind were the price which had to be paid for a larger unity, 'and they ought not to be allowed to dwarf in anyone's mind the real gains which the completion of union promises to secure.' These newspapers had also given considerable coverage to those who opposed the union, and in particular to the activities of the United Free Church Association and the views of James Barr. One correspondent complained about the space devoted to Barr, that it gave him far more prominence than he deserved.[8] Since such controversy is 'news', it was inevitable that the press would concentrate on those in both Churches who disagreed openly with the policies of the union committees. As we have seen, members of the minority adopted the strategy of writing letters to the press as a way of

[5] Ibid.
[6] *Scotsman*, 22.11.28.
[7] *Glasgow Herald*, 22.11.28.
[8] *Glasgow Herald*, 19.7.28.

gaining greater publicity for their cause.[9] We also noted, however, that the amount of press coverage given to James Barr tailed off during the second half of 1928 following the decision of a significant number of the minority to support the union.[10]

Throughout the twenty years of discussions it had been recognised that the union of the Churches was not an end in itself. At an early meeting Archibald Henderson had held up the famous map of Scotland that showed the disparity between the density of the population on the one hand and the concentration of the resources of the two Churches on the other. John White had also been concerned to see a greater efficiency in the work of the Church. One of the main motives in bringing about the union was the need to combine the resources of the two Churches 'for effective Home Mission and Church Extension Work'.[11] Writing in the Church of Scotland magazine as moderator in 1926, White said that the urgency and greatness of the challenge facing the Churches required 'the marshalling of all the forces of the Presbyterian Church in Scotland if the best results are to be achieved'.[12] He thought that the unchurched masses of the big towns and cities called on the Churches for 'unity of effort, unity of counsel, and unity of direction'. The union should lead to a rationalisation of the work of the Church in relation to the needs of the nation. In the next issue of the magazine, Lord Sands spoke of the waste of men and resources due to the rivalry and duplication of congregations at the local level.[13] One minister, he said, had told him that his neighbouring ministers in both Churches were 'just eating their hearts out owing to this overlapping and curtailment of sphere and the constant struggle under depressing surrounding competition'. This situation, said Sands, was unacceptable in view of the overall needs of the nation. The 'churchless million' was always the concern of those most responsible for the union.

Did the union fulfil its promise? Even John White would later have doubts about the answer to that question, as he made clear in presenting his report as convener of the Home Mission and National Church Extension committees to the assembly in 1935.[14] In assessing the union in the following year, he thought that much had been done in terms of the structures of the Church, and that its organisation tended to be 'more efficient and less wasteful'.[15]

[9]   See above, p. 212.
[10] See above, p. 240.
[11] John White, Union and Home Mission (W) 99.
[12] *LW*, April 1926, pp. 83–4.
[13] *LW*, May 1926, p. 103.
[14] *LW*, July 1935, pp. 270–1.
[15] John White, The Union — Seven Years 1929–1936 (W) 100.

But he also felt that in many respects 'less has been accomplished than was looked for'. Alexander Martin agreed that much remained to be done in blending the two traditions in the one Church.[16] One problem outwith the control of the Church was the sudden collapse of world prosperity. The union of the Churches took place during the first week of October, 1929; the Wall Street Crash took place during the last week of October. As White lamented, 'at the very moment that re-union took place, that year saw the Nations become bankrupt'.[17] The economic conditions faced by the united Church were most unfavourable for expansion and advance. In spite of those difficult circumstances, the Kirk sought to live up to its claim to be 'a national Church representative of the Christian faith of the Scottish people'.

(a) evangelism, efficiency, extension and ecumenism

The united Church had a total communicant membership of over one and a quarter million people.[18] But its position as a national Church also involved the obligation to minister to the people of Scotland as a whole. The first post-union meeting of the general assembly approved the launch of the Forward Movement, a mission of rededication by the restored national Church.[19] Twelve commissions were set up to explore different issues and the reports were later published as *The Call to the Church*, edited by the minister and journalist, J. W. Stevenson.[20] Stevenson was the editor of *The Scots Observer* and in 1930 he brought out a collection of papers by contributors to the magazine entitled *The Healing of the Nation*.[21] The occasion of the union of the Churches was seen as a new opportunity for the Church to re-examine and redefine its role in relation to Scottish society. A Forward Movement Congress was held in Glasgow in October 1931 and was followed by several regional 'Missions of the Kingdom' 'aimed at inspiring and mobilising congregations for local action'.[22] *The Call to the Church* identified the challenge facing the Kirk. There were about one and a half million people in Scotland who were outside any of the Churches.[23] The

---

16 'Principal Martin Looks Back' in *LW*, June 1934, p. 245.

17 White, The Union—Seven Years 1929–1936.

18 Fleming, *Story of Union*, p. 170.

19 Stewart J. Brown, 'The Social Ideal of the Scottish Churches during the 1930s', in Andrew R. Morton, ed., *God's Will in a Time of Crisis*, Centre for Theology and Public Issues, University of Edinburgh, Occasional Paper No. 31 (Edinburgh, 1994), p. 16.

20 Church of Scotland, *The Call to the Church*. The Book of the Forward Movement of the Church of Scotland (Edinburgh, n.d.).

21 J. W. Stevenson, ed., *The Healing of the Nation: the Scottish Church and a Waiting People* (Edinburgh, 1930).

22 Brown, 'Social Ideal', p. 16.

23 C of S, *Call to the Church*, p. 17.

2,800 congregations of the reunited Church of Scotland were numerically adequate but not ideally distributed. Congregational unions had already taken place, and it was optimistically assumed that the duplication of resources in small communities would soon be brought to an end. In addition, the task of church extension was seen to be a priority and one to which the Kirk must give its strength if it was to justify its claim to be a truly national Church.[24]

As has been pointed out, the emphasis of the Forward Movement was on reviving 'the parish and community ideal'.[25] Visitations of the parish were to be carried out by ministers and elders, while members were to be encouraged to become involved in the various organisations connected with the congregation, such as those for children, young people, and the unemployed. The parish ideal cherished by Thomas Chalmers in the early nineteenth century was to be made to work for the good of the whole of society in the early twentieth century. Its success would not only strengthen the pastoral care of the people but would also facilitate the evangelisation of Scotland. The Forward Movement, however, proved to be a disappointment.[26] The people of Scotland were beginning to feel the effects of the world economic depression. The Forward Congress had coincided with the general election of October 1931, called to seek support for the National Government in its efforts to meet the crisis. Public attention was necessarily given to the political and economic problems of the nation. At the local level, too, the results were less than had been expected by the promoters of the movement.

One question raised by the Forward Movement was whether the united Church was committed to the territorial principle of the parish unit as had been set out in Article III of its constitution. We have already noted the controversy aroused over the renaming of churches, a seemingly unimportant matter that nevertheless symbolised the unease of former United Free congregations over assuming a parish role. One minister told John White that even in a former Church of Scotland charge, that of St Enoch's-Hogganfield in the presbytery of Glasgow, 'The particular devil that resists my powers of Exorcism is a selfish Congregationalism'.[27] Another minister in the same presbytery hoped that one of the immediate results of the union would be that all congregations 'will be encouraged and enabled to do real Territorial work'.[28] In some

[24] Ibid., p. 47.
[25] Brown, 'Social Ideal', p. 16.
[26] Ibid., p. 17.
[27] A. C. Kennedy to J. White, 27.12.29 (W) 14.6.
[28] R. Howie to J. White, 23.10.29 (W) 14.2.

small towns, however, parish boundaries were not drawn up at first. And in the cities parish boundaries sometimes made little sense in terms of community.

What was required, too, was an energetic programme of union and readjustment that would make sensible provision for coherent parish communities. Alexander Martin had hoped that the 'larger view' would be taken when this issue arose at the local level.[29] He hoped that religion should cease to be a divisive force in the village life of Scotland. John White told the assembly in 1935 that the policy of union and readjustment could do much 'were it not for a sentiment that sometimes became an obstinacy'.[30] The task of bringing about sensible local unions has continued to be difficult. The 'U and R' committee, as it came to be known, was one of the least popular of church bodies, and the issue has continued to cause controversy in the Church. Before the union it was thought that charges not actually required for the needs of a parish would be suppressed, regardless of size.[31] Yet separate congregations have been allowed to continue in communities provided that they have sufficient resources. The rivalry between neighbouring congregations has often continued, and additional resources have not always been released for more needy areas.

Doubts were raised, too, about the viability of the traditional parochial structure of the Church. John White was himself involved in assessing the effectiveness of the parish system during the Second World War as part of the work of the Commission on the Interpretation of God's Will in the Present Crisis convened by Professor John Baillie.[32] The presbyteries were asked to supply information and many provided full reports. It became clear that in many towns there was often competition rather than co-operation between congregations. Church members did not necessarily pay attention to parish boundaries in relation to their own attendance at worship. Many people retained a loyalty to the congregation in which they had grown up and did not become members of their parish church. The alteration of parish boundaries, where it had taken place, had not generally fostered a sense of community within the area. In the large cities it appeared that the parish system worked badly, while in rural areas there was little criticism.

[29] Alexander Martin, The *Re-union of the Scottish Church*, An Address delivered at the opening of the General Assembly of the United Free Church of Scotland, 21st May 1929 (Edinburgh and Glasgow, 1929), p. 6.

[30] *LW*, July 1935, p. 271.

[31] *LW*, March 1926, p. 54.

[32] *JW*, pp. 397–8.

In spite of the results of this survey, White did not think that the territorial principle itself had failed.[33] Instead of calling in question the organisational basis of the strategy, he wished there to be a greater realisation by kirk sessions and members of their parish responsibilities. Yet he also recognised that more trained workers were required, not necessarily based permanently in any one parish, but able to move from one area to another. Some presbyteries, too, had suggested the grouping of parishes in the larger towns and the development of team ministries. White himself favoured the creation of Church Councils in towns where the population was under 50,000 in order to foster a unity of spirit and intention among the different congregations. A more effective supervision by presbyteries was also required. This was a subject which had been of concern to White since the 1920s, and the Church and Nation Committee had examined the issue.[34] White preferred the appointment of individuals as superintendents as had happened immediately following the Reformation in Scotland. He also envisaged the moderators of synods undertaking this role, and the place of former moderators of the general assembly acting as roving ambassadors in the Church for several years after their moderatorial year was over. The union had not led to this matter being carried forward in any significant way. White concluded that the union had not led, either, to the Church realising its role in the community:[35]

> Have we been using our great united forces for the winning of Scotland? The Church is not infiltrating through the Community as it can and as it ought ... We are all to blame. Too many of our good respectable Church folks still think of their own church as if it were a private religious club. They miss the main function of Church life and worship— to go out to their brothers and sisters and compel them to come in. As for the ministers, today they preach well and effectively, but a cordial wave of the hand from a motor-car travelling at thirty miles an hour is not in any sense an effective pastoral visit.

White could take heart that the parochial system appeared to be working better in the new housing areas using the churches built as a result of the Church Extension Campaign. Even in those areas, however, some church members still travelled back to their former parishes to worship on Sundays and were encouraged to do so by the ministers of the older churches.[36]

[33] *JW*, p. 398.
[34] John White, Superintendence (W) 49.
[35] *JW*, p. 399.
[36] Brown, 'Social Ideal', pp. 25–6.

As convener of the Home Mission Committee, White had convinced the assembly in 1933 to launch a national appeal for money for a National Church Extension Fund.[37] It was a bold venture in a time of economic difficulty, and it came in for an expected amount of criticism for that reason.[38] The aim was to raise £180,000. More than half the total had been gathered in at the end of two years, and the target was realised before the end of 1936.[39] Nevertheless the Church still found it impossible to keep pace with the growth of the new housing areas. Since it cost over £10,000 to build a church, the committee decided to erect hall-churches instead.[40] These buildings also came in for criticism but they provided a place of worship as well as facilities for other activities in these new communities. The Church was often the only public building in the area. A second national appeal for £90,000 was launched in 1936, but it met with a disappointing result.[41] After two years less than half the total had been raised. The level of giving was not helped by public criticism from White and other members of the committee of those congregations that had not given significant amounts to the campaign. In addition a national revival campaign, 'Recall to Religion', failed to create much new enthusiasm for the work of home mission.[42]

The disappointing response to such an initiative had been foreseen by one observer at the union assembly in 1929. He had thought it ominous that when both John White and Lord Sands had given priority to the work of home mission in their respective speeches, the assembly had not made 'the slightest sound of assent or approbation'.[43] If this meant that the idea of the Church as a religious club for the elect was still strongly held, then, it was said, the union held 'less for Scotland than Scotland needs'. One Glasgow minister, J. L. Morgan, voiced this concern during the debate on the report of the Home Mission Committee at the assembly in 1936.[44] He did not think that there had been progress since the union in reclaiming the unchurched. Church membership had fallen and the work of home mission had not captured the imagination of the people. Radical new methods and principles of mission had to be considered.

---

[37] *JW*, p. 288.
[38] *JW*, p. 291.
[39] *JW*, p. 295.
[40] *JW*, p. 326.
[41] Brown, 'Social Ideal', p. 25.
[42] Ibid.
[43] *The Scottish Chronicle*, 11 October 1929.
[44] Ibid., p. 24.

The standing of the Church of Scotland among the population of the new housing areas, and the poorer sections of society generally, was not helped by its conservative social outlook during the 1930s.[45] In this respect, however, the united Church was continuing the policies of the two Churches during the decade before the union when they had abandoned the policies of social progressivism and support for post-war reconstruction.[46] In the early 1920s the Churches required the co-operation of the government in relation to their union proposals, and thus hesitated to voice criticism of government policies. In the face of rising unemployment in the 1930s, and the introduction of the hated 'means test' by the National Government, the general assembly did not adopt a stance that would appear critical of the government or that might call for the increased state control of the economy.[47] Instead the Church took limited measures to ease the plight of the unemployed by providing recreational facilities and moral support at the parish level. White and other church leaders argued that the Church lacked the competence to make pronouncements in the economic and political spheres. The Church should not criticise the State or take sides in the economic struggle, but do all it could to alleviate the suffering of those who suffered as a result of the crisis.

The united Church also continued the campaign against Irish immigration that had been begun in the 1920s before the union. In 1923 the general assembly of the Church of Scotland had approved a report of the Church and Nation Committee, convened by John White and Lord Sands, which spoke of the need to resist the menace of Irish immigration.[48] In this campaign they were joined by the assembly of the United Free Church in 1924 and a joint committee was formed along with other Protestant Churches.[49] White headed a deputation which met government ministers in 1928, and called for Irish immigration to be restricted and for the deportation of those who were dependent on state support or who had committed a crime.[50] The campaign was futile and its basic premise, that the Irish population in Scotland was continuing to increase, was shown by both the government and the press to

[45] Ibid., p. 17.

[46] Stewart J. Brown, 'Reform, Reconstruction, Reaction: The Social Vision of Scottish Presbyterianism c.1830–c.1930', in *Scottish Journal of Theology*, 44 (1991), p. 508–11.

[47] Ibid.

[48] Stewart J. Brown, 'Outside the Covenant: The Scottish Presbyterian Churches and Irish Immigration, 1922–1938', in *The Innes Review* 42/1 (1991), pp. 19–45.

[49] Ibid., p. 27.

[50] Ibid., p. 31.

be false. The Presbyterian Churches were feeling apprehensive about their declining role in society, and there was a political concern over the supposed support being given to the Labour Party by Roman Catholic voters. Behind it all, too, was there not a concern for the claim, made in Article III of the Articles Declaratory, that the Church of Scotland was 'a national Church representative of the Christian faith of the Scottish people'? The basis for that claim, as we have seen, was that the united Church would indeed be the largest Church in Scotland in terms of membership. The increasing size of the Irish-Catholic population could result in that claim no longer being justified. By the end of the twentieth century, the Roman Catholic population is of a similar size to the membership of the Kirk which has declined to less than three-quarters of a million.

The same observer who had detected a lack of enthusiasm for home mission at the union assembly also thought that the references by John White to the future inclusion of the Scottish Episcopal Church and the Church of England in a united Church were met with 'but a partial and hesitating response'.[51] The issue of future unions with other Churches was not only mentioned as a possibility in the Articles Declaratory, but spoken of as a duty laid on the Kirk. Apart from the union with the United Original Secession Church in 1954, no other union has taken place since 1929. The responsibility for this outcome, however, cannot be laid at the door of the Church of Scotland alone. Attention was turned in the 1930s, and then again in the 1950s, to the question of union with the Church of England. The problems of inter-communion, recognition of ministries, and the role of bishops, proved to be the stumbling-blocks in this case. To its credit the general assembly in 1934 followed the lead of John White and approved the recommendations of a joint statement. The statement set out the points of agreement between the two Churches as well as matters that required further consideration.[52] A similar willingness to take the matter further was not forthcoming south of the Border at that stage.

It would be a mistake to think that the union of 1929 of itself would revive the national mission of the Church, give it a new social vision, and automatically lead to further ecumenical advance. In one respect, the union simply changed the structures and combined the resources. Alexander Martin recognised that 'mere Union would not cure all ills'.[53] An amalgamation of

---

[51] *The Scottish Chronicle*, 11 October 1929.
[52] *JW*, pp. 305–6.
[53] *Glasgow Herald*, 17.10.27.

ecclesiastical machinery in itself and of itself was, he said, 'a very secondary thing'. What was wanted was 'a warmer temperature, in which everything in either Church that was contrary to the mind and will of the Church's Lord would melt and disappear.' In addition to the economic circumstances of the country not being conducive to further change, the whole process of union had taken a long time. One detects that an element of exhaustion had entered into the leaders and members of the Church and that this played a significant part in the failure of the Forward Movement and the other attempts at renewal after 1929. The goal of union was enough of a challenge without seeking radical reform in the life of the Church.

(b) unfinished business

It has been noted that the initial task of removing the obstacles had taken much longer than had been originally anticipated. It had taken time to reach agreement within the committee itself on the wording of the new constitution of the Church and some measure of compromise had been necessary over the content of Article I. The Church then had to wait for parliament to enact the necessary legislation that recognised the Articles Declaratory. During this process the First World War had put a stop to negotiations for the best part of four years. Following the passing of the Church of Scotland Act of 1921, the church leaders then grew impatient as they waited for the government to set up the departmental committee to examine the issue of the teinds and the endowments. Compromise was again required, on this occasion with the landowners, before the terms of a bill could be agreed. It then took some time for the bill to make its way through parliament. Thus when these two obstacles were finally removed, the Churches did not wish to take long over the framing of the Basis and Plan of Union. The union provided a new constitutional basis and structure for the Church of Scotland, a framework within which the Church could carry out its primary tasks within the nation and beyond. Yet there were several important questions which were left unresolved and which would have to be decided by the united Church.

The key matter of the doctrine of the Church was one such issue. It had been difficult to frame the doctrinal declaration in Article I, and in view of the subsequent failure of the Church to agree to any further change in this respect, this Article stands as a considerable achievement. Because of the problems surrounding the framing of this Article, however, the union committees had not tried to define what was meant by 'the fundamental doctrines of the Christian faith', to which ministers subscribed, or to tackle the place of the Westminster Confession itself. A special committee was set up by the assembly in 1930 to examine the whole question of 'Creed revision', but this did not result in either a new confession or a new statement of the fundamentals of the faith.[54] The outcome of this committee's deliberations was a short statement of the Christian faith for the purposes of instruction and guidance. The committee came to the conclusion that it was not the time to propose any radical change to the position of the Westminster Confession. Later attempts in the 1970s to seek change in this area would also fail.[55] The Church has therefore not succeeded in lifting the burden from the shoulders of ordinands who have to decide for themselves what constitutes the 'fundamental doctrines' when they sign the formula. The Articles have given the Church considerable scope for the restatement of its faith. As one observer noted after the union, 'short of going over formally to Rome or becoming Unitarian, there is precious little in the way of amendment of creeds that the Scottish Church cannot perform.'[56] But the Kirk has not exercised that freedom, and Article I remains as the one authoritative statement of the Church's creed. The Article, however, was not intended to serve that purpose and it was framed to allow for differing interpretations. As has been noted, the Preamble, which was based on the Article, has become a reference point for what constitutes the essence of the Church's faith.[57] The issues surrounding the place of the Westminster Confession and the definition of the fundamentals of the faith, however, were not grasped at the time of the union.

Since the union the Church has also only made one change to its constitution as set out in the Articles. In 1992 the words 'Provincial Synods' were deleted from Article II, thus enabling the Church to abolish these courts which had ceased to perform a useful function. The flexibility of the constitution has not been utilised and James Barr has been proved correct when he saw the procedure for change in Article VIII as a 'triumph for stagnation'.[58] The possibility for change is there, but the mechanism is cumbersome and does not lend itself to reform. It is worth noting, too, that the proposals in the 1970s to change the position of the Westminster Confession as the Church's principal subordinate

---

[54] *FR*, pp. 111–14.

[55] See *FR*, ch. 6.

[56] George Malcolm Thomson, *Will the Scottish Church Survive?* (Edinburgh, 1930), p.18.

[57] See above, p. 169.

[58] *FR*, p. 98.

standard, and to introduce a short statement of the fundamentals to be subscribed by ministers, also failed to be approved under this mechanism. In this case, however, the presbyteries approved the proposals by the required two-thirds majority, and it was the general assembly which failed to pass them in the end.[59]

In other areas different traditions and practices were allowed to continue in the united Church and there was no attempt at harmonisation. The two Churches represented different views of the eldership, the Church of Scotland tending towards a 'low' view, and the United Free Church towards a 'high' view. The difference came to light over the involvement of elders in the ordination of ministers and the rights of kirk sessions with regard to worship and the sacraments. In both Churches, too, there were more extreme views. In the Church of Scotland, high churchmen could speak of 'lay eldership',[60] while the UP tradition continued to speak of ministers and elders belonging to the one office, as teaching and ruling elders.[61] The different views of the eldership have survived, although the higher view of the UF Church has become more widely held. The constitution of individual congregations has been left as it was in 1900 so that UP and *quoad omnia* constitutions still exist side by side. Again, the model constitution, drawn up in 1935, was to be encouraged, but congregations have been able to maintain the particular way in which they are governed. Differences remained and time was left to give the answer. That answer has not always been the result of careful theological reflection and has not always enabled the Church to meet the needs of a changing society.

(c) the lasting legacy

What, then, can be said to be the lasting legacy of the union? The statement of the Church's spiritual freedom in the Articles, and the way in which this was further enshrined in the Basis of Union, has proved to be of great significance. There were no legal challenges to the union by a disaffected minority as happened in 1900. Those who formed the United Free Church (Continuing) did so without making such a challenge in the civil courts. The legal basis of the spiritual independence of the Church as set out in the Articles Declaratory has, however, been the subject of several cases since 1929.

---

[59] *FR*, p. 125.
[60] H. J. Wotherspoon and J. M. Kirkpatrick, *Manual of Church Doctrine* (London, 1919), p. 176.
[61] Woodside, *Soul of a Scottish Church*, p. 243.

The first such case, *Ballantyne* v. *Presbytery of Wigtown* in 1936, arose because the presbytery of Wigtown sought to carry out readjustment following a vacancy in the parish of Kirkmabreck. Some members objected to this policy and argued that the congregation had a statutory right to elect a minister under the Patronage Act of 1874 which was unaffected by the Act of 1921.[62] It was held, however, that this was a spiritual matter which was subject to the terms of Article IV of the Articles Declaratory, and that the jurisdiction of the civil court was thereby excluded.[63] Article IV declared the Church's power 'subject to no civil authority to legislate, and to adjudicate finally, in all matters of doctrine, worship, government, and discipline in the Church'. Lord Aitchison observed that this Article declared the self-government of the Church, and that the rights of the Church in its own sphere were recognised rather than conferred by the State.[64] It has been noted that there was one dissent to this judgement and that it was a pity that the decision should stand simply on the basis of two judges.[65] Since that comment was made, however, there have been two other cases whose judgements have recognised the Church's spiritual jurisdiction in an unambiguous way.

The case of *Logan* v. *Presbytery of Dumbarton* was brought to the Court of Session in 1995 by a minister who sought a judicial review of the decisions of the presbytery which were of a disciplinary nature.[66] Counsel for the presbytery referred to Article IV of the Articles Declaratory and to the previous judgement in *Ballantyne* v. *Presbytery of Wigtown*.[67] Although an interim decision had been made to stop the carrying out of the judgement of the presbytery, Lord Osbourne recalled those interim orders, holding that the case involved a spiritual matter. Since the passing of the Act of 1921, he said, the position was quite clear: 'There was a supreme jurisdiction in the Church courts in relation to ecclesiastical matters.'[68] He quoted the opinion of Lord Aitchison in 1935, which has already been noted, that the Act of 1921 did not confer rights upon the Church but rather recognised that in the Articles the Church claimed to have an inherent power. The fact that the Articles only became operative after they had been freely adopted by the Church was

---

[62] *Scots Law Times* (1936), p. 436.
[63] Ibid.
[64] Ibid., pp. 446–7.
[65] Francis Lyall, *Of Presbyters and Kings* (Aberdeen, 1980), p. 73.
[66] *Scots Law Times* (1995), p. 1228.
[67] Ibid., p. 1232.
[68] Ibid., p. 1233.

an assertion by the Church of its autonomy in matters affecting its own life and polity.

This more recent case was quoted in subsequent decisions made by an Employment Tribunal in 1998, and by an Employment Appeal Tribunal in 1999, in the case of *Ms Helen Percy* v. *Church of Scotland Board of National Mission*.[69] Following complaints made against her, Ms Percy had demitted her status as a minister in the presbytery of Angus, where she had held a post as an associate minister. In addition she had held a part-time appointment with the Board of National Mission as a prison chaplain. Ms Percy complained of constructive dismissal, and of discrimination against her contrary to section 6 of the Sex Discrimination Act of 1975. Before the Employment Tribunal, counsel for the Board of National Mission referred to the Act of 1921, and in particular to the terms of Article IV of the Articles Declaratory, and to the case of *Logan* v. *Presbytery of Dumbarton*. Counsel submitted that the Employment Tribunal was part of the civil authority, and did not have the power to review the way in which the courts of the Church dealt with the demission of a minister, which was a matter of discipline as specified in Article IV.[70] In its ruling, the Tribunal referred to both the Logan case and the earlier Ballantyne case, which had held that such matters were spiritual and came under the terms of the Church of Scotland Act of 1921.[71] Before the Employment Appeal Tribunal, counsel for Ms Percy argued that, in the modern context and against the European background, the secular court should not attribute a wide definition or construction to Article IV, so as to deny the opportunity to individuals covered by its provisions from asserting their rights.[72] In rejecting these arguments, the Tribunal concluded as follows:[73]

> The important matter is that Parliament has allowed the Church an exclusive jurisdiction and if, therefore, a particular matter falls within that jurisdiction as defined in this case by Article IV, the Church is immune from interference in whatever it does in the furtherance of matters contained

[69] The Employment Tribunals (Scotland), Case No. S/300120/98 Held at Dundee on 7 September 1998; Employment Appeal Tribunal, Appeal No. EAT/1415/98, 22 March 1999.

[70] The Employment Tribunals (Scotland), Case No. S/300120/98 Held at Dundee on 7 September 1998, p. 5.

[71] Ibid., pp. 10, 14.

[72] Employment Appeal Tribunal, Appeal No. EAT/1415/98, 22 March 1999, pp. 5–6.

[73] Ibid., p. 8.

within that Article, which must extend not only to natural justice but also to any statute which could otherwise apply such as the Sex Discrimination Act.

In these recent cases, therefore, the spiritual independence of the Church as declared in the Articles, and recognised by parliament in the 1921 Act, has been fully upheld.

The position of the Church has also been recognised in relation to the incorporation of the European Convention on Human Rights into United Kingdom law. In 1998 the general assembly called on the government to give an assurance that the Human Rights bill was entirely consistent with the provisions of the Act of 1921 or to amend the bill so that it would be consistent.[74] This issue was raised by other Churches and religious bodies and the government introduced a clause by which a court had to have particular regard to the way in which the Act would affect the exercise by a religious organisation of its freedom of thought, conscience and religion.[75] In parliament the Secretary of State for Scotland, Donald Dewar, assured the house that it was not the government's intention to disturb the recognition of a spiritual jurisdiction to courts of the Church of Scotland.[76] It would only be if the Church was acting as a public authority that it would be subject to the provisions of the Convention on Human Rights.[77] In other words, the separate and distinct spiritual authority of the Church was recognised and the position under the Church of Scotland Act was affirmed. The third clause of that act, however, affirms the jurisdiction of the civil courts in matters of a civil nature,[78] and the Church remains subject to civil law in those areas where it applies. For example, with regard to the rights of an employee of the Church in its offices or eventide homes, the Church is subject to the same laws as other employers. With regard to matters affecting one of its ministers, however, the Church has a separate spiritual jurisdiction.

The recognition by parliament of an exclusive jurisdiction outside of its own authority was indeed a remarkable resolution of the problem of relations between Church and State. The Church of Scotland Act, in recognising the independent jurisdiction of the Church in spiritual matters, represents a singular breach of the supreme authority of parliament. As has been pointed out, in passing the Act 'Westminster punctured its own most sacred

[74] *C of S Rep.*, 1998, pp. 40/8–10 and Deliverances, p. 3.
[75] *C. of S. Rep.* 1999, p. 1/5.
[76] Hansard HC, 317, 21 October 1998, Col. 1345.
[77] Ibid., Col. 1346.
[78] See Appendix I, p. 284.

doctrine of parliamentary sovereignty'; the House of Commons could be said to rule all of Britain with this one notable exception.[79] The Act was thus a vindication of those who had left the Kirk at the Disruption in 1843 because they rejected the notion of a unitary state.[80] It was also designed to prevent the occurrence of another Free Church Case in which the body that had claimed spiritual independence from the State was subject to an adverse judgement in the civil courts. In the view of the judges in that case, the Church 'did not exist at all' in the sense of having 'an inherent spontaneity of life which is not imposed but original, which though it may be regulated by the civil authority is not derived therefrom.'[81] Thus the importance of the Church of Scotland Act cannot be underestimated.[82]

In addition, the Church still has a relationship with the State as a national Church. The role of the Church in the nation is recognised by the State and the services of the Church are used on State occasions. This relationship is symbolised by the continuing attendance of the Lord High Commissioner at meetings of the general assembly. Such recognition can lead to the appearance of the Kirk being an 'established' Church, but as we have seen such a term would be quite inappropriate to describe the continuing relationship between Church and State as set out in the Articles. The Church is neither established nor disestablished, but can best be described as both national and free.

The constitution of the Church as set out in the Articles Declaratory also gives considerable freedom to the Church to change and develop as it sees fit. It was important that the Church be able in the future to change its constitution without losing its identity as a Church in the eyes of the law. The constitution had to have the power of change, a power which had not been recognised in the Free Church Case. The mechanism in Article VIII provides the Church with the freedom to alter its constitution, always consistently with the provisions of Article I. Those who drafted the Articles were clear that significant modifications could be made to the Articles under the terms of Article VIII. It would be possible, for example, for the Church to replace the Westminster Confession with another doctrinal standard, to abandon Presbyterian government, and to change

---

[79] Andrew Marr, *The Battle for Scotland* (London, 1992), p. 40.

[80] Harold J. Laski, *Studies in the Problem of Sovereignty* (New Haven, 1917), p. 65.

[81] John Neville Figgis, *Churches in the Modern State*, 2nd ed. (London, 1914), p. 36.

[82] *PRS*, p. 374.

its understanding of itself as a national Church. None of these matters are contained in Article I and hence are subject to change. Indeed they were deliberately left out of Article I for that very reason. But is such wide-ranging reform permitted by the constitution of the Church? The claims of those who drafted the Articles might appear to be far too sweeping and unrealistic. Are there no limits to the extent of change other than the provisions of Article I?

The question arises as to what constitutes a 'modification'. In his book *The Constitution and Laws of the Church of Scotland*, James L. Weatherhead writes that 'a possible criterion would be that any proposed alteration which would in normal procedure be treated as a counter-motion would go beyond modification, and would therefore not be competent'.[83] However it is for the Church to decide in this as in other matters relating to the interpretation of the Articles. In the case of a proposed modification of the Articles, 'the procedure is such that there would be a presumption that any modification approved by three successive Assemblies, and by two-thirds of the Presbyteries in two successive years would be one which the Church had thereby agreed to be competent.'[84] In other words, anything consistent with Article I, as interpreted by the Church, would be an amendment rather than a counter-motion. A proposal in relation to a particular Article may appear to be a counter-motion, but will be an amendment in relation to the Articles as a whole. Article VIII speaks of the modification of the Articles as such, 'these Articles', and not 'any of these Articles'. There are few precedents in this area, since the only change to the Articles which the Church has approved has been with regard to the abolition of provincial synods. In this case, however, looked at simply in relation to synods, the proposal to abolish them might have appeared to be a counter-motion, but in relation to Presbyterian government, and the Articles as a whole, it was an amendment.[85] Thus, as has been argued elsewhere,[86] the Church has a wide scope for reform outside of the provisions of Article I.

As we have seen, the Articles were modelled on the United Free Church Act of 1906 Anent the Spiritual Independence of the Church that had been passed in the aftermath of the Free Church Case. Both the Articles and the 1906 Act are listed in the Basis of Union as leading documents setting forth the constitution of the

---

[83] James L. Weatherhead, *The Constitution and Laws of the Church of Scotland* (Edinburgh, 1997), p. 21.

[84] Ibid.

[85] I am grateful to the Very Rev. Dr James L. Weatherhead for making these points in correspondence.

[86] *FR*, pp. 139–40.

united Church. In other words, the two documents have an equal status. Any further doubt regarding the scope of the Church's claim to spiritual freedom should be dispelled by the wording of the first of the declarations in the Basis of Union. It speaks of 'the inherent liberty of the united Church as a branch of the Church of God to determine and regulate her own constitution and laws as duty may require, in dependence on the grace of God and under the guidance of His Word and Spirit.' The freedom of the Church of Scotland is stated not only in the Articles and in the Act of 1906, but also in this first declaration. Since the Articles have been recognised by parliament, attention has so often been focused on them. But the Articles should be interpreted in the light of the other two statements of the Church's freedom as the body of Christ.

The Basis of Union thus provides a foundation for the Church which is strong yet flexible. The freedom of the Church is declared both in relation to the State and within its own sphere. The Church is thus free to change and develop in response to the leading of God's Spirit, but always consistently with the catholic faith in the trinity and the incarnation as set out in Article I. The structure which was built upon this foundation in the Plan of Union was not as adventurous as it might have been, and some matters were left for the united Church to decide. Yet these matters were capable of change if the Church had a will. Union of itself could not provide the impetus for reform and renewal. The remarkable feature of the union of 1929 is that the freedom of the Church to change is enshrined in the constitution of the Church itself. Those who rebuilt the Kirk in the union of 1929 laid the foundations well.

Appendix I The Church of Scotland Act and the Articles Declaratory 1921

An Act to declare the lawfulness of certain Articles declaratory of the Constitution of the Church of Scotland in matters spiritual prepared with the authority of the General Assembly of the Church.

WHEREAS certain articles declaratory of the constitution of the Church of Scotland in matters spiritual have been prepared with the authority of the General Assembly of the Church, with a view to facilitate the union of other Churches with the Church of Scotland, which articles are set out in the Schedule to this Act, and together with any modifications of the said articles or additions thereto made in accordance therewith are hereinafter in this Act referred to as "the Declaratory Articles":

And whereas it is expedient that any doubts as to the lawfulness of the Declaratory Articles should be removed:

Be it therefore enacted by the King's most Excellent Majesty, by and with the advice and consent of the Lords Spiritual and Temporal, and Commons, in this present Parliament assembled, and by the authority of the same, as follows:—

Effect of Declaratory Articles

1. The Declaratory Articles are lawful articles, and the constitution of the Church of Scotland in matters spiritual is as therein set forth, and no limitation of the liberty, rights, and powers in matters spiritual therein set forth shall be derived from any statute or law affecting the Church of Scotland in matters spiritual at present in force, it being hereby declared that in all questions of construction the Declaratory Articles shall prevail, and that all such statutes and laws shall be construed in conformity therewith and in subordination thereto, and all such statutes and laws in so far as they are inconsistent with the Declaratory Articles are hereby repealed and declared to be of no effect.

Other Churches not to be prejudiced

2. Nothing contained in this Act or in any other Act affecting the Church of Scotland shall prejudice the recognition of any other

Church in Scotland as a Christian Church protected by law in the exercise of its spiritual functions.

Jurisdiction of civil courts
3. Subject to the recognition of the matters dealt with in the Declaratory Articles as matters spiritual, nothing in this Act contained shall affect or prejudice the jurisdiction of the civil courts in relation to any matter of a civil nature.

Citations and commencement
4. This Act may be cited as the Church of Scotland Act, 1921, and shall come into operation on such date as His Majesty may fix by Order in Council after the Declaratory Articles shall have been adopted by an Act of the General Assembly of the Church of Scotland with the consent of a majority of the Presbyteries of the Church.

SCHEDULE

Articles Declaratory of the Constitution of the Church of Scotland in Matters Spiritual

I. The Church of Scotland is part of the Holy Catholic or Universal Church; worshipping one God, Almighty, all-wise, and all-loving, in the Trinity of the Father, the Son, and the Holy Ghost, the same in substance, equal in power and glory; adoring the Father, infinite in Majesty, of whom are all things; confessing our Lord Jesus Christ, the Eternal Son, made very man for our salvation; glorying in His Cross and Resurrection, and owning obedience to Him as the Head over all things to His Church; trusting in the promised renewal and guidance of the Holy Spirit; proclaiming the forgiveness of sins and acceptance with God through faith in Christ, and the gift of Eternal Life; and labouring for the advancement of the Kingdom of God throughout the world. The Church of Scotland adheres to the Scottish Reformation; receives the Word of God which is contained in the Scriptures of the Old and New Testaments as its supreme rule of faith and life; and avows the fundamental doctrines of the Catholic faith founded thereupon.

II. The principal subordinate standard of the Church of Scotland is the Westminster Confession of Faith approved by the General Assembly of 1647, containing the sum and substance of the Faith of the Reformed Church. Its government is Presbyterian, and is exercised through Kirk Sessions, Presbyteries, Provincial Synods, and General Assemblies. Its system and principles of worship, orders, and discipline are in accordance with "The Directory for the Public Worship of God," "The Form of Presbyterial Church Government," and "The Form of Process," as these have been or may hereafter be interpreted or modified by Acts of the General Assembly or by consuetude.

III. This Church is in historical continuity with the Church of Scotland which was reformed in 1560, whose liberties were ratified in 1592, and for whose security provision was made in the Treaty of Union of 1707. The continuity and identity of the Church of Scotland are not prejudiced by the adoption of these Articles. As a national Church representative of the Christian Faith of the Scottish people it acknowledges its distinctive call and duty to bring the ordinances of religion to the people in every parish of Scotland through a territorial ministry.

IV. This Church, as part of the Universal Church wherein the Lord Jesus Christ has appointed a government in the hands of Church office-bearers, receives from Him, its Divine King and Head, and from Him alone, the right and power subject to no civil authority to legislate, and to adjudicate finally, in all matters of doctrine, worship, government, and discipline in the Church, including the right to determine all questions concerning membership and office in the Church, the constitution and membership of its Courts, and the mode of election of its office-bearers, and to define the boundaries of the spheres of labour of its ministers and other office-bearers. Recognition by civil authority of the separate and independent government and jurisdiction of this Church in matters spiritual, in whatever manner such recognition be expressed, does not in any way affect the character of this government and jurisdiction as derived from the Divine Head of the Church alone, or give to the civil authority any right of interference with the proceedings or judgments of the Church within the sphere of its spiritual government and jurisdiction.

V. This Church has the inherent right, free from interference by civil authority, but under the safeguards for deliberate action and legislation provided by the Church itself, to frame or adopt its subordinate standards, to declare the sense in which it understands its Confession of Faith, to modify the forms of expression therein, or to formulate other doctrinal statements, and to define the relation thereto of its office-bearers and members, but always in agreement with the Word of God and the fundamental doctrines of the Christian Faith contained in the said Confession, of which agreement the Church shall be sole judge, and with due regard to liberty of opinion in points which do not enter into the substance of the Faith.

VI. This Church acknowledges the divine appointment and authority of the civil magistrate within his own sphere, and maintains its historic testimony to the duty of the nation acting in its corporate capacity to render homage to God, to acknowledge the Lord Jesus Christ to be King over the nations, to obey His laws, to reverence His ordinances, to honour His Church, and to promote in all appropriate ways the Kingdom of God. The Church and the State owe mutual duties to each other, and acting within their respective spheres may signally promote each other's welfare. The Church and the State have the right to determine each for itself all questions concerning the extent and the continuance of their mutual relations in the discharge of these duties and the obligations arising therefrom.

VII. The Church of Scotland, believing it to be the will of Christ that His disciples should be all one in the Father and in Him, that the world may believe that the Father has sent Him, recognises the obligation to seek and promote union with other Churches in which it finds the Word to be purely preached, the sacraments administered according to Christ's ordinance, and discipline rightly exercised; and it has the right to unite with any such Church without loss of its identity on terms which this Church finds to be consistent with these Articles.

VIII. The Church has the right to interpret these Articles, and, subject to the safeguards for deliberate action and legislation provided by the Church itself, to modify or add to them; but always consistently with the provisions of the first Article hereof, adherence to which, as interpreted by the Church, is essential to its continuity and corporate life. Any proposal for a modification of or addition to these Articles which may be approved of by the General Assembly shall, before it can be enacted by the Assembly, be transmitted by way of overture to Presbyteries in at least two immediately successive years. If the overture shall receive the approval, with or without suggested amendment, of two-thirds of the whole of the Presbyteries of the Church, the Assembly may revise the overture in the light of any suggestions by the Presbyteries, and may transmit the overture when so revised to Presbyteries for their consent. If the overture as transmitted in its final form shall receive the consent of not less than two-thirds of the whole of the Presbyteries of the Church, the General Assembly may, if it deems it expedient, modify or add to these Articles in terms of the said overture. But if the overture as transmitted in its final form shall not receive the requisite consent, the same or a similar proposal shall not be again transmitted for the consent of Presbyteries until an interval of five years after the failure to obtain the requisite consent has been reported to the General Assembly.

IX. Subject to the provisions of the foregoing Articles and the powers of amendment therein contained, the Constitution of the Church of Scotland in matters spiritual is hereby anew ratified and confirmed by the Church.

Appendix II The United Free Church Act anent the Spiritual Independence of the Church (1906)

"WHEREAS the General Assembly judged it necessary in the circumstances of the Church to pass the following Act, and although the principles set forth therein involve no new departure and are not in any sense a constitutional novation, but have been always accepted and maintained by this Church, yet in respect of the importance of making manifest to all that the whole Church explicitly adheres to these principles, the General Assembly deemed it right to send it down as an Overture under the Barrier Act: the General Assembly hereby, with consent of a majority of Presbyteries, declare and enact, as follows:—

"Considering the situation created by the decisions of the House of Lords on 1st August 1904, in the Cases of *Bannatyne and Others* v. *Lord Overtoun and Others*, and *Young and Others* v. *Macalister and Others*, and the grounds on which these decisions were based; considering also the Resolutions relative thereto of the Commission of Assembly at its ordinary Meeting on 10th August 1904, of which Resolutions the Assembly hereby approve; and considering that it is needful to make clear the position in which the United Free Church of Scotland stands in reference to the questions thus raised, the General Assembly resolve and declare as follows:—

1. "They assert and protest that those branches of the Church of Christ in Scotland now united in this Church have always claimed, and this Church continues to claim, that the Church of Christ has under Him as her only Head independent and exclusive jurisdiction and power of legislating in all matters of doctrine, worship, discipline, and government of the Church, including therein the right from time to time to alter, change, add to, or modify, her constitution and laws, Subordinate Standards, and Church Formulas, and to determine and declare what these are.

2. "The General Assembly accordingly declare anew and enact that it is a fundamental principle and rule of this Church that, in dependence on the grace of God, recognising the authority of the Word of God, contained in the Scriptures of the Old and New Testaments, as the supreme unchangeable Standard, and looking

to the Head of the Church for the promised guidance of the Holy Spirit, this Church has the sole and exclusive right and power from time to time, as duty may require, through her Courts to alter, change, add to, or modify, her constitution and laws, Subordinate Standards, and Formulas, and to determine and declare what these are, and to unite with other Christian Churches; always in conformity with the Word of God, and also with the safeguards for deliberate action and legislation in such cases provided by the Church herself—of which conformity the Church herself, acting through her Courts, shall be the sole judge—and under a sense of direct responsibility to the ever-living Head of the Church, and of duty towards all the Church's members.

3. "The General Assembly also declare and enact that in all the Courts of the Church a decision of the Court given either unanimously, or by a majority of its members present and voting, is the decision of the Court, and the decision of the General Assembly so reached is final. With respect to Acts which are to be binding Rules and Constitutions of the Church, the Assembly shall have regard to the safeguards referred to in the foregoing resolution.

4. "The General Assembly further declare that the Church holds her funds and property, present and future, in conformity with these principles; the Church reserving her right to accept and hold benefactions, subject to specific conditions attached to them by the donor, when and so long as she judges these conditions to be consistent with her liberty and her principles, and to be expedient in the circumstances of the time."

Appendix III The Memorandum of 1912

1. The most pressing duty at the present time is to make a real effort to show how the problem of State relationship can be dealt with in such a manner as shall satisfy the most cherished ideals of both Churches.

2. In the Joint Report submitted to the Assembly of 1911 the view was indicated that it would be difficult, if not impracticable, to secure concurrence in any attempt to define special State relations in a modern Statute, and that in this connection legislation would probably have to be limited to the recognition by Parliament of the freedom which must be a condition of any possible union, and the repeal in general terms of all enactments in any way inconsistent therewith.

3. Before any approach can be made to Parliament the Churches must be in agreement as to the Constitution of the United Church. It would not meet the views of either Church that the Constitution should either in form or in substance be prescribed by Parliament. But there seems to be no reasonable objection to Parliamentary recognition of the Constitution in a form which would not in any way fetter the Church in her own spiritual legislation and administration, or interfere with such power of future modification of any of the terms of the Constitution as the Constitution itself contains. The Constitution must therefore be a concordat between the Churches themselves. Questions of State relations do not necessarily enter into the framing of such a Constitution, but care must be taken that the Constitution contains nothing inconsistent with the claim of the United Church to recognition by the State as national preserving her continuity with the Church of the Reformation.

4. In the course of these negotiations both Churches have accepted the principle that in matters spiritual the Church shall be free from external authority and shall be governed or limited only by her own Constitution. Two questions of difficulty have emerged in this relation which are closely related to each other—doctrinal testimony and the limits of the power of the Church under her own Constitution to alter the Constitution itself. But these are not questions as between the Church of Scotland as an Established Church and the United Free Church as a non-Established Church.

Even if the Church of Scotland were non-Established these difficulties would still have to be met. It is not proposed on the part of the Church of Scotland that such matters, even as they may affect civil rights, should be governed by special State relations.

5. The position of other Churches is not prejudiced by these negotiations. The Church of Scotland has expressed her sympathy with the suggestion that these Churches might be given an improved status in the eye of the law, and beyond this it is not easy to advance by way of seeking any changes as regards these Churches which they are not at present seeking for themselves. But, on the other hand, one of the obstacles to union is the view that exclusive recognition of a National Church infers positive injury to all other Churches by depressing their position in the eye of the law. There are expressions in some of the Statutes which give colour to this argument, and it seems desirable to endeavour to meet it, if not by positive legislation for these Churches, at all events by a statutory disclaimer of any exclusive claim of the Church of Scotland to recognition by the State in Scotland as a Christian Church.

6. As regards endowments and ecclesiastical law in its civil relations generally (fabrics, churchyards, banns, city churches, university chairs, &c., &c.), the matter is one of great complexity, and it would be very difficult for the Churches to come to any complete agreement by negotiation between themselves, even if it were proper for the Churches to treat these as domestic matters to be settled by themselves alone. The Church of Scotland maintains that the endowments are to be conserved for the United Church, and will go forward in the matter of union only upon the footing that the United Free Church and the Government of the day, which is to make itself responsible for the necessary legislation, accept the position that the endowments are not to be secularised. But the details of the manner in which the ancient endowments are to be dealt with under the new conditions must be intrusted to a strong and sympathetic Parliamentary Commission. Such matters have been recognised as appropriate to Parliament throughout the whole history of the Church since the Reformation.

7. The manner in which union might be carried out on some such lines as these above indicated deserves careful consideration. It is obvious that legislation is necessary, and it would appear that this legislation should be subsequent to (1) the adjustment of a Constitution for a United Church, and (2) its approval by both Assemblies with the consent of Presbyteries, but prior to (3) the formal completion of a union by Acts of Assembly upon the basis of that Constitution. There are thus three steps. The Act would be

an enabling measure as regards the Church of Scotland, in her civil and temporal relations, and the union would be the voluntary act of both Churches. It is not overlooked that there may be objection to take steps (1) and (2) on a tentative basis, the consummation of the union on the lines approved of being dependent upon the action of Parliament. It is hoped, however, that this objection is only theoretical, and that it will not be allowed to stand in the way of negotiations for union if other difficulties are removed. Antecedent assurances may ensure the assent of Parliament to the necessary measure, and there is reason to believe that there will be no difficulty in obtaining such assurances.

8. Suggestions as to the form which the necessary legislation might take must in the meantime be tentative. But to avoid any misunderstanding as to the suggestions which follow, it must be understood that they presuppose antecedent approval of the Constitution by the United Free Church and agreement to unite with the Church of Scotland upon the basis thereof. Although this agreement might not be expressly referred to in the Bill, if that course were more acceptable to the United Free Church, the conclusion of the agreement would be a public fact within the cognisance of Parliament when Parliament was invited to assent to the proposed measure. In the view of the Church of Scotland, legislation—such as is here indicated—would be desirable only if union following thereupon were assured, and union would not be assured or in any way advanced by legislation to which both the great Presbyterian Churches in Scotland were not cordially assenting parties.

9. The terms of the Preamble to the Bill would be a matter of much importance. Some such Preamble as the following might be framed:—

Whereas the Treaty of Union between the kingdoms of Scotland and England makes provision for the security of the doctrine, government, worship, and discipline of the Church of Scotland, and Acts of the Parliament of Scotland in that regard are thereby ratified, approved, and confirmed: Whereas it is expedient to remove any obstacle which present law may be deemed to place in the way of the union of other Presbyterian Churches with the Church of Scotland, as the Church of Scotland claiming historical continuity with the Church of the Reformation as the same was recognised as the national Church of Scotland by the Act of the Parliament of Scotland, 1592, cap. 8: Whereas the Constitution in the Schedule to this Act has been approved of by the General Assembly of the Church of Scotland, with the consent of a majority of the Presbyteries of the Church: Whereas it is expedient that this Constitution should be recognised by Parliament as the Constitution of the Church of Scotland, and that it should also be recognised that the Church possesses and enjoys thereunder, in relation to the State and to the law, all the liberty, rights, and powers in matters spiritual therein claimed and set forth, and that no limitation thereof is to be derived from any Statute or law affecting the Church of Scotland at present in force, such Statutes and laws in so far as they may be inconsistent with said liberty, rights, and powers being herein repealed and declared of no effect: Whereas stipends modified out of the teinds, parish churches, manses, and glebes, and sundry other property and revenues possessed and enjoyed by the Church of Scotland under public law, have from time immemorial, or for long periods, been dedicated to religious uses and to the maintenance of a territorial ministry throughout Scotland: And whereas it is expedient that the same should not be diverted therefrom, but should continue to be devoted to religious uses, and to the maintenance of a territorial ministry under provisions adapted to the conditions created by the union of the Church of Scotland with any of the said Churches, and always in a manner consistent with the terms and provisions of the said Constitution of the Church, and the liberty of the Church in matters spiritual therein set forth and herein recognised.

10. In the enacting part of the Statute provision would have to be made for the following matters:

(1) The recognition of the Constitution in the Schedule (with any modifications of the same which may hereafter be made by the Church under the powers contained in the Constitution itself), as the Constitution of the Church of Scotland and the repeal of all statutory provisions and laws inconsistent therewith, or which would derogate from the liberty, rights, and powers in matters spiritual of the Church as therein set forth.

(2) The appointment of a Commission, the duties of which would be

(a) To prepare, subject to any conditions which might be prescribed, and consistently with the Constitution of the Church, a scheme for the administration and application of the property and revenues possessed and enjoyed by the Church of Scotland under public law; and the adjustment of the civil law generally in relation to or as affected by the present arrangement of parochial and other ecclesiastical areas to the new conditions created by union upon the basis of the said Constitution.

(b) To make temporary orders, either general or particular, with reference to such matters of civil right in order to obviate difficulties which might otherwise arise during the transition period.

(c) On the application of the General Assembly of the Church of Scotland or of any Commission appointed by the same, and after hearing all parties interested, to make orders modifying the trusts under which any property or endowments are held by the Church or by any congregation or organisation in connection therewith other than the property and revenues possessed and enjoyed by the Church of Scotland under public law in so far as may be necessary in order to bring the said trusts into legal harmony with the conditions created by the union of Churches, but always in such a manner as will most satisfactorily give effect to the purposes and objects to which the property and endowments are at present dedicated, or to cognate purposes and objects, due regard being had to the rights and interests of particular localities and congregations.

(d) To make all such vesting orders as regards the property and endowments of the Church of Scotland or of any Church uniting with it or of any congregation or organisation in connection with the same as might be necessary to carry out the said union in terms of the said Constitution.

Provision would have to be made for the conservation of all vested life interests.

11. It is a matter for earnest consideration whether a provision might not be embodied to the effect that nothing which is contained in any Act of the Parliament of Scotland, or of Great Britain, or of the United Kingdom, in relation to the Church of Scotland, should be construed to the prejudice of the recognition by lawful authority of any other Church in Scotland as a Christian Church protected by law in the exercise of her spiritual functions.

Appendix IV The Draft Articles of 1914

I. The Church of Scotland is a branch of the Holy Catholic or Universal Church, believing in one God the Father Almighty, and in Jesus Christ His only Begotten Son Incarnate for our salvation, and in the Holy Ghost, three Persons in the unity of the Godhead; owning obedience to its once crucified, now risen and glorified Lord, as the sole King and Head of His Church; proclaiming the forgiveness of sins and acceptance with God through faith in Christ, the renewing of the Holy Spirit, and eternal life; and labouring for the advancement of the Kingdom of God throughout the world.

II. The Church of Scotland adheres to the principles of the Protestant Reformation. The Word of God which is contained in the Scriptures of the Old and New Testaments is its supreme rule of faith and life. The Westminster Confession of Faith, approved by the General Assembly of 1647, is its principal subordinate standard, subject always to the declarations in the sixth and eighth Articles hereof. The government of the Church is Presbyterian, and is exercised through Kirk-Sessions, Presbyteries, Provincial Synods, and General Assemblies. The system and principles of the worship, orders, and discipline of the Church are set forth in its authoritative historical documents.

III. The Church is in historical continuity with the Church of Scotland which was reformed in 1560, whose liberties were ratified in 1592, and for whose security provision was made in the Treaty of Union of 1707. The continuity and identity of the Church of Scotland are not prejudiced by the adoption of these Articles. As national it is a representative witness to the Christian faith of the Scottish people, and acknowledges its divine call and duty to bring the ordinances of religion to the people in every parish of Scotland through a territorial ministry.

IV. The Lord Jesus Christ, as King and Head of His Church, hath therein appointed a government in the hands of church office-bearers, distinct from and not subordinate in its own province to civil government. The Church of Scotland, while acknowledging the Divine appointment and authority of the civil magistrate within his own sphere, and holding that the nation acting in its corporate capacity ought to render homage to God and promote in all appropriate ways the interests of His kingdom, declares that it receives from its Head and from Him alone the right and power subject to no civil authority to legislate, and to adjudicate finally, in all matters of doctrine, worship, government, and discipline in the Church, including the right to determine all questions concerning membership and office in the Church, the constitution of its Courts, and the mode of election of its office-bearers, and to define the boundaries of the spheres of labour of its ministers and other office bearers.

V. The Church affirms that recognition by civil authority of its separate and independent government and jurisdiction in matters spiritual, in whatever manner such recognition be expressed, does not in any way affect the character of this government and jurisdiction as derived from the Divine Head of the Church alone and not from any civil authority, or give to the civil authority any right of interference with the proceedings or judgments of the Church within the sphere of its spiritual government and jurisdiction.

VI. The Church has the inherent right, free from interference by civil authority, but under the safeguards for deliberate action and legislation provided by the Church itself, to declare the sense in which it understands its Confession of Faith, to modify the forms of expression therein, or to formulate other doctrinal statements, and to define the relation thereto of its office-bearers and members, but always in agreement with the Word of God and the fundamental doctrines of the Christian faith contained in the said Confession, of which agreement the Church shall be sole judge, and with due regard to liberty of opinion in points which do not enter into the substance of the faith.

VII. The Church of Scotland, believing it to be in accordance with the will of Christ that His disciples should be all one in the Father and in Him, that the world may believe that the Father has sent Him, and recognising that other Churches, in which the Word is purely preached, the Sacraments are administered according to Christ's ordinance, and discipline rightly exercised, have richly contributed to the spiritual life of the nation, owns and declares anew the obligation to seek and promote union with these Churches; and welcomes conference with them on matters affecting the moral and spiritual wellbeing of the community, and participation by their ministers on national and public occasions in religious services conducted according to the usages of the Church of Scotland; and finally affirms the right to unite without loss of its identity with any other Church on terms which this Church finds to be consistent with these Articles.

VIII. The Church has the right to interpret these Articles and, subject to the safeguards for deliberate action and legislation provided by the Church itself, to modify or add to them; but the Church, as a branch of the Catholic Church, unalterably adhering to the declaration of faith and duty set forth in the first Article hereof, and solemnly recognising its sacred trust to defend and to transmit the faith once for all delivered unto the saints, declares that acceptance of the Word of God as the supreme rule of faith and life, and fidelity to the fundamental truths of the Christian faith which are founded upon the Word of God, and received in His Church, are essential to the continuity and identity of the corporate life of this Church. The Church also holds that Presbyterian Church government being agreeable to the Word of God and consonant with the religious traditions of the Scottish people is the only form of government of the Church of Scotland.

IX. Subject to the provisions of the foregoing Articles and the powers of amendment therein contained, the Constitution of the Church of Scotland is hereby anew ratified and confirmed.

Appendix V The Preamble, Questions and Formula, 1929

PREAMBLE

The Narrative shall be read and, the Ordinand having taken his place before the Presbytery, the Moderator shall declare as follows:—

In the name of the Lord Jesus Christ, the King and Head of the Church, Who, being ascended on high, hath given gifts unto men for the edifying of the body of Christ, we are met here as a Presbytery to ordain A. B. to the office of the Holy Ministry by prayer and the laying on of hands by the Presbyters to whom it doth belong, and to induct him into the pastoral charge of .... In this act of ordination the Church of Scotland, as part of the Holy Catholic or Universal Church worshipping One God — Father, Son, and Holy Spirit — affirms anew its belief in the Gospel of the sovereign grace and love of God, wherein through Jesus Christ, His only Son, our Lord, Incarnate, Crucified, and Risen, He freely offers to all men, upon repentance and faith, the forgiveness of sins, renewal by the Holy Spirit, and eternal life, and calls them to labour in the fellowship of faith for the advancement of the Kingdom of God throughout the world.

The Church of Scotland acknowledges the Word of God which is contained in the Scriptures of the Old and New Testaments to be the supreme rule of faith and life.

The Church of Scotland holds as its subordinate standard the Westminster Confession of Faith, recognising liberty of opinion on such points of doctrine as do not enter into the substance of the Faith, and claiming the right, in dependence on the promised guidance of the Holy Spirit, to formulate, interpret, or modify its subordinate standards: always in agreement with the Word of God and the fundamental doctrines of the Christian Faith contained in the said Confession—of which agreement the Church itself shall be sole judge.

Then the Moderator, addressing the Ordinand or Minister to be inducted, who is to stand and make answer to the questions put to him, shall say:—

A. B., in view of this Declaration, you are now required to answer these questions:—

QUESTIONS TO BE PUT TO MINISTERS BEFORE THEIR ORDINATION OR ADMISSION TO A CHARGE.

1. Do you believe in one God—Father, Son, and Holy Spirit; and do you confess anew the Lord Jesus Christ as your Saviour and Lord?

2. Do you believe the Word of God, which is contained in the Scriptures of the Old and New Testaments, to be the supreme rule of faith and life?

3. Do you believe the fundamental doctrines of the Christian faith contained in the Confession of Faith of this Church?

4. Do you acknowledge the Presbyterian Government of this Church to be agreeable to the Word of God; and do you promise to be subject in the Lord to this Presbytery and to the superior Courts of the Church, and to take your due part in the administration of its affairs?

5. Do you promise to seek the unity and peace of this Church; to uphold the doctrine, worship, government, and discipline thereof; and to cherish a spirit of brotherhood towards all the followers of the Lord?

6. Are not zeal for the glory of God, love to the Lord Jesus Christ, and a desire for the salvation of men, so far as you know your own heart, your great motives and chief inducements to enter into the office of the Holy Ministry?

7. Do you engage in the strength of the Lord Jesus Christ to live a godly and circumspect life; and faithfully, diligently, and cheerfully to discharge the duties of your ministry, seeking in all things the advancement of the Kingdom of God?

8. Do you accept and close with the call to be Pastor of this charge, and promise through grace to study to approve yourself a faithful Minister of the Gospel among this people?

The questions having been answered to the satisfaction of the Presbytery, and the Formula having been signed, the Ordinand shall kneel, and the Moderator, by prayer with laying on of hands, in which all the Ministers present join, shall ordain him to the Office of the Holy Ministry.

Thereafter the Moderator, except in cases in which there is no induction to a pastoral charge or any office, shall add these words:

I now declare you to have been ordained to the office of the Holy Ministry, and in the Name of the Lord Jesus Christ, the King and Head of the Church, and by authority of this Presbytery, I induct you to this charge; and in token thereof we give you the right hand of fellowship.

The following Question shall then be addressed to the Congregation, who are asked to signify assent by rising and standing in their places:

Do you, the members and adherents of this Congregation, receive A. B., whom you have called to be your Minister, promising him all due honour and support in the Lord, and will you give of your means, as the Lord shall prosper you, for the maintenance of the Christian Ministry and the furtherance of the Gospel?

FORMULA

I believe the fundamental doctrines of the Christian faith contained in the Confession of Faith of this Church.

I acknowledge the Presbyterian government of this Church to be agreeable to the Word of God, and promise that I will submit thereto and concur therewith.

I promise to observe the order of worship and the administration of all public ordinances as the same are or may be allowed in this Church.

This Formula shall also be that to be signed by Elders on admission to office.

Bibliography

Unpublished sources

New College Library, Edinburgh
Lord Balfour of Burleigh's Papers, MSS.BAL.1–92.
A. R. MacEwen's Papers, Box 12.1.1–245.
Alexander Martin's Papers, Boxes, 1–21 (M).
New College Archives and Edinburgh University Faculty of Divinity Archives, AA1.1–2.
— Theological Faculty Minute Book, 1921–33, Vol. IV, AA1.2.4.
— Senate Minute Book, 1913–33, AA1.1.4.
United Free Church of Scotland Papers (UFC).
John White's Papers, Boxes 1–106 (W).

Scottish Record Office, Edinburgh
Lord Sands' Papers (LS), CH1/10/1–25.
Records of the Scottish Land and Property Federation (SLPF), GD325/1/203, 305, 327–8.
Church of Scotland, Papers of the General Assembly (PGA), CH1/25/1–4.
Minutes of the Presbytery of Edinburgh, 1927–8, CH2/121/38–9.
United Free Church of Scotland, Minutes of the Presbytery of Edinburgh, 1927–8, CH3/111/50.
Minutes of the Presbytery of Hamilton, 1927–8, CH3/171/23.
Minutes of the Committee for Conference with the Church of Scotland, 1908–29, CH3/1389/1–3.

Glasgow City Archives, Mitchell Library, Glasgow
Church of Scotland, Minutes of the Presbytery of Glasgow, 1927–8, CH2/171/30.

Office of the Clerk of the Presbytery of Hamilton, Hamilton
Church of Scotland, Minutes of the Presbytery of Hamilton, 1927.

Offices of the United Free Church of Scotland, Glasgow
Minutes of the United Free Church Association, 1919–29 (UFCA Min.).
Papers of the United Free Church Association, 1919–29 (UFCA).

The Secretary of the Scottish Church Society, Paisley Abbey, Paisley
Minutes of the Scottish Church Society, 1909–29.
Papers and Memoranda relating to Church Union (SCS).

Glasgow University Archives
Minutes of Half-Yearly Meetings of the General Council, 1907–9, DC183/1/4.
Minutes of the University Court, 1907–9, 1926–34, C1/1/15, 34–9.
Camera Minutes of the University Court, 1926–34, C1/2/9–10 (GUC).
Minutes of the Senate of the United Free Church College and of Trinity College, 1924–54 DC84. 1/2/3.
Minutes of the Faculty of Divinity, 1923–33, DIV 1/6–7.

St Andrews University Library, Special Collections
Minutes of the University Court, 1927–34, UY505 (StAUC).
Minutes of the Faculty of Divinity, St Mary's College, 1923–31, UY408.
Papers of Principal Sir James Irvine, UY 875 Irvine (IRV).

Edinburgh University Library, Special Collections
Minutes and Papers of the Faculty of Divinity, 1927–58, 1VA, 3VA (EUD).
Signed Minutes of the University Court, 1924–34, Vols. XIV–XVI (EUC).
Minutes of the Senatus Academicus, 1924-32, Vols. IV–V.

Aberdeen University Library, Special Collections and Archives
Minutes of the University Court, 1924–36, Vols. X–XII (AUC).
Diaries and Papers of James Cooper, MS.2283/1–44 and Box (JC).

Published works

Article VIII: Its Provisions and Safeguards, by a Parish Minister (Paisley, n.d.).
Lady Frances Balfour, *A Memoir of Lord Balfour of Burleigh, K.T.* (London, 1925).
Lord Balfour of Burleigh, *Presbyterian Reunion in Scotland* (Edinburgh, 1919).
— 'The Ecclesiastical Situation in Scotland', in *The Contemporary Review* 117 (1920), pp. 45–54.
G. F. Barbour, *The Life of Alexander Whyte* (London, 1923).
James Barr, *The Scottish Church Question* (London, 1920).
— *The United Free Church of Scotland* (London, 1934).

— *The Origin, Nature and Destination of the State Endowments of the Church of Scotland* (Dundee, 1924).

R. W. A. Begg, *The Renovation of Kippen Parish Church 1924–1991*, 6th edn. (Kippen , 1991).

A. N. Bogle, 'Church Union in Scotland: An Account of the Movement and Present Position' in *Record,* September 1925, pp. 383–6.

Albert Bogle, 'James Barr, B.D., M.P.' in *RSCHS,* 21 (1983), pp. 189–207.

Stewart J. Brown, 'The Ten Years' Conflict and the Disruption of 1843' in Stewart J. Brown and Michael Fry, eds., *Scotland in the Age of the Disruption* (Edinburgh, 1993), pp. 1–27.

— 'The Social Vision of Scottish Presbyterianism and the Union of 1929' in *RSCHS* XXIV (1990), pp. 77–96.

— 'Reform, Reconstruction, Reaction: the Social Vision of Scottish Presbyterianism c.1830–c.1930', in *Scottish Journal of Theology*, 44 (1991), pp. 489–517.

— 'The Social Ideal of the Scottish Churches during the 1930s', in Andrew R. Morton, ed., *God's Will in a Time of Crisis*, Centre for Theology and Public Issues, University of Edinburgh, Occasional Paper No. 31 (Edinburgh, 1994), pp. 14–31.

— 'Outside the Covenant: The Scottish Presbyterian Churches and Irish Immigration, 1922–1938', in *The Innes Review* 42/1 (1991), pp. 19–45.

Stewart J. Brown and Michael Fry, eds., *Scotland in the Age of the Disruption* (Edinburgh, 1993).

W. Brown and J. Rutherford Hill, *Church and State in Scotland: where are we today?* (Edinburgh, 1925).

John Buchan and George Adam Smith, *The Kirk in Scotland 1560–1929* (Edinburgh, 1930).

David S. Cairns, *Life and Times of Alexander Robertson MacEwen, D.D.* (London, 1925).

Nigel M. de S. Cameron, ed., *Dictionary of Scottish Church History and Theology* (Edinburgh, 1993) (*DSCHT*).

Andrew J. Campbell, *Two Centuries of the Church of Scotland 1707–1929* (Paisley, 1930).

A. C. Cheyne, *The Transforming of the Kirk* (Edinburgh, 1983).

— *Studies in Scottish Church History* (Edinburgh, 1999).

J. Robertson Christie, *Church of Scotland Endowments* (Edinburgh and Glasgow, 1923).

Church of Scotland, *The Principal Acts of the General Assembly of the Church of Scotland* (Edinburgh, 1908–29) (*AGA*).

— *Reports on the Schemes of the Church of Scotland* (Edinburgh, 1908–29) (*C of S Rep.*).

— *Reports to the General Assembly of the Church of Scotland* (Edinburgh, 1930–) (*Cof S Rep.*).

— *Proceedings of the Union Assembly 1929* (Edinburgh, 1929).
— *The Layman's Book of the General Assembly* (Edinburgh, 1909–29) (*Layman's Book*).
— *The Call to the Church*. The Book of the Forward Movement of the Church of Scotland (Edinburgh, n.d.).
James Cooper, *The Approaching Union between the Free Church of Scotland and the United Presbyterian Church*, Introductory Lecture, Session 1900–1901 (Glasgow, 1900).
— *A United Church for the British Empire* (Forres, 1902).
— *Church Reunion in Scotland*, its claims and prospects (Edinburgh, 1906).
— *Church Reunion: the Prospect in Scotland* (Dublin, 1910).
— *The Historical Side of the Reunion Question* (Dublin, 1914).
— *Reunion: A Voice from Scotland* (London, 1918).
— 'The Present Call to Witness to the Fundamental Truths of the Gospel', in Scottish Church Society, *Conferences*, First Series (Edinburgh, 1894).
— 'Present Position of Negotiations for Presbyterian Reunion in Scotland', in *the Church Quarterly Review*, 88 (1919), pp. 271–90.
J. T. Cox, ed., *Practice and Procedure in the Church of Scotland*, 1st edn. (Edinburgh, 1935), 6th edn. (Edinburgh, 1976) (Cox).
A. W. Cowe, 'General Trustees', in *DSCHT*, p. 356.
William A. Curtis, 'Reunion in the Scottish Church and the proposed Articles', in *The Hibbert Journal*, 18 (1919–20), pp. 240–58.
The Disestablishment Council for Scotland, *The Haldane Report and the Haldane Declarations* (Dundee, 1924).
Gordon Donaldson, *Scottish Church History* (Edinburgh, 1985).
— *The Scottish Reformation* (Cambridge 1960).
James Denney, *Jesus and the Gospel* (London, 1908).
Dictionary of National Biography, Vols. 1–63 and Supplements (London, 1885–1949).
A. L. Drummond and James Bulloch, *The Church in Late Victorian Scotland 1874–1900* (Edinburgh, 1978).
Robert J. Drummond, *Lest We Forget* (London, 1951).
A. I. Dunlop, 'The Paths to Reunion in 1929' in *RSCHS*, 20 (1980), pp. 163–78.
Sir Alfred Ewing, 'The Scottish Universities: The Effect of a United National Church', in *Scots Observer*, 3 October 1929.
W. Ewing, ed., *Annals of the Free Church of Scotland, 1843–1929* (Edinburgh, 1914).
John Neville Figgis, *Churches in the Modern State*, 2nd ed. (London, 1914).
J. M. Finlayson, *The Church of Scotland in Danger: Objections to the Policy of the Union Committee* (Peterhead, 1919).

J. R. Fleming, *A History of the Church in Scotland, 1843–1874* (Edinburgh, 1927).

— *The Story of Church Union in Scotland*, its origins and progress 1560–1929 (London, 1929).

— *A History of the Church in Scotland, 1875–1929* (Edinburgh, 1933).

The Form of Presbyterial Church Government.

W. R. Forrester, *Christian Unity and Church Union, A plea for federation* (Edinburgh, 1925).

Alexander Gammie, ed., *General Assemblies Annual, 1929* (Glasgow, 1929).

A. J. H. Gibson, *Stipend in the Church of Scotland* (Edinburgh and London, 1961).

R. B. Haldane, *Richard Burdon Haldane: An Autobiography* (London, 1929).

G. D. Henderson, *Heritage, A Study of the Disruption* (Edinburgh and London, 1943).

Andrew Herron, *The Law and Practice of the Kirk* (Glasgow, 1995).

Historical Papers submitted to the Christian Unity Association (Edinburgh, 1914).

Robert Howie, *The Churches and the Churchless in Scotland* (Glasgow, 1893).

I. G. C. Hutchison, *A Political History of Scotland 1832–1924* (Edinburgh, 1986).

A. Taylor Innes, *The Law of Creeds in Scotland* (Edinburgh and London, 1902).

James Kirk, ed., *The Second Book of Discipline* (Edinburgh, 1980).

J. A. Lamb, ed., *Fasti of the United Free Church of Scotland 1900–1929* (Edinburgh and London, 1956).

Harold J. Laski, *Studies in the Problem of Sovereignty* (New Haven, 1917).

Robert Lee, *The Popery of Spiritual Independence* (Edinburgh, 1845).

James F. Leishman, *Linton Leaves* (Edinburgh, 1937).

David Lyall, 'Christian Ethics and Practical Theology' in David F. Wright and Gary D. Badcock, eds., *Disruption to Diversity: Edinburgh Divinity 1846–1996* (Edinburgh, 1996), pp. 135–150.

Francis Lyall, *Of Presbyters and Kings* (Aberdeen, 1980).

C. G. McCrie, *The Church of Scotland, her divisions and her reunions* (Edinburgh, 1901).

A. R. MacEwen, *A History of the Church in Scotland* (London, 1913).

H. R. Mackintosh, 'The Building of Church Union in Scotland' in the *Dalhousie Review*, 1 (1921), pp. 221–32.

— 'The Great Church Union in Scotland' in *The Expository Times*, 41 (1929–30), pp. 15–19.

Norman Maclean, *The Years of Fulfilment* (London, 1953).

Donald Macmillan, 'The Ecclesiastical Situation in Scotland', in *The Hibbert Journal*, 4 (1910–11), pp. 391–410.

— 'Presbyterian Reunion in Scotland: The Draft Articles', in *The Hibbert Journal*, 17 (1918–19), pp. 309–18.

Ian Machin, 'Voluntaryism and Reunion, 1874–1929' in Norman Macdougall, ed., *Church, Politics and Society: Scotland 1408–1929* (Edinburgh, 1983), pp. 221–38.

William Mair, *A Digest of Laws and Decisions Ecclesiastical and Civil*, relating to the constitution, practice, and affairs of the Church of Scotland (Edinburgh, 1887), 2nd edn. (Edinburgh and London, 1895).

— *Churches and the Law* (Edinburgh, 1904).

— *The Scottish Churches: Two Papers* (Edinburgh, 1907).

— *My Life* (London, 1911).

Andrew Marr, *The Battle for Scotland* (London, 1992).

Alexander Martin, *Assembly Addresses on Church Unity and a 'Fundamentals Creed'* (Edinburgh, 1920).

— *Church Union in Scotland: the first phase* (Edinburgh, 1923).

— *Church Union in Scotland: the first stage completed* (Edinburgh, 1925).

— *Church Union, The Proposed Uniting Act*: Speech by Rev. Principal Martin D.D. at the General Assembly of the United Free Church of Scotland, 27th May 1927.

— *Church Union in Scotland: nearing the goal* (Edinburgh, 1928).

— The *Reunion of the Scottish Church*, An Address delivered at the opening of the General Assembly of the United Free Church of Scotland, 21st May 1929 (Edinburgh and Glasgow, 1929).

— *A Twofold Appeal*, the Closing Address delivered at the General Assembly of the United Free Church of Scotland (Edinburgh, 1929).

A. Martin and R. J. Drummond, *Church Union*, Speeches delivered at the adjourned meeting of the General Assembly of the United Free Church of Scotland, on 21st November 1928 (Edinburgh, 1928).

William H. Marwick, 'James Barr: Modern Covenanter', in *Scottish Journal of Science*, 1 (1973), pp. 183–98.

Stewart Mechie, *The Office of Lord High Commissioner* (Edinburgh, 1957).

— 'Education for the Ministry in Scotland since the Reformation II', in *RSCHS*, 14 (1962), pp. 161–78.

— 'Education for the Ministry in Scotland since the Reformation, III' in *RSCHS*, 15 (1965), pp. 1–19.

— *Trinity College Glasgow 1856–1956* (Glasgow, 1956).

Augustus Muir, *John White, CH, DD, LLD* (London, 1958) (*JW*).

Douglas M. Murray, *Freedom to Reform: the 'Articles Declaratory' 1921* (Edinburgh, 1993) (*FR*).

— 'James Cooper (1846–1922) at Glasgow: Presbytery and Episcopacy', in William Ian P. Hazlett, ed., *Traditions of Theology in Glasgow 1450–1900* (Edinburgh, 1993), pp. 66–74.

— 'Matthew Leishman of Govan 1821–1874: the Middle Party and the middle way', *Society of Friends of Govan Old*, Sixth Annual Report, 1996, pp. 4–17.

Robert Low Orr, ed., *The Free Church of Scotland Appeals 1903–4* (Edinburgh, 1904).

Parliamentary Debates, Official Report, Fifth and Sixth Series, House of Commons (London) (Hansard HC).

Parliamentary Debates, Official Report, Fifth Series, House of Lords (London) (Hansard HL).

Robert Pitcairn, ed., *The Autobiography and Diary of Mr James Melvill* (Edinburgh, 1842).

C. L. Rawlins, ed., *The Diaries of William Paterson Paterson* (Edinburgh, 1987).

G. M. Reith, *Reminiscences of the United Free Church General Assembly* (Edinburgh and London, 1933)

Kenneth R. Ross, *Church and Creed in Scotland: the Free Church Case 1900–1904 and its Origins* (Edinburgh, 1988).

Lord Sands (Christopher N. Johnston), *Dr. Archibald Scott of St George's, Edinburgh, and his times* (Edinburgh and London, 1919).

— *Life of Andrew Wallace Williamson, K.C.V.O., D.D.* (Edinburgh, 1929).

— 'Church Union in Scotland', in *The Quarterly Review*, 233 (1920), pp. 205–25.

The Scots Confession of 1560, A modern translation by James Bulloch (Edinburgh, 1984).

Hew Scott, ed., *Fasti Ecclesiae Scoticanae*, 1–7 (Edinburgh, 1915), 8 (Edinburgh, 1950), 9 ed. J. A,. Lamb (Edinburgh, 1960).

Scottish Church Society, *Reunion: the necessary requirements of the Church of Scotland*, Conferences, Fourth Series (Edinburgh, 1909).

Notes on the Revised Basis and Plan of Union (Edinburgh, 1928).

D. W. D. Shaw, 'Dual Identity: Church College and University Faculty, in David F. Wright and Gary D. Badcock, eds., *Disruption to Diversity: Edinburgh Divinity 1846–1996* (Edinburgh, 1996), pp. 169–185.

P. Carnegie Simpson, *The Life of Principal Rainy* (London, 1909), 2 vols.

Rolf Sjölinder, *Presbyterian Reunion in Scotland, 1907–1921*, Its Background and Development (Edinburgh, 1962) (*PRS*).

J. Sommerville Smith, *Miller of Ruchill* (Glasgow, n.d.).

Jock Stein, ed., *Ministry for the 1980s* (Edinburgh, 1980).

J. W. Stevenson, ed., *The Healing of the Nation: the Scottish Church and a Waiting People* (Edinburgh, 1930).

William Swan and A. W. Wotherspoon, *Nec Tamen Consumebatur. Statement differentiating the Minority Report from the Majority Report of the Church Union Committee* (Edinburgh and London, 1914).

George Malcolm Thomson, *Will the Scottish Church Survive?* (Edinburgh, 1930).

W. R. Thomson, 'Presbyterian Reunion in Scotland', in *The Hibbert Journal*, 17 (1918–19). pp. 449–57.

T. Thomson, ed., *The Acts of the Parliament of Scotland* (London, 1814), Vols. II–III.

J. Hay Thorburn, *Gold May be Bought too Dear: An Appeal to the People of Scotland and a Challenge to the Promoters of the Draft Articles of Union* (National Church Defence Association, n.d.).

Thomas F. Torrance, ed., *The School of Faith* (London, 1959).

United Free Church of Scotland, *The Proceedings and Debates of the General Assembly* (Edinburgh, 1909–29) *(UFC Proc.)*.

—*Reports to the General Assembly of the United Free Church of Scotland (UFC Rep.)*.

—*Speeches delivered by Archibald Henderson, John Young and James Denney at the General Assembly, 30 May 1911 (Edinburgh, 1911)*.

— *Manual of Practice and Procedure in the United Free Church of Scotland*, (Edinburgh,1905), 2nd edn. (Edinburgh, 1927).

—*The Handbook of the United Free Church of Scotland (Continuing) and of the United Free Church of Scotland, 1931–9 (UFC Handbook)*.

— *Supplement to the Manual of Practice and Procedure of the United Free Church of Scotland*, containing changes adopted from 1929 to 1935 (Glasgow, 1936).

A United Free Churchman (J. M. Macfie), *The Union of the Churches: A Plea for Readjustment* (Edinburgh, 1926).

Hugh Watt, *Thomas Chalmers and the Disruption of 1843* (Edinburgh, 1943).

— *New College, Edinburgh: A Centenary History* (Edinburgh, 1946).

James L. Weatherhead, *The Constitution and Laws of the Church of Scotland* (Edinburgh, 1997).

Gavin White, 'Whose are the teinds? The Scottish union of 1929', in W. J. Sheils and Diana Wood, eds., *The Church and Wealth*, Studies in Church History, 24, (Oxford, 1987), pp. 383–92.

John White, *Efficiency*, Address delivered at the Close of the General Assembly, May 28, 1925 (Edinburgh and London, 1925).

— *Reunion and International Friendship* (Oxford, 1930).
— 'Church and State' in *Scottish Legionary*, 1949, pp. 16–18.
Donald J. Withrington, 'The Churches in Scotland, c. 1870 — c. 1900: Towards a New Social Conscience?', in *RSCHS*, 19 (1977), pp. 155–68.
— 'Non–church-going, church organisation and "crisis in the church" c. 1880 – c. 1920', in *RSCHS*, 24 (1992), pp. 199-236.
David Woodside, *The Soul of a Scottish Church* (Edinburgh, 1919).
H. J. Wotherspoon, *A Free Church in a Free State* (Edinburgh, 1914).
— *James Cooper, A Memoir* (London, 1926).
H. J. Wotherspoon and J. M. Kirkpatrick, *Manual of Church Doctrine* (London, 1919).

Pamphlets
The Church Union Association, *The Coming of One United Church for Scotland* (rev. ed. 1910).
— *Report of Conference on the Union of the Theological Colleges*, held on 7 March 1912.
J. Rutherford Hill, *A Frankly Critical Commentary* (n.d.).
Notes on Church Union.
Plain Words on Church Union, Tracts Nos. 1–4.
United Free Church Association (UFCA), *Annual Report and Statement.*
— *The Proposed Union: Guide to Members of the United Free Church of Scotland*, August 1927.
— Leaflet No. 1, *Back to Establishment.*
— Leaflet No. 2, *Would Union be Strength?*
— Leaflet No. 3, *Country Kirks and Union.*
— Leaflet No. 4, *Support of Church Ordinances in New Testament Times and Today.*
— Leaflet No. 5, *"Establishment with Freedom".*
— Leaflet No. 6, *"A State-Endowed Church.*
— Leaflet No. 7, *Compulsion in Religion.*
— *Annual Report and Statement on Report of Lord Haldane's Committee on the Property and Endowments of the Church of Scotland.*

Unpublished PhD thesis
Douglas M. Murray, 'The Scottish Church Society, 1892–1914: the High Church Movement in the Church of Scotland' (Cambridge Ph.D. thesis, 1975).

Newspapers and Periodicals
The Scotsman.
Glasgow Herald.
Life and Work, the Magazine of the Church of Scotland (*LW*).
The Record of the United Free Church of Scotland (*Record*).

Index